Lord Gnome's Literary Companion

Lord Gnome's Literary Companion

Edited by
FRANCIS WHEEN

VERSO

London · New York

First published by Verso 1994
© Private Eye 1994
All rights reserved

Verso
UK: 6 Meard Street, London W1V 3HR
USA: 29 West 35th Street, New York, NY 10001–2291

Verso is the imprint of New Left Books

ISBN 1–85984–945–8

British Library Cataloguing in Publication Data
A catalogue record for this book is available from the British Library

Library of Congress Cataloging-in-Publication Data
Lord Gnome's literary companion / edited by Francis Wheen.
    p.   cm.
Includes index.
ISBN 1-85984-945-8
    1. Literature, Modern—20th century—History and criticism.
I. Wheen, Francis.
PN771.L63   1994
028.1—dc20

Typeset by Solidus (Bristol) Limited, Bristol
Printed in Great Britain by Biddles Ltd

CONTENTS

INTRODUCTION

by Francis Wheen

Speaking seriously, we know that a really good book will more likely than not receive fair treatment from two or three reviewers; yes, but also more likely than not it will be swamped in the flood of literature that pours forth week after week and won't have attention fixed long enough upon it to establish its repute. The struggle for existence among books is nowadays as severe as among men. If a writer has friends connected with the press, it is the plain duty of those friends to do their utmost to help him. What matter if they exaggerate, or even lie? The simple, sober truth has no chance whatever of being listened to, and it's only by volume of shouting that the ear of the public is held . . . Suppose it were possible for me to write a round dozen reviews of this book, in as many different papers, I would do it with satisfaction. Depend upon it, this kind of thing will be done on that scale before long. And it's quite natural. A man's friends must be helped, by whatever means . . .

George Gissing, *New Grub Street*, 1891

Let Walter Savage Shelleyblake be a young author. Let his book be called *Vernal Aires*. Soon will come the delicious summons from the literary editor of the *Blue Bugloss*. 'Dear Shelleyblake, I was so interested to meet you the other night . . . I have been wondering if you would like to try your hand at a little reviewing for us. We are looking for someone to do the Nonesuch *Boswell*, and your name cropped up.'

The Nonesuch *Boswell* alone is worth four guineas, and soon a signed review, 'Expatriate from Auchinleck' by Walter Savage Shelleyblake, appears in the literary supplement of the *Blue Bugloss*. It is full of ideas and Mr Vampire, the editor, bestows on it his praise. The next book which Shelleyblake reviews, on Erasmus Darwin, is not quite so good but his article, 'Swansong at Lichfield', is considered 'extremely bright'. Suddenly his name appears under a pile of tomes of travel; the secrets of Maya jungles, Kenya game-wardens, and ricocheting American ladies are probed by him. In a year's time he will have qualified as a maid-of-all-work and be promoted to reviewing novels. It is promotion because more people read them and because publishers 'care'. If he is complimentary and quotable he will be immortalised on the dust wrapper and find his name in print on the advertisements. And eight to ten novels a fortnight, sold as review copies, add to his wage.

Cyril Connolly, Enemies of Promise, 1938

Half hidden among the pile of papers is a bulk parcel containing five volumes which his editor has sent with a note suggesting that they 'ought to go well together'. They arrived four days ago, but for 48 hours the reviewer was prevented by moral paralysis from opening the parcel. Yesterday in a resolute moment he ripped the string off it and found the five volumes to be *Palestine at the Cross Roads*, *Scientific Dairy Farming*, *A Short History of European Democracy* (this one is 680 pages and weighs four pounds), *Tribal Customs in Portuguese East Africa*, and a novel *It's Nicer Lying Down*, probably included by mistake. His review – 800 words, say – has got to be 'in' by mid-day tomorrow.

. . . At about 9 pm his mind will grow relatively clear, and until the small hours he will sit in a room which grows colder and colder, while the cigarette smoke grows thicker and thicker, skipping expertly through one book after another and laying each down with the comment, 'God, what tripe!' . . . Then suddenly he will snap into it. All the stale old phrases – 'a book that no one should miss', 'something memorable on every page', 'of special value are the chapters dealing with, etc etc' – jump into their places like iron filings obeying the magnet.

George Orwell, 'Confessions of a Book Reviewer', in
Shooting an Elephant and Other Essays, 1950

With one or two exceptions the English novel is consistently let down by a deferential reviewing establishment with an engrained reluctance to condemn inferior work. Book reviewing – I speak as someone who reviews about 50 books a year – is a racket, a pleasant and sweetly conducted racket, but a racket all the same, in which everybody more or less knows everybody else and gamely conspires in mutual backslapping. It is important to emphasise at this juncture that the literary world is not *obviously* corrupt . . . Obviously, no one is going to telephone a reviewer and offer him money to write favourably about a particular book. Similarly, few literary editors these days send out novels to a reviewer with the instruction 'not to be too hard on poor old X' (though they may make the job easier by sending the book to somebody known to be well-disposed towards X). But sooner or later anyone involved in the world of books will find that he or she operates by way of a subtle network of compromises . . .

D.J. Taylor, *A Vain Conceit: British Fiction in the 1980s*, 1989

Has Grub Street changed at all in the century since George Gissing composed his gloomy masterpiece about literary hackery? At first glance one would say that of course it has changed, changed utterly: in the age of videos and computer games, people are less dependent on the printed word for diversion or stimulation. And those who might once have earned a meagre living in Grub Street can now exercise their verbal facility in more profitable or comfortable careers. As Bernard Bergonzi has pointed out, the denizens of *New Grub Street* would today have little point of contact. Take the embittered critic Alfred Yule and his bright daughter Marian, who acts as his researcher and ghost-writer. 'Nowadays,' Bergonzi writes, 'since the rise of English as a university subject, both of them would be more at home as academics.' (Like Professor Bergonzi himself, one might add.) As for Jasper Milvain, the ambitious young opportunist with a facile pen, he 'would probably be destined for a job in advertising or public relations'.

John Gross has made the same point (in *The Rise and Fall of the Man of Letters*) by imagining what might have happened to the sons of Connolly's Walter Savage Shelleyblake: the older boy is now a senior lecturer in English at a new university, while the younger brother 'was marked down for success the moment he went into television. Today he is probably best known to viewers as the anchor-man of a weekly satirical review of the arts, although he also turns up regularly in paperback symposia, at Happenings, in the colour supplements, and indeed throughout the media generally.' Gross adds, however, that both brothers 'occasionally review for the *Blue Bugloss*'.

That last touch is perhaps the most significant. Literature is no longer central to our culture: as Gross notes, alternatives to reading have prospered, and, among the young at least, the compact disc and the television 'offer excitements which the written word cannot begin to rival'. Even so, the Shelleyblake boys still turn out their reviews for the *Blue Bugloss* just as their father did before them.

Books pour forth from the press in an unceasing torrent; publishing, once a quiet occupation for tweedy types in dingy Bloomsbury offices, is now a multi-million dollar business with all the paraphernalia of any other modern enterprise – share options, buy-outs, marketing gimmicks, management consultants, corporate strategies. If books have indeed retreated to the margin of the culture, one might expect the amount of attention given to them to diminish accordingly; but it isn't so. Newspapers that formerly had 'a books page' now fill three or more pages a week with reviews (the *Sunday Times* book section, Cyril Connolly's old stamping ground, runs to 16 pages every week). Glossy magazines are crammed with profiles of fashionable metropolitan novelists – Will Self, perhaps, or Rachel Cusk – while news editors titillate their readers with stories about six-figure advances paid to unknown authors. Bookselling, too, has confounded expectations. In a 1991 postscript to a new edition of *The Rise and Fall of the Man of Letters*, John Gross wrote: 'It is video stores that have sprung up on every side, not bookshops.' Actually, what is most striking about the contemporary urban landscape is how many new bookshops there are – Waterstones, Dillons, Books Etc, Ottakars – rather than how few. We are continually warned that almost nobody reads books any more, and that those few people who do will soon prefer to imbibe their literature from CD-ROM disks anyway. But it hasn't happened. With the sale of film options and foreign rights, and the proliferation of lavishly sponsored awards (the Booker Prize, the Whitbread Prize, the NCR Prize, the *Sunday Express* Prize, the W H Smith Prize, the *Esquire*–Volvo–Waterstone's Prize and many others, some of which sound more like trophies for minor-league football), it is today surprisingly easy for a fair-to-middling novelist to make a living. Literary journalists, too, have seldom had it so good: in the mid-1980s, largely to keep up with Rupert Murdoch's *Sunday Times*, many national newspapers belatedly started paying their reviewers properly: contributors who had been accustomed to receive £50 for a 700-word review suddenly found that it was now worth £200. As we lurch towards the new, bookless millennium, literature and its service industries are in surprisingly robust financial health.

But at what cost? The new publishing corporations may pay their authors higher advances than the little old Bloomsbury houses could ever manage, but they are commensurately less willing to take risks. Hence their fondness for the 'non-book': take someone who is already well-known – Ivana Trump, Britt Ekland, Naomi Campbell, Joan Collins, Edwina Currie – and pay her a fat fee to put her name to a blockbuster novel. Whether the putative author can write scarcely matters: unseen hands will always be ready to assist. The important thing is the author's celebrity, which guarantees acres of newspaper publicity, appearances on chat-shows and lucrative serializations; the book will thus become a bestseller regardless of its quality. (Or so they suppose, in their simple way: it is gratifying to record that some apparently fail-safe efforts in this line have come a cropper, including Ivana Trump's *Free to Love* and *For Love Alone*. Not that she'll complain. Her advance for the two novels was $3 million.)

The publishers' quest for 'promotability' is pursued just as breathlessly at the other end of the scale, when launching a young, unknown writer: often, more care will be taken to produce a glamorous publicity photo than to edit the tyro's typescript. If the author has an exotic past – one thinks of Will Self's much-publicized heroin habit, or Esther Freud's Bohemian childhood, or Joseph O'Connor's relationship with his pop-star sister, Sinead – so much the better. Any aspirant novelist who thinks that it is enough merely to write a book had better think again.

The demise of the small independent publisher, and the concentration of power in a few large conglomerates, also makes it much more likely that writers will fall victim to a conflict of interests. Suppose you are a novelist published by Hutchinson, and you are asked to review a new novel published by Jonathan Cape. You will be aware that both Hutchinson and Cape are part of Random House; indeed they inhabit the same offices in the Vauxhall Bridge Road. As a conscientious reviewer you will do your best to produce an honest piece, but at the back of your mind you may hear a small voice warning: Best go easy on it, we don't want to upset the powers-that-be at Vauxhall Bridge Road, do we?

Or, to take an admittedly extreme case, imagine that you are commissioned by the *Sunday Times* to review Anna Murdoch's new novel. You may well discover that the book is tosh and drivel (I speak as someone who has read two of Anna Murdoch's novels); but you can't help noticing that the author is married to the *Sunday Times*'s proprietor, Rupert Murdoch; and that he also owns HarperCollins, the firm that publishes her. You have been hoping that the *Sunday Times* will serialize your forthcoming biography of David Frost; or perhaps your agent has just told you that Fontana (prop. R. Murdoch) is interested in buying the paperback rights to your last book, a history of computers. Whatever, it seems silly to risk antagonizing the entire, global Murdoch empire just because of one negligible novel; you have a living to earn, after all. And so, gritting your teeth, you switch on your computer and start to write: 'Anna Murdoch's lively, intensely readable new saga . . .'

Literary conflicts of interest are as old as Grub Street itself; the difference today is not one of kind but of degree. Authors have always tended to seek the company of other authors (writing is a lonely business), and only the most high-minded have managed to resist the impulse. 'You ask,' George Orwell once wrote to Stephen Spender, 'how it is that I attacked you not having met you, & on the other hand changed my mind after meeting you ... Even if when I met you I had not happened to like you, I should still have been bound to change my attitude, because when you meet anyone in the flesh you realise immediately that he is a human being & not a sort of caricature embodying certain ideas. It is partly for this reason that I don't mix much in literary circles, because I know from experience that once I have met and spoken to anyone I shall never again be able to show any intellectual brutality towards him, even when I feel that I ought to ...'

Now, however, there are so many opportunities for meeting your fellow practitioners that it is hard to preserve such wilful isolation. Even a first-time novelist living in a semi in Warrington will, once she starts to attract attention, find herself invited to attend parties at the Groucho Club, or sit on *Late Show* discussion panels, or speak at the Hay-on-Wye literary festival, or join a group of 'young British writers' on a British Council tour of Prague and Budapest. Once you have been recruited to this travelling circus, can you still criticize your colleagues without inhibition? As D.J. Taylor observes, in *A Vain Conceit*: 'You are writing a review of a first novel, for instance, to which the only honest reaction is to say that the author ought to have chosen some other career. But then you remember that you are publishing a first novel yourself in six months' time, and nobody wants to be thought ... ungenerous. Consequently, you produce the usual persiflage about "prom-ise" and reach exceeding grasp.' Turn to the books section of any national newspaper, any week, and you will find at least one piece written by a friend of the author whose book is under review. Only about once a year, however, will you find any declaration of this interest. A few years ago, in a sudden fit of self-righteousness, the *Sunday Times* announced loudly that it would not permit the sort of back-scratching and log-rolling that infest other literary pages to pollute its own reviewing. *Private Eye* undermined this at once by printing a long list of all the interlocking friendships (or, less often, enmities) that lay behind the paper's choice of reviewers.

How can one escape the network of debts and allegiances that is literary London, bearing in mind that 'London' in this sense reaches out to include even our promising young writer in Warrington? One answer is to bypass Grub Street altogether and commission reviews from academics, who, insulated from the hubbub of the Groucho Club, can write freely about new books without nervously wondering how it will affect their standing in the

Groucho or whether their invitation to Jonathan Cape's Christmas party will be rescinded. Alas, it isn't as easy as that. Literary criticism is a comparatively new academic subject: the Merton professorship of English Language and Literature at Oxford was established in 1885, and Cambridge did not have a professor of English Literature until 1911. The Merton chair is currently occupied by John Carey, the *Sunday Times*'s chief reviewer, but he is the exception who proves a rule: that in the past few decades the gulf between English academics on the one hand, and the general reader (and literary editor) on the other, has become so vast as to be almost unbridgeable. There is no longer a common language.

If you listen to dons, you will be told that this is all the fault of the literary editors and their coteries, who stubbornly refuse to acknowledge the usefulness or importance of 'theory' and continue to review books in an old-fashioned, amateurish way. See, for example, the famous essay by Terry Eagleton, Warton Professor of English at Oxford, attacking the 'theoretical paucity' and 'common-place philistine empiricism' of old-style reviewing; his predecessor in the Warton chair, John Bayley, who often wrote for the national press, is accused of having ratified 'English criticism's inability to confront its own intellectual nullity'.

He may have a point. But the dons should not escape blame: over the past 20 years, while enjoying themselves enormously in the ever-more inaccessible labyrinths of deconstruction and semiology, they have wilfully cut themselves off from any possibility of dialogue with the ordinarily intelligent book-reader outside the ivory tower. You do not have to be a philistine to believe that the work of, say, Derrida is mostly just a game, amusing enough for those who wish to play it but ultimately of no great assistance to anyone else.

And yet, ironically enough, there is one line of Derrida's that literary editors and reviewers seem to accept enthusiastically: *il n'y a rien de hors texte* (there is nothing outside the text). In their narrow concentration on the work before them – without reference to the cultural or commercial forces that may have shaped it – they can be every bit as blinkered by their own methodology as any Yale academic. The choice of texts is severely limited, too: a new life of Bonar Law or Hugh Walpole will get ten times as much space as, say, a biography of Madonna or Paul Gascoigne; a run-of-the-mill 'literary' novel will be treated far more seriously than a superior thriller. (The *Daily Telegraph* deals with *genre* fiction – romance, crime, horror, science fiction – by giving a one-sentence summary of the plot and awarding a 'star rating', in the manner of the *Michelin Guide*. It would never occur to the paper to judge Jeanette Winterson or Will Self in such slapdash fashion.) In their own way, literary editors are as out of touch with the reading public as any Eng. Lit. lecturer. Many of the authors who regularly dominate the bestseller lists – Jean M. Auel, Shaun Hutson, Barbara Taylor Bradford, Delia Smith, Rosemary Conley – are *never reviewed at all*. Matters are not improved by the existence of a cultural populist claque in academia which does attend to such authors but with an ostentatious contempt for critical standards.

This is where *Private Eye* comes in. The 'Literary Review' page at the back of the magazine is just as likely to notice Jack Higgins or Catherine Cookson as Iris Murdoch or Sir Kingsley Amis. Whatever the genre there is a willingness to appraise critically. More importantly, it attempts to explain the unseen forces that police this literary culture – the literary agents, the editorial directors, the hype-merchants, the back-scratchers.

In keeping with *Private Eye* tradition, the articles are anonymous. Just as the news pages of the *Eye* have long provided a sanctuary for stories that journalists are unable to get into their own newspapers, so the literary section allows professional reviewers a freedom that they can't find in the other papers for which they write. Gathering together the *Eye*'s reviews for this book, I winced to see several friends of mine – Candia McWilliam and Ian McEwan, for instance – being given a fearful drubbing. Still, it can't be helped. The whole point of the 'Literary Review' page is that there are no sacred cows, no inhibitions, no special favours, no treacly euphemisms. Messy work, but someone's got to do it.

1

PUBLISHING

Lunch, anyone?

Save our trees

The Bookseller: Organ of the Book Trade (Autumn Books 1986, Issue No. 4207)

*A*PPROXIMATELY 1,000 books are published in Britain every week. In the early 1980s this rate fell slightly, but now it is rising again. About 50,000 new titles, including re-issues and academic books, arrive on the market each year. At an average print run of 4,000, this makes a physical quantity of 200 million books.

In the view of Paul Johnson, writing recently in the *Spectator*, this rising tide of new books is a good thing. He takes it as proof that the British are becoming more civilized. But as usual this dogmatic ninny is talking through the top of his hat. 50,000 new books a year is too many. The good ones get lost in the flood of mediocrity. Even the commercial ones, which might help to pay for the good ones, are swamped.

The dynamic at the heart of this excess is the need of the small general publisher to fill up the list in his catalogue. Each year he will find a few good books, worth doing on merit or popular appeal, but to justify his company's existence, to keep the reps busy and pay for lunches in Soho, he will need to bring out at least 30 more. So he fills up his list with anything to hand.

The best place to see this phenomenon in action is the bumper autumn issue of *The Bookseller*, where 9,000 forthcoming titles are listed. A flip through the first 186 pages of publishers' advertisements, from A to Deutsch, will reveal what civilization has in store.

From W.H. Allen we have *Pink Goddess: The Jayne Mansfield Story.* From Allen & Unwin comes *The Shaping of Middle Earth*, 4th volume, ed. Christopher Tolkien. Angus & Robertson have *The Working Camera: The World's First Pop-up Guide to Photography*, by Professor John Hedgecoe. Among the many books offered by ABP is *The Big Smoke: A History of Air Pollution in London since Medieval Times.* Also from ABP we have *Faggots* (modern fiction) by Larry Kramer and *All By Myself: The Toilet Training Book*, 'based on proven psychological principles'.

From A&C Black we have *50 Favourite Wet Flies* and *The Dinky Toy Price Guide.* Bulking up Blackie's list is *The Manual of Ready-Mixed Concrete*, 320 pages. From Blandford we have *Combat Helicopters since 1942* and *The Power of Holistic Aromatherapy.*

From Bodley Head, a sinking firm, we have *The Titanic* by Michael Davie, 'full story of a tragedy'. In their children's list is *I'm Having a Bath with Papa* by Shigeo Watanabe.

From Century, a rising firm, comes the *Lark Rise Recipe Book* and *The I Ching of Business Decision Making.* Century have *Captain Mark Phillips on Riding* by Captain Mark Phillips. Constable have *Not the Whole Truth* by Patrick Lichfield, 'the human story behind his rise to fame'.

Big publishers can play this game too. In fact Collins have given up trying to do anything else. Their list is fillers from end to end. The only title that catches the eye is *Care for Your Kitten* by Anna Mews.

Nor are literary publishers exempt. Chatto pack their list with cheap foreign novelists from Latin America or Eastern Europe. This time they have *Dvorak in Love* by Josef Skvorecky, and the trend has spread to Jonathan Cape, whose fiction includes *The Stones Cry Out* by Molyda Szymusiak. Also from Cape we have *In These Times* by Bernard Levin and *Dogwatching* by Desmond Morris.

Finally we come to Andre Deutsch, who has a better eye for a filler than any small publisher in London. This time his best is *Following the Drum: Women in Wellington's Wars*, by Brigadier F.C.G. Page. One can guess how delighted the brigadier is to be in print. One can guess how little he was paid.

Passed over in this brief summary of publishers A–D are the following assorted titles: *Homeless Person's Handbook*; *Australian Wine Guide*; *Knit Your Own Skyscraper*; *Entertaining with Alcohol*; *The Ambridge Book of Country Cooking*; *Pooh's Workout Book*; *Floella's Fabulous Bright Ideas Book*; *Grandma and the Ghoulies*; *The Lonely Little Mole*; *Indoor Cricket*; *Coming to Terms with Menopause*; *Making Timeless Toys in Wood*; *Sneaky Tricks to Fool Your Friends*; *Turk, the Border Collie*; *Vogue Bedside Book II*; *Diary of a Zen Nun*; *English Garden Embroidery*; *The Smoker's Addictionary*; *The Complete Book of M.A.S.H.*; *American Football Rules in Pictures*; *Celtic Knotwork*; *Practical Deerstalking*; *Antique Typewriters.*

22 August 1986

Catalogue of crime

ORDINARY readers don't usually get to see publishers' catalogues. It's a pity. If they did, they might have a better idea of publishers' desperation. And bafflement. And contempt. They might, indeed, take our tidal book-production business less seriously.

Good books are few and publishers are many. There are not enough good or even decent books to go round. So bad books, boring books, pointless books have somehow to be titivated up to look better than they are. The process begins with the publishers lying loudly about them in their catalogues, in the hope of conning booksellers and the media.

Notionally most entries in publishers' catalogues are written by the editors of the book. Notionally they have *read* them and can remember one from another. It's a handicap soon overcome though.

After all, they've been doing it for years. The methods are known, the key words few. This year's spring catalogues of forthcoming books display the old routines nicely.

One favourite is to cast a bald lie in the form of a well-known fact. Hence the present tense, hence 'confirms'. 'It confirms Pete Davies as a provocative and powerful voice in modern fiction' (*Dollarville* from Cape); 'These qualities ... confirm his standing among such classic humorists as Dickens, Waugh and Flannery O'Connor' (*Sort of Rich* by James Wilcox, Secker).

It helps here not to look too stressed about it. *Dottie*, by Abdulrazak Gurnah (Cape), 'places Gurnah firmly in the company of our most distinguished novelists' – but 'firmly' confirms only nervousness.

There are two main ways of getting round the fact that it's just the same old boring rubbish. You can say it's *better* same old boring rubbish ('In his finest novel yet, David Malouf ...'). Or you can pretend it is completely *new* or *different* same old boring rubbish. 'There is simply no *precedent* for the chilling crescendo of its narrative power ...' (*The Innocent* by Ian McEwan, Cape); 'A.S. Byatt has a *unique* reputation as a novelist who combines passion and intellect ...' (Chatto).

Here, too, an appearance of confidence helps the confidence trick: 'Dorris Collins is an extraordinary woman with extraordinary talents, and this volume makes extraordinary reading' (*Positive Forces*, Grafton) is *not* the way to do it.

Encouragingly, many catalogue entries have evidently been composed in resentment and malice. 'He follows the graceful flight of osprey and merlin, and encounters the curious otter and comical tree-creeper' (Jim Crumley's study of the Cairngorms, Cape).

'Brought up by a clan of hyenas and then by the Kalahari Bushmen, Kala keeps in her shuttered mind the secret of the ancient city which lies submerged in the Okovango Swamp' (*Kala* by Nicholas Luard, Century).

Sometimes puffers admit defeat (as well they might), and rather downplay the promise, large promise, which is the soul of an advertisement. 'Each photograph is fully captioned, *to enable readers to identify what is shown*' (*Wales from the Air*, Barrie & Jenkins).

But most are shameless. 'If we could drive a hole through the earth at the centre of the Bermuda Triangle, we would emerge at the centre of another triangle, dubbed the Devil's Sea, or The Dragon's Triangle by seafarers over the centuries' (*The Dragon's Triangle* by Charles Berlitz, Grafton). (Thinks: If we could gimmick together a follow-up, we would rake it in.)

In this dreamy world, where all biographies are definitive and none interim, where all novels are the author's 'most assured, most complex and resonant work to date' and none not as good as the last one, the few noteworthy books sink in a bubbling effusion of drivel.

This year those few include a new collection of stories by William Trevor (Bodley Head, January), a duff new novel by Thomas Pynchon (Secker, February), V.S. Pritchett's travel pieces (Chatto, February), more Primo Levi (Methuen, February), another North London alcoholic novel by Kingsley Amis (Hutchinson, March), another Barbara Vine thriller (Viking, March), a juvenile novel by John Kennedy Toole (Viking, March), a Brian Moore (Bloomsbury amazingly, April), a big new Vargas Llosa (Faber, April), another Theroux novel (Hamish Hamilton, April), and maybe that McEwan (Cape, May).

And there's also *Something Leather* by Alasdair Gray from Cape in April. 'Since *The Canterbury Tales* no other British fiction has shown such a convincing social range in such embarrassing detail.' If the book's half as good as that, it could even be worth having.

5 January 1990

Catalogue of despair – 1992

CATALOGUES are publishing at its most seductive, its most glamorous – and its most fake. No amateur student, thumbing through the glossy booklets advertising publishers' wares for the coming six months and eyeing the conveyor belt of apparently fail-safe money-spinners would ever divine the real state of British – correction, Anglo-American – publishing today.

The book trade flounders in recession, hundreds of its employees lost their jobs in 1991, and it is a truth universally acknowledged that publishers publish too many books, unimaginatively, and at prohibitively expensive prices. But is this something you would gather from their catalogues? No. All is fame, lucre and triumphant achievement.

Or almost. Reading between the lines of these breathless accumulations of publicists' prose, it is possible to detect the mild, though insistent, note of unease. What do you do, after all, if fewer people are buying your products and the big retailers – Smith's and wicked Mr Maher – keep squeezing your margins? The answer seems to be that you concentrate on the tried and trusted: royalty, or sub-royalty (this spring brings a biography of Princess Alexandra, not to mention Captain Mark Phillips' *The Horse & Hound Book of Eventing*); or stock bestsellers (the HarperCollins list comes bristling with new work by the likes of Susan Howatch, Craig Thomas and Barbara Erskine). There are blockbusters and mesdames Steel, Cookson and Wesley, and, down in the literary basement, new offerings by Peter Ackroyd, Graham Swift and Ian McEwan. What you will not find is anything that smacks even vaguely of risk.

In fact a slight air of fatigue hangs over several of these puff-sheets, the fatigue of publishers whose strategy to contain the recession has been to dig in, pump the stuff out and hope that, miraculously, turnover will see them through. The result is a torrent of singularly uninteresting books. The Hutchinson catalogue – 50 pages long – contains nothing much more than new novels by Kingsley Amis and Ruth Rendell. Nadir is reached with the Weidenfeld & Nicolson catalogue, which offers memoirs by Eric Hammond and Frank Bruno and, when summarizing a book by David Benedictus entitled *Sunny Intervals and Showers*, squeaks with desperation: 'This is not an arid and specialist work; though detailed it is infected with a real love for the subject.' Golly.

As a touchstone for the way the industry is going, though, catalogues are invaluable. What will the future bring? The answer, apparently is: more celebrity 'novels', commissioned on the basis that punters are more likely to buy books by people they've heard of, their exemplar a hugely unappetizing work by Rupert Everett entitled *Hello Darling, Are You Working?*; more refusals to learn from past mistakes (only this failing, surely, could explain the appearance of second novels by Tariq Ali and Julian Critchley); and more transatlantic psycho-crap, the highlight being a Simon & Schuster offering called *Awaken the Giant Within*, described as 'how to take immediate control of your mental, emotional, physical and financial life'.

What else? Pious attitudes are struck about the various new trade paperback lists (Chatto, Secker and Hamish Hamilton). These, which offer original novels in softcover, have been puffed all over the place as the future of publishing – 'we care a great deal about these books ... They are representative of the very best writing that we most wish to publish,' says Hamish Hamilton – a concern with the bottom line masquerading as altruism.

What, the reader might wonder, is actually going to *sell* among all this contrivance? These books, regrettably, can be found in places like the Headline catalogue and have titles such as *Brain Damage*, *The House of the Red Slayer* and *Games of the Hangman*. Oh, and in case you hadn't already twigged, it's the Tolkien centenary. Z–z–z–z ...

3 January 1992

Season of lists and mellow dreadfulness

*A*UGUST is a dead month for the publishing trade. In fact, given the current economic gloom, every month is a dead month in the publishing trade, but August is deader than most.

A few beach books creep out unnoticed into the pale summer sun, the publishers slumber on the patios in Pont St Esprit, Jeffrey Archer, Joanna Trollope and David Lodge battle it out at the airport bookstalls, and the only sound comes from the slap of fat autumn catalogues falling on to reviewers' doormats.

Publishers love the autumn. They do two-thirds of their business in it; half of the average firm's turnover can be chalked up in the six week lead-in to Christmas. The fun of autumn catalogues, though, lies not in marking down the row of surefire bestsellers from the likes of Maeve Binchy and Len Deighton, but in wondering whether what is so confidently advertised will actually be vouchsafed.

Pride of place in the HarperCollins catalogue, for example, is occupied by Ben Pimlott's long-awaited life of Harold Wilson, a work apparently incomplete even at this late stage. Similarly, the literary editor of the *Sunday Times* recently filled much of a Radio 4 books programme with a lavish encomium of Paul Bailey's new novel, *Sugar Cane*. As it happens, this has been put back to the spring for the simple reason that the old boy, a famous procrastinator, hasn't finished it yet.

Certain to appear, alas, is a hulking load of publishers' traditional autumn offerings – extraordinary books that nobody will want to buy. Who, for instance, is going to pay hard-earned money for Cecil Parkinson's memoirs, David Owen's poetry anthology or Tony Benn and his research assistant's *The Agreement of the People: A New Constitution for Britain*?

The autumn crop of anthologies – normally a fail-safe way of bumping up turnover – is more than usually desperate: lowlights include A.N. Wilson on Church and clergy (Faber), John Mortimer on villains (Oxford) and – something that at first glance looked like an amusing joke on the part of the catalogue compilers – *The Penguin Book of 20th Century Speeches*, edited by Brian MacArthur.

It being the autumn, famous names predominate on the fiction shelf. Most of them can expect short shrift from the angry young critics, in particular Malcolm Bradbury with *Dr Criminale* (Secker) – Bradbury's conspicuous merits as a novelist have become overshadowed in the public mind by his reputation as a literary log-roller, and of course it's so much more interesting to review the novelist rather than the novel.

In the same department, A.S. Byatt's *Angels and Insects* (Chatto), two abstruse novellas about Victorian intellectual life, will be read with great bewilderment by a small proportion of the 300,000 or so people who shelled out for the paperback of *Possession*.

Here and there as usual lurks the faint smell of controversy: A.N. Wilson's *Jesus* (Sinclair Stevenson) – very faint, that; what was to have been a biography of Stephen Spender by Hugh David, now reduced to 'A Portrait with Background' as a consequence of the subject's nervousness over revelations from his early life; Neil Lyndon's *No More Sex War... The Failure of Feminism* (yawn); and Humphrey Carpenter's life of Benjamin

Britten, the latter no doubt crammed with salacious details of the Britten/ Pears ménage.

All in all, a very typical autumn lies ahead: some predictable money-spinners, crowds of largely indifferent novels in search of the Booker, which should be won by Barry Unsworth's *Sacred Hunger* (Hamish Hamilton), and, all too typically, some real horrors. It is early days yet and the autumn deluge has still to begin, but already one would give a lot of money not to have to possess Jeremy Reed's biography of his eponym, Lou, Sean French's *Fatherhood: Men Write About Fathering* or Bel Mooney's *Perspectives for Living: Conversations on Bereavement and Love*.

14 August 1992

Withering hype

*A*UTUMN in the world of books invariably has a depressing ring of familiarity: factitious excitement about the Booker Prize; columns of po-faced exegesis on live-wire topics such as 'Whither the Novel?'; the third and fourth recapitulations of other people's good ideas; and lurking away in the depths of this grey, gloomy pool, careless of the splashings of excitable smaller fry, the big fish, the Clancys, the Eddingses and the Deightons, whom there is some commercial point in publishing.

For 1993, repeat the mixture as before. The Booker circus starts even earlier this year, with this season's literary contenders – Murdoch, Ackroyd, Boyd – upon us by the end of August. The smart money is already on the Indian writer Upamanyu Chatterjee (*The Last Burden*, Faber) who shares with Vikram Seth the inestimable advantage of being foreign, but beats him hands down when it comes to over-writing. Never mind, if the book can be said to follow all the prescriptions with which 'Bookworm' flagged Michael Ondaatje's victory last year (foreign, funny name, 'poetic' prose style and so on) then this is it.

The 'Whither the Novel?' chatter, too, can be expected to roll on until at least November. Not only are various deeply serious young writers standing by to inform us once again that the novel is dead (has the *Guardian* books page no other *raison d'être*?), but they will be joined by a serious older man, in this case Malcolm Bradbury, whose compendious *The Modern British*

17

Novel comes from Secker. Even worse, to mark the 25th anniversary of the Booker, there will be a 'Booker of Bookers' event to add to the existing party, and no *Late Show* discussion worth its salt will be free from its enveloping tentacles.

Publishing, it will perhaps come as a surprise to learn, is about good ideas, or, rather, the amount of repetition that good ideas will bear before they become bad ideas. Remember Jung Chang's *Wild Swans*? Well, somebody at Gollancz clearly thinks this one will run and run: stand by for *Red Azaleas* by Anchee Min, billed in that catchpenny way so beloved of book publicists as 'the most powerfully erotic and moving autobiography to emerge from modern China'. Elsewhere, the scent of *déjà vu* hangs heavy. Philip Ziegler's biography of Harold Wilson would look more exciting if we hadn't had a first instalment (if a rather more sycophantic one) last year from Ben Pimlott. Similarly, Sean French's life of the endlessly underrated English novelist Patrick Hamilton (Faber) would be that much more alluring had not Nigel Jones got in first back in 1991.

Other bandwagons will be less easily derailed. Gollancz, again, have had the very bright idea of getting Nick Hornby (*Fever Pitch*) to put his name to a collection of essays by a gaggle of thirtysomething wannabes maundering about their obsession with soccer (*My Favourite Year*) – expect acres of coverage from media chums. Another minority interest suddenly having money thrown at it is the gay market, most obviously in the launch of Cassell's 'Sexual Politics' list. Early offerings include Mark Simpson's *Male Impersonators* ('examines ... whether male body-builders are covert transsexuals, football matches are one vast "circle jerk", and how gay men play with manliness as a kind of drag') and the Sisters of Perpetual Indulgence's (*Who they? – Ed.*) safer-sex postcard book *Get the Rubber Habit*, a shocking comment on the business sense of a fine old English firm.

Will any of the above actually sell? Answer: no. And what will sell, then? Answer: Tom Clancy's *Without Remorse*, Len Deighton's *Violent Ward*, and a dozen other stodgy transatlantic techno-thrillers. Oh, and the initial print run for volume one of Mrs Thatcher's memoirs *The Downing Street Years* (HarperCollins) – the autumn's bestselling book – is a cool 200,000.

27 August 1993

Sale of the century

The Illustrated Kilvert

*T*HE *Illustrated Kilvert* (Century Books) is already beginning to feature in the bestseller lists – not always a reliable guide to popularity. It is a little-known fact that booksellers who stock large quantities of a book may name it as a bestseller simply to help the hype and so get rid of their copies. All the same, it is a fair bet that come Christmas a number of desperate punters will be forking out the required £15.95 for something to give to Granny or Aunt Matilda.

The formula – a classic text with a rural theme, re-vamped with a plenitude of sepia photographs, inferior water-colours and facsimiles of pressed flowers – is one that has been pioneered by Century Books and its bold brash proprietor Anthony Cheetham, and imitated by many other publishers. But the original money-spinner whose success has inspired a host of such books was *The Diary of an Edwardian Lady*, Michael Joseph's greatest money-spinner ever.

Anthony – son of diplomat Sir Nicholas Cheetham – who has been described as 'an Old Etonian shit' by a fellow Old Etonian publisher (not a shit), is a softly spoken, pushy 43-year-old who began his publishing career in Sphere and moved on to found Futura, specializing in soft-porn books like *Confessions of a Window Cleaner*.

Bought up by Maxwell, Cheetham soon fell out with Captain Bob. With the help of generous City backing, which he has never lacked, he set up his own firm, Century, which has recently bought up Hutchinson.

Produced by 'packager' Julian Shuckburgh, Cheetham's 'gift market' books like *The Illustrated Kilvert* are done on the cheap, like most of his books. Printed in Spain, the original Kilvert text has been decorated with illustrations by an unnamed and therefore, presumably, inexpensive water-colourist. It is not really a book at all but a present and it proclaims the fact that its publisher is primarily interested in making as much money as he can – like his hero Sir Clive Sinclair – rather than in producing real books for people to read.

Apart from other considerations Revd Kilvert's famous diary (originally published by Cape in 1944) is not a book that gains anything from being illustrated. The Victorian country parson's descriptions of life in the Welsh border country and more especially of nature and wild flowers, make their own pictures in the mind and the addition of photographs, dredged up from local libraries and museums, add nothing at all to the reader's pleasure and are, in many instances, merely a distraction.

Unfortunately for Cheetham, there are signs that the bottom has now rather dropped out of this particular industry. Despite the continuing success of the *Illustrated Lark Rise to Candleford*, its sequel, the *Illustrated Cider with Rosie*, like most sequels, flopped and has recently been seen in remainder shops along with spin-offs like the *Lark Rise Portfolio*, a box of cheap prints on shiny paper suitable for throwaway place mats.

27 June 1986

Arentcha Secker them?

Martin Secker & Warburg: The First Fifty Years; *A Memoir*
GEORGE MALCOLM THOMSON (Secker & Warburg)

S ECKER & Warburg have for fifty years been the most eclectic of our 'literary' publishers. In 1959 they brought out young Malcolm Bradbury's first novel, *Eating People Is Wrong*; in 1974, under the imprint of The Alison Press, they shocked the world with Piers Paul Read's *Alive*, which might more appropriately have been called *Eating People Is Right*.

By the end of the 1960s, the firm had been losing money for five successive years. Thomas Tilling, who owned the Heinemann Group which embraced Secker's, decided that Fred Warburg, the Humphrey Bogart lookalike who founded the firm in 1936 with Lytton Strachey's last lover, the eccentric Roger Senhouse, should be put out to grass. But who to succeed him? The last heir apparent, in the 1960s, was the gaunt, crazed-looking Maurice Temple-Smith, whose sole claim to fame was in having been the 97th editor to have read John Braine's *Room at the Top* but the one who decided to publish.

Unfortunately Temple-Smith quarrelled with Warburg and departed, the ancient Warburg assuming command again. There was definitely a crisis.

Heinemann's managing director, the sinister Charles Pick, had been trying to get rid of Warburg for years, less because Secker's made so little money than because Warburg was openly contemptuous of his literary acumen. Pick persuaded his colleague Alan Hill to sound out Tom Rosenthal (the man at Thames & Hudson responsible for cutting down Scandinavian forests to provide enough paper for the firm's art books) on a likely successor to Warburg, by then aged over 70. It was a curious mission because Rosenthal was not thought to know anything about fiction, which he had never published.

At lunch at the Garrick Club, Hill asked Rosenthal if he had any ideas. As Thomson hilariously records in his elegant history of the firm, Rosenthal responded: 'Alan, if you are offering me the job, I would like to take it.'

Rosenthal is a curious mixture of qualities: ludicrous pomposity, and genuine humour; ignorance of the simplest professional procedures, and great literacy; mean as hell with his authors, but capable of huge warm-heartedness; a proud husband and father and an office lothario. The apocryphal story of his interviewing a potential secretary, clearing his throat, adjusting his polka-dot bow tie and saying 'I have reached the stage in life when a man ought to have a mistress, and I think you might be fitted for this role' is believed because that is what his colleagues *think* he is like.

While he was at Secker's, no one ever knew whether he was in love with the place or merely using it as a rung in the ladder of his preferment. He probably did not know himself. He actually read, and admired, many of the firm's authors, particularly the foreign ones. On the other hand, when any of them appeared in the office, they might be treated to some extraordinarily pompous speech by Rosenthal about his own career, starting, 'As managing director of this firm, and potential chairman of the overall Heinemann group . . .'

As a businessman he can drive self-destructively hard bargains. For example, a number of 'his' authors, like Tom Sharpe, were late to get published in paperback because Rosenthal insisted (without their knowing) on making his 'popular' authors part of a double package-deal with the paperback company. Pan, Corgi or Penguin could only 'have' Sharpe or Bradbury or David Lodge on condition they also bought some German or South African bore who had taken Rosenthal's high-brow fancy.

Rosenthal's blunders have usually been his own fault. His triumphs probably owe much to the acumen of his wife Ann who is probably the cleverest literary agent in London. He knows how far he can go.

For all his obvious defects of character, many would look back on Rosenthal's time at Secker and Warburg as a sort of golden age. Unfortunately for the firm, he departed for the more hysterical pastures of Andre Deutsch in 1984 after a series of rows with BTR, then owner of Heinemann.

He was succeeded as managing director by Peter Grose, an ex-literary agent and aviator, not noted for reading his clients' manuscripts – but then literary agents don't. Thomson writes, 'When Peter Grose, a lively-minded, popular Australian became Publishing Director in 1980, he already had a clear idea of what the firm stood for.' This sounds ironical now since Grose himself has recently been kicked upstairs by his new boss, Paul Hamlyn.

George Malcolm Thomson concludes his account of the firm, 'Now, having charted its course through half a century, it seems a good moment to turn the page and begin a new chapter.' It surely isn't significant that when you turn the page there is a blank.

8 August 1986

Pop-boiler

Michael Joseph: Master of Words RICHARD JOSEPH (Ashford Press)
At the Sign of the Mermaid: Fifty Years of Michael Joseph (Michael Joseph)

'MICHAEL Joseph should never have been a publisher,' reveals his son Richard, halfway through his relentless biography of his father. This seems an unfair verdict as, it could be argued, Michael Joseph Ltd survived as a profitable, independent publishing house for as long as it did because its founder, his colleagues and his successors had an infallible, unremitting eye for the middle-brow and mediocre.

That may well be why this biography is published not by the family firm but by the enterprising Ashford Press. Richard Joseph, in an act of filial piety, sifted 'through trunks of old letters, piles of press cuttings, and an attic bursting with literary riches' and then spent two years on the manuscript. Michael Joseph, the firm, then rejected it, preferring a self-congratulatory 'festschrift' instead.

Michael Joseph the man was a successful literary agent with Curtis Brown before founding his firm at 38, and thus understood what publishing was really about: the making of money.

Apart from that we learn that Michael Joseph wrote books himself including the ones about cats. 'His famous cat books were tremendously popular,' says the son, but he also remembers 17 other books, and goes so far as to list all the father's published and unpublished articles as well.

We learn that Michael Joseph had three wives (one divorced, one died, one outlived) but are left remembering most that 'Michael was well known for his love of cats and he was renowned internationally for his affections.'

Insight into Michael Joseph is rather thin on the ground in the back-slapping *At the Sign of the Mermaid*. Those who provide recollections of the firm, if not necessarily of the founder, include H.E. Bates, Monica Dickens, E.S. Turner, Rumer Godden, Dickie Bird (not the cricket umpire, presumably, as there's a photograph of her), Richard Gordon, Keith Waterhouse, Derek Tangye, Henry Cecil, Miss Read, Arthur Hailey, Elizabeth David, Jane Grigson, Dick Francis, James Herriot, and improbably, James Baldwin, who writes of Michael Joseph's third wife and one-time secretary, Anthea: 'When she produced a contract out of her handbag, I signed on the spot. I never forgot that.'

The other authors are not much more interesting as they fatuously tug their forelocks. Listen to Barry Hines: 'When, a few weeks later, I went to the Bloomsbury Street office to meet Anthea I was extremely nervous. But that good and charming lady was immediately sensitive to my feelings and asked if I would like some tea or coffee. When I said that tea would be nice, she enquired, "Indian or China?" Then I knew I had arrived: from where I came from (sic) we just had tea.'

The pictures make up one of the few interesting sections. They are, one suspects, what being in publishing is all about. Photograph after photograph shows the bespectacled face of one Charles Pick (with Alec Guinness or Monica Dickens or Roald Dahl or someone else whose books he would have been unlikely to enjoy). Pick started as a salesman, became joint managing director of Michael Joseph, flounced out when Roy Thomas bought the firm, and went on to become chairman of Heinemann.

Last year, when Michael Joseph was being sold by the Thomson Group, negotiations were conducted by Thomson ex-chief executive Sir Gordon Brunton. He writes, with the only touch of asperity in an unctuous book: 'A persistent interest was shown by Heinemann in the guise of its former chairman, Mr Charles Pick, an approach which you will not be surprised to hear I considered singularly inappropriate.'

Quite so, but 50 years of Michael Joseph ended instead with the company being swallowed up by Peter Mayer's new commercial Penguin which shows every sign of carrying on the great tradition of the Founder.

14 November 1986

Naim droppings

Women NAIM ATTALLAH (Quartet)

R EADING books written by publishers is usually a bit of a blood sport. Mostly all they're up to is fondling their sensibilities. Sir Rupert Hart-Davis rubs himself up against the classics; Jeremy Lewis of Chatto is fascinated by his own adolescence; Christopher Sinclair-Stevenson of Hamish Hamilton witters on about his cultured holidays. The summit of modern publisher–lit. is undoubtedly the late Michael Joseph's prose poems about eroticism with his cats ('Sleep, coquette, your blandishments avail no more. Now I am delivered of your tyranny awhile', etc. – soon to be re-issued in a deluxe edition).

In this appalling genre Naim Attallah has gone straight to the top. For his hobby is a little more interesting: women. And he likes them not just one at a time, not in twos or threes, but in great gabbling throngs. Poshly gabbling, for preference. Namara House, where he concocts his phallic perfumes and saucy picture books, is thickly carpeted with gorgeous pouting Naimbirds of noble birth, if little brain. They are popularly known as Naim's harem. But really what they find themselves in is that other rich man's fancy: a private zoo.

Now, with oriental generosity, Mr Attallah has flung open the doors and allowed us all a peek. Indeed he has been out on safari and brought back no less than 289 prime specimens of ripe womanhood from around the world. The old, the young, the rich, the mad; from Koo Stark to Barbara Cartland.

The noise from this collection is, frankly, appalling, not to mention the smell. None of these women agree; all want to be heard.

Most of this snuffling and screeching is pretty dull. Yet Naim listened to it all, or at least he recorded it. Surely he did not believe any one of these women would suddenly tell him the answer to anything? Obviously not. All seem to have been pitifully eager to talk. Perhaps they didn't take the grinning Naim and his 'pocket-sized machine' seriously? Were there magic mushrooms in the 'Quartet salad'? Is the Attallah presence irresistibly idiotizing? Did they think he was their friend?

Whether it's him or them, he has captured some prize specimens. This book will become an invaluable *Who's She* work of reference. Unlike Anna Ford's awful *Men*, it gives you the names. Suppose Miss Arabella Weir was being friendly. A quick check would tell you that she herself promises she will 'usually come up with the goods'. And if you had your eye on Margaux Hemingway, how labour saving this tip would be: 'I need to have it when the moon is less full. I think it's all gravitational pull.'

Mr Attallah has most kindly asked all these women what sort of man pleases. Collectively, the responses amount to a tall order. Regine Deforges looks for 'almost a caveman spirit'. Beatrice Dalle selects 'men who are physically handsome'. Tina Brown, however, quite likes men who are extremely ugly. Shirley Conran doesn't mind short, fat or bald, but she does prefer millionaires, so throw it away quickly. Molly Parkin won't do it with Tories but she isn't picky about age. One 80-year-old 'was a wonderful lover, he had a very active tongue. I don't say that his member was great, but it didn't seem to matter at the time.' No, I expect not.

What do women think men are actually like? Victoria Glendinning seems to have been a mite unlucky here. 'I always imagine men more like railway trains chugging along, just wanting to go bang-bang-bang when they can.' Bang bang *bang?* Crikey. Teri Garr says quite firmly that 'they can have sex with a wall'. Oh dear, I'm sure she's right. I probably just haven't met the right wall yet.

And what do women think women are like? Miss Glendinning has the answer to this, too: 'A lot of women live almost like my dog Sophie – in the present.' Marie Helvin has a distinct theory: 'A woman's emotional feelings are stored in her sexual organs.' So does Melissa Sadoff: 'Our brain is different.' Just the one? Ah, well, Mary Kenny puts it all down to 'the atavistic ear' which women have, listening out for babies. Christina Monet points elsewhere: 'A hole is more passive than a penis.'

And what about Aids then? 'Nature's way of dealing with sexual liberation,' says Mirella Ricciardi amiably. Baroness Plowden agrees: 'One wonders whether God hasn't sent AIDS to make us pull ourselves together.' Isabel Goldsmith chirrups: 'Thank God for AIDS.' Millions may die, but at least it'll stop the Frogs pestering her. Lady Lothian doesn't think condoms are the answer. She believes they give you cancer 'from the friction of the rubber', although she is anxious to point out that she herself was 'never a refrigerator'.

Women is a triumph. Naim writes, quite superbly: 'Women have always been instrumental in whatever I have achieved.' I bet they're sorry now.

16 October 1987

Buffalo Bill's rodeo

Granta 20: *In Trouble Again* (Penguin)

'NEARLY every movement in Britain in the twentieth century has managed to find a forum in the place we normally turn to for such things, which is the literary magazine,' runs a quotation from *Encounter* printed in one issue of *Granta*. 'If one were looking, as writer or reader, for such a magazine, it would be hard at this minute to avoid the claims of *Granta*.' The author? The inexplicably ubiquitous Malcolm Bradbury, who by chance is listed among the magazine's editorial board.

Disinterested examination does not bear out his claims. Although touted by its publishers as the 1980s successor to John Lehmann's wartime *Penguin New Writing*, *Granta* was in fact started by his father, Rudolph, while a leisured and well-connected graduate in the 1890s. After pootling along, off and on, for 80 years the magazine found itself being commandeered in 1979 by a rather different figure.

Bearded and overweight, the American postgraduate Bill Buford might easily have been mistaken for a member of ZZ Top but it soon became apparent that behind the boozing, laid-back exterior was a shrewd operator. After the first, hesitant issues, which remained largely of Fenland interest, he hit on that trusty standby, the 'publishing crisis'; familiar names – Brigid Brophy, David Caute – were invited to trot out their party pieces and the issue duly came to metropolitan attention.

Buford was not slow to realize that such spurious pigeon-holing was the way to sustain attention among the capital's slack-minded media pundits. In the space of a few months he was no sooner off one telephone, flattering and cajoling the blonde publicity girls at trendy publishers to provide extracts from whatever Latin American novel was forthcoming, than he had picked up the receiver and was seeking interviews in the *Guardian, Bookseller, Tatler* and *Time Out* to promote the wonderful new talent he had discovered. No party was too marginal for him not to be on the late afternoon train to Liverpool Street; no amount of cheap red plonk could stop him enthusing, to all who would listen, about his magazine.

Such tactics brought him the sobriquet Buffalo Bill from sharp-tongued literary agent Pat Kavanagh but duly endeared him to Peter Mayer, brash new chief at Penguin who was looking for a way to restore his firm's intellectual credibility after such disasters as *The Four Hundred* and the loss of a lucrative backlist.

Ken Dickson (Marketing) Ltd of Sunninghill was dropped and *Granta* put itself in the hands of a corporation which has since swallowed up other independent imprints, such as Salamander, all the while maintaining that each will retain an 'individual identity'.

As far as *Granta* is concerned, this is limited to its office remaining in Cambridge. Whatever quirks of character it acquired in the long intervals between each issue have vanished with the need to produce a fresh movement every three months. Each issue bears a stark headline – 'Science', 'Autobiography', 'Dirty Realism' and, naturally, 'More Dirt'. Despite one piece of good fortune in having James Fenton in the Philippines during a coup, *Granta* is evidence more of skilful PR than of editorial talent. Far from representing Bradbury's 'movement', much of each issue is provided by eager publishers, Faber and Picador prominent among them.

Almost 40 pages of one issue contained fragments from an already heavily publicized novel by Milan Kundera, the Czech author who has been around for donkey's years. Most bizarre of all Buford agreed to print 100 pages from a monumentally pretentious and sub-literate account of a late-1960s Rolling Stones tour by an ageing druggie taken on by Heinemann's desperately trendy David Godwin.

To be fair, one might doubt whether Buford really likes what he prints. As a member of the panel at one publishers' bash he agreed to choose the year's worst books, something from which Lady Rachel Billington and Hilary Spurling demurred. Among the extracts read out with heavy derision by the galloping Buffalo was one from the Revd A.N. Wislon's *Scandal*. This self-same scene was heralded by *Granta* a few months earlier.

The latest issue is given over to travel writing, and the editorial board has vanished. At least 110 of its pages are shortly due out in hard covers. A fair proportion is very readable, notably Hanif Kureishi's piece on Bradford which has the eye for detail shown in his Ealing-like *My Beautiful Launderette*, but the impression is of a magazine assembled, not edited. One begins to wonder how long it can continue. Penguin's *Firebird* series has been put out to grass after four issues, and Peter Mayer might seek inspiration in the fact that Allen Lane called a halt to *Penguin New Writing* with issue 40. Long before then, the Buffalo will have disappeared across the prairie in search of another watering-hole.

6 February 1987

Prose and cons

Granta 34

THERE is no doubt that *Granta* has published exciting writing over the years. Unfortunately the years were 1983 and 1984, when editor Bill Buford coined the term 'dirty realism' and produced a series of issues containing the good and the unexpected: from Milan Kundera (in the days when literary editors thought he was an Italian football team) to the Rolling Stones.

Buford used to find new writers. Today he jumps on whatever literary bandwagon is passing. Simon Schama wins a prize? Why, let's commission him to do something for *Granta*. Allan Gurganus being hyped? Commission him. *Granta* claims to be 'A Paperback Magazine of New Writing', but 'new' in the sense of 'we've seen it all before'. *Granta* 34 does for new writing what *Rambo 94* would do for the art of cinema. There's as much chance of finding a new writer in *Granta* these days as of finding a Pogues' song on a Pavarotti album. (A few more literary lunches and the bearded Buford will soon bear a startling resemblance to the Nessun Dormobile.)

For all his faults as an editor (and Buford has many, as anyone who has ever heard his lunchtime 'Oh damn, I've left my wallet at the office' story will testify), the thinking man's Snipcock could produce an adventurous and readable magazine. But these days he's more concerned with expanding his publishing empire, and the magazine's content has suffered. For at least a couple of years it's been possible to predict *Granta*'s contents quite easily. Each one is guaranteed to contain (and the latest is no exception):

• *One concerned piece about Eastern Europe/Russia*: This time it's the Russia/Afghanistan question; last time it was Romania; in 32 it was Moravia; in 31 it was Bucharest and Timisoara; while *Granta* 30 went all the way and devoted an entire issue to ramblings on 'New Europe', just like every other publication in the land. Buford used to set trends, now he's about as trend-setting as the *Telegraph Magazine*. He'll be doing a Gulf War issue next. Or maybe a royal family one.
• *Several pages of self-promotion*: Buford used to allow other publishers the privilege of advertising their wares in *Granta*, but now it seems that he no longer needs the money so he can shut them out and advertise Granta Books instead. The current issue has five pages of self-promotion, including both

inside covers. Last time it was six pages, and check out the all-important inside covers of issues 32, 31, 30, 29, 28 . . .

• *Several pieces by 'new' writers who have appeared in* Granta *too often before*: Out of 12 pieces in the current issue, eight are by old *Granta* hands.

• *One piece by Martin Amis, Julian Barnes or Jonathan Raban*: See issues 34, 33, 32, 31, 30 and 29. Issue 28 was a self-indulgent birthday special so merely had something by *everyone* who's ever written for the magazine before.

• *Several pieces by people writing books for Granta Books*: Strangely this doesn't include Buford himself, who has allegedly been writing a book on football hooliganism for almost a decade. Maybe these days he finds the Groucho Club more amenable than sharing a stadium with a load of drunken illiterate yobs (he can get that every year at the Frankfurt Book Fair, anyway). In this issue it includes an extract from Simon Schama's book, 'published by Granta Books next spring', and a piece by Amitav Ghosh, who will be 'published by Granta Books in the autumn'. Why not just condense the books like *Reader's Digest* and have done with it?

• *At least one dead body*: In *Granta* 34 it's Soweto in the concerned photo-journalist's flashlight, with the dead body laid out on page 254. It's not as if the photos are well reproduced, though given the subject matter perhaps we should be grateful for all the grain we can get. Last time it was Bolivia (dead child, page 180), with harrowing photos of Romanian orphans for good measure. In 32 we got off lightly: the Czech bodies lying down were merely dead drunk. Issue 31? A cheerful set of photos of Bucharest funerals, not intruding on private grief in the least. Issue 30? 'The Death of Merab Kostava'. Issue 27 was actually called 'Death', and centred round a gruesome set of photos of people dead or dying in hospital casualty wards, with another dozen dead faces at the back for those who hadn't yet thrown up.

Quite what this says about the psychological state of the editorial team is uncertain, though it may reflect subconscious concerns with the increasingly likely death of *Granta*, unless someone operates soon.

1 February 1991

Mommie dreariest

Book Marketing Council: Mother's Day Promotion

*T*HE Publishers' Association, like any other trade body, is a company of wolves at heart. Its active arm is called the Book Marketing Council. This was set up in 1979 to flog more books – not by getting more buyable books published but by trying to shift the garbage with which booksellers were already lumbered.

It works by identifying potential buyers first and then selecting plausible titles to shove their way. The results have included such distinguished campaigns as 'Teenread' and, under the former director Desmond Clarke, the production of fatuous lists of Twenty Best Novels of Our Time and the Twenty Best Writers on War (tastefully called 'The Bloody Muse', that one).

Now the council has targeted a new bunch of suckers – mothers and their doting sprigs. For Mother's Day on 5 March, the BMC has launched a huge campaign to persuade people to consider books as similar to flowers or chocolates. A million promotional leaflets have been printed, to be distributed in bookshops, inserted in some editions of the *TV Times* and delivered door-to-door. Punters are invited to buy from a list of 12 'recommended' titles, directly, through the post, or via a 'Hotline'. The present will then be delivered in 'a choice of two beautiful wrappings'.

The beauty of the scheme from the publishers' viewpoint is that the books don't have to be any good.

The leaflet itself is impressively contemptuous. 'What would be a more perfect gift for Mother's Day than a book? It won't shed leaves or droop. It can't make her fat and she certainly doesn't need to water it.' Mothers, eh? Too lazy to look after plants properly, eat themselves stupid given half a chance.

The Janet Marsh Birthday Book (Century Hutchinson) for recording the family birthdays is ideal, isn't it? It caters to the mother's sole interest, it has little quotes from poets to keep up the pretence of a text, and it is embellished with fatuous water-colours of children with fairy wings capering about with mice in dungarees, for mothers love nature.

Flowers for all Seasons: Spring by Jane Packer (Pavilion) is good because it consists of pretty pictures with a central monomaniac's section on spring weddings, by the woman, mark you, who did up Fergie's step on the path to motherhood. 'Pew ends are a natural site for decoration', of course.

Enquire Within on Everything by Moyra Bremner (Century Hutchinson) recognizes that mothers are homemakers and you can get better service out of them with an instruction book. *Love* by Sheila Pickles (Pavilion) pays tribute to what keeps them on the production line. This 'scented book' is a packager's triumph: an anthology of unreadable extracts, accompanied by Victorian illustrations, it smells like a bijou loo. 'Gentle reader, please close your eyes, rub the marbled endpapers of this book, and dream of sitting in an English rose garden on a still midsummer afternoon.' Anything but read it. Bloody reading gets on a publisher's wick.

The World of Thrush Green by Miss Read (Michael Joseph), again enriched with cutesy-pie pictures, confirms that mother lives in a rustic never-never land in which she bakes scones (recipe provided) for grateful children. *Louisa Elliot* by Anne Victoria Roberts (Chatto) titillates her fancy of being courted, in the nineteenth century, by alternately a poet ('reserved, chaste and steadfast') and an officer in the Royal Dragoons ('dashing and hard-living').

Mother loves doctors and in *Doctors* by the infamous Erich Segal (Bantam) there is a medical heroine who not only has a child herself but brilliantly saves its life. However, the husband hero's comment before conducting his first pelvic examination – 'the vagina is really one part of the body we've actually been on both sides of. In one way we could look at it as a sort of homecoming' – seems a little too close to, well, home, even for Mother.

The thematic appeal of *Darling Ma* by Joyce Grenfell (Hodder), letters to her mother, was plainly irresistible, as was that of another winsomely illustrated picture book, *The World of the Baby: A Celebration of Infancy through the Ages* by Georgina O'Hara (Michael Joseph), combining the great subject with Mother's chronic nostalgia. *Hammers and Tongues* by Michele Brown and Ann O'Connor (Grafton), a mediocre anthology of women's quotes, seems, apart from not being a real book, almost a reasonable choice. But *Romancing the Stars: The Astrology of Love and Relationships* by Penny Thornton is a prodigy of silliness, more than 500 pages of lubricious tosh about what Virgos do in bed with Tauruses, supplemented by 'personality profiles' of the likes of Jeffrey Archer, Barbara Cartland and Uri Geller. 'Jeffrey Archer is all Ram.' Having been published in 1986, its nervous attempts at prediction already stand revealed as rubbish. Not that addled Ma is capable of knowing as much.

The Teeny Weeny Cat Book by Martin Leman (Pelham), the most negligible of all these non-books, leads the way, a state-of-the-art job. It contains just 12 tiny and inept pictures of cats with 12 non-original rhymes opposite ('C was a lovely pussy cat; its eyes were large and pale; And on its back it had some stripes, and several on its tail.') Mother, you see, goes weak at the knees when presented with anything tiny, all right teeny weeny, because it reminds her. And if she can't have babies any more, cats will do.

3 March 1989

Zzz . . . it's Booker bedtime

*T*HE Booker shortlist is dreary and predictable, the fault lying as much with dreary, predictable writers as with the dreary and predictable judges.

Suggestions that this may have been an even more than usually grim year for British fiction are confirmed by the fact that – despite the ritual cries of dismay about the make-up of the shortlist – critics have struggled to identify books that ought to have been chosen instead.

The *Evening Standard*'s A.N. Wislon called for more famous names – Anita, Sir Kingsley, P.D. James, Malcolm Bradbury – but this old farts' manifesto seems unlikely to attract much enthusiasm beyond the office of Wislon's new editor, Stewart Steven, who regards Dick Francis as literary fiction.

Otherwise, the only shock-horror omission anyone could find was Rose Tremain's semi-pisspoor sexchange yarn *Sacred Country*. This was amusing, as most of the literary editors and critics bemoaning her exclusion included in their pieces the traditional denunciation of the influence on the shortlist of the University of East Anglia Writing School (represented in the 1992 list by Ian McEwan). Fact: Poor, sad, non-shortlisted outsider Rose Tremain teaches this notorious course.

The prize will be announced on 13 October, with most of the money at the bookmakers on Michael Ondaatje's identikit Booker book and most of the industry rooting for Unsworth's 19th-century Thatcherite yarn, *Sacred Hunger*. But in the interim a number of sub-Booker prizes should be awarded.

THE HUBRIS SHIELD A strong shortlist this year. The early contender was former lit.-ed. Sebastian Faulks who for some reason decided to autograph the copies submitted to judges of *A Fool's Alphabet*: a Booker first in 24 years.

However, Faulks's doomed vanity was soon eclipsed. In 1992, a surprising number of authors have behaved as if they had a divine right to the prize. 'Yes. I expected to be on the shortlist,' Edna O'Brien told *The Guardian*. Capping even this arrogance, Secker & Warburg fixed the launch dinner-party for Malcolm Bradbury's Euro-pisspoor *Doctor Criminale* for the evening of the day the shortlist was announced, anticipating celebrations. In fact, neither Bradbore nor O'Bore made the final 20. The dinner was reportedly a maudlin affair.

THE GOOD EGG CUP The likeliest reason for the foolish certainty of literary timeservers that this would be their year is the presence on the judges' panel of Dame Harriet Harvey Wood, doyenne of the British Council. For decades her job has been to fly writers like Bradbore, O'Bore and P.D. James around the world to discuss their work in Eastern Europe and the Commonwealth. Hence the older writers were hoping she would book them a place on the shortlist with the efficiency with which she had arranged their tickets to Budapest. But the word is that – with an integrity which is to the credit of the British Council – she declined, when it came to the judging, to back her mates if they turned in sub-standard work.

THE POLLY (PUBLICISTS' ECONOMY WITH TRUTH) AWARD On the jacket of Paul Watkins's sub-sub-Hemingway *The Promise of Light*, Faber excitedly claim that the young man's first novel was 'nominated for a Booker Prize'. Juvenile critic Tom Shone was so impressed by this information that he made it the intro to his loving profile of Watkins in *The Indescribablyboring*. Fact: You can't be nominated for the Booker; you are entered by your publisher. What Faber means is that Watkins was entered for the Booker. In this sense, 100 books a year – including, this time round, bodice-ripper Dorothy Dunnett – are 'nominated' for the Booker.

THE POST-FEMINIST AWARD There has been the usual criticism of the lack of female writers on the list (1 out of 6 in 1992, slightly up from 0 last year). This makes people like Carmen Callil angry and generally leads them to call for more and more female judges. They should be careful. In many years, women judges have kept off women writers proposed by male judges. This year impeccably feminist chairperson Victoria Glendinning described one of the chaps as 'a condescending bastard' when he worried about the small number of women on the list. The *Sunday Times* tried to whip up some hysteria with the suggestion that the only book out of the six by a woman didn't make the original longlist of 24 and was mysteriously inserted into the shortlist at the last minute. Not true.

FALL FROM GRACE MEDAL In recent years, Faber has seemed to have a

lock on the shortlist, providing at least one of the six and – in several years
– the winner. Now the Queen Square magic seems to be fading. No Faber
books made the 1992 list and while two were close – Michael Dibdin's
thriller *Cabal* and Nigel Williams's comedy *They Came From SW19* – neither
was actually entered by the company. They were called in by the judges. The
official Faber trio – Watkins, P.D. James and dreary Deirdre Madden –
finished nowhere. Are Matthew Evans and fiction chief Robert McCrum
losing their touch?

THE CLEAN-UP PRIZE   The real winner this year is Peter Straus, Picador's
publisher and last of the great bookmen, who regards publishing as servicing
literature as opposed to progressing his own career. He is less morose and
Eeyore-like than usual at present as no fewer than four of the six shortlisted
books will be gracing Picador's paperback list next year, the imprint's 21st
anniversary. In addition, Straus has just published *The Butcher Boy* in
hardback. Coincidentally, Straus for the first time this year became a member
of the Booker board of management which appoints the judges and Mark
Lawson, one of the judges, is published by Straus.

THE OVERALL LOSER   The main loser this year is Terry Maher of Dillons.
As none of the shortlisted titles is published by Secker & Warburg or
Heinemann or any other imprint of Reed International, for the first time in
three years Dillons won't be able to cock a snook at the net book agreement
and discount certain shortlisted titles.

25 September 1992

2

REVIEWERS

The sound of one hand back-scratching

Fogey bared

Penfriends from Porlock A.N. WILSON (Hamish Hamilton)

O NCE upon a time there was a good novelist called A.N. Wislon. He was asked, as novelists often are, to undertake a little light reviewing work for the lowbrow market – *Spectator, Sunday Telegraph*, that sort of thing. He accepted. Indeed, he acquired a taste for it. He rose through the ranks, becoming literary editor of the *Spectator*. Finally he was promoted to chief book critic of *Private Eye*. Wealth and fame were his.

But he threw it all away. In a moving valedictory article he explained that he was giving up book reviewing to devote himself to his Art. When the person from Porlock next came knocking on the door trying to interrupt his creative frenzy with offers of work, Wislon would simply ignore him.

How moved we all were!

And what a lot of nonsense it turned out to be. For within months of hanging up his black cap Wislon had moved into an even gamier branch of journalism: tapping out 'why oh why?' pieces for the leader page of the *Daily Mail* in the persona of A.N. Cabdriver. ('That Archbishop of Canterbury – what's his game then? There's only one language them arse-bandits understand ... Oh, a 500 quid tip, ta very much guv...') The only literary works on which his opinions are sought these days are *Dandy* and *Beano*.

And what of his Art? He is reduced to writing pompous introductions to coffee-table books of photographs. 'The chief glories of France are comestible and potable,' he babbles in one such, *Landscape in France* (Elm Tree Books). 'This land of Cockayne, fat with food, runs with rivers of wine, "O fortunate Burgundy, whose breasts produce so good a milk!" Many a traveller must have echoed Erasmus's words when driving, or better still cycling, through the gentle landscape of Burgundy...' Bernard Levin would be proud of him.

If there's one thing drearier than a coffee-table book it's a collection of old reviews. *Penfriends from Porlock* is just such a collection, bunged together by Ms Rachel Boulding of Hamish Hamilton. To make matters worse, it doesn't include any of the few Wislon pieces one might care to re-read: the farewell to criticism, the deranged attack on Marina Warner, the *Private Eye* columns. He has the grace to admit in his preface that when he saw what Ms Boulding had retrieved from the Wislon archives '[he] was appalled'.

The dust-jacket promises a book that 'represents the wide range of A.N. Wilson's interests', but this must be the blurb-writer's little joke. Few ranges could be narrower or more creakingly predictable: not for nothing was Wislon the *fons et origo* of Young Fogeydom. Much of the book is an exaggerated genuflection to the 'genius of John Betjeman and of Barbara Pym', plus G.K. Chesterton ('such a wholesome antidote to the humourless-ness of our age') and Thomas Love Peacock ('as agreeable as it is possible to imagine') and, inevitably, the Great Cham ('Johnson's talk is an inexhaustible mine'). He has nothing memorable to say about any of them.

And then there's God. Wislon begins to mince uncontrollably at the delicious thought of 'soutane, amice, alb, girdle and violet Mass vestments'. He drools over birettas and breviaries, rosaries and ivory crucifixes. 'How many lovely baroque High Mass sets moulder in Anglican sacristies,' he simpers, 'while the celebrant (sorry, President) wears hideous floppy linen vestments?'

And so he goes on, a ridiculous mixture of grumbling blimp and preening nancy-boy, dreaming himself back to an age when he could camp it up in church and then repair to his club for roast beef and stilton.

'Cecil Beaton,' Wislon damningly suggests in one of his pieces, 'had no fear of the obvious and no fear of overdoing things in his quest for the beautiful.' The criticism could equally well apply to Wislon himself. He ends his review of Beaton's biography thus: 'I closed the book merely feeling that he was rather silly, and a little bit sad.' Precisely.

5 February 1988

Ford Bollox Ford

Wildlife RICHARD FORD (Collins Harvill)

IN the last couple of years book reviewers have got younger and so book reviewers' prejudices have changed.

Middle-aged or old writers of modest abilities – Margaret Drabble, Iris Murdoch, say – have suddenly found their books rudely rebuffed after 20 years of fawning from their contemporaries, themselves ejected from their positions.

The younger critics who have replaced them naturally believe they are free from any such unthinking fealties. They ain't, of course. It's only that time has not yet revealed them for what they are.

What these sprigs have in common is a belief that English fiction is shagged out (or daintier words to that effect) whereas American fiction is big-cocked and bouncing (ditto).

In its higher forms this involves some argument that American English is living and vital in a way that middle-class English English is not, now. In its dimmer ones, it's just that it's a lot more fun to read about mobile homes in Mississippi and Oldsmobiles in Montana than it is to read about concrete campuses in the Midlands and tatty squats in Lambeth.

Every young book reviewer and *Arena*-reader is barmy about the 'dirty realists' promoted by Bill Buford in *Granta*. Everyone worships the late Raymond Carver and adulates his successor and mate, Richard Ford. In a few years, or sooner, these tastes will look as quaint as the vogue enjoyed by the hoolahoop.

Like Saul Bellow's last two books, Richard Ford's new novel, *Wildlife*, is really just a short story dressed up as a book. It is also self-parodically poor. You wouldn't know it from the reviews. In the *Sunday Correspondent* James Wood called him 'the leading storyteller of his generation'; in the *Sunday Times* Penny Perrick gushed 'Every sentence Ford writes illuminates'; in the *Independent* Anthony Quinn was asked to make an unenthusiastic review enthusiastic by the literary editor, Robert Winder.

Ford made his name in this country with *The Sportswriter* (quite a good book ripped off from Walker Percy's brilliant one, *The Moviegoer*, written 20 years before). It's the maundering reflections of one aimless man, Frank Boscombe.

As one character's voice this was okay. What *Wildlife* catastrophically shows is that it's the only one Ford can do.

Wildlife is about a 16-year-old boy, Joe, watching his parents' marriage break up. Absurdly everybody in it, including the boy, not to mention the birds in the air, talks Fordese about Life and Luck and Happiness and Going Wrong, all the time. Existential questions are chewed over in the vocabulary of a dimwitted cowboy. Sub-Hemingway, sub-Brando, it's about as authentic as a 501 ad.

It's a succession of sub-philosophical little speeches. Dad tells his boy: 'Everything seems arbitrary. You step outside your life and everything seems like something you choose. Nothing seems very natural.'

The boy himself tells the story of his mother's lover in ludicrous Brandoesque cadences. 'Maybe, I thought, he was not to blame for kissing my mother and holding her dress up over her hips. Maybe that's all he could do. Maybe no one was to blame for that, or for much of what happened to anyone.'

So infectious is this rubbish that when the boy sees a wee boidy out of the window he credits it with a Fordian crisis of identity. 'It just sat as though it was waiting for something to start to happen that would give it a reason to move or to fly or even look in one direction or the other.' Feathered twat.

Ford has an incredibly over-worked vocabulary. 'Thing', 'anything', 'something', 'nothing', 'maybe', 'happiness', 'sadness', 'luck', 'life', 'light' – these words are combined into sentences like symbols in a slot machine. 'Words' is another Ford word, of course. 'And there are words, significant words, you do not want to say, words that account for busted-up lives, words that try to fix something ruined that shouldn't be ruined and no one wanted ruined, and that words can't fix anyway . . .' And so cretinously on.

This isn't vigour, it's decadence. Our critics are yet more decadent for admiring it. *Wildlife* is Adrian Mole, aged 16-and-a-half, taken seriously. So what if Americans believe the *Of Mice and Men* delusion – that the harder you find it to be articulate the more true and moving you are? That way lies Arnold Schwarzenegger.

31 August 1990

The Read Brigade

Books of the Year

*E*VERYONE likes 'Books of the Year' features. Editors like them because they don't have to pay for them. Contributors like them because it's flattering to be asked and they can conspicuously do favours. Booksellers like them because they come at Christmas, helping baffled donkeys spend their money. And intelligent people like them because they mount a finer display of bookworld sottishness than anything else all year.

This time round, though, there were signs of self-consciousness in the Books of the Year ranks. The *Listener* had no Books of the Year because of some childish objection to the Cult of Personality. The *Guardian* had none because nobody wants to have anything to do with its new literary editor, Waldemar Thing. The *Newstatesperson* didn't get it out on time (disorganised). The *Literary Review* missed altogether (drunk).

However, those that managed it came up with the goods, from the intelligent person's point of view. This was the year of spreading oneself thinly. Poor was the pundit who secured only one showing; anyone who was anyone opined multiplely.

Eighteen people chose their Book of the Year more than once. In other words, everyone whose name remains in the head of a literary editor after lunch. Any feeling of *déjà vu* this year was not supernatural.

Debrett gives few clues as to whether it is more genteel, when choosing one's book of the year several times, to be toughly loyal to the same title or to hint at the rich scope of one's reading by choosing differently on each occasion. Most people opt for the latter. The energetic Richard Cobb, for example, managed to prefer differing books for the *Spectator*, the *Sunset Times* and the *Daily Torygraph*.

But other, seasoned, pound-a-word pros like Mortimer elected for the former method, as less labour-intensive. In the *Sunset Times* Mortimer thought Marquez's novel *Love in the Time of Cholera* 'a wonderfully funny, tender account of physical love postponed until old age; a novel written with all of Nabokov's brilliance, but a better book than Nabokov ever managed'. In the *Spectator* his inimitable wit had refined this to 'an extraordinarily touching story of sex postponed until the partners are very old and can enjoy it. The best book Nabokov never wrote.' Sheer professionalism.

Arse-licking took a back seat in 1988. In the *Financial Times* Douglas Jay achieved full lingual extension by choosing as his book of the year that captivating narrative *The Financial Times: A Centenary History*. And in *The Times* Isabel Raphael scored a more personal application by selecting the paperback of that incisive study *Word-Watching* by Philip Howard, bonehead literary editor of *The Times*.

Otherwise it was all a matter of dull old log-rolling and autofelicitation. It was reassuring to see Number Two *Spec* poetry bore Peter Levi sucking up, in a number of venues, to Number One *Spec* poetry bore P.J. Kavanagh, in the time-honoured manner, but shocking that Kavanagh, unlike last year, failed to reciprocate with recognition of Levi's awful Shakespeare biography. How rude. Turn and turn about, please.

In the self-love section there were good showings from Anthony Blond (who chose a book he himself had published) and Roy Strong, who in the *Torygraph* chose *The Garden in Winter* because, as he put it with his usual scholarly elegance, 'my garden happens to be in it'. But runaway victor here was Barbara Cartland, again in the *Telegraph*. 'My favourite book is *Barbara Cartland's Year of Royal Days* (Lennard), which I wrote myself. I only read history and therefore this book, which has an historical anecdote for every day of the year, was a test of my memory and my research, mostly among my own Library which contains over 1,000 books. To me, because it was historical, this book was a sheer joy.' Here Cartland sets a standard for years to come.

The most popular choice of book this year was Philip Larkin's *Collected Poems*, with 19 mentions, or Tom Wolfe's *Bonfire of the Vanities*, with 20 mentions, some repeat appearances. Twelve brains chose Marquez; eleven liars Holroyd's *Shaw*; eleven more honest men Primo Levi. Ten dullards preferred David Lodge's *Nice Work*. A.N. Wilson has eight friends. Seven citations were won by Stephen Hawking, Peter Carey, Raymond Carver, Penelope Fitzgerald, Bruce Chatwin and, unexpectedly, by Roy Foster for his *Modern Ireland*. It may even be a good book.

Melvyn Bragg demonstrated his genius for arts journalism – which is a matter of becoming a thirsty depersonalized sponge – by choosing the three winners, Larkin, Wolfe and Marquez, all by himself. In the barefaced category, high marks were won by Matthew Parris for honouring the dead with *Russell Harty's Grand Tour*, and by Galen Strawson, for honouring the brain-dead with Jay McInerney's *Story of My Life*. In the come-off-it stakes Germaine Greer triumphed with *Poems on Affairs of State: Augustan Satirical Verse – Vol. IV*, from Yale, 'edited by Galbraith M. Crump and published in 1968'. It was the 'M.' that pleased.

This was a good year for ludicrous encomiums. Somebody called Geoffrey Bailey praised Susan Hillmore's *The Greenhouse* for telling 'the sad drama of a family lovingly watched over by the greenhouse'. Next year the outside toilet? Jasper Griffin was hearteningly concerned for the fittings too. 'Best reading of the year for any literate loo must be J.D.N. Kelly's *The Oxford Dictionary of Popes*,' he asserted.

Martin Amis thought his mate Redmond O'Hanlon's book *In Trouble Again* was 'hallucinogenic, scrotum-tightening'. Personal problems, no doubt. Bimbette Kate Saunders said of bimbo Candia McWilliam: 'She writes like Henry James in a ballgown and tiara.' Dozy John Grigg favoured Roy Foster because 'his book is large, but light and comfortable to hold'.

But this is a time for tradition and this year's Anthony Burgess Shield goes once more to Anthony Burgess. He took it with a masterful two-pronged attack. In the *Observer* he simply listed without comment eleven books (such profusion of interests). In the *Independent* he went for the kill. 'I deliberately limit myself to two books that have lighted autumn bonfires in my mind,' he opened. One was a study of 'the imaginative faculty ... the death of humanism, the sign as self-referential phenomenon, the image as an image of an image'. The other was a novel about 'semiological obsession', 'books talking to books', by Umberto Eco. This, he lightly commented, is 'not out, I think, in English until next year'. Olé!

23 December 1988

Drooltide greetings

CHRISTMAS 'Books of the Year' features resemble nothing so much as that other Christmas trinket, angel chimes. Both go tinkle, tinkle, tinkle; both go round and round and round again; and both are fuelled by hot air.

It's not even the log-rolling that appals any more. When there's nothing out there but logs, what does it matter? So what if Malcolm Bradbury infallibly chooses a book by a graduate of his creative writing course, Ian McEwan, as the one 'which deserved more attention than it got'? Or that there was the usual little clique of Oxford bodies sophisticatedly taking it in turns to lick one another. Ian McEwan choose Craig Raine who chose Galen Strawson who chose Ian McEwan ...

And who cares that Anthony Powell had the foresight to select as book of the year the latest book by 'the sensitive hand of Hilary Spurling' – as it happens, his own future biographer? Or that Powell's other choice, by his old mate V.S. Naipaul, was in turn assiduously selected by the very same Ms Hilary Spurling in the general interests of sociability?

Or that in the *Independent on Sunday* five people contrived to choose books by other people choosing books on the same page – in one case (Julian Barnes cosying up to Joan Smith) despite the book having come out a couple of years back? Or that in the *Sunday Times* Humphrey Carpenter blithely nominated a book by his gardener, 'set in our garden', and chosen by nobody else at all?

Never have there been so many Christmas books pages; never have they been so dull. Nicholas Shakespeare, literary editor of the *Telegraph*, showed his contempt by issuing the *same* Christmas books supplement with both the Saturday and Sunday *Telegraphs.* Nobody noticed.

Question: How many times can one person choose his or her books of the year? Answer, somehow: as many times as he or she is asked. And this year everybody was asked many times.

So we got, contain your excitement please, John Mortimer choosing his books of the year in the *Sunday Times.* There his 'trio of prizewinners' is made up of Muriel Spark, Claire Tomalin and Ruth Rendell. But wait a tic and, trumpet tootling, here he comes again, in the *Spectator.* There his holy trinity still includes Tomalin and Rendell, but Spark has been mysteriously transmogrified into Peter Ackroyd, the gargantuan biographer.

What a pro, what economy of effort. Such fatigued, minimal alteration was a tactic adopted this year by many other multiple entry merchants, including John Banville, Patrick Leigh Fermor, Doris Lessing, Colin Thubron and Penelope Fitzgerald. Other noted carousel-riders – the Bragg itself, Anthony Burgess, D.J. Taylor and A.S. Byatt – preferred to show their creative powers by somehow contriving to choose entirely different books of the (same) year for different reasons in different papers.

Ruth Rendell fouled up, betwixt and between. She lavishly praised A.S. Byatt's Battenburg cake of a book *Possession* in the *Telegraph* but, when she did it again in the *Sunday Times*, let herself down badly, simply saying 'there remains nothing new to say about it'.

Feeble! Be nerd enough and there's always something new. You can say, for example, as Craig Raine did of Galen Strawson's *The Street Connexion*, a study of 'causation and David Hume', that 'it stretched me till I twanged'. You can say, as Hugo Barnacle did of Salman Rushdie, that he can 'still make words bounce and scamper'. You can be dork-brain enough to name no fewer than 15 books as your book of the year, as did Christopher Hawtree.

Or you can make sure your books are chosen by nobody else – because – perchance! – they're in a foreign language. (Traditionally this manoeuvre is known as the Burgess Finger, but this year even Burgess was out-fingered by Gabriel Josipovici who chose three books in French, of which one was translated into French from the German and one from the Czech).

Or you can cover yourself by – waggishly! – choosing books that aren't actually books of the year at all, not by a long stretch, like the one chosen by Noel Malcolm in the *Spectator* – John Paget's *Hungary and Transylvania* (2 vols, John Murray, 1839).

Or, please may we all go home now, you can take *ishoo* with one of the topical books of the year by making it – controversially! – your *worst* book of the year. Burgess's autobiography, Rushdie's children's story, Ackroyd's *Dickens*, Noel Annan's *Our Age*, A.S. Byatt's stuffed turkey, Nobel winner Naguib Mahfouz's *Palace Walk* – all got the pro and con treatment, as if one way or other it mattered.

It didn't and it doesn't; it just wasn't a good year for books ('a year not remarkable for fiction,' said Burgess, 'a vintage year for fiction,' said Grey Gowrie).

The books most often nominated were all tediously obvious. Counting on my bleeding stumps, they were led by Byatt (the gangrenously boring *Possession*), followed by Claire Tomalin (*The Invisible Woman*), Penelope Fitzgerald (*The Gate of Angels*) and John Updike (*Rabbit at Rest*). Others listed a lot were John McGahern's *Amongst Women*, Robert Hughes's essays, *Nothing If Not Critical*, Alice Munro's stories, *Friend of My Youth*, Burgess's autobiography, Ray Monk's biography of Wittgenstein and Hilary Spurling's life of Paul Scott. The only surprise was the support for Derek Walcott's epic poem *Omeros*.

Maybe it's even good. And then again maybe it was a better year for video games. Or petunias.

21 December 1990

Prose . . . and cons

Books of the Year

Not only has this been a poor year for books, it's been – far more importantly – a poor year for books of the year. There's been a ruinous outbreak of shame among literary editors. At the *Independent on Sunday*, Blake Morrison did not even let his reviewers tip each others' books. Dimwit, spoilsport, wally! Why does he think we read them except to see who's licking whose arse, and who has churlishly failed to reciprocate?

And, worse, this year he and others have had the bright idea of setting each reviewer to choose books in his or her own area only. This robs us of the pleasure of seeing people pretend to make a measured selection from all the books published over the last 12 months (say, 65,000).

No publishing year could ever be dire enough completely to defeat the kind of people asked to choose their books of the year. But this year's books have approached closer to acknowledged tedium than those of any year in living memory.

Some reviewers have actually confessed it. In the *Independent* Gabriel Josipovici firmly blamed the books: 'This is the first year for as long as I can remember when I cannot think of a single book that really moved me.' In the *Sunday Times*, Peter Kemp got the bad news over quickly: 'In what has been a dismal year for new novels, Pat Barker's *Regeneration* (Viking) shines out.' His editor, John Walsh, took exactly the same approach, adding only some phallic Celtic poncing: 'While several good novelists seemed to be operating at half-strength this year, William Trevor's *Two Lives* (Viking) stood out like a dolmen in a playground.' (Presumably meaning 'huge' – as in 'have I got a dolmen for you, darling!')

Even Anita Brookner thought things looked a bit flat. 'Not an adventurous year,' she observed in the *Spectator.* 'All the established novelists appeared at their most characteristic and therefore their most predictable.' Including her. Usually, Ruth Rendell nominates Anita Brookner and Anita Brookner nominates Ruth Rendell. Not this year. Too tired, perhaps.

It was a struggle for anybody to find a bright side to look on. Numerous frauds protested that it had been a good year for literary biography. Anthony Burgess, bless him, went one better. 'This has been a good year for scholarly compilations,' he announced; an elegant way of allowing that it has been pisspoor for everything else (certainly nobody chose his silly book about Mozart).

The classic Burgess Manoeuvre, of ostentatiously selecting books in foreign languages, was almost universally adopted this time around, though not so much to show off as to hint that, *franchement*, English books had been terrible. Richard Cobb chose a book by the 'parish priest of the village of Vattetot-sous-Beaumont in the Pays de Caux from 1945 to the late 1980s'; Hilary Spurling improved on this by choosing *La Femme Lapidée*, 'an Iranian journalist's laconic account of the stoning of a woman taken in adultery four years ago in the Ayatollah's Iran'. That's one in the eye for English writers, anyhow.

Wallflowers abounded. Michael Ignatieff chose Julian Barnes, but nobody at all chose his dreadful novel (definitely not Julian Barnes).

The most pointed snubs came to Woy Jenkins. His autobiography, *A Life at the Centre* (Macmillan), was actually the second most popular choice of the year, cited nine times – but it was ignored by both David Owen and Michael Foot. Choosing instead a life of Bob Boothby, poor old Worzel said hopefully: 'Sometimes the lesser lights, properly displayed, can illuminate the political scene better than the blazing assurance of their leaders as presented by biographers and autobiographers' – yes, and sometimes they can just fizzle out, can't they?

Easily the most popular choice, rather ridiculously, was Nicholson Baker's charming little essay about his obsession with John Updike, *U & I* (Granta). This was followed by Woy's memwoirs, and *Wise Children*, the novel by Angela Carter (Chatto), with most of her supporters expressing a friendly wish that she had won a prize. Immediately behind came John Richardson's *A Life of Picasso Vol. 1* (Cape), and the biography of Darwin by Adrian Desmond and James Moore (Michael Joseph). The latter 'brings the hot historiography of science to the life of this sweet-natured *rentier*, and inserts him authoritatively into the violent class conflict and religious disputes of his time,' said that authoritative inserter, John Ryle, hotly, in the *Sindi*. Helen Zahavi said that it was 'as if Oscar Wilde had written Death Wish'; Ian Thomson said of Iain Sinclair's *Downriver*, 'he writes like Dickens on lysergic acid'; and Frederic Raphael said of *Hitler and Stalin*, it 'just shows what Plutarch could have done if he had had a word-processor'. A thin year indeed.

6 December 1991

Books of the Year

*F*OR several years this column has tracked the log-rolling in 'books of the year' choices: the cheery waves over the page to pals, publishers, lovers, former pupils and even old tutors.

It's become a Christmas tradition. Ruth Rendell and Anita Brookner bob and curtsey to one another; Peter Levi and P.J. Kavanagh stand each other a round; Malcolm Bradbury sends his best wishes to the alumni of his course in creative writing; Craig Raine licks the arse of Ian McEwan, his old friend and near neighbour in north Oxford – everybody gets into the festive spirit. It's the book trade's office party.

But this year people have become a little shy, shame-faced even. To be sure, Julie Burchill, Jan Morris and Alice Thomas Ellis chose only books by their friends, but the party-poopers admitted it. In the *Independent on Sunday*, shockingly, contributors were again disallowed from nominating books by colleagues.

There remain, however, one or two valiant outposts of old-style plugging. Hilary Mantel, who this year wrote a pre-publication puff for Adam Thorpe's *Ulverton* and then somehow 'reviewed' it too, made it her book of the year in the *TLS* ('displays a unique brand of talent, virtuosity, energy and warmth of heart'), the *Spectator* ('an amazing technical feat but also warm, funny and very moving') and the *Daily Telegraph* ('not so much a novel as a theatrical performance: uncanny, accomplished and moving').

Kate Kellaway, in the *Observer*, bravely selected her dear friend James Lasdun's wretched stories; and Craig Raine did the business for McEwan's *Black Dogs* in the *IOS*. A.S. Byatt recommended Christopher Hope's *Serenity House* in the *Sunday Times*, Byatt and Hope being old chums. And Alice Thomas Ellis plugged Beryl Bainbridge's *The Birthday Boys* in the *Spectator* – Bainbridge's publisher, Colin Haycraft of Duckworth, being ATE's husband.

But generally it was a pitiful performance. All the bitchy reviews of reviews have finally killed the spirit of giving that used to prevail at this time of year. Happily, though, mutual aid has been replaced by something even funnier: sustained self-advertisement.

Books are now chosen primarily to display the chooser's character. You still can't find out which books to buy, but you can discover how all these people like to think of themselves.

Nicholas Shakespeare likes to think of himself as an exotic, so he chooses foreign novels and adds: 'I finished this on a glacier 16,000 feet in the Andes.' Anita Brookner is sorry for herself and so writes: 'Colin Dexter's *The Way Through The Woods* is beguiling enough to make one forget a high temperature, as it did in my case, and other winter ailments.' Jocelyn Targett is consumed with ambition and self-importance, so he believes *Black Sun* by Geoffrey Wolff must be the book of the year, even though it wasn't published this year, because 'Of the books I've read this year, it is the one I am most jealous of.'

Craig Raine is sex-mad and so in the *TLS* said quite simply: 'I enjoyed the sex in three books: Garrison Keillor's *Radio Romance*, Nicholson Baker's *Vox* and Susan Wick's *Singing Underwater*', as though he was the one who had it (no doubt, in the privacy of home, he did). Malcolm Bradbury's recent novel was slaughtered by the reviewers, so he begins: 'In the chaotic and often bitter spirit of reviewing this last year, two books that have given me great pleasure seem not to have won the careful attention they deserve.' Sadly, neither was actually his own.

That perfection was left to Jeanette Winterson, who famously chose her own effort as 'book of the year', rightly suspecting perhaps that nobody else would. 'My own *Written on the Body* is this year's most profound and profoundly misunderstood book. A fiction which dismantles the scaffolding of the 19th century novel, replacing time, place, situation, character, even gender, with an intense consciousness. An exaltation of love. An exultation in language. Words unclothed.' Mind unhinged? No, Winterson has merely grasped that these choices exist purely for self-display and acted decisively, praising her own intelligence overtly, rather than covertly like everybody else. She has set a standard.

The prize for axe-grinding goes to Paul Johnson, recommending in the *ST* Lady Antonia Fraser's *The Six Wives of Henry VIII* and claiming it was attacked by 'envious' academics. In fact the academics' complaints were at inaccuracy and emotiveness.

The widespread recognition that 'book of the year' choices are for waggling your bum seductively, rather than choosing the books of the year, has led to the phenomenal number of multiple entries this year.

William Boyd, Alastair Forbes, John Biffen, Penelope Lively, Julian Barnes, Auberon Waugh, Craig Raine, Tom Paulin, Gabriel Josipovici, Jonathan Keates, D.J. Taylor, J.G. Ballard, Ruth Rendell, A.S. Byatt, Lorna Sage, Jonathan Raban, Terry Eagleton, Paul Johnson and Frederic Raphael – all made two or three appearances in various papers, some choosing the same, some different. Vote early and vote often, eh?

Adding up total nominations is therefore best done on the one, two, oh hell, heck of a lot, system. Much the most mentioned title was the *Selected Letters of Philip Larkin* (with Anthony Powell's commendation – 'The selection contains much to ponder' – the most poignant, since what Powell must be pondering is the discovery that although Larkin wrote to him politely enough, in letters to Kingsley Amis he regularly called him 'the horse-faced dwarf').

Victoria Glendinning's *Trollope* and Miranda Seymour's *Ottoline Morrell* were the most popular biographies, and *Ulverton* would have been the most-cited novel even without Hilary Mantel's heft. Other books that may well be quite good are Nick Hornby's *Fever Pitch,* John Gross's *Shylock*, Charles Sprawson's *Haunts of the Black Masseur: The Swimmer as Hero*, Thom Gunn's poems *The Man with Night Sweats*, Richard Ford's *Granta Book of the American*

Short Story, and perhaps even Donna Tartt's debut novel, *The Secret History*. Who knows?

One thing is certain, however. Michael Ignatieff, Edmund White, Valentine Cunningham, Cressida Connolly, Chloe Chard, Zara Steiner and Richard Eyre all chose Michael Ondaatje's completely bogus book, *The English Patient*. They have therefore proved once and for all that they have no literary judgement whatsoever and we need never pay any attention to them again. Thanks very much. A lovely Christmas present.

18 December 1992

You scratch my book . . .

YOU felt you'd read many of this year's 'book of the year' choices before? Well, you had, you had.

An astonishing number of reviewers chose their books of the year twice or thrice, showing conclusively what a small circuit the reviewers tread. Round and round, whoops, it's you again, *luvly* to see you.

Those who gave us the benefit of their advice more than once included Paul Johnson, Hilary Mantel, Jonathan Raban, Roy Foster, Robert Harris, Michael Palin, Michele Roberts, William Boyd, D.J. Taylor, Julie Burchill, Jilly Cooper, Gerald Kaufman, J.G. Ballard, Alastair Forbes, Hilary Mantel, Paul Johnson . . . Nice for them, but an incey-wincey bit claustro for the rest of us.

There are two techniques: one is somehow to try to find that you have chosen different books of the year, the other to brazen it out and short-change your readers.

Trying the second, Hilary Mantel worked hard. In the *TLS* she told us that Glyn Maxwell's poetry book *Out of the Rain* has 'energy, wit and style'. In the *Spectator*, she found it 'supple, witty and ambitious'. In the *Daily Telegraph*, she had been 'enchanted, haunted and amused'. Mantel's readers of course may well feel duped, done over and despised.

Michele Roberts was simply contemptuously lazy. In the *Sunday Times*, she offered this: 'The novel I most enjoyed this year was *Aquamarine* by Carol Anshaw (Virago), a tender and wry examination of the choices its heroine might have made. Three completely different versions are given of how her life might have turned out, linked by the image of the aquamarine water in the swimming-pool and the women athletes who meet in it. A new issue of a classic cookery book is Edouard de Pomiane's *Cooking with Pomiane* (Serif): both serious and funny, never pompous, enjoyably anti-slimming. Giovanni di Paolo's ravishing illustrations of Dante's Paradiso are reproduced in an edition by John Pope-Hennessy (Thames & Hudson), hideously expensive but pure delight.'

By a strange coincidence, on the same day (28 November) she offered this to readers of the *Sunset Times*: 'The novel I most enjoyed reading this year was *Aquamarine* by Carol Anshaw (Virago), a funny, tender and wry examination ... Three completely different versions ... linked by the image of the aquamarine water ... classic cookery book ... serious and funny, never pompous, and enjoyably anti-slimming ... Dante's Paradiso ...' and so on, word for word. Truly, the word-processor is a labour-saving device.

Then we have the old-fashioned shameless plug. In the *Spectator*, Alice Thomas Ellis carelessly called it that, naming a book published by her husband, Colin Haycraft: 'I make no apology for this shameless plug, any more than I would for our superb cheese pudding. *Le patron mange ici.*'

In the *Daily Telegraph*, Nicholas Mosley was similarly upfront with his ad: 'The book I have most admired this year is *The Green Book of Poetry* (Frontier), compiled and with a bold running commentary by my son, Ivo Mosley ... I can imagine no better Christmas present.'

Slyer was Jeanette Winterson. Last year she made herself the first person other than her soulmate Barbara Cartland ever to choose her own book as the book of the year. This had the disadvantage that almost anybody who could read could see that he was being cheated. This year, much more subtly, she chose *The Penguin Book of Lesbian Short Stories* edited by Margaret Reynolds, saying 'this focused and purposeful anthology will pleasure its readers'. That way she didn't have to mention that Margaret Reynolds is the woman she lives with, nor that the climactic story in this collection is the only work published this year by Jeanette Winterson, which, as it happens, is all about her *grande affaire* with Margaret Reynolds. Move over, buggins, c'est moi, Jeanette!

Similarly underhand log-rolling came from John Keegan (*Torygraph*), who chose Hugh Thomas's *The Conquest of Mexico* '... because Hutchinson should be congratulated for publishing a work of high scholarship as a commercial venture. It deserves a great success.' As, presumably, does Keegan's own *A History of Warfare* (a work of scholarship blah blah blah ...) coincidentally published by ... Hutchinson.

The *Torygraph*'s readers were also treated to Martin Cropper plugging his great friend Jonathan Meades's 'swaggering *Pompey*' and Rose Tremain doing likewise for *May the Lord in His Mercy Be Kind to Belfast* by her East Anglian neighbour Tony Parker.

Meanwhile in the *Sunset Times*, Lucy Hughes-Hallett eulogized *Paddy Clarke Ha Ha Ha* by Roddy Doyle: 'as remarkable for the subtlety of its prose as for the unsentimental clarity of its vision of childhood'. By some mischance, Roddy Doyle neglected to mention his publisher, Dan Franklin of Secker & Warburg, in his list of thanks when he won the Booker Prize. Lucy H-H is Mrs Dan Franklin, so she's presumably repairing the damage. One of her other chosen books, *Trainspotting* by Irvine Welsh, was also published by her hubbie at Secker.

In the area of simple old-fashioned, straightforward, artisanal arse-licking – all cricked necks and furred tongues – there was little competition for Penny Perrick of the *Sunday Times*. Alone among reviewers she thought the book of the year was '*Highgrove: Portrait of an Estate* (Weidenfeld) by HRH The Prince of Wales and Charles Clover ... the heir to the throne reveals where his talents really lie: in creating thyme walks, drainage systems, wild flower gardens and turning a fairly dismal country house into an earthly delight ...' Well, the interest in drainage systems we knew about.

Sadly, this was the last year of Anthony Burgess's books of the year and it wasn't a classic performance. Happily, the profoundly pretentious position he has vacated has been confidently assumed by the libidinous ivory-plonker Alfred Brendel. In the *Sunday Telegraph*, he confidently selected only books not available in English: 'Julio Cortazar's last collection of stories *Deshoras* (Unzeiten, Suhrkamp, 1990) laconic and masterful. Felisberto Hernandez's *Hortensias*, hallucinatory prose from an Uruguay (1902–1964) ...' An Uruguayan. Olé. Or whatever the equivalent is in Latvian.

The book most chosen: Alan Clark's *Diaries*, named 17 times, by almost everybody on the *Sunday Telegraph* (at last somebody's had the guts to say how despicable and smelly women and the working classes are, arf arf) but by nobody at all at the *Observer.*

Next, surprisingly, came the thoroughly disappointing *Dr Johnson and Mr Hyde* by Richard Holmes (11 votes), trailed by *The Marriage of Cadmus and Harmony* by an Eyetie, Roberto Calasso, and Blake Morrison's weepie about his dad's death, *And When Did You Last See Your Father?* (10 each). Calasso must be good. Blake Morrison, on the other hand, is the literary editor of the *Independent on Sunday*, which is thought not to have spoiled his chances among those who plan to publish a book themselves in the next year or two.

Paddy Clarke Ha Ha Ha got more than five mentions, as did Sebastian Faulks's novel *Birdsong*, published by Hutchinson and praised by Faulks's friend, and Hutchinson editor, Euan Cameron in the *Torygraph*. Others with more than *cinq points* were Andrew Motion's *Philip Larkin: A Writer's Life*, Vikram Seth's *A Suitable Boy*, Carol Shields' *The Stone Diaries*, the *Flaubert-Sand Correspondence*, and Cormac McCarthy's Wild West novel, *All the Pretty Horses*.

17 December 1993

Personality disorders

*T*HE most cursory glance at the literary history of the past 150 years swiftly dispels the illusion that books were ever reviewed simply on their merits.

Thackeray, Trollope and Gissing – to take only three eminent Victorians – have left terrifying accounts of the back-scratching and wire-pulling that necessarily accompanied any attempt to get your works favourably noticed in the 19th century. Then, as now, book reviewing had fallen victim to the fatal tendency of the critic to confuse whatever he might think of a writer's politics or eagerness to hand out dinner invitations with the writing itself.

In the 20th century this tendency has plumbed even more bizarre depths. In the 1940s, for example, any High Church journal worth its salt could be guaranteed to grow apoplectic in its attacks on anything that could be described as 'modern' or 'highbrow' – except when it happened to be written by T.S. Eliot. Eliot, you see, was an Anglo-Catholic and 'one of us'. Consequently, his poems had to be well reviewed, even if they were full of incomprehensible statements that didn't rhyme.

Sixty years later the cult of personality remains the single factor most likely to reduce the average book review to biased nonsense. Its current victim, inevitably enough, is the late Philip Larkin. Not only have the up-market arts pages in recent weeks been full of assaults on Larkin's character, as revealed in Anthony Thwaite's edition of the letters and Andrew Motion's biography (both Faber) – as if the old boy's drooling over tit-mags mattered; there has also been a great deal of concentrated sneering about his poetry, with the assumption that the two are somehow linked.

The complaints about Larkin generally take two forms. On the one hand there is the suggestion that because he was (or affected to be) racist and anti-Semitic, no child reared according to the stifling dictates of political correctness should be allowed to read his work – an argument so fatuous one despairs about the intellects of the people putting it forward. On the other there is the suggestion – a slightly more plausible one – that the costive, negative aspects of Larkin's character seep through into his verse, thereby rendering it 'limited', narrow and so on.

This line of thought is arguable, for there are aspects of a writer's life and opinions that will always surface in his or her work, but in Larkin's case it is always liable to founder when set against the motives of the people propounding it. For what Professor Eagleton and Mr Tom Paulin really dislike about Larkin is what he represents, his Englishness, his liking for Mrs Thatcher, in fact his ordinariness.

Larkin is a characteristic figure of his time, not a singular one, and it is this that makes his detractors gnash their teeth. Also there's the fact that he isn't *lofty* enough, don't you know – even his fear of death is somehow made to seem immature, as if everyone weren't afraid of dying. At any rate it can be safely predicted that if Larkin had ever written a sonnet to Arthur Scargill, Professor Eagleton wouldn't hear a word against him.

But this tendency is ingrained in the modern reviewing establishment, to the point where large numbers of contemporary writers regularly find themselves reviewed not for what they write but for who they are. Malcolm Bradbury's last novel *Dr Criminale*, for instance, was by no means as bad a book as a host of angry young critics made it out to be, but then Bradbury is a licensed Aunt Sally these days and *therefore* his books are worthless.

Curiously this attitude doesn't always work to a writer's disadvantage. One of the most amusing sights of literary London at the moment is the spectacle of reviewers (white, male reviewers) trying to be polite about Ben Okri's new novel, for Okri happens to be Nigerian and the suggestion that he ought to consult a dictionary now and then would probably be taken as racist.

The same disregard for objective standards affixes itself to gender, where a book about Aids by a gay male novelist is nearly always thought to be above criticism by the earnest reviewer. Among a tribe of OK writers acclaimed for what they represent rather than the quality of their writing, only Jeanette Winterson seems to have been found out, her last novel being so bad as to be unignorable.

But just as it is possible for works of genius to be written by a moral invertebrate, so novels by homosexuals are not *necessarily* any good. And is it a terrible heresy to say that the current Best of Young British promotion reeks of tokenism of this sort?

9 April 1993

3

BESTSELLERS

A million readers can't be wrong –
can they?

Ford fiasco

Ford ROBERT LACEY (Heinemann)

ONDAY 14 July was Bastille Day. It was also publication day for *Ford* by Robert Lacey, price £15.00, pages 778, weight 3lb 2oz. To celebrate this mighty event William Heinemann, Lacey's publisher, threw a launch party at the Groucho Club. Parked outside was a Ford Model T. Inside the club, thick across the ceiling, were hundreds of gas-filled balloons inscribed with the single word 'Lacey'. All went well until the author himself attempted to make a speech, at which point balloons with his name on began to descend around his head.

There are probably several morals in this. But to watchers of the book trade, such frantic publicity means only one thing. The publisher has spent more money than the book is worth. Thanks to the muscle of Lacey's British agent, Michael Shaw of Curtis Brown, *Ford* cost Heinemann and Pan more than £100,000. This advance was considerably higher than Lacey's former publishers, Hutchinson and Fontana, thought the market would bear. They could not see the British public rushing to buy a fat, expensive book about 'America's royal family of the road'. And many booksellers agree with them, having noticed the utter lack of interest aroused in their customers by the muck-raking serialization in the *Sunday Times*. The British, it seems, don't want to know about the wives of Henry Ford II. The trade's view is that Heinemann will be pushed to sell their print run of 65,000 copies, despite a deal with Book Club Associates.

But this won't worry Brian Perman, Heinemann's managing director, who also made a rapturous speech at the Groucho. Perman, according to a former colleague, 'wouldn't know a good book if it jumped up and hit him in the face', but he is acknowledged to be a whizz at marketing. Back in the 1970s, when he was at Hutchinson, Perman helped to invent the Lacey phenomenon. Now he has bought the man for himself, and even if *Ford* turns out to be a dud, Lacey's next will probably pay off.

Lacey himself admits that *Ford* is aimed at the American market, for which 140,000 copies have been printed by Little Brown of Boston. Informed guesses put the author's advance at around £400,000: a figure that includes the expense of two years spent living in style near Detroit.

So what's the secret? Instead of swilling free bubbly at the Groucho, literati who want to make money should study the techniques of Robert Lacey, 42. First, choose a good commercial subject. Lacey used to write history books, until he had the bright idea of doing the Queen. *Majesty* (1977) was a triumph of pop biography. The Lacey phenomenon was born. Books followed on the Princess of Wales, the Saudi royals, and aristocrats in general (a TV tie-in).

Dynastic gossip is Lacey's forte. To get it he puts on his best suit and charms his way into inside circles, who don't twig his game until too late. 'This is just a sex book!' roared Henry II when he realised what had been done to him. (Source: Virginia Mather, Lacey's research assistant, who will tell this story with pride and glee to anyone that rings her up and asks her.)

Lacey's second trick, learned at the *Sunday Times*, is to pad out his subject with superfluous trivia. To be fair to him, he really does work at this. 'A massive achievement of research' are probably the truest words in the book's blurb. In case we should miss the point, Lacey himself provides no less than 116 pages of notes, bibliography and sources. He has read *The Jesuits in North America* (2 vols, 1905) and consulted the Hans Tasiemka Archives, he informs us, and to put it all together he has had the help of an 'IBM PC-XT personal computer using SSI Wordperfect 4.0'.

Hot gossip and pseudo-academic research, inflated with publicity balloons: that is the Lacey formula. And it works. Lots of people like it. To enjoy this latest book, you need strong wrists and an interest in the motor industry, but it is efficiently written, and just when you're starting to wonder if the subject measures up to the Queen of England, the author sets you straight on page 9:

'Tales of Henry Ford's mechanical prowess, his devising of gadgets and tinkering with tools, have clustered around the accounts of his youth like miracles around the boy Jesus.'

25 July 1986

Ready for the knacker's yarn

Driving Force DICK FRANCIS (Michael Joseph)

*D*ICK Francis occupies an important place in English letters. He is the favourite writer of people who hate reading. He serves as a club to beat the rest with. Philip Larkin called him 'always 20 times more readable than the average Booker entry'. Kingsley Amis hasn't even tried to focus his bloodshot eyes on anything else since about 1968.

And in a new anthology on *The Pleasure of Reading*, the grumpy old playwright Simon Gray boasts that he too uses Francis to condemn all other modern novels. 'The truth is you know exactly where you are with a Dick Francis, especially the early ones, which seem to me infinitely superior as works of literature to the razzamatazz stylistics of the highly publicised and award-winning novels by young X, who jives egocentrically across the page, but fails to make one wish to turn it.' *Jiving*, . . . eh? What will the young come up with next?

As a final seal of approval, Dick Francis is the only writer enjoyed by the queen and the queen mother, otherwise hardline print shunners.

Dick Francis has become an institution – the one author you can ostentatiously say you like if you actually loathe them all, the squits. Francis himself has always done his best to play along by suggesting that he's no writer johnny, no fear. 'The process of producing fiction is a mystery which I still do not understand . . . My first draft is IT . . . I start at Chapter 1, page 1, and plod on to THE END,' he wrote in his autobiography, *The Sport of Queens.*

The books arrive seasonally, year after year, like the Grand National and the queen mum's birthday. By his own account, every year Dick Francis begins a new book on 1 January, delivers the manuscript to his publisher on 8 May, and sees it published in September. He began this process in 1961, five years after ceasing to be a professional jockey. *Driving Force* is thus his 31st novel, or rather his 31st edition of the same novel. For just as a race is run round the same course each year without anybody complaining, so Dick Francis's readers positively rejoice that each book is basically the same as all the others. Less trouble, what?

All are set, more or less, in the world of horse-racing. (Francis's occasional treks away from this setting have his readers whinnying in dismay.) All are narrated by a male hero. Although this hero begins with a handicap, whether physical or psychological (bereavement, divorce, unrequited love, family tragedy, whatever), he always comes out a winner, proving himself brave and honest, honourable and taciturn, heterosexual but horse-loving, one of nature's gents.

The plot sees his hero assailed by nature's bastards. The bad bastards always want to nobble the 'orses (noble beasts). The good guy sets out to stop them, and does, although only after enduring physical torture (bravely borne) at their hands.

Francis takes a simple view of human nature, which he shares with the Tory party and the police force – there's good and there's bad. The hero, we know, is good. The plot consists of working out who the bad bastards are and then punishing them. Got that?

The morality underpinning these stories could not be simpler. Breeding, don't you know. Francis believes in distinctions of birth for ponies and people equally. So the narrator says: 'Her high cheekbones, long neck and calm eyes reminded me of noble ancestor portraits, bone structure three hundred years old.' It's a miss, not a mare, he's describing but the principle's the same, isn't it?

Again: 'The brown sensation with the white blaze, recognisable afar off, swept effortlessly up the track towards us in the smooth coordination of muscle and mass that was nature's gift to the lucky few, horses and humans, in whom grace of movement equalled speed.' An 'orse, as it happens, not Linford and his lunch box, but who's to know?

All those blessed with 'nature's gift', whether on two legs or four, have of course to face the mean-minded assaults of the bad bastards, or as it might be, the rotten *socialists*. They want to nobble their betters. Francis explains, about the wonder horse: 'Not everyone had rejoiced with Michael over the emergence of a prodigy in his stable. Human nature being what it was, a certain portion of the racing world would have been happy to hear that ill had befallen the horse. Michael shrugged it off. "There will always be spite and envy. Look how some politicians encourage it! It's not my problem if people bitch and grudge and bitch, it's theirs."' So there you have it. Life's unfair but it's only natural. Stop worrying.

For those who don't want to think – and by definition Dick Francis readers don't – it's all wonderfully soothing. Unfortunately, the 31st time round the track, Francis is flagging.

Driving Force is unbelievably dull. To set up some kind of detective story, Francis has his good guy running a fleet of 'motor horseboxes' transporting nags to races and back. The bad guys seem to be surreptitiously using the hero's horseboxes for their nefarious purposes.

Nearly the entire book consists of the hero checking his logbooks, schedules and computer records to find out which of the drivers must be involved – possibly the most laborious and unappealing method of disclosure Francis has ever devised.

And when finally all is revealed, it's a con. The reason everything's been so inexplicable is that there have been two entirely unconnected sets of baddies at work, both using the horseboxes to transport two entirely different methods of nobbling horses. One is vials of virus to be squirted up the hossie's nostrils, the other is rabbits bearing noxious ticks. Yes, *ticky rabbits*. That's what we've been hanging on for, through nearly 300 pages, *poxy bunnies.*

Giddy up, Dick! Not that it'll matter to Francis's fans. It'll still be their book of the year. Reading's not their thing anyway.

28 August 1992

Macho ado about nothing

A Season in Hell JACK HIGGINS (Collins)
The Negotiator FREDERICK FORSYTH (Bantam Press)

O NE of the ironies of the book trade in this country is that most of the attention is paid to the books that nobody buys. The young novelist commended by the Sunday newspapers as 'a writer to watch out for', the biographer neatly anatomizing some Bloomsbury hanger-on: both may receive plenty of review coverage, both add lustre to a publisher's list, but nobody much will actually pay money for their work.

The great British book-buying public reserves its book tokens for the great stodgy monsters which will pay a publisher's Garrick Club bill long after the slim first novels are nestling in the remainder bin.

Jack Higgins and Frederick Forsyth are two of the biggest of these great stodgy monsters. *A Season in Hell* has so far sold nearly 50,000 copies in hardback. *The Negotiator*, with book club sales taken into account, will probably do twice this. Both will be enormously successful paperbacks. There will be films. And in a year – in Forsyth's case perhaps two or three years – the wheel will start to roll round again.

So what is the secret of this vast financial success (Higgins must be worth several million by now, Forsyth even more)? Is it because the books are well-written? No. Small editorial miracles have to be achieved before this kind of material is fit for the printer and even then cracks still show.

Is it because they have a distinctive style? No again. Higgins's book might have been written by a computer. Forsyth, in all his 448 pages, allows himself one stylistic flourish: he describes an American secretary of state as resembling 'a flamingo *en route* to a funeral'.

Is it because their stories are particularly plausible? No, emphatically. Higgins's is about an ex-SAS man on a revenge mission against drug-runners, Forsyth's describes an East–West confrontation over the oil running out with the president's son kidnapped along the way and both are preposterous. Either could be exploded, as Martin Amis once said of a Brian de Palma movie, by a phone call or five minutes' thought.

No, both these books pull in their thousands of purchasers simply by appearing to be *au fait*, because they present an insider's view of this fraught, complicated planet in which everything is subservient to and can be explained by the author's superior knowledge. Part of the trick is the accumulation of technical detail. Just as Forsyth beguiled the readers of *The Day of the Jackal* with an account of how to forge a passport, so he takes a page or two of *The Negotiator* to explain the written-off vehicle racket.

Another part of the trick is to stuff the book with real people. Higgins has his heroine stopping off for a quick chat with Henry Kissinger. Forsyth wheels in Margaret Thatcher, Mikhail Gorbachev and anyone else you care to name. When the president's son arrives for his first tutorial at Balliol and meets a certain Dr Maurice Keen, you are suddenly stopped by the recollection that, yes, there is a Dr Maurice Keen on the Balliol history staff.

Occasionally this technique degenerates into sheer one-upmanship. Someone in *A Season in Hell* orders a bottle of 'non-vintage Krug', which is better than vintage champagne, don't you know, because of 'something they do to the grapes'. Forsyth does better than this, though, explaining that the wine-growing regions of Southern Andalusia don't produce the sherries of Jerez, as one might have thought, but 'a rich, strong red wine'.

It has to be said that Forsyth is more adept at this game than Higgins, whose frequent elucidations, such as Concorde providing 'the fastest passenger flight in the world', are a touch self-evident. However, Forsyth does tell us that Oxford's greatest sporting rivals are Cambridge.

In fact, *The Negotiator* is a better book altogether. Leaving aside the mass of superfluous detail it does at least stoke up an atmosphere and the scenes in which Quinn, 'the negotiator', treats with the kidnappers are genuinely compelling. Also, Forsyth keeps his dialogue to a minimum. This in comparison with an author whose idea of an incidental remark is to have a character say 'Bloody weather... Always seems to be pissing down' is a relief.

What else to say? Both books are, of course, disgustingly violent, though surprisingly sex-free (Quinn, it must be said, has a jolly time with a female American agent sent to cover him). Higgins displays an attitude to women that could best be described as shameful. If one wanted a word to sum up their varying attractions it would be 'macho'. In the wake of the Rushdie affair we hear a lot from publishers about the moral worth of books and the civilizing, liberal values that they are thought to promote. Odd then that the novels that make them their money should be such simple exercises in emotional fascism.

9 June 1989

The Eagle has crash landed . . .

The Eagle Has Flown JACK HIGGINS (Chapmans)

*A*RE sequels a good idea? More precisely, are sequels 16 years on a good idea? Jack Higgins's publisher seems to think so.

According to the blurb writer's confident testimony, 'millions have waited' for this exceedingly belated follow-up to *The Eagle Has Landed*, the novel about a Nazi attempt to assassinate Churchill in 1943 which single-handedly transformed its creator from run-of-the-mill thriller writer to international bestseller. But this is Higgins's third publisher in three years – vanity and greed seem to have seen off the other two – and the thought of a career grown static hangs over any examination of *The Eagle Has Flown*.

Did I say static? Jack Higgins's novels are generic. Their characteristic is that they resemble other novels by Jack Higgins, in some cases literally so, as whole passages of dialogue and description have a habit of being rolled on from book to book.

Like his characters, perhaps, our Jack is a man of few words. Consequently

The Eagle Has Flown, in which a plot is hatched to spring Colonel Steiner, survivor of the Churchill debacle, from the Tower of London through the agency of the obliging IRA terrorist Liam Devlin – the Canaris plot against Hitler lurking all the while in the background – is an agreeably familiar work. Like any Higgins excursion it has the over-researched bits (no doubt an RAF Lysander *did* fly at 270 mph and require a 240-yard runway) and the under-researched bits (the Birmingham train, you fear, arrives at Euston rather than King's Cross). It has the same perfunctory attitude to scene, character and death – notably page 235 in which no fewer than four people get blown away – and the same bizarre invocations of famous writers – in this case Dickens, Browning and Whitman – just to show that the author has read a few books.

It also has that typical Higgins thumbprint, the complete absence of any description that actually describes. The characters here tend to be 'a small man, sallow skin, black hair carefully parted', 'a small frail man with very white hair', or to have 'olive skin, hollow cheeks and a pencil moustache, his hair carefully parted in the middle'. Punctilious, perhaps, over the single question of hair, Higgins's evocations of scene are yet more minimalistic. A garden? 'Flowers everywhere.' The London docks? 'Ships everywhere.' Dialogue is strung together with a few stage inflections – Irish blarney (from Devlin), upper-class twit (from the English fifth-columnist Sir Maxwell Shaw) serving to differentiate the speakers.

However, *The Eagle Has Flown* has one novel dimension, a feature of earlier Higgins novels now given a new and overwhelming importance. Nominally a book about World War II counter-espionage, *it's actually a book about the weather.* Climatic conditions brook very large in *The Eagle Has Flown*. In fact they seem to be the only phenomena in which Higgins takes the slightest interest. 'Damn rain. I suppose the driver of the car skidded,' says the detective on page 21. Subsequently the weather becomes a vital hinge on which the story turns, dwarfing plot – there never was very much of that – and character – there never was very much of that either – into insignificance.

'Looks as if we're going to get some fog. Bloody weather,' someone remarks on page 70 when the English top brass review their custody of Steiner. By page 72 there is an animated account of a fog, which is 'yellow and acrid and bit the back of the throat like acid'. The scene then switches to Germany where, naturally enough, 'the weather was bad in Berlin, the kind of winter that wouldn't make up its mind'. 'Jesus, the rain,' Devlin reflects, a bit later on. 'That's London for you.' Just how central all this mist, rain, wind, snow and so forth is to motivation and the course of the action can be gauged by the scene in which a German general asks Devlin why he can never take anything seriously. 'It's the rain,' the IRA man replies sincerely. As for the book's climax when the plane flies in to whisk Devlin and his prize back to France, the lavish descriptions of another pea-souper make it clear from the start that the enterprise is doomed to failure.

Fog, fog, nothing but fog. *The Eagle Has Flown* might be an indifferent novel, but as a climatic resumé of the period December 1943 to January 1944 it is in a class of its own.

29 March 1991

Moonraking it in

Win, Lose or Die JOHN GARDNER (Hodder & Stoughton)

IAN Fleming, who started it all, died in 1965. Ironically it was James Bond's *annus mirabilis*. Fleming left only a meagre £289,000, but with the film of *Goldfinger* a huge commercial success and *Thunderball* in the can, worldwide sales of the Bond books hit 29 million copies in that year. Glidrose, the firm established to administer the expanding Bond empire, declared a pre-tax profit of £353,000.

It was a lot of money for the mid-1960s – Bond, along with The Beatles, was one of Britain's most successful exports – and by this stage a lot more people wanted a piece of the pie: Fleming's Japanese translator, a Bulgarian spy novelist – there was even a work allegedly dictated to a lady amanuensis from beyond the grave. Glidrose, who had qualms about the quality of this torrent of unlicensed imitation, eventually hired Kingsley Amis to write an 'authorized' Bond continuation (it appeared as *Colonel Sun* in 1968 under the pseudonym 'Robert Markham') but by then the floodgates were opened. The author might be dead, yet ersatz Bond remained.

John Gardner came late to the party – late, but enthusiastically. In fact, since the appearance of *Licence Renewed* in 1981 there have been a further eight of his Bond escapades, including the 'novelization' of *Licence to Kill*, the current Timothy Dalton disaster. Each has been presented to the public under the banner of authenticity: 'captures that high old tone and discreetly updates it' according to *The Times*; 'a remarkably successful recreation of every lady's favourite action man' in the opinion of the *Sunday Times*. Each – and *Win, Lose or Die* is no exception – takes James Bond a further step or two away from the tall, resourceful ladykiller who first appeared as long ago as 1953 in *Casino Royale*. The reader can be forgiven for going along with all this, for to anyone under 35 the Bond atmosphere is mostly a matter of increasingly silly films, fast cars and Roger Moore's dinner jackets. Yet the films, even the early ones, were no more than parody Bond. Even Fleming's later books are not a reliable guide to the odd mixture of genteel sadism, womanizing and detailed knowledge of espionage techniques that made up Bond style: he grew sick of his creation towards the end and the last novels have an oddly tongue-in-cheek air. For 'that high old tone' you have to go back to the 1950s, to *From Russia With Love* or *Moonraker*, to Eden, Macmillan and Suez. *Win, Lose or Die*, set on a Mediterranean aircraft carrier and featuring a plot to kidnap various assembled world leaders, bears a halting resemblance to the recent crop of films, but the real Bond atmosphere has been dead for upwards of 30 years.

At heart it's a question of plausibility, a question of the awful grinding noises that occur whenever you take a character whose allure is based on sharply constructed incidentals out of his time, out of his milieu. According to the SMERSH dossier on him in *From Russia With Love* (1957), Bond started working for the secret services in 1938. That makes him . . . 70? 75? Spymaster M, references to whose 'Victorian upbringing' are strewn around the Fleming books, must by now be getting ready for his telegram from the Queen. The defective timescale is perhaps less important than the fact that by adapting Bond to the 1980s – by giving him a 'nice little BMW' instead of an Aston Martin, by making him a non-smoker and markedly more considerate to women – Gardner manages to remove most of the characteristics that made him interesting. Even the violence, the gallery of explosions, throat-cuttings and neck-breakings, has an odd, perfunctory quality.

This is not to say that Gardner hasn't acquired some of the characteristic Fleming tricks – the preposterous plots, the deliberate cultivation of danger in which the Bond warning, gaily ignored, duly leads to disaster – but *Win, Lose or Die* has none of Fleming's ability to build up tension or introduce detail casually. When Gardner talks knowledgeably about aircraft specifications the effect is only to reassure us that he read the appropriate flight manual.

Above all, there is the drawback that Gardner, a clever man aware of the pitfalls of this type of task, can't quite bring himself to take it seriously. The queer feeling that this is a skit rather than a recreation reaches its height when Bond is introduced to Thatcher, Bush and Gorbachev. Thatcher thanks him for saving her life on a previous occasion; Bush conveys a warm message from his predecessor; Gorbachev weighs in with a few words of *glasnost*-induced approbation.

So much for the silent, fleeting, anonymous assassin of the 1950s. Thirty-five years on Bond is not much more than the man in the Milk Tray advert.

4 August 1989

Bestial seller

A Time to Die WILBUR SMITH (Heinemann)

*H*ERE we have the current bestselling novel in the country, the number one choice of airport airheads. Heinemann have printed no less than 317,000 in hardback and spent £100,000 on hype.

They needn't have bothered. Last year, Wilboid's South African rhapsody *Rage* was Britain's biggest-selling paperback, outshifting even Catherine Cookson. Altogether, Smith has sold over 20 million in this country.

It adds up to about one pulp-pack for every sexually active male. For these books are hormonal stews – or rather poultices, to be applied to the private parts of flagging commuters. That's what the sweaty suit opposite you in the 7.35 with his nose in a Wilboid is up to – encouraging himself that he's still a bit of an animal.

Wilboid writes beastie books, about big, hard men – 'Oh God, my darling. You are so big, so hard. Oh please, quickly, quickly!' – giving it to women and animals, and for good measure blacks, indifferently.

You don't need to know your Freud to see that cocks and shooters are interchangeable here. The Freudian input of these stories is crude enough to get through to those who are literally unconscious.

A Time to Die is about a girl called Claudia who idolizes her father. She goes on an African hunting trip with him ('The thought of her father firing that sinister glistening weapon made her angry') but he is past it and gets shafted himself, by the tusk of an elephant.

The girl then takes up with Sean, the white hunter who organized the trip and a big gun-shooter in both senses. He's even got a good digit: 'He touched her on the hip with one finger . . . The touch was light but she felt the disconcerting male strength in his single finger.'

Throughout the book Sean bangs away tirelessly, giving it not only to Claudia but to lions and errant darkies too.

Just to show you what can happen if you're not harder than the next guy, there is a scene in which his great enemy, a wicked negro called China, sticks a red hot poker up a commie's arse.

'The metal smoked and sizzled and spluttered, as China rotated his wrist, twisting the rod deeper and deeper into the Russian's body. Now his screams were great explosive gusts of sound . . .' Later big Sean shoots up China too.

The animal analogy is pressed home remorselessly. Claudia and a lioness get done in unison. 'The lion covered her body with his own, standing astride her, and as he lowered his haunches over hers, his penis unsheathed from its pouch, glistening pinkly, and the lioness laid her tail forward along her back.

'Sean ran the tips of his fingers up to the juncture of Claudia's thighs, and he could feel the springing mattress of pubic hair through the cloth of her breeches. Her thighs opened slightly under his hand. The lion humped his back over the female in a series of convulsive, regular spasms . . .'

Wilbur not only thinks sex is animal, but that animals are sexy. Take elephants: 'The tips of the trunk are as sensitive and dextrous as the fingers of the human hand and Tuketala reached down between her back legs and groped for her vaginal opening . . .

'As he manipulated her, so her oestrus discharge flowed down freely drenching his trunk and the aroma of it filled his head. His penis emerged from its fleshy sheath, as long as a man is tall . . .'

Or maybe you'd rather not take elephants? No worries. Even the birds are at it chez Smith. 'In the undergrowth a lourie called "Kok! Kok! Kok!" as raucously as a parrot . . .'

And the leeches too. 'Sean found they had crawled up into the cleft between his buttocks and were hanging like black grapes from his genitals. He shuddered with horror as he worked on them, while safely in the dugout Riccardo made a facetious comment: "Hey, Sean, this must be the first time you've ever objected to a bit of head!"'

In Sean's eyes Claudia is a nice little menagerie herself. 'He took pleasure in watching her hard little buttocks oscillating in those tight blue jeans. They reminded him of the cheeks of a chipmunk chewing a nut.' When they go to it they are, naturally, 'as lithe as mating otters'.

Blacks are pettable too, the best of them following orders 'as unquestio-ningly as a gun dog sent to retrieve a downed pheasant' and getting his reward: 'Sean touched his woolly head as he would his favourite gun dog . . . Matatu swelled with self-importance.'

Both women and blacks beg for it. 'Is that an invitation, sir?' grovels Claudia, 'I wouldn't mind a little abuse – from you.'

'Vote? You can't eat a vote. You can't dress in a vote, or ride to work on it. For two thousand rand a month and a full belly you can have my vote,' declares an Uncle Tom, told he will have no vote in South Africa where Sean is taking him.

And this is the Nation's Choice. The effect on those commuters does not bear thinking about. Hide your hamsters now. Especially if they're coloured.

23 June 1989

Is he not flagrant?

In For A Penny: The Unofficial Biography of Jeffrey Archer
JONATHAN MANTLE (Hamish Hamilton)

JEFFREY Archer's most triumphant bestseller is the unfinished saga of imaginative genius that is his own life story. The problem is that literary culture has laid down a convention whereby autobiography and fiction are supposed to be separate genres.

In For A Penny is not, of course, an autobiography but is instead a mildly unflattering, extended review of the autobiography that Archer has been writing, and rewriting, ever since he decided that a career as a deckchair attendant in Weston-super-Mare was not for him.

To borrow the words of Michael Hill QC, Jeffrey Archer has 'lied, and lied, and lied' about himself. He has claimed that his father – a local journalist – was a British Consul in Singapore and a colonel in the Somerset Light Infantry.

He has claimed that he attended Wellington, which suggests the famous Berkshire public school and not Wellington School, Somerset, where he had earned an assisted place.

He once invented a story about travelling to America after leaving school, working his passage on a tramp steamer up the Panama Canal.

His CV, when applying for his first full-time job, boasted that he'd taken the physical training instructor's course at Sandhurst and won an honours diploma from the International Federation of Physical Culture, University of Berkeley, California.

His *Who's Who* entry said that he was educated at Brasenose College, Oxford, whereas in reality he took a teaching course at the Oxford Institute of Education and befriended the principal of Brasenose, Sir Noel Hall.

He deceived his Oxfam colleagues about obtaining the support of The Beatles for a fund-raising campaign and allowed the myth to grow up that he had successfully brought The Beatles and Harold Macmillan together at the dinner table. He fiddled his expenses while working as a fund-raiser for the United Nations Association. The litany of lies, as a libel silk might say, is seemingly endless.

Archer's wife Mary evidently despises Fleet Street journalists for being what Mantle calls 'merchants of fear'. The reason, simply, is that she fears they will expose Jeffrey's lies or his 'gift for inaccurate précis', as she once dubbed this quality of her husband's. Yet Jeffrey himself only despises journalists when they become 'knockers'. Up until that point they are the medium through which his lies are purveyed.

When Jeffrey tells *Mail* diarist Nigel Dempster that an American toy manufacturer has bought the title of his first novel, the puff enters the record and the myth of his success is suitably enhanced. And when Jeffrey tells another hack that Mary, the wife of whom he is always proud, got her PhD at the age of 16, that too, although wildly inaccurate, somehow becomes part of the Archer myth.

Or what about his claim to have enjoyed constant access to No. 10 Downing Street while he was briefly deputy chairman of the Conservative Party? His personal assistant David Faber, Macmillan's grandson no less, is adamant that Jeffrey made no more than four or five visits to Downing Street during his tenure of office.

A couple of years ago the *Eye* ran a story about how the Father's Day race at St John's College School, Cambridge, had been stopped. Miffed fathers had phoned to tell us that it was because of Jeffrey Archer, whose two sons were pupils at the school. Apparently, the former Oxford Blue had a neurotic desire to win the race and even saw to it that he ran in a heat where all the younger fathers, and hence all the competition, were absent.

Jonathan Mantle doesn't mention this curious though highly telling anecdote. You see, Jeffrey can't bear to lose, whether at sport, politics or 'literature'. When asked about his political allegiance, Jeffrey baldly responded: 'If you want to get on, why join the losers?' He once seriously enquired of publisher Tom Maschler whether, if he were to read John Fowles' *The French Lieutenant's Woman* another five times, he might stand a chance of winning the Nobel Prize for Literature.

Jonathan Mantle, it must be said, is unlikely to win the Nobel Prize either. Archeresque writing and extravagant metaphors abound in Mantle's text. When Michael Hill QC cross-examined Mary Archer, a Cambridge chemistry don, during the *Star* libel trial in 1987, Mantle says that the barrister found himself 'countering the chill winds of a Newnham corridor'.

Now the author's vagueness on the dust-jacket about his own education assumes significance. Did Mantle go to Cambridge? Has he ever been in a Newnham corridor? Suddenly, one can hear Jeffrey Archer coming to Mantle's aid . . . 'At least Jonathan's a "doer". When are you going to write a biography that gets serialized in *Today*?'

Jeffrey will always have the ultimate moral justification. He is a 'doer'. His critics are, by definition (his definition, that is), not doers. More often than not, Archer implies, critics are 'knockers', cynics who are jealous of the success of 'doers'. Thus Jeffrey blocks out criticism, most of which is adverse.

However, lest the *Eye* be accused of knocking Jeffrey Archer, it should be said in mitigation of his vanity and dishonesty that he is frequently nice to others in his desperate quest to be loved and recognized. As a Tory researcher who worked for him put it: 'It would be the easiest thing in the world to say "Archer's a complete shit". But he isn't.' Quite.

5 August 1988

Blockhead busters

The Night Manager JOHN LE CARRÉ (Hodder)
Honour Among Thieves JEFFREY ARCHER (HarperCollins)

*H*ow hard is it to produce a bestseller? Here we have the big boys' books of the summer, both designed to flow smoothly out of the airport bookshops, as the once-a-year hardback purchase of reluctant readers.

They're similarly packaged, identical in size and feel. Both have a martial image on the cover – a knight with a spear on the le Carré, a ceremonial sword on the Archer. Both are the required length, a little over 400 pages. Both have titles echoing previous titles by their authors – such as *First Among Equals* for Archer, and *The Secret Pilgrim* for le Carré – to facilitate product recognition among their dopey customers.

Both, too, are cried up in exactly the same way in the blurb. First comes the beginnings of a plot summary, then the closing pitch. 'In *The Night Manager* le Carré has given us his best novel to date: a story of majestic reach, funny, sad, captivating and constantly thrilling . . .' 'In *Honour Among Thieves* Jeffrey Archer has created a novel of intrigue and passion . . .'

Easy, then, is it, bestseller production? Unfortunately, *tragically*, somebody still has to choose and arrange the words that fill up the inside. The publishers would obviously rather avoid this expensive and unreliable section of the manufacturing process. Many disappointed readers would probably prefer it too. But there – we just don't have the technology yet. Sure enough, in their different ways both authors duly botch the job.

Archer's defects are the less interesting. He is simply too thick, too devoid of normal human responses, to write an adequate thriller. The most exciting thing about *Honour Among Thieves* is just how stupid it is.

The plot is quite hair-raisingly crass. Saddam Hussein wants to get at President Clinton. So he pays some criminals to steal him the American Declaration of Independence and leave a fake in its place, so he can spitefully burn the original live on television! The hero, a Yale prof (Archer *still* wishes he had really gone to university) and amateur spy, goes to Baghdad to get it back, along with the love interest, an Israeli agent and, phwoar, former model.

At the end, it is revealed that Saddam's copy is a fake too, and the real one is therefore perfectly safe. This revelation has, in fact, been excruciatingly obvious to any reader of normal intelligence since page 84, but Archer evidently considers it one of those 'twists in the tale' that only an absolutely top-notch master storyteller, such as himself, can hope to pull off. He really, truly doesn't know any better.

The Archer prose, meanwhile, remains as moronically inept at delivering the necessary information as ever. A typical sentence: 'As the plane lifted off from Tel Aviv's Ben Gurion airport for Heathrow, Hannah pondered once again what had caused a twenty-five-year-old woman at the height of her career as a model' (hard to credit, I know, but it is herself she's supposed to be thinking of) 'to want to apply to join the Institute for Intelligence and Special Tasks – better known as Mossad – when she could have had her pick of rich husbands in a dozen capitals.' It would be hard to devise a single sentence that could more concisely demonstrate its author's incurable incompetence as a novelist.

It is often rumoured that Jeffrey Archer does not write his own books. This is obviously not true because they would be so much better if he didn't. As it is, the personal touch, that dead hand, shows through everywhere. The only smart thing about *Honour Among Thieves* is that it is set in the United States. This is because America is a bigger country and so there are more people there who may be dumb enough to buy it. Perhaps Archer had professional advice to this effect?

Le Carré, in comparison, is a literary whiz. But he too spoils the product, not through incapacity but sentimentality. In *The Night Manager* he has once more worked through his obsessions with class, infidelity, male masochism and the enslaving attractions of young women. The fact that he now has to do without the cold war as a theme has made no difference at all: the books always were about his own compulsions anyway.

The Night Manager reworks characters introduced in *The Secret Pilgrim*. A fine young man (close-combat expert, etc.) has inadvertently betrayed his lover. After her death, he is offered the opportunity to redeem himself by becoming an undercover agent, spying on 'the worst man in the world', an arms dealer and drug merchant who lives in the Bahamas. While doing this, he becomes infatuated with the dealer's girlfriend, young, beautiful, equestrian, innocent, lovely nipples, etc. Inevitably, the hero is himself betrayed by the cads back at base in London. But, no less inevitably, after prolonged tortures, heroically withstood, he gets the girl and escapes.

This perfectly good, if standard issue, story is made insufferable by le Carré's pitiful crooning about the girl, 'Jed'. The way she knows 'how to do that with your hips when you walk', her 'unsupported breasts', her 'long waist', 'the satin planes of her back', 'the surprising sharpness of her athletic shoulders, which were the tomboy bits of her', 'the white underneath to her arms and the flow of her hips as she rode', her 'endless' not to mention her 'baby-pink' legs, and 'her skin all one soft tan' notwithstanding.

But this character with whom le Carré is so besotted never has any reality whatsoever (few erotic fantasies do). Far from operating as a prime motive for the story, the character wrecks it, and the narrative disintegrates. The reader becomes embarrassed to eavesdrop this privy pornography, especially since le Carré has tried to make this absurd female represent the solution to all his hero's pain and insecurity.

But there you are, boys will be boys – not that Archer shows any signs of ever having been anything so lifelike. Hatched from an egg, perhaps?

2 July 1993

Yankee doodle, not so dandy

The Touch of Innocents MICHAEL DOBBS (HarperCollins)

ONCE upon a time, people used to write novels and then try to sell them. Not any more.

Now you identify the market first and then produce the book. Everything else works this way round, so why not fiction too? *The Touch of Innocents*, Michael Dobbs' attempt to capitalize on the success of *House of Cards* and *To Play the King*, shows you *exactly* why not.

Dobbs, like Jeffrey Archer, wants to break out of Britain and into the American market. You might suppose this would be no problem. You don't have to live in a book's setting to read it. We're used to soaps and cop-shows set in the States aren't we? Can't they read about us?

Americans, however, do not take this liberal attitude. Americans take only America and Americans seriously. If, like Michael Dobbs, you want to put some dollars in your pocket, you have to find a way of setting at least half your book there. So here we have yet another literary equivalent of one of those revolting co-productions, with an American heroine and a British villain.

But brand continuity is important too. So Dobbs has given us another version of Francis Urquhart, this time called 'Paul Devereux'. All he needed to do was to find a story linking this character with the Yankee heroine, Isadora Dean.

Here he has not had a great deal of luck. The plot is ludicrously incoherent – not that *that* will matter once it's been turned into telly.

Isadora is an American television reporter, working in Europe with her two small children. Her horrid, soon to be divorced husband, back in America, is a defence contractor whose future depends upon the commissioning of a new fighter plane, which will only happen if the British agree to come in on the project.

Isadora has a car crash in Dorset and is taken to hospital unconscious with her children. But lawksamercy! While she is here, her youngest is, by pure chance, stolen away by a heroin addict who sells children for adoption by lustful Arabs.

No, here's the coincidence! This adroit heroin addict is none other than Paulette Devereux, the daughter of this Paul Devereux, who – would you believe it! – happens to be secretary of state for defence, the very man who is to take the crucial decision on the new fighter plane.

Well, well, what a tangled web we weave, when first we practise to deceive, eh? Devereux duly covers up for his daughter. Everybody tells Isadora that her child died in the crash and has already been cremated. Devereux even takes her into his house and tries to seduce her himself! But intelligent Isadora has her suspicions and sets off to rescue the infant, never minding that she is to lose her husband, her job, her new boyfriend and her other child in the process. Wrath of the tigress, what?

She recovers the brat at the last moment (Gatwick airport). But it seems that the beastly Devereux, and her horrid husband too, will still get away scot-free. Indeed Devereux seems certain to succeed as the next prime minister. Dear me! But, on the very last page, Isadora suddenly remembers that she has a copy of Devereux's diary, in which he has unwisely recorded the fact that he has been screwing the prime minister's wife whenever the PM's away on official business!

This story is so batty, so fruitily silly, that it is almost endearing. You begin to feel sympathy for poor Dobbs, as he haplessly tries to find some way of joining up all the special selling points he wants to get in. The task so obviously defeats him: he labours so painfully under the grossly unfair handicap of not being able to write for toffee. If there were some way of avoiding this embarrassing intermediate stage between the advance and the television adaptation, he'd take it, you just know, and spare us all.

But what a loss that would be. For *The Touch of Innocents* is no mere escapism, Dobbs assures us. It is a deeply serious study of the difficulties faced by working mothers. 'Until now, I have lacked the courage and certainly the experience to write about the largest group against whom there is widespread discrimination – mothers. Particularly working mothers,' he says, beating his ample breast, in the Acknowledgements.

'As my various careers have flourished I have watched female colleagues being torn between maternal instinct and professional ambition, conscious of my own male advantage rather than their dilemma. Perhaps, with the help of this book and of many friends I now understand that problem rather better – and the conflicting, often tormenting, emotions of which it is composed.'

Yes, that's right, there's a message here. And it's this: If you try to be a working mother, scheming colleagues will steal your job as soon as you fall ill. Heroin addicts will abduct your children and tell you they are dead. You will find yourself obstructed at every turn, by the corrupt secretary of state for defence, who will have personally nobbled every single doctor, bank manager, police officer and newspaper editor with whom you come into contact. It will be no good turning to your husband, either, because he'll already be divorcing you as a liability in his work for the military.

Most mothers will recognize the justice of this description. It is if anything an understatement of the obstacles all working women face. But it has taken the courage – as he himself so blushingly calls it – of Michael Dobbs to bring this terrible state of affairs to light. It can hardly be denied that he has finally tackled one of the most pressing social problems of the day – just as he did when he warned us that nearly all Conservatives have already murdered at least one mistress.

He deserves every success. The publishers have surely been right to assume, as their pricing suggests they have done, that *The Touch of Innocents* will top the bestseller list for months to come. And yet people still complain about the state of the British novel!

14 January 1994

Down at eel

The Legend of Te Tuna **RICHARD ADAMS** **(Sidgwick & Jackson)**

ORIGINALLY published in a 'limited edition' by Sylvester & Orphanos, Los Angeles, this latest book by Richard Adams was rejected by Penguin. It comes to Britain through Sidgwick & Jackson (director: the Earl of Longford) who got the book because they once employed the author's daughter Juliet.

Jacqueline Korn, the author's agent, refuses to make any comment on the deal. At a guess, Sidgwick paid around £25,000. They are certainly delighted with their catch. Despite a refusal by *The Bookseller* to carry their pre-publication advertisement, they report advance orders of 11,300 copies. They will shortly be putting the paperback rights up for auction.

Te Tuna has 71 pages. Twenty-nine of them are blank. Of the rest, 18 are filled by the colour illustrations of the Finnish artist Ul de Rico. 'I asked Ul to reflect the unashamed naturalness of Polynesian eroticism,' Adams told *Publishing News*, who accepted the ad refused by *The Bookseller*. Male browsers who wish to quench their curiosity should try pages 15 (masturbation), 25 (anal exposure) and 34 (unusual position, forest floor). Women should not look inside the book at all.

The story comes from Tahiti, and can be found in any old book of South Sea legends. But Adams says he heard it on a visit to the island in 1975. 'I felt I had to try to write it for people this side of the world.'

The gist of it is that Te Tuna, a gigantic eel, lives at the bottom of the ocean with his woman, Warm Hina of the Sky. But Hina is bored of the Eel. She runs off through the 'humid woods where, pendent in the shade, the red hibiscus thrusts from out the bloom its long, erectile stamen'. Eventually Hina finds a real man, whose name is Maui Tikitiki Ataranga. They set up house together. The Eel, enraged, rises from the ocean. Maui makes a stand on the beach. He swallows the monster, sicks it up again, then crawls inside it. Te Tuna droops and dies, but later sprouts back as a tall erectile palm tree whose nuts fall off and feed the human race for ever.

To bring this important myth to Western attention Richard Adams has turned it into verse, one stanza per page. He did this, he says, 'as an act of homage to Keats and Spenser'.

Penguin have endured such manic conceit since 1972 when Adams, a former assistant secretary at the Department of Environment, tried to insert the following description of himself in the author's details of *Watership Down*: 'He is within that tradition, now fast disappearing, of the scholarly and literary civil servant. Marvell, Lamb, Arnold and Trollope are his precursors.'

Relations took a further dip when the whole first printing of *Girl in a Swing* had to be destroyed because of a libel. (A few copies escaped, however, and were unwittingly signed by the author. They change hands now at about £500.)

For Penguin the final straw came when Adams tried to insert a poem called *The Albatross* into a book about the Antarctic written with the naturalist Ronald Lockley. The poem ('Zig-zag astern, I am your albatross') was one of three about the lady purser of the expedition's ship, with whom Adams had an affair on the voyage.

Peter Mayer, chief executive of Penguin, protested that the poem was irrelevant to the book and offensive to the author's wife. In a letter dated 28 May 1982, written from his home in Whitchurch, Richard Adams replied: 'It is a writer's duty to wear his heart on his sleeve and be damned. From the Dark Woman sonnets onward, this has formed a vital feature of English literature. For possible adverse consequences one must care nothing, as Shelley, Matthew Arnold and others were aware, to say nothing of Boswell. You will, I hope, be familiar, to take a living instance, with the poetry of John Betjeman . . .'

There was more. But Penguin prevailed. The poem was removed and can now be seen in *Occasional Poets*, an anthology that came out in 1986: editor Richard Adams, publisher Penguin Books. So the link is not yet quite broken. Penguin may have rejected the eel of Tahiti, but they won't want to pass up the memoirs of Traveller, the horse of general Robert E. Lee. That's Adams's next, and the awful thing is it will be a bestseller.

28 November 1986

Rug addict

Weaveworld CLIVE BARKER (Collins)

CLIVE Barker is correctly named. Or so one might have assumed, until one saw that this book has just entered the bestseller lists, having already earned its perpetrator over a million dollars.

Barker began his literary career with six downmarket Sphere paperbacks, boldly called *Clive Barker's Books of Blood*, vols 1, 2, 3, 4, 5 and 6. On the title page they had the promising if not terribly well-rhymed verse: 'Every body is a book of blood; /Wherever we're opened, we're red.' So it was. There was no prissy nonsense about plot development. Nearly every page offered a generous spurt of gore, usually supplied by something dead carving up somebody living.

So far so good. No problem with the Trades Description Act there. If it was a spot of gagging you fancied, with maybe a little nausea and throwing up thrown in, you knew where to go. Now, however, Clive Barker has moved on from being an honest grooh! yuurgh! merchant and become an Artist. He has already written one full-length novel, *The Damnation Game*, about a chap decomposing. He had directed his own film, *Hellraiser*, about a man being torn apart with meat hooks and then becoming a blood-slurping incomplete corpse ('really nice pictures,' he crows, 'we've got women dislocating men's jaws with hammers'). And with *Weaveworld*, his new publishers, Collins, have begun pushing him hard as a class act. It even has a drippy picture of athletic Clive by none other than Linda McCartney on the sleeve.

Barker, say Collins, is 'a writer of enormous vision, imagination and elegance', adding hopefully that he is 'working within a popular genre and extending that genre, lending it a legitimacy it doesn't usually have'. He himself embarrassingly considers *Weaveworld* to be 'fantastique fiction', rather than just plain 'orror. What this actually means is that after about 100 pages of regular raw liver effects, you get another 600 odd of hobbity tosh about a magic carpet.

In this carpet (in its *weave*) live some agreeable otherworldly folk called 'the Seerkind'. They are hiding there from the evil 'Scourge'. They use all sorts of terrific spells called 'raptures' to ward it off. They don't think much of ordinary people, or 'Cuckoos'. But two young Cuckoos, Cal from Liverpool and Suzanna from London, get drawn into the tremendous struggle between the Seerkind and the Scourge. They end up having the most amazing adventures.

None of this stuff, conveyed in pretentious and leaden prose, is of any conceivable interest whatever to anybody, which is presumably why Barker has packed the first part of the book with his usual splatter stories. Now these *are* interesting.

For though Barker has been taken up by radical magazines for using 'inner city' settings, and for such winning ways as making the most repulsively evil character in the book a zealous member of the Special Branch, these trendy fans are under a misapprehension. What really winds Barker up, what drives his writing, is something far more traditional and less right on: fascination with female sexuality and its revoltingness. Most of his horrid bits connect with this, some overtly, some metaphorically. It is presumably the source of his appeal to the tired men in suits whom one sees so carefully studying his works on the 5.35 and the 6.15. All that slime, all those raw bits. That gruesome appetite. Yes indeed. How telling, how true.

The most animated characters in *Weaveworld* are three evil sisters, Immacolata (alive), the Hag and the happily named Mama Pus (both dead, but active). Mama Pus in particular is a bit of a stunna, basically resembling 'cold, wet threads of phlegm', occasionally 'laced with strands of bloody tissue'. She has the habit of supernaturally raping men ('he felt his manhood drawn up into a channel that might have been flesh, but that it was corpse cold'). No sooner is this accomplished than she gives birth to 'byblows', 'less born than shat'. These are none too comely. 'No perversion of anatomy had been overlooked amongst them: bodies turned inside out to parade the bowel and stomach; organs whose function seemed simply to seep and wheeze . . .' (I expect that semi-colon is what Barker's publishers mean by 'elegant'.)

This is all fairly straightforward of course and not so different from the home life of any Liverpool Catholic. (Barker's a Liverpudlian, obviously.) Just to make sure we get the point, the heroine Suzanne is equipped with a supernatural force of her own with which to fight the baddies and this is called the *menstruum*. At key moments it 'spills' from various orifices. The men have to keep 'a respectful distance'. As one of the Seerkind explains to Cal, women have powers, men just have pricks.

So there's a moral for you. That's why it is men who read and write books of blood. Women don't have to. They're bloody enough anyway, eh?

How clever of Collins to slip this stuff upmarket. Indeed, their only worry now must be that Barker might spend some of that advance on analysis.

13 November 1987

Eco disaster

Portent JAMES HERBERT (Hodder)

THINK of James Herbert and you think of rats. Richard Adams scored with rabbits. William Horwood made it with moles. But James Herbert? He's the rodent operative.

His first novel, *The Rats*, was a proper literary nasty: rats behaving badly; rats rather falling down on the highest standards of behaviour. Herbert smartly followed it up with *Lair*. As the title delicately hints, this wasn't quite the sort of book that Anita Brookner favours either. There was a degree of unpleasantness involved.

But horror writers, no less than other men, are affected by success. They begin to think more highly of themselves. They may have started by grovelling in the dirt, but now they fancy something a bit nicer, a bit less . . . well, *horrid*. Rats, they say to themselves, are all very well for a younger man, but as one gets older one prefers something a bit more refined: stars, for example, stars that twinkle bwightly in the sky.

Portent, already gaily ascending the bestseller list, is one of the silliest excuses for a horror story ever issued. Or to put it another way, it's a New Age horror story.

In the near future, there's a big hole in the ozone layer and lots of pollution everywhere. Suddenly, pwetty, pwetty little twinkly balls of light start appearing all over the world, causing climatic upsets wherever they appear.

Whatever can it mean? Why, it's a sort of spiritual thingy. It's just like the 'Gaia' theory of that Lovelock chap. Mother Earth is, as it were, herself alive, a kind of single organism, and she's not just interested in self-preservation either. No; she's changing purely to help mankind survive the damage done by his own ecological naughtiness. And who is helping her make this change? Sweet little New Age children, from all round the world, equipped with special psychic powers, of course. And who finds about this? Um, a man who works as a sort of elevated weather forecaster, actually.

It is not hard to imagine the dismay when this steaming pile of tosh appeared on the desk of Herbert's publisher. Very nice, James, but where's the ketchup? Where are the hideous gnawings, the vile pustulences, the rendings limb from limb? You've got until the weekend to put it right.

Herbert has duly attempted to dramatize this wretched fairy story by putting in a big, bad witch, who doesn't want any of these lovely new meteorological developments to happen. As a result of her opposition, they're all more violent than they need be. Yup, violent.

So a Canadian 'silviculturalist' is roasted to death in a forest fire. An Australian diver is shredded in an underwater eruption. A Londoner is sliced in two by a sheet of glass in an earthquake. An Indian boy is steamed until he's done by a boiling geyser. A Californian girl is battered to bits by giant hailstones. Mass incinerations abound.

All very nice and juicy, too. Unfortunately, in the process Herbert has completely blown his New Age credentials. Far from being too nice, this is a very nasty book indeed. For his witch, the principle of all evil in the world, is a crudely caricatured black woman. Hugely fat, stupid and stinky, she drinks blood and excrement, insatiably tortures her sexual partners to death and tries to chomp up the dear little white children. She is revoltingly described: 'thick, savage lips', 'flat, misshapen nose', 'gross belly', 'protu-berant nipples', 'sweat-soaked stench'.

Nor is this the casual racism usual in bestsellers – although Herbert has plenty of that too (when trying to imagine the effects of apocalyptic weather on different countries around the world, he comes up with this classic: 'In Ireland potatoes were cooked in their fields').

This is sustained vilification. All the evil characters are black, all the black characters are evil. At one point, the genial weatherman, Rivers, is mugged by a black youth ('hate-filled eyes', 'muscled brown arm', etc.) and you are meant to enjoy it when Rivers strikes him with a stick: 'The blow was short, sharp and very hard. The black youth's broad nose became even broader, flattening itself with a cracking sound. The youth grunted and spittle shot from his mouth', etc.

Herbert should go back to rats. To be sure, as the bloody millennium approaches, we're all going to go very silly indeed, freely interpreting hosepipe bans in the light of the Book of Revelations, worshipping Freddie Mercury and taking John Major seriously. It's inevitable, we're already getting used to it.

But irrationality of this kind – hatred and bigotry worked up into apocalyptic fantasy – can well be avoided. And if, by the way, you fancy a bit of meteo-horror, J.G. Ballard was ten times better at it 20 years ago.

4 December 1992

Top of the friction list

The Plains of Passage JEAN M. AUEL (Hodder & Stoughton)

O NE thing alone makes this book worth knowing about – its sales. It climbed to the top of the fiction list in this country as soon as it came out and it's still squatting there, flatly. In America it had an initial hardback print run of *1.5 million*. As a milch cow, Jean M. Auel (pronounced *Owl*) is in the Wilbur Smith league.

Look at the book review pages and you'd think that publishing revolves around long-awaited translations from the Czech and the previously uncollected essays of Isaiah Berlin and V.S. Pritchett.

It don't. Publishing's about trash like this. Sensitive publishers may have to hold their noses and don rubber gloves to handle such books, but they keep the business going. And, what with dumpbins, who needs books pages?

Or wants them? It's probably a relief to the publishers that *The Plains of Passage* nearly defies review. *Nearly.* 'Ere we go.

The Plains of Passage is the fourth volume, 'the *long-awaited* fourth volume', in a series of six, following on from *The Mammoth Hunters* of 1985. It describes a journey ('a Journey') made across Ice Age Europe by a super-glamorous blonde Cro-Magnon woman, Ayla, and a super-glamorous Heselteeny Cro-Magnon man, Jondalar, accompanied by two tame horses (Racer and Whinney) and a tame wolf (Wolf).

There is no plot. They just keep on trekking. They cross rivers. They climb mountains. They find food, they cook it. They make herbal teas. They think they've lost the wolf but they find it. They think they've lost the horses but they find them. They meet some Neanderthals ('the clan') and other Cro-Magnons ('the others'). They bonk. They bonk again. They bonk more. They bonk ever and anon. Then they arrive. And that's it.

Never before in the history of human stupidity – surely, *please* God, cross my heart and hope to die – has a worse book been read by so many. The sleeve modestly hails Auel as 'one of the world's most esteemed and beloved authors'. By Hodder's accountants perhaps? Not, I think, by William Golding, on whose great novel of early man, *The Inheritors*, she so heavily and ineptly relies (though Golding may have less of a case against her than the producers of *The Flintstones*).

Mrs Auel (pronounced *Bonk*) bores away for pages about the Ice Age flora (rushes) and fauna (mammoths, giant hamsters) and the Ice Age climate (most chilly), but she makes no attempt to create a world or a language for this couple.

When some strangers flee at their approach, Ayla moans 'I was so looking forward to visiting with these people.' When summer comes, she says 'I'm sick of this hot weather, and these terrible gnats!' Jondalar has obviously been reading the subject up. 'Woolly rhinos are unpredictable and can be vicious,' he warns. He sees a giant deer. 'That animal sure can run!' he exclaims.

Mrs Bonk is dreadfully infatuated with her blond bombers. They're faultlessly fit, matchlessly pretty, uniquely sensitive and unprecedentedly thoughtful. All by themselves, for example, they have solved every major problem of human development: animal-taming, high technology weapons, democracy, anti-racism, oral sex, even the pill (though not the wheel).

'Jondalar,' says Ayla, 'you're an unbelievable man.' He is.

A great lay though. Like, you know, he always goes down on her first, even on a windswept glacier. You see, 'Jondalar had been trained as a flint knapper . . . Women responded to his perception and sensitive handling the way a fine piece of flint did, and both brought out the best in him. He sincerely loved to see a fine tool emerge from a good piece of flint under his deft touch, or to feel a woman aroused to her full potential, and he had spent a great deal of time practising both.'

More time perhaps than Mrs Owl has spent practising how to write. Her sex scenes are cretinously repetitious. Hop-skip-jump. Fold, shaft, well.

First, the folds. 'He reached his tongue forward and found her hard nodule buried deep in her folds', 'his tongue found the familiar folds, reached into her deep well, and then reached up higher for the small hard node' . . .

Then the shaft.

'He sunk his shaft deeply. . .'

'His long shaft withdrew and penetrated again . . .'

Then the *well*, the *deep* well.

'He straightened up behind her, moved in closer and found her deep well with his eager straining manhood', 'she reached for his manhood and guided it to her well' . . .

Well, well. Well, I never. Mrs Bonk's book has a use after all. At least we know now why Radclyffe Hall's lesbian epic was called *The Well of Loneliness*.

23 November 1990

Dungeons drag on and on

Seeress of Kell: Book Five of the Malloreon DAVID EDDINGS (Bantam)

*E*NJOY reading reviews of Angela Carter, Milan Kundera and William Trevor, do you? You do? Actually, it doesn't matter whether you do or you don't. Obviously, the literary editors all think you do, or they think you should. Because though these novelists don't sell a lot, they always get the main coverage in the books pages.

Seeress of Kell, on the other hand, has not been reviewed at all. Yet it is currently the bestselling hardback novel in this country – as was, last year, its equally witless predecessor, *Book Four of the Malloreon, Sorceress of Darshiva*; as were, before that, the three previous books in the series; and, before that, the five books of the previous series of associated claptrap, *The Belgariad*.

So why no reviews? Let's be fair. Obviously it wouldn't be easy to find anybody capable of getting through such tripe and then testifying to his or her response in joined-up writing. And then again, if you found a reviewer, could he – however gifted – accurately convey the book's true asininity? Could he even vestigially describe it without making it seem a lot more coherent and appealing than it is?

Seeress of Kell is a sword and sorcery book. Literally. You might think that just as shopping and fucking books aren't all about shopping and fucking – you keep getting those shamefaced digressions about relationships and stuff – that sword and sorcery books aren't just about swords and sorcery. But they are. *Sorceress of Kell* is about stabbing and tricks and nothing else.

The setting is an invented, cod-medieval world, in which the bloody forces of good are battling the bloody forces of evil. The fate of the entire universe is at stake, as per usual, and the whole caboodle is in fulfilment of some crappy old prophecy or other. There are only a few main characters on each side, well even they're not characters really, though hordes of evil gremlins, sorry 'Gromlims', keep cropping up to be bumped off.

There's also a dragon, a regular issue dragon – you know, the scaly, fire-breathing, flying kind. There's a jousting tournament, a trip in a sailing boat, a bundle of silly spells, many talking animals and a number of personal appearances by 'the gods'.

Eddings writes for the people who find Tolkien too taxing. If he has taken any pains, it's to make his style halfwit-friendly. The only flourish is the ridiculous names. Whole sentences exist merely to display silly titles, and are repeated from book to book. From the last one, *Sorceress of Darshiva*: 'Urgit, High King of Othol Murgos, sat on his garish throne in the Drojim Palace of Rak Urga.' From *Seeress of Kell*: 'Urgit, High King of Othol Murgos, was wearing a blue doublet and hose, and he sat up straight on his garish throne in the Drojim Palace.'

The plot is equally dumb. Two magic balls, 'the Orb' and 'the Sardion', have to be brought together in a magic place, and this Seeress person has to choose between two contenders, the Child of Light and the Child of Dark, as to who will be God. A tough one, eh? Which is it going to be? You're right. It's the Child of Light. Even one of the characters notices it's not really much of a choice. 'I can't see where all the difficulty was then. Doesn't everybody prefer the light to the dark?' 'You and I might, but the Seers have always known that Light and Dark are simply opposite sides of the same thing,' replies God brightly.

But isn't this just harmless fun for the hopelessly dim? No, it ain't. It's not so harmless.

How do you explain the popularity of a book such as this? It's certainly not because it's a good read. It's a *dreadful* read, it's one of the worst reads you ever could find. The book works in the way it does on so many because it is successfully parasitic on pre-existing needs.

Essentially, it is perverted religion. Eddings has invented a mythology and his readers have swallowed it. L. Ron Hubbard began as a writer of rubbishy science fiction and only opportunistically turned his fantasies into a cult when he realized that his readers might be induced to take it seriously.

Eddings isn't up to that – but the appeal of his fiction is to the same starved appetite for mythology and the supernatural that makes people vulnerable to anybody with the crassness to offer to feed it. You don't need to do it coherently, tastefully, sensibly. Eddings does it on as low a level as you'll meet. Compared to some of the competition, indeed, his very ineptitude makes him less offensive than he might be. William Horwood's Duncton trilogy, another religiose fantasy bestseller, was all about *moles* (talpids, not spies) and ended with an actual mole crucifixion, and a mole ascension into heaven, all of which Horwood managed to imbue with sickening intensity.

Eddings's pastiche of the Bible is merely incompetent – 'Know ye that all adown the endless avenues of time hath division marred all that is – for there is division at the very heart of creation', and so, poopily, forth. His attempts to make his story eternally significant are simply laughable – 'You may know,' explains his hero with typical woodenness, 'that from time to time in the past there have been meetings between the Child of Light and the Child of Dark. We're going to the last one there's ever going to be. The meeting's going to decide the fate of the world.' Oh, right, better pay attention.

Eddings, presumably through native numbness, manages to churn out this garbage without lapsing into facetiousness himself. And that alone is enough to sell his books on an enormous scale. His success is built on his readers' emotional and intellectual deprivation, but who cares? Let them fight dragons.

21 July 1991

Odd hobbits

The History of Middle Earth 9: Sauron Defeated J.R.R. TOLKIEN, edited by Christopher Tolkien (HarperCollins)
The Tolkien Family Album JOHN AND PRISCILLA TOLKIEN (HarperCollins)

J.R.R. Tolkien wrote *children*'s stories. *The Hobbit* was originally read to his three boys when the eldest was 13. The publishers, Allen & Unwin, accepted it because in 1936 the Chairman's son, Rayner Unwin, wrote this enthusiastic report:

'Bilbo Baggins was a hobbit who lived in his hobbit-hole and *never* went for adventures, at last Gandalf the wizard and his dwarves persuaded him to go. he had a very exciting time fighting goblins and wargs. at last they got to the lonely mountain; Smaug, the dragon who gawreds it is killed and after a terrific battle with the goblins he returned home – rich! This book, with the help of maps, does not need any illustrations it is good and should appeal to all children between the ages of 5 and 9.'

The age limitation was finely placed. Rayner Unwin was 10 at the time.

No better appreciation of Tolkien has been written or is needed. With the qualification that Tolkien's writing appeals also to those with the mental age of a child – computer programmers, hippies and most Americans – it was an accurate assessment of the market, too. Alas, there are so many such retards in the world that it profited his publishers to pretend that Tolkien was a *proper* writer.

For years, Tolkien was the milch cow of Allen & Unwin, and then Unwin Hyman, until even his royalties failed to save the firm from being gobbled up by Murdoch's HarperCollins. This month is the centenary of Tolkien's birth. Accompanied by new editions of *The Silmarillion* and *The Lord of the Rings*, these two books are HarperCollins' attempt to cash in.

The 'family album', by Tolkien's eldest son and his daughter, is a harmless collection of banal snaps – Tolkien's hideous retirement villa in Bournemouth, the family on holiday in Lyme Regis, some of the hens the family kept during the war – introduced with an harmoniously banal text.

'The study was very much the centre of Ronald's [Tolkien's] home life, and the centre of his study was his desk ... We vividly remember a row of coloured Quink and Stevenson inks and sets of sealing-wax in different shades to match his large supply of stationery.' Wow! Sure beats the incest and infidelity, the boozing and buggery you get in most modern memoirs! Or maybe not.

Sauron Defeated, assembled from Tolkien's wastepaper basket by his youngest son, Christopher, will, however, be enthusiastically welcomed by all right-thinking people. For, inadvertently, it does more damage to Tolkien's reputation than a dozen critics ever could. Everything published by Tolkien's estate since his death has made him seem an ever-greater bore, but this volume is an unparalleled triumph of tedium.

Christopher Tolkien was originally supposed to keep this 'account of the writing of *Lord of the Rings* ... within the compass of three fat volumes'. He has stretched it to nine by including every draft and repetitious jotting, all carefully collated. His scholarly approach serves nicely to show up Tolkien's infantilism.

'The name of the sole surviving orc beside Shagrat is *Radbug* in both C and D (*Shaga* in RK: see LR appendix, F, p.409), *Radbug* being retained in the final story as the name of an orc whose eyes Shagrat says that he had squeezed out (RK p.182); in C the orcs whom Sam saw running from the gate and shot down as they fled are *Lughorn* and *Ghash Muzgash* (*Lagduf* and *Muzgash* in D, as in RK)', reads a typical note – for all the world as though it mattered.

These *Lord of the Rings* off-cuts fill only a third of the book. The rest is padded with an astonishingly silly story about the members of an Oxford discussion club who start dreaming themselves into various Norse sagas, somehow connected to Atlantis. Capping even this is a final section in which Tolkien gives a full grammar of one of his nauseating invented languages, 'Adunaic', complete with declension tables and pronunciation guides ('The continuants W, Y, L, R, Z are pronounced voiceless after the aspirates, but otherwise suffer no change').

'Literature,' admits one of the members of the discussion club, 'may have a pathological side.' That Tolkien should, for whatever reason – religion, wartime trauma, or routine bad taste – have wanted to turn out such trash is depressing enough. That his least scribble should subsequently be dignified by such laboriously scholarly publication is grotesque.

And if Tolkien did us all a bad turn by making it possible for the likes of David Eddings and other lo-talent drudges to make money by droning on about dungeons and dragons, he did something worse to his own family.

Originally he made fantasies appealing in order to entertain his children. Now his children are employed by his fantasies. It's usual for the offspring of famous writers to find themselves in their parent's shadow. But the fate of Christopher Tolkien, adjudicating between orcs, volume after volume, is surely nearer to penal servitude.

17 January 1992

Shocking filler

A Sensible Life MARY WESLEY (Bantam)

JUMP on to any rush-hour train or bus, peer over the shoulder of the Sloaney-looking girl standing next to you and in among the clutch of drinks invitations and letters from Jonjo and Harriet you can be pretty sure of finding the upturned pages of a Mary Wesley novel.

Such is the *réclame* of Ms Wesley's productions (this is the seventh) and the celebrity of their author – a spry old bird in her late 70s – that *A Sensible Life* (currently number one in the bestseller list) threatens to displace Wilbur Smith and even Jeffrey Archer as the book people read on public transport.

This is quite an achievement. Looking to explain it, turning initially to the bouquet of critical garnishes which adorns the jacket, one is led irrevocably to consider the role of *The Times* newspaper. *The Times* has been rooting for

Mary Wesley since way back, since *Jumping the Queue* ('a virtuoso performance') and *The Camomile Lawn* ('exceptional grace and understanding'). It thought *Harnessing Peacocks* (No. 3) 'hugely enjoyable'. By the time of *Not That Sort of Girl* (No. 5) it wheeled out Philip Howard to commend 'a witty and charming love story... One of the things that I love about Mary Wesley is that she has reached an age where she can say dangerous or naughty things without shocking.'

Indeed, if anything exceeds the absorption of *The Times* in Mary Wesley's novels, it is Mary Wesley's absorption in *The Times*. Their relationship is entirely reciprocal. *A Sensible Life* is stuffed full of references to the *Thunderer*, right from the moment Nigel emerges from his pre-dinner drink (it is 1930 or thereabouts) to instruct the ingénue heroine: 'If you want to understand what makes people tick, you read this paper.' Subsequently *The Times* becomes the novel's window on the world, where Flora reads about the hatches and matches that keep the plot ticking on, where she finds out about her Dutch lover's death at the hands of the Nazis. So great is her reliance on Printing House Square that it sometimes seems to be her only means of verification. 'Not your father?' she enquires of Cosmo on page 321, having been apprised of old General Leigh's death. 'I did not see it in *The Times*.'

Elderly generals. People called Cosmo and Nigel. *The Times* newspaper. It will have become apparent by now that *A Sensible Life*, like elderly generals, people called Cosmo and Nigel and in fact *The Times* newspaper, is of the past rather than the present. And to be sure, like much of what catches the literary tube-traveller's eye in these backward-looking times, it is primarily an exercise in nostalgia: a glorious wallow in a bath composed of butlers, dressing for dinner and crêpe-de-Chine underclothes, a genteel saunter around a map composed of tea at Gunters, drinks at the Ritz and passages to India.

So Ms Wesley passes one important test of literary marketability with flying colours: she writes knowingly about the past. At the same time she clears another significant hurdle, which is to say that she writes avidly about sex but with sufficient gentility to commend herself to the refined sensibilities of her readership. *A Sensible Life* is distinguished by a persistent undercurrent of libidinousness, full of delicious young things feeling the hot breath of their country house hide-and-seek compatriots, randy parents and creaking bed-springs. The trick is that it is all done in exquisite good taste, so that when Flora, who has fancied Felix since she was a 10-year-old, finally manages a wartime bedding, it's 'a love making, expert but impersonal, slow, slow, quick, quick, slow, ending with a thunderous chord'. The coyness is characteristic: sexy (sort of), witty (up to a point). The type of book you might give to an elderly relative without embarrassment.

Mary Wesley writes sharply, although her dialogue sparkles with a little too much lustre ever to convince, and can be very funny ('The poor dog,' Flora ripostes when it is revealed that her hated *memsahib* mother has been bitten by a rabid Airedale), but none of this explains the titanic sales of this genteel, ladylike, rather diffuse and mildly tedious novel.

What does, perhaps, explain it are her themes: typically the habit of her posh yet raffish heroines to kick against the pricks (no pun intended), to defy convention and to do their own thing – in Flora's case declining to rejoin her indifferent parents in India and set out on the husband-hunt. In the annals of English fiction there is perhaps no more alluring figure than the toff who rebels, the upper-class raff, the disaffected classy lady with the roving eye. So *outré*, my dear. Small wonder, then, that Caroline on the 8.23 is entranced or that Auberon Waugh thinks she should win the Booker Prize.

27 April 1990

All mouth and trouser

A Dubious Legacy MARY WESLEY (Bantam)

You can find out how decrepit a horse is by inspecting its teeth. Exactly the same goes for human beings, Mary Wesley believes. All her characters bare their fangs, as they appear. Seldom has a writer shown such devotion to dental condition. It's just one of the things that have made her such a popular Oldie novelist.

Here comes the first person in *A Dubious Legacy*. 'Margaret parted her red lips, showing excellent teeth.' Here's her brother, Basil: 'Good but slightly wayward teeth'. Here's gay Jonathan: 'His mouth, not so wide, showed excellent teeth.' Here's a foreigner, Pilar: 'She smiled, showing her large teeth.' And her son, Ebro: 'He had the same parrot jaw and the outsize teeth.' Here's Jonathan and his lover making up to Ebro: 'The Jonathans said, "Lovely boy, *lovely*" and "My dear! What virility", and were rewarded by a flash of Ebro's enormous teeth.'

When one of the young women complains about her father's attitude to her ageing mother, we know just what to expect. 'His references to a crêpey neck, greying hair, double chin, veiny legs and yellowing teeth make me sick, she thought. The remarks about teeth are particularly vile.' As we do when a boy and a girl hit it off. 'He approved the pert nose and full mouth which, the evening before, he had kissed, sliding his tongue between the slightly irregular teeth, which had nipped quite sharply.' And so we are not in the least surprised when an actual nag gets in on the act. 'One of the horses leaned forward and nibbled her shirt, its grey lips making a plopping sound. It tweaked at the shirt with yellow teeth.'

Mary Wesley's appeal seems so straightforward. Hosses, gels, rumpy pumpy in the country, all that – sex and class, nostalgia and gossip. She's a snob's delight, a *Sunday Telegraph* natural. For once, nobby readers are only too pleased to have the mucky bits. They always did think that sex was too good for the proles. That was what was so disgusting about the 1960s – the plebs acted as though they'd invented it. Wesley could teach them a thing or two, eh, gamey old bird! Why, if you only knew – the things they got up to when they were young! In the proper place, of course, and without shouting about it from the rooftops.

Superficially, *A Dubious Legacy*, her eighth novel, fits this pattern nicely. The story runs from 1944 to 1990. Henry Tillotson owns a country house, Cotteshaw ('Its walls played host to roses and honeysuckle'). However, his life is blighted. During the war, he heard that the woman he loved had married another man. In deference to his father's dying request, he then married a woman he did not know, in order to give her British citizenship. Margaret turns out to be an uncooperative loony, who stays in bed all day and won't let him divorce her.

Two young couples come for the weekend and end up permanently sharing the house with Henry, in a kind of toffs' commune. Eventually, the two girls have children, their children have children, and the novel turns into a family saga. Henry remains chastely married to lunatic Margaret until she dies. Eventually, he dies himself, attended by the second and third generation – a kind of happy end.

In the meantime, there are all Wesley's usual accessories to enjoy. Loyal servants. Dear old gays. Faithful hounds. Henry's fine old Bentley. Skinny-dipping in the private lake. Grey flannels, Fair Isle sweaters, Dior dresses. Pheasants cackling in the wood. Bucolic dinner parties. No money worries. Eggs and bacon for breakfast.

But something odd happens in this book. There is real malignancy here. The character of Henry's wife is so evil as to make their marriage entirely implausible. She tears a pet cockatoo apart. She tries to drown a child. She bites and stabs Henry. We are expected to rejoice – as all the characters do – when she is drowned herself.

We are also expected to sympathize with Henry's life outside the marriage. Mad Margaret tells people he has sex with horses, though the girls don't quite believe it. '"I believe that suggestion about horses is a hoax", said Antonia when he was out of earshot. "It would be more likely to be dogs." She joined Barbara in a refreshing burst of giggles.'

In fact, dear old Henry succeeds in secretly seducing both these young wives and fathering their children without their husbands ever becoming aware of it. It is his own two children, Clio and Hilaria, who unwittingly tend him on his deathbed.

All this is presented as a pastoral. According to the jacket, 'It is the story of a man whose flaws are redeemed by kindness, generosity and wit. It is a gloriously funny, human story.' Actually, beneath the rustic charm, it's peculiar and perverse, a lesson in immorality – an Oldie's fantasy of a most disturbing kind.

Mary Wesley is a genuine novelist in the sense that she does have a moral world to communicate and the means to do it. What seems to have escaped notice, as her giggling readers revel in her country house parties, is her extraordinary indecency. She may be long in the tooth, but she has a truly nasty bite.

13 March 1992

Art imitating lifelessness

A Spanish Lover JOANNA TROLLOPE (Bloomsbury)

EXTRAORDINARY how what starts out as an imitation can sometimes take on a life of its own and end up further down the track than the thing it was set to study! And so Joanna Trollope, conceived, promoted and retailed as a cut-price Mary Wesley, now finds herself at the very top of the heap, a staple of the bestseller lists and the darling of the *Daily Telegraph*.

In fact this progressive improvement in Ms Trollope's fortunes – does anyone remember her, I wonder, when she wrote historical romances created by her distinguished ancestor? – was bound to happen. Though the English book-buying public has always been fascinated by Mary Wesley's upper-bourgeois merry-go-round, it invariably remained somewhat in awe of her – which is never a good relationship to exist between an author and her public. She was at once too upper class and too astringent, too haughty and too Bohemian – and the characters were mostly complete bastards, too. Anyone who could refine the formula – a little cosier, a little more English, a little more provincial – would consequently be quids in.

In case this sounds like ritual highbrow disparagement of the books that the great British public – bless the dears – presses to its heart, it should be said that there is a case to be made for Joanna Trollope. It goes something like this. Perhaps the greatest failing of the contemporary English novelist is his or her inability to write about 'ordinary life'. Martin Amis's John Self and Keith Talent are very funny, terminally droll even, but they are grotesques, not human beings. What we want is the English provincial scene, the log-fire roaring and the silent majority getting on with its bustling domestic business.

An excellent case it is too, up to a point. Above all, your average fiction fancier wants something that takes place *outside London* – which, after all, is where most of us live – away from the crack dealers and the jungle jive. And they certainly get it in *A Spanish Lover*, in which no aspect of the roseate bourgeois vista goes unremarked. There is the familial contrast – two sisters, one running a gallery with her husband, the other a travel agent embroiled with a Spanish boyfriend – there are the roguish children, there is even the *pressing social issue*, don't you know, when Lizzie and Rob's livelihood is threatened by the recession.

What there isn't, regrettably enough, is any sign of a creative intelligence working in anything but the most trivial way. Ms Trollope might be writing about the sort of people who deserve to appear in fiction, but she writes about them in a desperately uninteresting manner, and despite the carefully measured out ingredients the whole is as flat as a pancake.

Mostly this is the result of a quite exquisite perfunctoriness of incident and characterization, in which the plot is intermittently cranked up with alarming haste – the gallery starts to founder almost in a matter of days – and the characters jink around the conversational openings until they can deliver themselves of the epic, sententious statements that Ms Trollope has prepared for them, as when Rob tells Lizzie: 'It's just life itself that deals you a nasty when you aren't looking, it's life that keeps moving the goalposts. We haven't changed, it's just the things around us that have.'

In a sense none of this – plot (Rob, Lizzie and family surviving in reduced circumstances, Frances having a baby), moral (making the best of things) – matters, for *A Spanish Lover* is a nostalgia trip, pure and simple, back to a world of bustling, apple-cheeked families and bucolic satisfactions, full of detail that seems just a touch old-fashioned for the early 1990s, spiced up with a decorous sexual undertow but no smut (another tick on the reader's checklist).

The general effect is to remind the reader of Frances's apprehension (while checking out an Italian holiday jaunt) 'that she would find it all a cliché, done to death by the remorseless English mania for a civilised release from the shackles of a chilly Puritanism into an acceptable sensuality'. As it happens, the last three words would make a good title for Ms Trollope's next one. For the moment there is a certain amount of incidental pleasure to be gained from predicting who will feature in the TV film. That nice Kevin Whately as Rob, Patricia Hodge as Lizzie and Geraldine McEwan as the old mum, *I'd* say.

4 June 1993

A mint with holes in it

Polo: A Legend of Fair Women and Brave Men JILLY COOPER (Bantam)

*H*ELLO Paups! 'Ow's yer hovels? All right? 'Course they are. They're what you was bred to. Believe me, they *suit* you, they really do. Don't change a thing.

Not that you want to, do you? You're happy as you are. You must be, 'cos there's nothing you like better than to get home to yer own little 'ovel and have a good old read about the really really rich, is there? This summer you'll be tucking into *Polo* in the thousands, the 'undreds of thousands, won't you? Oooh, you'll *love* it.

It's about the nobs, you see, the absolutely stinkingly loaded, the bluest blue blue-bloods. Your favourites! And where else can you get them in such quantities these days? For, as the distinguished sociologist Nicholas Coleridge put it in the *Sunset Times*, your favourite weekly guide to sucking up to your betters, 'Jilly Cooper's great strength is that she is the only British author currently writing long, complex and sustained novels about the English middle and upper-middle classes' – upper middle to him that is, bleedin' stratospheric to you and me!

And you don't want to read about other bloody paups, do you? No way. What you want is great big dollops of dosh. And polo is dead good for that. It may be the most boring and silly game ever invented, after golf, but crikey, it costs. The ponies, you see. Expensive. Only trillionaires can possibly afford them. And then these trillionaires want to play in the polo teams they pay for, alongside the real riders, the proper posh who understand horses. Can you believe it?

Plenty of opportunity for patronizing nooves, there! And would your Jilly miss them? No fear, not her. It's specially for always telling you what's really nobby and what's not that you love her, isn't it? So you'd know, wouldn't you? If a nob or near-nob ever came nobbing round your hovel.

So Jilly introduces polo team owner Victor Kaputnik. Name tell you anything? Not like 'Rupert Campbell-Black', 'Ricky France-Lynch', or 'Sir David Waterlane, Bart', is it, quite? You're absolutely right. 'Originally Hungarian, Victor was a pharmaceutical billionaire', *not* a proper nob. And look at fat Victor's girlfriend, 'a red-headed nightclub hostess, whose heavy eye make-up was already running and whose uplifted breasts were already burning'. 'Blimey it's 'ot, she said. Why do the 'orses keep bumpin' into each uvver?' Well, what do you think? Not quite a nob? Right again! You're making those fine social distinctions already. You're getting stuck into another Jilly Cooper novel.

And you've still got the breasts and the bonks to come, you lucky paups. Jilly's got these nobby breasts on the mind or somewhere. They're always popping up. 'Breasts as rounded as scoops of ice-cream', 'breasts rising like pomegranates', 'breasts so small and firm they hardly splayed to the sides at all', 'breasts soft and white-gold in the sunshine with the nipples pink and spread', 'nipples as hard as biro tops', there's such a lot of breasts about.

And the bonks, the posh polo type bonks – Jilly's just so good at slipping in reminders about the poshness, the horsiness, of the bonks, isn't she? So you'll know. If ever a nob comes round your hovel bonking. 'Running his tongue up the smooth hillock of her breast, he fastened on her nipple and slid two fingers between her legs. Christ, he could restore polo sticks in the slippery linseed oiliness.' I spy a nob! Don't you? A sportsman, too. 'Even his cock seemed to have biceps as, with the ball of his thumb seldom far away from her clitoris, he drove her to extremes of joy.' Field sports of course. 'As he inserted a finger, she jumped like a branded filly. "It's OK, darling, you're tight, but not that tight. I'll get you so sopping beforehand, I'll slide in like a cartridge into a twelve bore."' And, by gum, you know how those slide in, don't you? Smoothly, if it's a good one – and it's bound to be.

And you get a quality plot too. Will England win the Westchester Cup? Will Ricky France-Lynch get his wife back? Will Perdita, a polo-playing bit with another full pair of those breasts, find out who her real father is? Yes, she will. He's a horsey nob!

I mean, look at Perdita's mum, Daisy, in the sack with polo-playing former Welsh Guard, Drew. 'I haven't shaved my legs or anywhere else. I'm like an old ewe,' says Daisy, friskily. Drew's not deterred. 'The Welsh Guards were always known as the sheep shaggers,' he ripostes. 'This is the only bit that needs cutting back,' he says, parting her pubic hair and gently fingering. 'All you need is a bit of spit and polish.' What a soldier!

All this, plus prolonged accounts of fictitious polo matches and packs of laboured puns. 716 pages full. Fortunate paups. At £14.99 it's positively cheap. Though not to you, of course.

24 June 1991

The first cuckold of spring

The Man Who Made Husbands Jealous JILLY COOPER (Bantam)

HERE'S a neat trick. People buy Jilly Cooper books to read on the beach to stop their brains disturbing their rest. They make good escapist reading because, on the one hand, they are marginally more interesting to look at than a faceful of sand but, on the other, they are less mentally demanding than a packet of crisps.

This makes them the idjit's choice – just perfect for the one book a year readers, the half a book a year readers, the couldn't-get-on-with-it-at-alls. But this summer Cooper's troopers are in for a little surprise. Although superficially appearing an acceptably escapist confection, *The Man Who Made Husbands Jealous* is one of the most depressing novels ever published. Despite being set in 'the idyllic Rutshire village of Paradise', it's actually, quite unmistakably, an Inferno.

It's not just the appalling prose, the caricature characterization, the absence of a plot or the shameless resort to padding that make the book hell to read. Her fans have never minded these before – although they are possibly just a little worse this time around.

Silly Jilly's style depends on a few tawdry verbal counters: 'utterly', 'seriously', 'marvellous', 'mega', 'blissful', 'heavenly', 'ravishing' and the like. She is unable to construct a plot, but that doesn't matter because her readers are unable to hold one in their minds. So her people just dawdle around for 500 pages behaving in character, until she makes the right man get the right girl. The gaps are filled up with horribly protracted set pieces, mostly sporting – here we get a polo match, a cricket match, a concert, a village fete, a nativity play, a skiing trip, a horse race, a tennis tournament and a dismal sort of orgy.

The miserable personnel are differentiated by such subtle devices as making one main woman character speak refained ('Ay don't think that's in the raight spirit') and another Cockney ('Fank you for everyfink'). But if these prove too complex, a cast list is provided at the beginning, which tells you all you need to know ('Seb and Dommie Carlisle. The heavenly twins. Vastly brave professional polo players, whose serious wildness has been tempered by the recession.')

Every 20 pages or so, the desert wastes are embellished with an awkward attempt at a witticism – 'coq-up au vin', 'she doesn't kick against the lack of pricks', 'Think not for whom the telephone bell tolls', and so forth. Rather funnier than these are Cooper's inadvertent misadventures with the English language and the human body. 'Georgie's heart seemed to be beating between her legs,' for example, and 'Her splendid bosom soared above an enviously thin waist . . .' – which would be quite good had they been deliberate.

All this is bestseller standard issue. What's not is the extraordinarily brutish, dispiriting portrayal of marital infidelity. The mistress of Jilly Cooper's husband Leo took the unusual step a few years ago of publishing her story in the *Grauniad*. This book is evidently a long-term product of that kerfuffle.

It begins in a wish-fulfilment fantasy. Lysander Hawkley is 22, 'broad-shouldered, heart-stoppingly handsome, wildly affectionate, with a wall-to-wall smile that withered women', as Cooper haplessly puts it. This paragon moves into a posh Cotswold village called 'Paradise' to help the neglected and betrayed wives of the area, one after the other, to regain their husbands' affections by making them jealous.

He duly sleeps with them all. But then, as the book plods on, round and round the circles of hell, every single person in the village sleeps with everybody else. Halfway through the story, at the nativity play, it is suggested that instead of singing 'Oh come all ye faithful . . .', the lyrics should say 'Oh come both ye faithful' because there are only two such people in the village. By the end, it's been revealed that neither of these are faithful either.

As usual, Cooper does her best to make the sex appealing by making a menagerie of it. 'Plunging his face into her pubic hair, snuffling as appreciatively as a truffle pig . . .'; 'as joyously as an otter diving into a summer stream he plunged his cock inside her'; 'despite her wriggling away like a piglet, he kissed her'; 'her dark hair tickling his belly, she kissed him everywhere, her tongue as delicate and subtle as a lurcher's'; 'she's so peaceful, thought Lysander protectively, like a leveret, or a female mallard', etc.

But, pigs and dogs apart, the dominant mood of the book is one of excruciating jealousy and betrayal, real cruelty and pain. The men are all false, but then so are all the women. Cooper's views break out in grim little editorials.

'The only pleasure afforded a chronically cuckolded wife, of witnessing the anguish of one's husband's current mistress when he moves on to a new one, was denied to poor Kitty . . .'

'If you have a remotely attractive husband in the nineties . . . you have to be prepared to share him,' advises one wife. 'The most important thing in marriage is companionship and a huge bit on the side to cheer one through the bad patches,' counsels the other.

No sweet dreams in the sun-lounger then; nightmares, rather. Since this message of misery is automatically going to become the hardback bestseller of the summer and the paperback of next, it's quite a good con to have perpetrated. But hell hath no fury . . . Nice to see Andrew Parker-Bowles in her acknowledgements, too.

23 April 1993

Too many Cooksons . . .

The Year of the Virgins CATHERINE COOKSON (Bantam)
The House of Women CATHERINE COOKSON (Corgi)

CATHERINE Cookson is the last remnant of working heavy industrial plant in the North-east. She's been churning out books for over 40 years, and the sales have never stopped rising.

She's produced over 80 titles and sold more than 90 million copies. These two new ones each became the bestselling novel – one in hardback, the other in paperback – as soon as they were published.

And, owing to her unparalleled paup-appeal, even more people read her than buy her. The true register of her success is the Public Lending Right returns, in which she invariably scores far more loans than any other writer. In one year, no less than 35 of all the 100 most borrowed titles were by Cookson.

The greatest milch cow in publishing is now 86 years old and has been in poor health for some time. Her publishers, Transworld, are not unnaturally concerned – so much so that they have begun to think about ways of maintaining product continuity beyond the grave.

No publisher can see why an established line should go out of production just because its author has been selfish enough to expire. Various ways round the problem have been tried. The late Virginia Andrews has been trademarked: her ghost continues to turn out bestsellers, successfully flogged as 'The New Virgina Andrews' – one of these fabrications is in the bestseller list now. The late Alastair Maclean, on the other hand, has simply been posthumously impersonated by 'Alastair MacNeil', with both names appearing on the cover, the former in larger type than the latter, a ploy guaranteed to confuse the open-mouthed dimwits who buy such books.

Transworld has gone for the relatively tasteful option, launching a Catherine Cookson Award for new novelists. The first winner, Valerie Wood, is to be announced later this year. She gets £10,000. Transworld gets a Cookson-lookalike which it can legitimately publish with the words CATHERINE COOKSON blazoned large on the cover – a first step to being free from irritating dependency on the woman herself, immortalizing her mighty brand-name.

Yet with any luck this little scheme will fail. Many bestsellers and would-be bestsellers are synthetic, cynically written down by greedy hacks. Cookson's aren't like this at all. They really are as mad as hell. They obsessively rehearse terrible scenes and deranged longings. They pound away at painful places. They're Tyneside's answer to Greek tragedy.

The Year of the Virgins contains fantastic slaughter. Fat and crazy Catholic Winifred Coulson has a loveless marriage with husband Dan, who's doggedly knocking off Maggie the cook in their Tyneside mansion. They have three adult children in the house, mentally retarded young Stephen, adopted Joe and young Don, of whom Winifred is insanely and sexually possessive.

And now young Don is getting married to young Annette. Whoops! 'Appen as he drives off from the wedding, he's paralysed and rendered incontinent in a car crash. By heck though, that ain't all. 'Appen he's already impregnated his bride beforehand. Winifred goes bananas when she finds out and is carted off to the loony bin for shock treatment. 'Appen she escapes though, comes back home, catches Dan and the cook hard at it and batters everyone in the house to within an inch of their lives with a plank of wood. 'Appen at this point almost every character is in hospital. 'What had come upon them? It was like a curse. But it was no curse, it was simply mother-love, twisted mother-love.'

But all's well that ends well. Winifred dies of exposure. Annette has the baby, saintly paraplegic Don kicks the bucket in Catholic cheer, and adopted Joe reveals that he's always had the horn for Annette himself. She confirms that she has long had the hots for him too. And now the deck's been cleared. Whahey!

All of this is supposed to happen in the 1960s. The period detail is thin and implausible, but it doesn't matter. The story is told in a sort of continuous breathlessness, the over-explicit dialogue oriented by incessant use of the characters' names. Cookson shows little linguistic awareness but she has a fanatical grasp of structure, always dutifully telling you where people are at any time, and what they're doing. It's simultaneously quite unreal and peculiarly convincing because, improbable as the characters are, Cookson is committed to them. In fact, of course, they are all *her*.

For Cookson's own often-told story is at least as extraordinary as her novels. She was born illegitimate in Jarrow and, until told the truth by other children, believed her alcoholic mother was her sister and her grandparents were her parents; she was brought up in great poverty but saved enough as a laundry manageress to buy a large boarding house; she was childless but suffered four miscarriages; and she endured a severe mental breakdown, which took 10 years to recover from, before she began writing in her 40s . . .

These events and the pain they caused are what fuel her writing, reappearing again and again in very slightly different guises. Her current paperback, *The House of Women*, offers yet another mad matriarch, more infidelity and attempted murder, another lover who waits years for his beloved and, for good measure, a strong dose of father–daughter incest. All this is set off by an accidental pregnancy (Cookson's whole oeuvre depends on contraceptive failure).

The emotional pressure behind this writing is unmistakable. Cookson is a much better novelist than those – like Melvyn Bragg and Julie Burchill – who have tried to fake their way into bestsellerdom. All those stock scenes may be imitated – but the manic intensity is not so easily faked. Her publishers are right to be anxious about her health. They don't make them like her any more, what with the Welfare State and all. Thank heaven it's being dismantled! Literature can only benefit.

26 March 1993

Penile servitude

The Bridges of Madison County ROBERT JAMES WALLER
(Minerva paperback)

WOMEN, observes a Russian proverb, have long hair but short brains. It must be true. Here's the proof.

You thought women were becoming smarter, men nicer, things fairer all round? No, no, no. How could you have been so silly?

The Bridges of Madison County is a monstrously successful book. It's been the bestseller in the States for a year now. Its publisher there believes it will be the biggest-selling hardback of all time, shifting four million copies. In Britain, it was published last year as *Love in Black and White* by the hapless Sinclair-Stevenson and it flopped. This time around the hype has hit home. It's already a bestseller and it's going to get worse. Your mother's going to read it.

This is the perfect cult book – basically, it's *Jonathon Livingston Seagull* humps an *Edwardian Country Lady*. The story is cretinously simple. If you don't know about it already, you're going to soon, whether you like it or not. In 1965, a 52-year-old photographer, philosopher and all-round wonder called Robert Kincaid meets a 42-year-old woman of Italian extraction, called Francesca, in rural Iowa. Her husband, a dork-brained farmer, is off on a business trip. So Robert bangs her blind for four days. Then he tactfully clears off and she piously resumes her life as a housewife and drudge.

In 1989, after they're all conveniently dead, Francesca's children find her mementoes of the affair and realize that this was the love of her life. And, though they never met again, it turns out she was the love of his life too. Well, well! Awfully, sad, eh?

It's an astonishingly simple male fantasy. The woman, Francesca, is hardly characterized at all, except by her nipples and her fantastic adulation of the man. Having had a four-day ration of a real hunk, she dutifully goes back to serve out a life sentence with her dreary family. Still, even a nibble of something as tasty as that should keep her going for the rest of her days, eh? And grateful with it, too, obviously.

The man, Robert, on the other hand, is attentively idolized throughout the book. This is a wee bit embarrassing because he so clearly represents the author himself. Robert James Waller and Robert Kincaid are both in their early 50s, the same height and build, with the same habits (smokers, joggers, vegetarian). Just to make sure you get the point, the book is illustrated with photographs of some crappy old bridges in Madison County which Kincaid takes in the book but which were actually taken by Waller himself.

Kincaid is portrayed as the greatest guy who ever lived. 'At 52 his body was all lean muscle, muscle that moved with the kind of intensity and power that comes only to men who work hard and take care of themselves', for starters. He's a trojan in the sack, naturally, as a former girlfriend is wheeled on to testify: 'Invariably, after they'd completed their lovemaking and were lying together, she'd tell him, "You're the best, Robert, no competition, nobody even close."' And he cleans the bath afterwards too.

Waller has got just enough nous to master the Cellini trick – instead of boasting how wonderful you are yourself, you slyly report how bloody wonderful everybody else thinks you are. Francesca is good value in this respect. The daft bint thinks to herself: 'There was a gazellelike quality about him, though she could tell he was strong in a supple way. Maybe he was more like a leopard than a gazelle. Yes. Leopard, that was it.' Later, she simply says: 'He was real, more real than anything she'd ever known.'

Finally, when they get down to it, she informs him: 'Robert, you're so powerful it's frightening.' And then we get this: 'The leopard swept over her, again and again and yet again, like a long prairie wind, and rolling beneath him, she rode on that wind like some temple virgin toward the sweet, compliant fires marking the soft curve of oblivion . . . She, who had ceased having orgasms years ago, had them in long sequences now. . .' Of course she did, of course she did, billions of them. In fact, 'it went on for days, almost without stopping'.

Less happily Waller tries to show what a great poet and sage this man is by quoting him directly. So the prannet gets to say things such as: 'Like two solitary birds flying the great prairies by celestial reckoning, all of these years and lifetimes we have been moving toward one another.' He also keeps lecturing away on the theme that 'male hormones are the ultimate cause of trouble on this planet'. Part of his supreme attractiveness to women is that he himself is 'hard . . . hard, physically'; he also knows that in future men are going to have to be different and wear sandals.

Meanwhile, here he is, 'one of the last cowboys', as he plonkingly describes himself. The message from Waller is that they don't make them like me any more, so get it while you can.

For what women want, if only they knew it, is a really good, thorough, old-fashioned shafting. 'She had become a woman again,' says Francesca, when she gets hers. 'He was an animal. A graceful, hard, male animal who did nothing overtly to dominate her yet dominated her completely, in the exact way she wanted that to happen at this moment.'

And you got to let them wild animals roam free, ain't yer? 'Don't you see, I love you so much that I cannot think of restraining you for a moment. To do that would be to kill the wild magnificent animal that is you, and the power would die with it,' the birdbrain tells the leopard (all the dialogue is that wooden, by the way).

So *The Bridges of Madison County* sets the relations between the sexes back about 30 years, before feminism had begun to bite. It's hardly surprising that Waller should have written it. But it's a little depressing that so many female dupes should have bought it. Women, eh? *Women.* But there you go. A chicken is not a bird and a woman is not a human being. Russian proverb.

22 October 1993

4

THE YOUNG AND THE HYPED

Never mind the quality,
look at the author photo

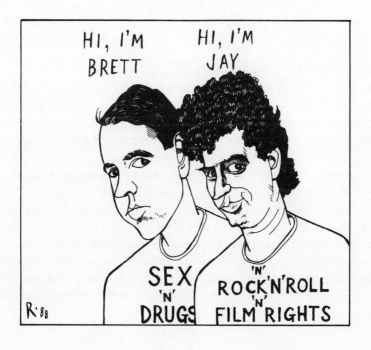

Grasping the nettle

The Darker Proof: Stories from a Crisis ADAM MARS-JONES AND EDMUND WHITE (Faber)

*A*DAM Mars-Bar's first collection of stories, *Lantern Lecture*, had the reviewers reaching for themselves. It was like the second coming. At last a new young writer! One excitable young man in the *TLS* demanded that something should be done to protect this National Treasure for the future of English Literature.

This was all some years ago now. Since then Mars-Bar's reputation has soared without the impediment of any further publications. He has successfully appeared on chat-shows in squeegee leather trousers; he has published a brilliant essay in *New Society* on the sauciness of Rambo. He has turned out a lot of waffle for the *Independent*; he has supervised an anthology of 'gay and lesbian fiction'. Gradually these endeavours have made him a Leading Writer.

But no more books. He had nothing to write about, you see. Never had had. Even in that first book the longest of the three stories had been nothing more than a reheated transcript of a trial presided over by his papa, Lord Chief Justice Mars-Bar. The National Treasure was all dressed up and nowhere to go.

But, just like Martin Amis, he has now found a Subject.

Amis decided that nuclear weapons were more fitting targets for his rhapsodically abusive prose than the London lowlife he had previously concentrated on, and he proceeded to knock out a collection of concerned stories, *Einstein's Monsters*. The idea was that because Nuclear Weapons are Important, stories about them must be Important too.

Mars-Bar had the same brainwave, only what he thinks Important is Aids. Like Martin Amis, his response has inevitably been short stories. 'Concerned stories' will henceforth be a new category in the bookshops. At least, I hope it will, because this stuff, like Soviet tractor fiction, is making its claim on us for reasons other than artistic excellence. Ironically it is ghetto-work.

It is painfully obvious from this collection that Mr Mars-Bar is more a man of decent feeling than instinctively a novelist. His stories progress firmly towards a moral of how to behave. The first is a sufferer's monologue (the most ambitious, and least successful, being an Amis pastiche). The second reports a death and its mourning. The third shows an infected couple coming to terms with the fact. The fourth, called 'The Brake', is the Message, demonstrating how a chap can change his lifestyle so as not to die before his time. There you are put right, 'braked'.

In a muddled way Mars-Bar does acknowledge that death, even premature death, is not uniquely a gay problem. The hero of 'The Brake' reforms his diet as well as his sex life; the last line of the story candidly admits that too much fried bacon can be just as killing as too much buggery (and moreover, showing you what a nice man Mars-Bar must be, harder to give up). But the admission betrays the pretention of the whole collection.

We are all mortal and *all* art exists in response to that fact. Recipes and tips for cautious frottage may be useful, and offered in all sincerity, but they are not what creative writing is about. Certainly Aids is going to affect fiction in the future but not as simply as this. *The Darker Proof* – wittily packaged by Faber & Faber in matt black – is just art as thermometer, art as Elastoplast. It will be brandished with horrible complacency in Islington.

Whether its authors realize it or not, what it will actually be read for elsewhere is its reportage of gay lifestyle. The stories by Edmund White, a not-so-decent Yankee gay narcissist, are comically absorbing on this level, with their obsession with musculature and organ size, their derision of heterosexuality. Even the decent heroes of decent Mr Mars-Bar are frankly preoccupied with the size of their balls. La Mars-Bar's hottest tip, by the way, is urtication. You tickle the scrotum with nettles. It feels 'only as sharp as curries are to a palate unused to spices'. Young nettles of course, so it's seasonal. Safe sex though.

24 July 1987

Gobblin' Teasmade

The Waters of Thirst ADAM MARS-JONES (Faber)

Poor Mr Mars-Bar has made a mistake. He has published a novel. Why has he been so silly?

In 1983 he was proclaimed one of *Granta*'s Best of Young British Novelists without ever having published a novel. Ten years later the honour was repeated. Not having blotted his copybook in the interim, he was one of the Best Young British Novelists–2, too. Now he's gorn and torn it, just when everything was going so well. If only he'd kept his head down, he'd have been a hot tip for the Booker, a certainty for the Whitbread.

It's not *much* of a novel, admittedly – only 180 pages long and obviously expanded from a short story – but that makes no difference.

Over the last ten years, Mr Mars-Bar has become an Aids specialist. In two collections of short stories, *The Darker Proof* and *Monopolies of Loss*, he has written a series of poignant little tales about what it is like for gay men facing the disease. Throughout them, his niceness is apparent – but in the sense of exaggerated fastidiousness, as well as goodness of heart.

These are the neatest, tidiest, most precious little contes ever constructed about such a large and overwhelming subject. They read like a displacement activity. It's as if he were trying to counter the huge mess of Aids by producing perfect miniatures, each tied up with a neat little bow or image. The one thing they do not do is tell a larger story.

Once or twice, nice Mr Mars-Bar has tried to broaden his approach – to make a novel of it. In the last story in *The Darker Proof*, called 'The Brake', he even went some way towards admitting that death, even premature death, is not uniquely a gay problem. The hero of that story realizes that if he wants to carry on living, he had better reform his diet as well as his sex life. Too much fried bacon can prove just as fatal as too much free-range buggery.

Ten years later, it is precisely this conceit that he has tried to expand into a novel, in another attempt to make an Aids story into something more universal. William is gay all right, but monogamous and not HIV positive. Instead, he has an inherited kidney disease. Twice a week he goes for dialysis; he can't eat anything salty or drink more than 25 fluid ounces of liquid a day. 'No bacon, no beaujolais' then. He dreams of a kidney transplant. But when he finally gets one, the organ is rejected and the drugs compromise his immune system so that he ends up in an Aids ward after all. Neat? Not *really*. It's a corny way of trying to take the Aids novel out of the ghetto.

And Mars-Bar has been so taken with the bacon idea that he has hammily organized the whole thing around it. William is a fanatical foodie and culinary images recur madly. 'I was afraid of finding out the hard way that transplant surgery has something in common with cooking. Everything depending on the freshness of the ingredients,' he says, tastefully. His heart, William says, is borne towards his boyfriend Terry 'on a strong current of catering. Love is not a convenience food. Love is not instant, freeze-dried or micro-wave compatible ... With tinned soup there is no love. With frozen pastry there is no love. Stock cubes likewise are the death of love.' But wot about pot noodles, Ad? *Lovely*, surely?

Even sex is made a foodie frolic. William's speciality is the 'hot-tea blow-job' (exactly what you'd expect). 'It's not an easy trick to do well, the hot-tea blow-job,' he says, proudly. 'Terry will never find anyone with a technique to match mine. And if love is measured by its cost there was a lot of love in that morning gesture, repeated so many times along the years. A teacup of average size contains five fluid ounces. Waking Terry as he loved to be woken would cost me 20 per cent of my daily ration, in the dialysis years.' Lor luvva duck. Saint Francis or what?

And then finally yer gets yer bacon. 'Streaky bacon done crisp' first appears as a theme on page 3. Later William discovers that he can eat what he likes while actually on the dialysis machine and breaks out into the sarnies. 'For me it was a sacrament in greaseproof paper,' he says, being a bit fancy in his speech like. But he just can't get no satisfaction. 'I tried every possible variation of ingredients, in my search for the elusive satisfaction of the bacon sandwich. Healthier bread, margarine instead of butter, bacon grilled instead of fried, bacon made by traditional processes or else from pigs that had led unusually fulfilling lives. And still in every sandwich there was an element that nullified the whole.' Sad, eh?

Tragic, more like. He concludes that it's not him, it's them. 'Perhaps there had been a general cancellation of flavour,' he suggests moodily. People who ate freely from day to day wouldn't notice the encroachments, on a broad front, of a creeping insipidity. Only I, after years of abstinence, was in a position to match present stimulus with memory and detect the progressive fading of taste-sensation from the world.' Well, la-di-da.

Bacon's off then. So, alas, is Mr Mars-Bar's fabulous career as the world's most abstinent novelist. It just never tastes as good as you imagined, does it?

18 June 1993

Over sexed, over paid and over here

Story of My Life JAY MCINERNEY (Bloomsbury)
The Rules of Attraction BRETT EASTON ELLIS (Picador)

*P*UBLISHERS, like everyone else, lust after young flesh. Or as they say, they are always on the look-out for new blood.

They can't get enough of it. There are few enough worthwhile American novelists under 30 and simply no British ones, as all the publishers, hesitating between the Beaumes-de-Venise and the Armagnac, mournfully agree. And the only reason there are any American ones is that they are not so easily embarrassed.

At the moment there are two young American novelists. They are called the literary bratpack, or as we say in England, the pratpack, much like a six-pack only smaller. Once upon a time there were three, because there used to be a lady called Tama Janowitz, whose first book *Slaves of New York* tickled Auberon Waugh's largish fancy hugely. Unfortunately her second, *A Cannibal in Manhattan*, about a cannibal in Manhattan, was very nearly as amusing as *Crocodile Dundee II*. Now nobody mentions her, and we are left with Tweedledum and Tweedledee.

Tweedledum, the senior of the two, wrote a clever first novel called *Bright Lights, Big City* about a chap coming to grief in New York. This was all in the hitherto unexplored second person present – it went 'you walk into the room and . . .' – so as to convey that things were happening without an agent, that the experiencing self was, you know, detached from the doing self, and that things in general were a bit out of control. A lot of bright young men on the BYM magazines naturally proceeded to do up their interviews this way for about a year ('You walk into the room and the man introduces himself. He is called Cliff Richard' and so on).

Tweedledum has now progressed to a third book, *Story of My Life*. By an ingenious twist, this is about a girl coming to grief in New York and it is written in the first person present. The thing about Alison is that she is a bear of no brain at all, not even a mini-portion. Her first sentence runs: 'I'm like, I don't believe this shit.' Nor do we, dear. Unhappily this proves to be one of Alison's more enterprising articulations.

Large helpings of sex and drugs follow, the only clean bit being where she tells us how to get 'a faucet orgasm' by thrusting at the bath tap (women only I should say). Though the book pretends to modernity, the morality tale is antique: too many drugs and too much promiscuity are bad for you and you end up with abortions and lunacy. Alison's final reflections on the matter are as impressive as her opening sally: 'Maybe I dreamed a lot of stuff. Stuff that I thought happened in my life. Stuff I thought I did. Stuff that was done to me. Wouldn't that be good.'

Americans of course believe that the fewer words you can manage the better class of person you must be. Marlon Brando, *Of Mice and Men*, President Ronbo – we mustn't blame Tweedledum for this phenomenon. What we might twitch our eyebrows about is the way he thinks the excesses of his characters make up for all stylistic inadequacies. There is something in this idea: people do persist in reading war books and the *News of the Screws*. But doing sex and taking drugs, like anything else, must be interestingly written about to be interesting to read about, and since they are both more repetitious activities than, say, gardening, this is difficult. Too hard for Tweedledum anyway.

Never mind. Bloomsbury have turned out their usual pretty book and there's a party at the Groucho. It'll go with the CDs. Tweedledee's package is aimed lower, in paperback for those unsure how hardbacks work.

Like *Story of My Life*, *The Rules of Attraction* presents a slice of female flesh on the cover. Originally this was a juicy bottom in knickers, but the publishers suffered a spasm of taste and changed this, at some expense, to less munchable shoulders, making the bum-cover a collector's item. It is not easy to see why they bothered, since the design still features both a diaphragm and what looks like a home-made tampon or is possibly an exotic cigarette. Like Dum's book again, Dee's has a pretentious epigraph about the perils of disorder. And like Dum's it has wildly unfortunate opening words ('and it's a story that might bore you but you don't have to listen').

Where it thrillingly differs is that instead of one stupid narrator, it has many stupid narrators. On the sleeve they call it 'kaleidoscopic', which very accurately means you can't tell one part from another. Otherwise it is exactly the same 20-year-olds fucking and drugging themselves to excess.

The reason these books are so threadbare is that they are not actually novels at all but ludicrously distended rock lyrics. The characters of both writers refer to rock songs incessantly and have the lives rock music promotes. Dee's first book was actually named after an Elvis Costello song, as is the heroine of *Story of My Life*, which is itself a Lou Reed song . . . Both have been aimed at people who have got used to buying only records. Youth culture is now rock culture and rock is what its books, like its films, must imitate.

Sad for the publishers of course, hoping to put themselves in touch with youth. They can only go back to Maggi Drabble's moving studies in sexual dysfunction in Hampstead. Or if they do really want to get closer to rock culture they should forget these hybrid forms, and go directly for the sort of thing that the splendid Omnibus Press are publishing in the autumn: *Johnny Rotten in His Own Words*. Well, word.

19 August 1988

Nursery crime

A Little Stranger CANDIA MCWILLIAM (Bloomsbury)

*B*AD female novelists are so much better than bad male novelists. Inept men turn out tedious and unreal fantasies. Inept women tell you about themselves and their preoccupations. They have at least that truth to life.

And some women are truly entertaining. Others, of course, are Anita Brookner. But Candia McWilliam is very entertaining indeed, as *Eye* readers may recall. Her place in literary history has been booked by the way last year she occupied the whole of Pseuds Corner one week – a triumph fully earned.

The *Telegraph* colour supplement had the droll idea of asking her to address the pleasures in her life. To such a towering egotist this was the opportunity of a lifetime, brilliantly taken. Her pleasures included singing 'bits of oratorio in empty train carriages', programming her dreams, 'reading Villiers de L'Isle Adam while eating a pomelo', 'the colours and trim of a pile of turnips', Kingsley Amis, and cooking – or, as she called it, 'beating against the tide in a homely coracle powered by well-deployed spoons'.

This last is presumably an example of what she declared to be her greatest pleasure of all: writing. 'It is where I live and what I do and how I am. I am making whale music in the hope and trust that there are listeners, but I should do it were there only krill.'

With this ingenious commission the *Telegraph* magazine had drawn out the best of McWilliam in one gush. But it didn't put her off whale music. Her first novel *A Case of Knives* won part of the Betty Twat Womantic Fiction prize and became notorious. It is about a rich homosexual heart surgeon who in his personal life coldheartedly experiments with people's hearts, McWilliam being no enemy to bad taste. The story is threadbare but the style is embroidered. McWilliam believes 'style' to be something you simply can't get enough of: the more fancy phrases and frilly turns per paragraph the better. She values words as she values turnips.

With a little splash of blood on the cover, and a full-page photograph of the stylish author on the sleeve, *A Case of Knives* was the quintessential Bloomsbury novel. Rebuffing of the plebs and their plain language continues apace in her second, *A Little Stranger*. Again, the tale itself is absurd. A tall, rich and aesthetic mother hires a short and common nanny for her first child. She gets pregnant again. The bulk of the book consists of her telling us, in a tone of fatuous hauteur, about the elegant pleasures of her life in a big house, as opposed to the ugly and stupid ones of the nanny. Finally this flow is interrupted when it is revealed that, in a terrifying reversal of the order of things, pregnant Daisy has become *fat*, while the nanny, with designs on madam's husband, has become anorexically *thin*. Horror of horrors. The wretched nanny, now gaunt, aspires to porky Daisy's place! Luckily she is soon seen off.

McWilliam achieves this amazing piece of plotting by simply not mentioning that anything has happened until the last minute, despite the fact that it is all narrated by the heroine. But no matter. This is not a novel but an anthology of brag and snub on the part of this McWilliamesque figure, Daisy. The boast may be simple: 'I am taller than most and have more hair.' Or recondite. Daisy talks of eating black olives, smoked roes, vinegared capers, raw steak and sweetbreads, while the nanny sups on garbage: 'For butter she had grease which reeked faintly of town water and her jam contained neither fruit nor sugar . . .'

But mostly it is a display of words – tall rare words, not short common ones: goffered, caret, bassinet, drugget, snoods, gynaecea, neonate, petersham, panicles, ahent, hetaira, zenana, flocci, darrows, eclampsia. Every object is described in ornate terms. A handbag closes 'with the short locked tusks of a gramnivore'. Old roses have 'bletted like fat tan onions'. Everything is awkwardly forced into food metaphors – or food itself is rhapsodized. Leeks are like organ pipes: 'sliced across, these monsters resembled white short-playing records'. You know the ones?

This parade of manner is what the book is about. The story, such as it is, exists only to add further piquancy to the prose. *A Little Stranger* may be unreadable or sickening – you can't eat a cake made all of currants – but it is still a triumph. Rarely has narcissism gone so far as to make the actual language an image of the writer. McWilliam is six foot tall, like a human saluki in appearance, and she has succeeded not only in telling a tall story but in getting her language up on stilts as well. The whole book is haughtiness embodied, looking down in disdain.

The other reason you'll be hearing about Candia McWilliam, apart from those lofty looks, is that she represents high society. She was brought up in one titled family, married into another, and is now again married to a Parsee Oxford don named Dinshaw (whose financier father used to support Jeremy Thorpe). The smart reviewers will no doubt be turning out in force to affirm their friendship. Nobs love to read books about uppity nannies being put down. It's a growing market. Never mind us krill.

20 January 1989

Hackney-ed

The Buddha of Suburbia HANIF KUREISHI (Faber)

*T*RENDY left-wing persons of a certain age adore Hanif Kureishi. If he didn't exist, they would have to invent him. It wouldn't be difficult.

Since he spared them the trouble, though, they're happy to ignore the fact that he has only about a fifth of the talent he's credited with. *The Buddha of Suburbia*, Kureishi's first novel, is awkwardly written and boring to read. But it's been reviewed with little whimpers of ecstasy by TLPs.

Angela Carter in the *Guardian* noticed admiringly that 'he remains Right On, politically, and lets the middle classes play little if any role in this world of squats, anti-racism and dishevelled integrity'.

That's all right then! For her it certainly was. 'It is a wonderful novel,' she concluded, adding subliterately, 'I doubt if I will read a funnier or one with more heart, this year, possibly this decade.' She must be intending to dedicate the 1990s to Enid Blyton.

The Buddha of Suburbia is hackneyed in everything except its racial subject matter, Asians in Britain. Kureishi knows that this is his unique selling point ('The material was quite fresh,' he has said, appreciatively) and he exploits his market monopoly with the eagerness of any small businessman.

'I write about the world around me, the people I know, and myself,' explains Kureishi. He does. This is in the worst sense an autobiographical novel; it resembles nothing so much as Paul Theroux's *My Secret History* without the irony.

It's the first-person story of Karim. Karim, like Kureishi, is the son of an Asian father and an English mother, growing up in the suburbs of south London. Like Kureishi, Karim makes it out of the suburbs into success (as an actor) in arty London north of the river. As soon as this happens the book turns into little more than bragging about a Bohemian lifestyle which, as anybody who saw his film *Sammy and Rosie Get Laid* knows, is all that Kureishi's Right On-ness amounts to.

Kureishi believes sexual promiscuity is politically liberating or is political liberation – a cretinous misapprehension presumably derived way back from somebody as mad as Wilhelm Reich and never examined. *Sammy and Rosie Get Laid* shows kissing and Kureishi pathetically speculates 'perhaps these kisses are subversive in some way'. It shows three couples having sex ('joyful lovemaking all over London') on a split-screen, and Kureishi opines that these 'avid fuckers' are 'running right up against the mean monogamous spirit of our age'.

In *The Buddha of Suburbia* Karim has sex with everybody, male and female. The bisexuality Kureishi promotes no doubt seems to him a logical extension of his basic belief that all transgression is good, all orderings wrong. But it reads only as a peculiarly grabby form of narcissism, wanting it all ('I felt it would be heartbreaking to have to choose one or the other, like having to decide between the Beatles and the Rolling Stones ... I could go to parties and go home with anyone from either sex').

Karim repeatedly stresses how very attractive he is, to both sexes, to everyone. For all its air of – thank you Angela – 'dishevelled integrity', the book is merciless. You are either 'interesting' or not. The key to the whole book is this little line: 'Thank God I have an interesting life, I said to myself.'

The Buddha of Suburbia is, then, a conventional book about a young man on the (sexual) make – a contemporary version of *Room at the Top* with added political cant.

Cant it is. In his diary of the making of *Sammy and Rosie Get Laid*, Kureishi announces as his political ideal 'that there should be a fluid, non-hierarchical society with free movement across classes and that these classes will eventually be dissolved'. Give me chastity and continence but not yet! in other words. A few pages later Kureishi is relishing one of the rewards of moving up: caviar in New York. 'Oh, how we eat! Oh, how I like life now! ... Each caviar egg explodes on my tongue like a little sugar bomb.'

And that's about how explosive Kureishi really is. When on *Start the Week* recently he said 'I think the riots at the weekend were terrific and I'm all for them' it was just his way of being interesting. Or not.

13 April 1990

Big Jimmy riddle

The Burn: Stories JAMES KELMAN (Secker & Warburg)

*A*ULD Jim gits oot of bed. Turns aff the alarm cloak. The wife sleeping the while. Gis straight ben the study. Sits doon in that and gives a wee look at the typewriter. Isni any good. Couldni move bit. Just isni any fucking good, cunts telling you yir a genius and that. The Jim fella knows. Just isni any fucking good at all.

Wee bit of time gis by. Hears the papers come through the door. Gits oot and brings them back, turns over the book pages. There he is. Fucking big picture of the guy, like he was Goad or something. Just sitting there holding this toty wee wine glass. A fucking wine glass, man! Auld Jim has a bit laugh about that. Guys in the pub seeing him holding a wine glass! Fucking bogging literary celebrity man, it was a joke, it was a fucking joke. This yin in the *Independent* says he's 'simply incomparable'. Ah mean, whit the fuck does that mean, saying yir simply incomparable? Other yin talking about the Scots literary renaissance, ah mean, whit a fucking carry on, eh?

Wee bit more time gis by. This Jim fella gis another squint it the typewriter. Isni any good, isni any fucking good at all. Hears the wife. Comes in and that ti stick oan the kettle. Sees auld Jim sitting there. Hasni started. Fucking advance out the windi. Goodnis sake Jim, she shouts, yir offi late.

Am no bothered.

Wife says: was this cunt writing in the *Guardian* saying youse the new James Joyce, did you ken that big fella?

Am no surprised.

Wife gis out agen. Jim sits ther, yonin. Stares at the bookshelf. All of them lined up there man, toty wee books in long fucking rows, a fucking *oeuvre*.

116

The Bus-Conductor Hines. Not Not While The Giro. A Chancer. Aye, that was a fucking good one, right enough. Was whin he wrote *A Disaffection* all the fucking trouble started, fucking Booker Prize shortlisting and folk thinking Jim now, he's fucking sellt himself out the while, be down the Guildhall next wearing a wee dinner jacket, but he wasni doing it for the money, he just wasni, and he wasno goan to wear no fucking dinner jacket neither. Ah, fucking banalities, ye just say them.

Looks oot the windi. Sees the wife taking the kids to school and that. Postman gis by up the path. Decent and leisurely process of the public mails yr lordship. Hears the letter come down oan the mat. Goad love us, another fucking cheque. It was just a fucking joke, a fucking joke the money they sent him and, Christ almighty, he felt so fucking bad, so fucking bad.

Coupla hours gis by. The wife comes in. Says: was this cunt on the phone wanting to know about a wee interview for the TV.

Ah couldni. Not with this fucking writer's block, I just couldni.

Could ye no write something else? Could ye no write a TV play, maybe, that the lassies could watch?

Fuck it, he says. Ah've got ma integrity ti think oaf. Fucking cunts'd eddit out most of the words.

Yir soft too, says the wife. Man, is awnly getting money out of the fucking English.

Auld Jim feels better. Sits doon ben the table, picks up the wee pen, starts writing another toty piece, aye, as if his fucking life depended on it.

10 May 1991

A bit Liffey

The Van RODDY DOYLE (Secker & Warburg)

JIMMY Sr came in the living room. You got used to it. In fact, it wasn't too bad. Not fair though. He was fuckin' eating far less, but he was getting fuckin' fatter. Veronica, Darren and the twins had the Ireland game on.

WE ARE GREEN WE ARE WHI'E

WE ARE FUCKIN' DYNAMITE

That was your man Darren, like the foul-mouthed bollix he was. Veronica walloped him across the head and made him put 10 pee in the swear box. You had to hand it to Veronica.

– Jaysis, I'm telling yeh, the hum in here is fuckin' atrocious, said Jimmy Sr.

– Wha' abou' you? said Darren to his da. Yeh step in some more of that dogshite?

– Be careful wha' yeh say, son, Jimmy Sr warned him.

– Wha' did you do in school yesterday? Veronica asked Tracy.

– She stabbed this fella with a compass, said Linda.

– I did not so, Linda; fuck off. She only saw me gettin' him with the compass. An' I did not stab him. I on'y . . .

– Shut up! said Jimmy Sr. Is a word I'm wanting with all of yis.

– He walloped Tracy with the homework journal, but not too hard. There was a penno in the game and they stopped to watch but your man Sheedy blasted it over, the headless fuckin' chicken.

– Wis down the library, it's the business in there yeh know, and your man Doyle's written another book.

– Wha'?

– He has indeed, Darren, son. Getting fuckin' embarrassing this is. Three books now. The one about Jimmy Jr and his mates, the one about Sharon having the kid, and now this one about me and Bimbo running the burger van. Makes us look right fuckin' eejits.

Jimmy Sr felt a fart coming. He didn't trust himself with it, but he carried on:

– Yeh, well that's had a bad psychological effect on me, son, reading it all. Beats me how the little shitehawk found out abou' everything. Time the baby's nappy got fried in the batter by mistake, time your man from the health department starts asking questions, fuckin' row I had with Bimbo over that wagon of a wife of his.

– Yeh, shouldn't worry about that, said Darren. Fuckin' literary critics that write for the English newspapers'll love yis.

– Wha's that?

– Look at yeh, da. You're a fuckin' working-class hero. Pissed out of yer brain and say "fuck" a lot but yeh've got a heart of gold. Fuckin' *Times Literary Supplement*'ll think yer a ride. Could be something by your man Kelman if it weren't for yer sense of humour.

– Yeh mean, yeh mean I'm *authentic*, son?

– Sure, da. You'll be a bestseller.

There was another penno in the game. Jimmy Sr watched it but your man Sheedy blasted it over again. He felt great though, he felt terrific. He said to Veronica:

– Give us a hug will yeh woman? I'm so happy I could shite.

30 August 1991

Chanel tunnel vision

Out to Lunch TANIA KINDERSLEY (Bantam)

O THERWISE entirely insignificant, *Out to Lunch* represents a new low in high-society publishing.

Its 24-year-old author, as the *Sunset Times Stuff and Nonsense* section obsequiously explained, is one of the Guinnesses, 'the legendary Irish dynasty, who all possess added froth and reassuringly large bank balances'. She has no other visible qualification for authorship. *Out to Lunch* is dimwitted to a fabulous degree. It very nearly comes out the other side into being positively captivating for its brainlessness, like the utterances of Lord Emsworth and Bingo Little. But not quite.

It's a tuneless hymn to snobbery. 'Venice Skye' is beautiful, posh and sociable; and her sister 'Alabama Skye' is beautiful, posh and brilliant, the best young playwright. The plot consists of Venice temporarily pretending to be cultured and Alabama temporarily pretending to be a party-girl, in order to attract the different boyfriends they want. Role reversal!

As the nauseating book-jacket puts it, 'When Venice takes to reading the *Spectator* and quoting James Joyce, and Alabama starts wearing St Laurent to the manner born and holding court in unaccustomed splendour, *le tout Londres* is amazed and amused. What *can* those dazzling Skye girls be up to? Could it possibly, just possibly, have anything to do with love?'

This gasping tone of auto-sycophancy is maintained throughout. 'They roared away down the M4, leaving London talking nineteen to the dozen in their wake.' 'The day after the party saw everyone reaching for their [sic] telephones.' 'She wore a perfectly cut, perfectly simple black coat and skirt, St Laurent's latest creation as only he knew how, the one that every woman worth her salt in London had been lusting after for the last month.' This fantasy that London is inhabited only by a tiny glob of nobs is essential to Tania Kindersley and her kind.

The poor are there only to be devastated by patronage. 'Alabama surveyed her wardrobe, shaking her head ... She bundled the lot over her arm, and took them to Oxfam, who almost fainted at the sight of half this season's Paris collections being dumped unceremoniously on their doorstep. "Well," said Alabama to the astonished assistant, "that should feed a few babies, at least."'

Inside the bubble, being 'deliciously witty' goes like this: 'He thought Chanel was something they were trying to build a tunnel under.' 'Oliver had the ability to make the bubonic plague seem a rather amusing trifle of gossip.' 'Well darling,' said Venice, who thought feminism was a type of sanitary towel, 'I'll tell you something for free. It never did a girl any good to let on that she has more than half a brain.' There is little danger of that troubling Tania Kindersley.

Conceivably she believes the book to be mildly satirical of its characters. But it could have been written by one of them, it *has* been written by one of them. The illiterate prose, with its wretched 'to die fors' and 'darlings', has no distance from what it describes. 'Alabama had taken her platinum locks off her face, to reveal her dangerous eyes, outlined in kohl. Her mouth was a wanton red, perfectly painted, setting off those startling bones. Her endless legs were clothed in sheer black stockings, and her shoes were suede.' This is simply drooling of the glossies, imperfectly aped.

Why has Kindersley written the book? Because it's smart to be known to have written a book. One of her characters is said to be 'the latest literary sensation', his friends 'all far too much flavour of the month at Hamish Hamilton or Deutsch'. Alabama is said to be popular with them – 'the young literary bucks laughed delightedly at her sallies, and fought, in spite of themselves, to light her cigarette'.

That the novel is no good doesn't matter because the people it is aimed at are incapable of reading it or anything else longer than a menu. Even if they could, they'd not understand that merely calling a book a novel doesn't make it a novel if the term is to have any value. So now Tania Kindersley is a novelist, although she knows as much about novel-writing as she does about Esperanto.

Why was it published? Because first novels normally sell such a small number of copies that anybody who has enough society friends to buy a few can be a good prospect for a snobbish publisher.

Another moronic toff, Simon Sebag Montefiore, had a non-novel, *King's Parade*, out earlier this year from Hamish Hamilton (a firm specializing in such vanity publishing). The *Sunset Times* again made much of the occasion and reported that the novel was 'a sell-out' because many of his acquaintances bought the book hoping to identify themselves in it. And Andrew Franklin, the Hamish Hamilton publishing director responsible, revealed that, apart from calling on family friends, 'his mother went round London bookshops and said "I am Simon Sebag Montefiore's mother, I will be coming back to see if you have given his book good space."'

A few years ago all these sprigs were writing not novels but travel books about traipsing around Peru or Bhutan. In a way that was better. Apart from getting them out of the country for a while, there was at least a small chance of their meeting with a fatal accident.

2 August 1991

Phew, what a stinker

Among the Thugs BILL BUFORD (Secker)

*B*ILL Buford, a portly American braggart, is the editor of *Granta*, the literary lad's rag. It's been a position of some influence. Over the last 10 years Buford has steadily promoted a particular style, essentially a bastardized form of travel writing – 'pre-eminently, a narrative told in the first person, authenticated by lived experience', as he once ploddingly defined it.

Such writing suits editors better than readers, because, unlike true imaginative writing, it can be commissioned. You pack somebody off to a spicy location and whether or not anything much happens to him, you get your piece at the end. If stuck for copy, the writer can gamesomely describe his toils while 'looking for' his story.

So off the boys go: to Peru, Afghanistan, the Philippines, the Amazon, Borneo, Bradford, all dependably getting 'In Trouble Again', as one dreadful issue of *Granta* called it, and then coming home to write it up, modestly pretending they hadn't been that brave *really.*

The only difficulty with this wonderful scheme is that literature can never be 'authenticated by lived experience'. It is well written or not. If it's not, the fact that the writer was actually there makes no difference whatsoever. And, pleasantly enough, Buford has fallen into just this trap. Appropriately, his own murderously boring book represents the last gasp of the *Granta* house-style.

It was meant to be one of the first breaths. But *Among the Thugs*, a study of football hooligans, has been prodigiously delayed. One measure of Buford's salesmanship has been the number of times it was confidently announced in Secker's catalogues throughout the 1980s. Year in, year out the poor saps were saying they expected the manuscript to arrive any day now. Buford's last great deadline was the World Cup. The book was *definitely*, for sure, cross my heart and hope to die, going to be ready for that. Wasn't it?

This autumn's Secker catalogue was one of the few of the last five years in which the book did *not* feature. The trick worked. Here finally we have it. And immediately it's obvious that Buford had a pretty good reason for his procrastination: his problem was not just idleness, but ineptitude.

The book is embarrassingly lame. The idea must have looked such a winner too. Being American, Buford could write a travel book about the British! Britain may be relatively trouble-free, but we have got football hooligans. All Buford had to do was get among them.

But that's all he has done. This book is a dim record of Buford's attendance at a number of football matches. Sometimes he went to the pub too. At other times he just watched on the television, listened on the radio, or got some press-clippings sent by an agency.

First he sees a football 'special' go by a station in Wales. Then, in 1984 he goes on a package to Turin with uncouth Manchester United supporters. Then he attends a National Front night in a pub in Bury St Edmunds. Then he watches an uneventful Cambridge United match and a rowdier one in Fulham. He goes to the 1988 European Championships in Düsseldorf – 'The city looked like Beirut,' he says pathetically – and listens to the Hillsborough disaster on the radio. Finally he makes it to Cagliari for the World Cup first round (where the journalists outnumbered the supporters), and gets beaten up by the Italian police, but he fails to make it to Turin for the finals.

His conclusions? Thugs are thuggish. No, really, they are; they're nasty. This smashing things and beating people up – it's bad news. Something gets into people in a crowd. You'd always assumed football hooligans were rather sweet and thoughtful? Well, you couldn't have been more wrong.

Buford ends up simply calling these hooligans 'stupid' and 'little shits' over and over again. Even he realizes that this does not make great reading. He watches a yob lobbing bottles. 'I was left with nothing more than the act of observing this little shit. Why was he of interest? What was there to say but: I have now watched a little shit?' Precisely. But no doubt he'd already spent the advance.

Buford tries to dramatize this dross by pretending, in best New Journalism style, that he himself becomes caught up in the thuggery. Sure, he doesn't become a hooligan; but after a match he does swear at an elderly couple obstructing him on the Underground. And when the fans vandalize Dawes Road in Fulham he has an orgasm, I think. 'There is glass breaking: it is a window. I hear it, but I don't see it, but the effect is sensational – literally sensational: it fills the senses, reverberates inside me, as though a blast of voltage has passed through my limbs. Something has burst, erupted.' Dearie me.

But the excitement doesn't last. The low point of Buford's attempt to make himself interesting is Hillsborough. 'Hillsborough: the most famous stadium in the world. What happened there confirmed something in me.' By which he means, hearing it on the radio makes him feel he has, for good and all, seen enough of football hooligans. His book, a different sort of disaster, has a similar effect on its readers.

25 October 1991

Sapphocated by love

Written On The Body JEANETTE WINTERSON (Jonathan Cape)

POOR Jeanette Winterson. One wants so much to like her. Lesbian, of what used to be called 'humble origins', admired by the type of people who don't generally read 'serious' fiction – just the sort of young iconoclast to set against the middle-class back-scratchers who run literary London and smash them into fragments.

And yet as *Guardian* Women's Page profile succeeds *Guardian* Women's Page profile, as Peggy, Ms Winterson's lover, brings in the tea again while Ms Winterson obligingly explains to her interlocutor how bad modern writing is, that task has become increasingly difficult.

None of it – the fawning interviewers, the tea or even the hauteur that leads Ms Winterson to look down her nose at nearly every living writer –

would matter if the books were any good. But *Written On The Body*, which for all its three-year gestation period still manages to read like a hastily written first draft, is an embarrassingly bad novel.

Its plot can be briefly summarized. Girl meets older woman. Each pleasures the other senseless. Alarmed physician husband reveals to girl that her lover has cancer, subsequently detaching her, with girl's acquiescence, for trip to foreign clinic. Girl goes away to Yorkshire where she becomes obsessed with her lover's anatomy ('If I could not put Louise out of my mind I would drown myself in her'), clavicle, scapula and all. Girl comes back to London to find lover supposedly recovered, divorced from husband and vanished, presumably on grounds of girl's betrayal.

A deliciously modern love story? Actually, no. According to the blurb, Winterson has 'fused mathematical exactness with poetic intensity and made language new'. In fact Winterson has made language very old. Part of this is to do with an addiction to the King James Bible, which leads her into improbable formulations of the 'The world will come and go in the tide of a day but here is her hand with my future in its palm' sort, but most of all it is a result of her decision to take the style back into the late Victorian period.

Here, for example, is a description of Louise the lover's mouth: 'full, lascivious in its depth, with a touch of cruelty'. An early moment of intimacy causes the narrator to reflect that 'In the heat of her hands I thought, This is the campfire that mocks the sun'. Testimonies to the power of love aren't far behind, naturally enough. 'No-one can legislate love; it cannot be given orders or cajoled into service. Love belongs to itself, deaf to pleading and unmoved by violence.'

Romantic fluff, then, but *old-fashioned* romantic fluff. And for some reason best known to the author this awesome level of sententiousness is maintained to the novel's end. No trick of the late-Victorian lady novelist escapes her. There is the magnificently bad dialogue – 'Louise, I don't know what you are. I've turned myself inside out to avoid what happened today. You affect me in ways I can't quantify or contain'/'Forget that you've been here before in other bedrooms in other places. Come to me new.'/'You are a pool of clear water where the light plays.' And there are the gloriously treacly mental salutations: 'Dear friend, let me lie beside you watching the clouds until the earth covers us and we are gone.'

Marie Corelli meets the Book of Revelations. And all this from a woman of whom the *Evening Standard* remarked: 'Many consider her to be the best living writer in the language.' It's not quite Jeanette's fault, of course. Editors these days are so scared of their major authors that they fear to tell them when they've written a turkey. *Written On The Body* consequently takes its place among recent horrors such as Peter Ackroyd's *English Music* and Graham Swift's *Ever After*, novels that one can confidently predict would have been returned to their authors if submitted anonymously. Meanwhile the conspiracy to promote Jeanette Winterson as a major talent continues – one of the most culpable examples of the present tendency to judge a book by criteria other than the ability of the author to write.

11 September 1992

Novel gazing

In the Kingdom of Air TIM BINDING (Jonathan Cape)

No doubt there is some sort of link between economics and the wider patterns of cultural achievement. At any rate, like the national economy and the national football team, the English novel – that pallid and scrawny beast – is widely believed to be careering down the long slide to obscurity.

No one buys English novels – the statistics show that – and now, apparently, no one writes them either. Only recently a sad young man took up several columns of the *Guardian* to reveal the shocking fact that neither he nor his collection of brainy acquaintances now considered novel writing a useful or profitable activity, and all over England silent tears were shed at the sight of so much nascent genius cast down by circumstance.

As a matter of fact, this idea is complete nonsense. Everyone is writing novels. I am writing a novel. John Major is probably writing one. Publishers' reception areas are cluttered with minor celebs convinced that launching into fiction is just the *dandiest* way to revive a flagging career. Only last week came the terrifying news that some poor hack has got to write one to which Britt Ekland can eventually put her name. Anyone can do it, it seems, or get it done for them.

In fact the trick is such an easy one to play that even publishers are picking up the cards. Here, as in so many areas of our national life, the recession is to blame. While there are a few *bona fide* publisher-novelists – Faber's cherubic Robert McCrum, for example – the majority are *ex*-publishers, laid low by retrenchment. Barely had the gates of Hutchinson slammed shut behind Robyn Sisman (sacked for editing the bestseller, *Fatherland*) than an outline of her *roman à clef* about Bill Clinton at Oxford (since sold for megabucks) was doing the rounds.

The book trade loves publishers who write, if only because showing that we can do it too is a splendid way of getting back at proper authors, whom nearly everyone in the book trade loathes on account of their vanity, petulance, arrogance and a conspicuous inability to write books without publishers' help. Its journals, consequently, have had a great deal to say about Tim Binding (formerly of Penguin and Mainstream) and his first novel, how Caradoc (King, predatory agent) liked it and David (Godwin, now, too, an ex-publisher – perhaps he's writing one) stumped up the readies, how it needed editing (an opinion cheerfully confirmed by the author) and its combination of talent and mass appeal.

For mass appeal, presumably read sex. *In the Kingdom of the Air* belongs to a rather familiar genre of modern English writing, the Graham Swift English-childhood-plus-lurking-mystery novel – in this case the attempt of a randy BBC weatherman to unravel the disappearance of the siren of his painstakingly evoked Kentish youth – and, like many another exercise in the genre, ruinously self-indulgent.

The first bit is a smug sex diary of the type Colin Wilson used to produce, full of who did what to whom and the pieces of furniture pressed into service, until about 60 pages in, it suddenly turns into Proust – all 20-line sentences and laborious recreations of past time.

The distinguishing note, though, is a sort of sub-Dickensian delight in saying the same thing in a number of slightly different ways. Thus, of climatic conditions, 'We fell asleep to rain's dull lullaby, we woke to rain's urgent whisper, and in the hours between it was rain's dreams, rain's wet dreams which we dreamt. We hurried from rain but could not escape . . .' (Memo to editor: this is an extraordinarily ugly piece of writing). Occasionally weather and randiness come together with unintentionally hilarious results, as when our hero sits in a wind-racked hotel room – the story reaches crescendo during the great storm of October 1987 – 'spread my legs and lifted my buttocks up into the air. Let the wind fuck me I thought. Let the wind find me naked in the dark . . .'

Well, yes indeedy. There are also lots of brackets (like this), full of irrelevant material (rather like this). But this is Tim's first novel and *everyone is being very kind*. However, the long-term consequences are too awful to contemplate. Where will it end? Which publishing savant will be next? Can we expect glittering first novels from, for example, Eddie Bell or Bill Buford? The publisher who writes, according to Arthur Koestler, is like a cow in a milk-bar. This is one herd instinct that ought to be stoutly resisted.

16 July 1993

Triumph of the Will

My Idea of Fun WILL SELF (Bloomsbury)

S AY what you like about Will Self – and in recent weeks many critics have said quite a lot – he looks the part. An 'ageing, cadaverous Ted', with an uncanny resemblance to Nicholas Cage in *Wild at Heart*, his gleaming canines and general ticket-collector-on-the-Oblivion-Express demeanour have struck terror into the hearts of many a literary chat-show audience.

Acts the part as well. A recent *Sunday Times* magazine profile provided an admiring and predictable resumé of the Self career to date – the philosophical studies at Oxford, sadly truncated by a drugs bust in the middle of finals, the heroin addiction – all calculated to awaken the envy of many a less turbulent writerly psyche. Sorry Anita, nice to have talked to you Iris, but you see you don't live an exciting enough life for our purposes. Stick a syringe in your arm and I'm sure we could manage a thousand words.

This preamble might seem to betoken an unnecessary concentration on the writer rather than the writing, but in the tangled media-governed forest we all inhabit, writing comes a poor second to personality. Why else should we all be so exercised by the thought that Martin Amis may or may not have left his wife for some literary groupie? You and I might think this indiscretion as newsworthy as the Scottish second-division football results, but no: Martin Amis's infidelities, Will Self's junkie past, it's news, it's *relevant*, darlings, and it's a great deal more alluring – at any rate to an unlettered journalist – than puzzling your way through that sea of print.

Which, in its way, is a bit of a comfort, because there isn't a great deal *to* the Will Self universe, as laid out in the bustling pages of *My Idea of Fun*; little interest in the arid, dusty landscape it patrols, only a few random figures lolloping over its stretched inclines (as the wordy, pleonastic Self prose would style it).

The book's plot – all about a marketing consultant named Ian Wharton and the manipulation of his psychic gift by a sinister familiar – and its incidental horrors (the penetrated pit-bull terrier's head and so on) – well, I think we can pass on them. There remains the more interesting question of how this Best of Young British Novelist, this 'master of dirty magical realism', actually writes.

Like many another writer of his age and susceptibilities, with extreme self-consciousness (no pun intended), so self-consciously, in fact, and with such an eye on the mirror that very few of his elaborate descriptions really describe anything, and the style, consequently, is wafer-thin. One character places 'a femurous receiver back on its pelvic cradle'. Now, does a telephone receiver look like a thigh-bone? Does it bollocks. The same goes for the description of a man whose smooth face is 'slashed open by his predatory mouth' – it's back to the early luxuriant Graham Greene, where revolvers droop like parched flowers and everyone is obviously *trying very hard*.

The tremendous 'look-at-me-ness', bequeathed by, among others, Uncle Martin – the whole dismal racket of being asked to admire not only the writing but the spectacle of the writer performing – also extends to the clutch of wayside barbarities on which so many reviewers have commented. Unhappily, or perhaps happily, they aren't in the least horrific (the reader who wants to be authentically scared would do much better to try an M.R. James ghost story) for you can almost visualize the spectacle of roguish Mr Self, brow furrowed and tongue hanging out, drooling over his desk in the hope of coming up with something really sick.

Ah yes, something really sick. This is a significant book, though. Far from breaking new ground, it's perhaps the last gasp of the 1980s Amis-fuelled screech-of-the-urban-psychotic tradition, books that for all their verbal dazzle have grown completely detached from anything that might be construed as ordinary life. The blurb's tough enquiries about the reader's notion of fun ('cocaine, nude teens and a hotel suite in Acapulco?' etc.) tell their own story, i.e. they're no one's idea of fun, not mine, not yours, only Will Self's. In much the same way, *My Idea of Fun* might tickle the author's vanity but it performs no other trick.

24 September 1993

5

MIDDLE–AGED SPREAD

Baby-boomers change their nappies

Fen and ink

New Writing Edited by Malcolm Bradbury and Judy Cooke (Minerva)

*E*NGLISH literature, as currently constituted, has any number of self-appointed guardians: Malcolm Bradbury, Professor of American Studies at the University of East Anglia, is perhaps the grandest of its grand panjandrums.

Novelist, critic, Booker Prize eminence, originator of the UEA's much-trumpeted creative writing course, he exerts an incalculable thraldom over the state of what in an earlier generation used to be called English Letters, an influence that extends through countless arid byways of Eng. Lit. and takes in any amount of patronage and beneficent wire-pulling.

Bradbury's children, consequently, can be found almost everywhere: pale, flinty statues rising up to dominate the dusty landscape of the bookshops. It is a power brokerage that extends not only to living writers – McEwan, Ishiguro and other UEA graduates too numerous to mention – but even to the dead.

The Angus Wilson revival, for example, which kicked into gear on television last year and will shortly proceed by way of publicized re-issues, is almost entirely the consequence of Bradbury bending some kindly disposed ears in publishing and TV. Do we need an Angus Wilson revival? It's a moot point; but Bradbury and a few like-minded chums will see that we get one, never fear.

The Bradbury message about the enduring health of English literature – a health which, let it be said, has been called into question a few times in recent years – is relentlessly up-beat, uncritical and inclusive. One of the salient features about his introduction to *New Writing*, with its chatter about 'strong new generations', is the number of names he manages to cram in. The other is a marked espousal of fashionable notions of de-centring and 'pluralism'. Pluralism turns up quite a lot here. English Literature as an entity scarcely exists of course and 'the dominant characteristic of new writing is its variety and pluralism, its multiplicity of expression, its breadth of voices'.

Curious then that a trawl through the pages of this handsomely produced,

British Council-sponsored paperback, with their promise of variety and multiplicity, should disclose such a queer narrowness of range. Of course we're all terribly ethnic these days, not to mention regional; so it's perhaps just a teeny oversight that there are in a collection of 40 writers just three colonials, one Irishman, one Welshman and a single Scot, the latter (Alasdair Gray) well past his sell-by date, and Doris Lessing to provide a whiff of the un-English.

An oversight too, certainly not an auspicious piece of pluralism, that nearly everybody here has some not very tenuous connection with Malcolm Bradbury. Christopher Bigsby and Lorna Sage? Colleagues from the UEA. Rose Tremain and Suzannah Dunn? Ancient and modern graduates, respectively, of the UEA creative writing school. David Lodge? An old back-slapping chum from way back.

But the truly deplorable feature of *New Writing* is its obviousness, its odd generic quality, the distressing way in which it reinforces all those wicked and of course erroneous prejudices that so many of us now share about the state of modern British writing. Interviews with Martin Amis, bits of Graham Swift's dreary new novel – for God's sake, the cry goes up, find us somebody else for a change, somebody a bit less self-admiring (pieces by Lucy Ellmann and Adam Zameenzad followed by Valentine Cunningham puffing Lucy Ellmann and Adam Zameenzad; David Lodge followed by Peter Kemp puffing David Lodge) – something a bit less redolent of the current dodgy state of British writing. The impression of a cosy little club, entrance fee now lowered to accommodate the Commonwealth, in which everybody thinks everybody else is just *dandy*, is quite invincible.

Fortunately one or two pieces – an A.S. Byatt story and a rallying cry by Ben Okri – transcend these limitations. Others – notably a tremendous piece of narcissistic breast-beating by Geoff Dyer – compound them. Presumably the blank pages which ruin stories by James Lasdun and Doris Lessing are printers' cock-ups rather than daring attempts at experimental truncation.

The really depressing thing, though, is the British Council imprimatur, which means that the book will be exported all over the place as an example of sparkling national excellence, when it is, in fact, an exposure of a profound *sectional* failure.

31 January 1992

McEwan's Expert

The Innocent IAN MCEWAN (Jonathan Cape)

'*T*HE top half swung on its hinge of skin towards the floor, exposing the vivid mess of Otto's digestive tract, and pulling the bottom half with it. Both tipped to the floor and disgorged onto the carpet . . . Before he made his run for the bathroom he had an impression of liverish reds, glistening irregular tubing of a boiled egg bluish white, and something purple and black, all of it shiny and livid at the outrage of violated privacy, of secrets exposed.'

'*Who wrote this?*' You can practically visualize the headmaster of the Academy of Modern Male British Fiction, one eye on the chalked blackboard behind him, turning to interrogate the idlers of the senior remove: 'Take that expression off your face Amis mi . . . Stop giggling Barnes . . . No need to cry Wilson, nobody thinks it was you . . . And now if somebody would go and fetch McEwan from the bootroom, perhaps we might be able to get to the bottom of this . . .'

Ian McEwan's early works, the short stories collected in *First Love, Last Rites* and *In Between the Sheets* stuck like a steely dart into the torpid flesh of late 1970s fiction. Grainy, intense, macabre, featuring a lemur-eyed collection of perverts and obsessives, invariably focused on the seamier side of human relationships, they were greeted with massed critical acclaim and enormous sales among that part of the reading public that likes 'serious fiction' even more if it has lissom young lovelies on the jacket (the paperback covers were famously lubricious). The prudish tried to earmark McEwan as a pornographer, a sensationalist, a *misogynist*, which was – and is – entirely disingenuous; his chief concern is with gender and most of the more outrageous little numbers about incest and so on turn out to be send-ups of male attitudes to women.

Such a stance was not indefinitely sustainable. The 1980s loomed and the *enfant terrible* tried hard to grow up. He did all the right things: he hooked himself onto the feminist bandwagon – should I say tumbrel – with *The Comfort of Strangers*, indicted the libretto for a CND oratorio, signed any amount of earnest petitions, and wrote one brilliant but flawed novel, *The Child in Time* (1987), a projection of Thatcherite England centring on a man's loss of his infant daughter. Now, three years later, along rolls *The Innocent* (for which Cape paid a quarter of a million pounds) whose chief conceit involves a man toting two suitcases' worth of dismembered corpse around mid-1950s Berlin.

The plot can be briefly stated. Leonard Marnham, whose dissecting skills are revealed in the passage quoted, is a gauche 25-year-old telephone engineer ferried out to work on an Anglo-American surveillance project involving no time in cultivating a more personal attachment to the alluring Maria ('Your eyes are beautiful and all the time they are hidden. Has no-one told you how they are beautiful?') However, there are problems about Maria, just as there are to be problems about the 'phone-tapping – principally, her drunken ex-husband who conceals himself in the wardrobe one night and, when sprung, turns nasty. At which Leonard and Maria turn nasty, and, though it was patently self-defence, there remains the trifling problem about what to do with the body....

Like *The Child in Time*, this is a book of good bits and bad bits. The private, human-interest bits – Leonard's relationship with Maria, his seduction, the waking nightmare of the death – are brilliantly done; there is perhaps no one now writing in England who can convey such a convincing impression of how men behave towards women (n.b. especially the scene in which mild Leonard conceives that he ought to slap his mistress about a bit). The public, wider-world bits, the accounts of the 'phone-tapping, are fairly tedious, stuffed with dutiful detail and slackly written. The thrillerish gloss is grafted on and sits oddly with what has gone before. The drawback about Ian McEwan's writing is not, as some people allege, that he is humourless, or disagreeably obsessed, but simply that he is *uneven*. Here, as elsewhere in his fiction, the world beyond the bedroom door lies before you, splayed out and inert, curiously unrealized and (unlike the people within) undeflowered.

11 May 1990

Dog daze

Black Dogs IAN MCEWAN (Cape)

*T*wo years on from *The Innocent*, Cape is giving Ian McEwan the Martin Amis treatment. For the uninitiated, the Martin Amis treatment consists of bulking out a 40,000 word novella – such an *effort*, this writing business – to maximal length, in this case 174 pages, so you can charge a wallet-lightening 14 quid for it.

It also consists of dispensing with any sort of exterior description of the book's contents, the implication being that these boys are now so famous we really don't need to know piddling details like what they're writing about, we can just take the stuff on trust.

Ian McEwan's novels – five of them now since the painfully wrought miniature of *The Cement Garden* back in 1978 – are generic. Their characteristic is that they resemble other novels by Ian McEwan. What can be said about them, consequently, are the same things, only on this occasion more so. Thus:

1. *He writes about boring people.* This year's models are an excruciating couple called Bernard and June Tremaine – he an ex-Communist turned intellectual Labour MP eager to witness the destruction of the Berlin wall at first hand, she a dying mystic obsessed by an encounter with the beasts of the title (on honeymoon in the Languedoc in 1946) which apparently revealed to her the nature of evil. Jeremy, the fortysomething son-in-law, a left-liberal publisher of educational textbooks and fascinated amanuensis – he is supposed to be writing a memoir of June – lacks even his subjects' occasional gestures at vitality.

2. *He writes about them in a boring way.* Mostly through dialogue of the breast-beating, super-revelatory and quite implausible sort. A page-long disquisition from June on her deathbed, endless self-justifying mono-logues from Bernard as he rambles round Berlin in November 1989. Jeremy, trying hard to reconcile the couple's opposed views of one another, chips in with bromides such as 'Isn't it for the best if some journey inwards while others concern themselves with improving the world? Isn't diversity what makes a civilisation?' To which June accurately replies: 'Jeremy, you're a dear old fruit, but you do talk such twaddle.'

3. *The architecture is even more boring. Black Dogs* swiftly declares itself as a contest between Bernard's rationalism and June's spiritual journey after truth, her conviction that the honeymoon encounter brought her 'face to face with evil', his dismissal of the whole business as 'religious cant'. Two entrenched positions, bereft of compromise, sustained investigation and, consequently, interest.

4. *He is still, at times, a terrific writer.* Describing Jeremy alone and terrified

in a silent French farmhouse, recreating June's horror as the giant dogs lope hungrily towards her on the path, McEwan is adept at conveying physical sensation. The last-page unravelling, when the dogs – Gestapo trained – are linked with the revival of Nazi sentiment witnessed by Jeremy on his trip with father-in-law (when Bernard narrowly avoids being beaten up by Fascist thugs) is brilliantly done, and the final sentence – in which June dreams of the dogs' retreat 'into the foothills of the mountains from where they will return to haunt us, somewhere in Europe, in another time' – quite masterly.

Ça suffit!, to use a catchphrase that recurs throughout the text. Examining the cragged, ageing visage that stares from the jacket, you are struck by how rapidly the whirligig of time brings in its revenges. Look back only a decade and a half and what were our bright young middle-aged novelists up to? Amis was writing his fine early novels; McEwan had just published *First Love, Last Rites*; Ackroyd was distinguishing himself as a slashing reviewer. And what are they now, other than fodder for the Young Turks? Go on boys, kick over the statues!

The cover is excellent.

19 June 1992

The Flaubert's parrot sketch

Talking It Over JULIAN BARNES (Jonathan Cape)

(Two anguished-looking thirtysomethings sit in a Covent Garden winebar.)

STUART: My name is Stuart and I'm a character in the new Julian Barnes novel. Do you know about Julian Barnes' novels? Apparently he wrote one a couple of years ago that everybody liked. *A History of the World in 10½ Chapters*, I think it was called. I haven't read it.

OLIVER: Hi, I'm Oliver, Oliver Russell, and I too play a not inconsiderable part in Mr Barnes' thrumming new opus. You'll have to excuse my chum Stu here, my slow-witted *amigo* in the suit. Fact is, sometimes I'm just megafuckstruck – to apply a favourite *mot juste* – at how dim our honest, workaday Stu can be. It would scarcely surprise me, forsooth, if the mogadonic Stuart, in search of said Julian's much-applauded *jeu d'esprit*, directed his stoutly shod feet to the non-fiction shelf at the public library, thinking it a work of history. He's the dull one, in case you hadn't guessed.

STUART: No, I suppose I'm not what you would call the sparkling type. Oliver's the clever one. He uses words like 'crepuscular' and 'steatopygous' all the time, so I suppose that makes him clever. Anyway he fancies my wife Gillian, which is what the novel's all about.

OLIVER: Apologies again (am I going to be doing this all the time? Yes, I fear I am) for my small companion's perplexity in the field of literary criticism. I do indeed, as humble Stu puts it in his quaint vernacular, 'fancy' the adorable Gillian (glimpsed tenderly at the wedding ceremony, ne'er forgotten thereafter). But what follows is an elegant fable of role reversal: hapless Stuart's failure to retain his wife's affections cleverly contrasted with my own spectacular and, if I say so myself, predictable triumph.

STUART: I suppose Oliver's right, though I get a bit of my own back at the end. At least I think I do – it's a bit difficult to tell. The thing is, I'm sure Julian Barnes is a very good writer and everything but you never really know what's going on. For a start it's all written in dialogue, so you can never decide who's telling the truth and who isn't. For instance when I find out about Oliver fancying Gill I end up head-butting him, but he calls it 'an unfortunate clash of heads'. Take your pick.

OLIVER: *Dear* Stuart. You see the way in which Mr Barnes' pleasing ambiguities altogether elude the poor boy? (It *was* an unfortunate clash of heads, by the way, and the account of my discomfiture is highly exaggerated.) An engaging display – you'll excuse me, but I'm quite a dab hand at the old lit. crit. myself – of the relativism that attends this jolly game called life.

STUART: I suppose, when you come to think about it, it's all about truth. About how it doesn't really exist because everybody's got a different version of what really happened. I think that's a silly way of writing a story. Surely if you read a book you want to believe that what happened really happened instead of arguing about it all the time.

OLIVER: *Truth*? Did you ever hear such bourgeois platitudinizing? The next thing you know he'll be telling you he likes a tune you can whistle.

STUART: Anyway he's quite funny, this Julian Barnes, but I wouldn't recommend you to read him. Everybody's a bit – what's that phrase? –

two-dimensional. And it's like watching one of those puppet theatres where you can see the person's hands.

OLIVER: Poor Stuart. A quite masterly contrivance, I'd say. I was megafuck-struck. No, not *contrived, contrivance.* Oh, you're hopeless.

19 July 1991

Skewered by time's arrow

Visiting Mrs Nabokov, and Other Excursions MARTIN AMIS (Cape)

FLICKING through the newspaper lists of famous people's birthdays to discover that Martin Amis is 44, as one was able to do a month or so ago, was a sobering experience – like registering the first crease on the loved one's previously flawless cheekline, or the incipiently pensionable status of Brigitte Bardot.

They're so *old*, these icons we grew up with, whose images we tacked on to our student bedsit walls, whose books we introduced gravely to our collection of dog-eared paperbacks, and it won't be long now, not that long, before time's dustcart comes to ferry them away.

Being a middle-aged literary hipster – the role Martin Amis seems to have acquired, without particularly wanting to, one imagines – must be a difficult business. On the testimony of *Visiting Mrs Nabokov,* even being a young literary hipster was something he had trouble with. The music was too loud (the Stones at Earls Court in 1976), the booze too plentiful (a famously drunken interview with Anthony Burgess), the late nights too wearying (the Cannes film festival back in 1977).

Worse was the posturing that editors clearly expected from their biro-toting protégés at this time – the sneers, the put-downs, all the effortful say-nays of the literary contender's repertoire. Because what young Mart – I think I can call him Mart after all these years – really wanted was to be nice to people. In fact, beneath the cockiness and the serious frown, Mart was really just a regular guy after all.

The title piece, for example, an early 1980s encounter with Vladimir Nabokov's widow and son in their Swiss hotel fastness, is quite wonderfully obsequious, references to Vera's 'deeply responsive face', which is 'still suffused with feminine light', Dimitri 'a figure of considerable interest himself', 'the accomplished translator of many of this father's novels' and so on.

This is Mart's second scrapbook of old journalism – the first, *The Moronic Inferno, and Other Visits to America* came out in 1986. Quality-wise, it falls some way behind the dizzying accomplishment of its predecessor. Not only does it lack the first book's coherence, the unity of theme and purpose, but there aren't so many literary pieces, and the journalist Amis is at his best simply as a literary critic rather than a souped-up cultural commentator or political bar-fly.

So while we get a hot-shit interview with Updike and a respectful obituary of Larkin, they rub shoulders with some of Mart's wackier peregrinations outside the agreeable rumpus-room of his study. I mean, do we want to know what he thought about a rock concert 17 years ago, or the experience of playing snooker with Julian Barnes (the Barnes snooker piece, by the way, is a perfect example of the shoulder-patting mateyness of literary London that people rightly complain about, as is the poker game with Al Alvarez and co.)?

Unsurprisingly, Mart's much better when he's writing about darts or football, subjects that allow him to do what he does best. Oddly, what Mart is *really good at* is patronizing the working classes. Those darts players, those fat bastards with their fisted lagers and piggy eyes! Just watch Mart take them on, that's all!

Actually one can extend this net to say that what Mart's really good at is patronizing unintelligent or venal people who don't know they're unintelligent or venal (the distinction is an unimportant one). Setting him down at the 1988 Republican Convention wasn't fair, neither to Bush and Quayle nor to Mart himself, because the tone gets a bit shrill and you just *know* that nobody here is really up to the smart boy's fighting weight.

In the end, though, it's Mart's slow, steady progress towards his half-century that you begin to worry about. There's a mock-terrible moment when he realizes that the interview with Nicholson Baker is the first he's conducted with a younger man. The style of the later pieces, too, is stuck halfway between youthful excess and uneasy maturity, and the result is the laboured formulations of a beetle-browed non-interview with Madonna ('From the start Madonna has included pornography in her array of cultural weaponry – because she understands its modern, industrial nature').

All this has got to stop, Mart. I mean essays on *Madonna*, every serious observation on whom could be fitted into a short paragraph, that rickety style which sacrifices everything – and I mean *everything*, plausibility, accuracy, clarity – in its eagerness to please? You've got to make your mind up where to go from here, Mart. This is the 1990s, darlings, and Keith Talent is dead.

8 October 1993

Iggy Pap

Francesca ROGER SCRUTON (Sinclair-Stevenson)
Asya MICHAEL IGNATIEFF (Chatto)

*H*ERE's a poser: why did the authors of these novels publish them? They're both brainy men. They've both got other things to do. And they're both old enough to know better.

It can only be that they believe that writing a novel will automatically waft them into the welkin. The humdrum philosopher and the dreary columnist will be left far behind as immortality beckons. They will be *artists*. Their names will go down to fame. Homer. Dante. Shakespeare. Scrotum. And Iggy. They can see it now.

Wrong. Novels have to be made novels, not just called novels. These novels are simply not novels to anyone more demanding than a cataloguer. Both are devoid of linguistic or formal interest. Both therefore have no interest at all except as reflections of their authors, should you for some reason be interested in their authors. If you are, they're rewarding enough. For *Francesca* and *Asya* both crudely project on to the main female character the qualities the author most aspires to: English poshness for Scrote; posh Russianness for Ig.

Francesca's the direr. Roger Scruton came from an ever so 'umble background but now he goes out with a nice bit of posh (Jessica, as it happens). Accordingly the hero of his novel, clever Colin, is the son of a lowly schoolmaster but he has a romance with aristocratic Francesca from the local big house ('the Hall'). It doesn't go well. Francesca's very doomy. Only at the end is it revealed why. She's had a fatal illness all this time!

This nerdy plot is told with dreadful ineptitude. No thought has been given to where the narrative voice comes from (so it just comes from

Scruton), or to what needs to be told and what not (so it's just whatever catches Scruton's eye). His own face shows through all the time and it's plug ugly. Colin and Roger believe in the importance of sucking up to aristocrats ('In his heart he believed in the legitimacy of institutions: he believed in law, in ceremony, in the colourful nonsense of condign punishment. He believed in the ruling class, in privilege, in heredity and customary power . . .')

The lower classes and racial minorities are dismissed with contempt. The novel cheerfully speaks of London's 'Pakistani peasants and proletarian Turks'. A fight at Colin's workplace is described in the disgustingly stereotyped language of the Worsthorne *Sunday Telegraph* comment pages. 'One day a gang of morons waited for him in the vat house, anxious to readjust his social standing to their own requirements. They leapt out, fists flailing, boots chopping the air. As luck would have it, Colin was carrying the ruler with which he checked the levels in the valves. It had a sharp edge of alloy, and by wielding it in a circle about his head, he was able to gash two cheeks, half sever an ear, and poke out a glutinous eye before running for the gate and safety.'

The relished cruelty of that has nothing to do with imagination or the art of fiction and is wretchedly typical of the book. Scruton cannot restrain his contemptuous urge to abuse common people, those 'stuffed puppets', so as to emphasize his distance from them. *Francesca* inadvertently tells you more than you wanted to know about the asperity of Scrote's character and politics. It will be useful to students of the psychopathology of the low-born theoretical, or as it used to be called 'New' Right, if to nobody else.

Iggy's *Asya* is a more amiable absurdity, being an expression of vanity rather than hatred. Ignatieff is, of course, a classic Canadian bore. But he likes to think of himself rather as soulfully Russian (as well as brilliant, scholarly, pretty, the thinking woman's Mr Spock). His last book *The Russian Album* was one long ad for this Russianness: a factual study of his own family background, all 'Tsarist adventurers, survivors of revolutions, heroic exiles'.

Then he said he found the idea of turning the subject into fiction 'tempting'. 'My characters would be just sufficiently grounded in a real past to be authentic and yet they would do my bidding . . . In creating them I would create myself. In the end the idea of fiction foundered on the realisation that such a novel would be peopled by characters neither real in themselves nor faithful to their originals . . . Fiction would be a betrayal.'

Asya is that fiction. Via the central character, Asya, it describes the history of the century.

Nearly every important scene of *Asya* has its precursor in *The Russian Album*. The estate Asya grows up on near Smolensk is where Iggy's grandmother Natasha grew up; Kislovodsk where she goes during the war is where his grandparents went; Asya's son is killed during the war on the family estate, fighting for the Germans, as was a member of Ignatieff's family; Ignatieff himself went looking for family graves in the cemetery of Novodevichy convent in Moscow; so does Asya in the last scene of the book.

Hurtling through the century, in cliché after cliché, *Asya* has no reality. The attempts made to tie this non-existent character into history, let alone the Meaning of Life, are pathetic, consisting of Asya perpetually asking herself ridiculous Russian questions ('did she, Asya, really know what happiness was?' – try it with an accent) and dodgy bits of historical context being bunged into the middle of already crappy sentences ('"Whether good or bad", she repeated, looking out through the windows of the car at the city on fire with the prospect of war: "he is my fate."')

True, Ignatieff has tried to shape the story with a dominant metaphor: but he's chosen the River of Life! Asya literally falls into it at the beginning of the book and the image comes clanging back at key moments. 'What a river of suffering still flowed deep inside her!' and so wetly forth.

Then the portrayal of Asya, feminist Iggy's pretence of seeing the world through her eyes, is comically undercut by his own male preoccupation with breasts and nipples. Whenever Asya's on the scene he always grabs an eyeful of her 'little ellipses with their raspberry nipples', 'her nipples tiny and erect', 'those adorable breasts'. He even works them into his history theme, when her husband returns from an absence – 'he kissed her and unbuttoned her blouse, parting its folds and caressing her breasts, drawing the memory of them and their reality together in his hands.'

This is *not* the way to outlive marble and the gilded monuments of princes. If Scruton and Ignatieff really want to be remembered, maybe they'd better start sponsoring park benches.

15 February 1991

You the Jewry

The Very Model of a Man HOWARD JACOBSON (Viking)

HOWARD Jacobson's literary career has proceeded in fits and starts. Two fine early novels: the first, *Coming From Behind*, about academic jealousy; the second, *Peeping Tom*, about Hardy. A travel book about Australia (*In the Land of Oz*). Most memorable of all, perhaps, was a finely judged appearance on the TV panel convened to discuss the 1988 Booker Prize, in which Jacobson's rudeness – to shortlisted authors, their books and anyone else who happened to be around – has been equalled only by Eric Griffiths' bravura performance two years ago.

Though now retired from academic life, Jacobson, like Griffiths, hails from Cambridge. There, according to the blurb on his new opus, he 'studied under F.R. Leavis' – a revelation that presumably explains the asperity, as it can't have anything to do with the book's contents.

The Very Model of a Man belongs to what has recently become a rather familiar genre – the early-civilization skit. The technique is a simple one. You take a self-aware narrative voice, whisk it back through time, point it in the direction of some elemental pageant – the Flood, say, or the creation process itself – and the result is something like the first chapter of Julian Barnes' *A History of the World in 10½ Chapters* or Martin Amis's short story *The Immortal*.

A splendid wheeze it is too. Jacobson, being Jewish, has settled on the post-Eden chapters of Genesis, specifically the story of Cain and Abel. *The Very Model*, consequently, finds a post-fratricidal Cain holed up in Babel, where everything is much more to his taste, giving a course of lectures and sporting with the daughter of a local civil servant. Meanwhile Sisobk the prophet is simultaneously casting his eye over the next thousand years or so of Jewish history to take in Jacob and Esau, Moses and Korah, and Isaac wondering 'Does that mean I'm on pottage tonight?'

As a skit it's exhaustively done: the jokes about Adam ('father with a small *f*'), the jokes about the divine presence Himself ('Long after dark, though, we could still hear Him pacing the vault of heaven, cracking His knuckles, chewing at the strands of His beard ...'), the devious arguments with the angel over the newfangled dietary prohibitions ('So an abused animal, I said ... is no more savoury to the Lord than a lightly prized one?'). There are also, à la Barnes, the bits of outrageous invented history, such as God becoming infatuated with Eve and an angelic attempted rape.

Framed as a modest short story, this might just have achieved some kind of fictive life. As a 100,000-word novel, though, it has all the drawbacks of the grossly extended gag: stretch-marks everywhere, repetitiveness, over-elaboration, and above all the sense of everything going untethered, existing only in terms of the dainty word-play and the Yiddish wisecracking. What did Jacobson think he was doing in writing it? Here and there come the glimmerings of a serious point about the nature of envy, Jewish misogyny and the arbitrariness of divine will, but the principal theme – the send-up of Old Testament aetiology – smothers it all.

The novel ends with another piece of myth-tampering when Cain's recently constructed tower at Babel is destroyed by divine wrath. To do Jacobson justice, some of the jokes are halfway reasonable – particularly the gang of hairdressers from Sodom ('We'll have no wife talk in this shop') – but the whole just creaks with *longueurs*. Moreover, should orthodox Jewry react to it in the same way that orthodox Islam reacted to *The Satanic Verses*, you hope that Jacobson has got his attic at the remote Welsh hotel and his brace of Special Branch minders already booked.

8 May 1992

Theroux the looking glass

My Secret History PAUL THEROUX (Hamish Hamilton)

A STILL boyish-looking 47, Paul Theroux is poised neatly in mid-career. It's been a bustling, non-stop, *relentless* progress, rather like that of the assorted trains that in *The Old Patagonian Express* provided him with his first big seller.

A lot of books have made their way on to the pages of Mr Theroux's fat writer's notebooks since the appearance of *Waldo* in 1967: 18 novels and short story collections, six plump travel books, a swathe of collected articles. The man is indefatigable. Over 20 years in the business and still, time after time, he shapes up.

The problem of the successful middle-aged writer is not stated often enough. What do you do as the advances get bigger, as your celebrity increases and the initial impetus that led you into writing, that far-off urge to scribble beneath the bedclothes and cover the backs of discarded envelopes, slowly works its way out of your system? The answer is that you do two things. You get bored, edgy and jealous of your reputation (Theroux's response to the odd bad review of *O-Zone*, his last novel, was a sight worth seeing). And, as it demands less exercise of the imagination, you start writing about yourself.

Which brings us nicely back to *My Secret History*, nominally a novel about the life of an American writer named André Parent, but actually a novel about an American writer named Paul Theroux. You can tell this from the avidity with which Theroux seeks to deny it. 'Although some of the events and places depicted in this novel bear a similarity to those in my own life, the characters all strolled out of my imagination,' he writes in one of those eye-catching little prefatory paragraphs.

Let's check this out. André Parent was born in 1942. So was Paul Theroux. Childhood in Massachusetts. *Check*. Early career teaching in Africa. *Check*. Lives in London and the States. *Check*. Parent even writes the same sort of books as Theroux. When he sits devising plots – 'I thought of another story, about an American in London ... I knew everything about this man, that he was my age, that he had been in Vietnam, that he was alone. Looking out of a window he saw a street sweeper being bullied by a young man' – the Theroux fancier knows that he has stumbled in on a repeat of the opening scene of *The Family Arsenal*.

Presumably the need for this sort of camouflage arises out of the subject matter, which comprises a) sex and b) the deceptions that are its inevitable consequence. André Parent can't get enough, whether as a pop-eyed Catholic altar boy, a pursuer of compliant African girls ('she balanced herself on an upraised root and we went at it like a couple of monkeys') or a 43-year-old taking first his mistress and then his wife on identically routed trips to India. It would all be jolly good fun were it not for the male fantasy gloss, a sort of awful lurid wistfulness, that colours the encounters with Lucy ('you can do anything you want with me') or his mistress ('If I'm bad you'll have to put me to bed'). The latter sets to work on a key part of the Parent anatomy 'more with eager greed than pleasure'. This is the side of Theroux that writes strangers-on-a-train seduction pieces for *Playboy* all about lustful older women and their 'sobs of pleasure' and causes you to wonder just how much adolescent wish fulfilment is compatible with the mantle of the serious writer.

The surest sign, however, that Theroux is running out of steam (to use another train metaphor), hitting that trough of middle-aged writerly spread, is the listless sprawl of his style, the terrible *easiness* of it all. *My Secret History* is stuffed full of callow formulations ('It's money, you know,' says the 19-year-old André. 'If you're rich you can have anything') and goofy climaxes: 'Almost an inch of cigarette ash was suspended over her shrimp salad. I did not want to see it fall.' It's quite entertaining and there are some good scenes – particularly one in which Parent confronts his wife's lover – but nowhere near as accomplished as the sharply written earlier stuff such as *The Family Arsenal* and *Saint Jack*. Fortunately Paul Theroux is a successful middle-aged author now and the critics, bless them, love it.

21 July 1989

Amissed again

Time's Arrow MARTIN AMIS (Jonathan Cape)

ONE of the more edifying cultural sideshows of the past few years has been the spectacle of an earlier generation of literary *enfants terribles* growing up in public.

This process of maturation, undertaken by, among others, Ian McEwan and Julian Barnes, has had several aspects. It has taken in stern pronouncements in newspapers – last month's letter to the *Guardian* about the attempted Russian coup was a shining example – public head-scratching over feminism, the Bomb and the state of the Labour Party, and slowly but all too perceptibly, attended by a levee of admiring publicists, an urge to upset has transformed itself into an anxiety to please.

In the old days, of course, writers simply got converted to Catholicism or sucked up to Stalin and had done with it. We inhabit a less confident world, alas, where the only refuge is humanism. Martin Amis, having begun his career with bodily fluids and then taken a shot at the Bomb is now having a go at children. Interviewers dwell amiably on the infant scrawls adorning his study wall, and the appearance of a couple of babies among the crowded cast list of *London Fields* was widely held to be a sort of Damascene turning point. What is this thing called maturity? Can *I* have some? The realization that people have kids and occasionally treat them in a less than scrupulous way scarcely counts as a heaven-sent revelation. But perhaps even this is a start.

The distinctive feature of *Time's Arrow* – a 40,000-word novella bulked out to standard length and costing an exorbitant 14 quid – has absorbed many a reviewer. The story of a man's life from grave to cradle, it is written entirely in reverse, though some mild cheating allows Amis to unscramble, or rather translate, the back-to-front conversation.

You see the trick? Tod Friendly, first glimpsed on his deathbed, gets younger by the second. The bewildered intelligence that is recording all this – what seems to be his soul – has trouble keeping up. Life is very puzzling. I mean, think about it. Tod works as a doctor: 'Some guy comes in with a bandage around his head. We don't mess about. We'll soon have that off. He's got a hole in his head. So what do we do? We stick a nail in it.'

Don't you just love it? Sex, in particular – Tod's frenetic, turbulent love-life – is a scream. Where does it take us? Why, backwards of course, back via conniving intermediaries and name changes to central Europe, the Auschwitz death-camps and a stolid Nazi named Odilo Unverdorben who helps out in the experiment labs and herds Jews into (or rather out of – it *looks* as if the cyanide is actually granting them life) the gas chambers. It's that old Martian device again – the cute perspective, the slantendicular angle – and what does it tell us about man's inhumanity to man? Nothing.

Not a shred of human feeling, not a tremor from the finger pressing the rewind button on the giant cine-camera. Think about it. This is real life. Real people died here. As in Auden's poem about Spain with the throwaway lines about the 'necessary murder', you get an impression – the image is from Orwell – of someone playing with fire who doesn't even know that fire burns.

Confronting the horrors of the 20th century is a necessary novelist's task. The books by Waugh and Powell might be very imperfect recreations of 1939–45, but at least they were written by men who had experienced some of its ghastliness at first hand. Amis's experience, naturally enough, is confined to reading the papers and watching the news. Even this, though, shouldn't automatically disqualify him. After all, the very best writers can get by on imaginative sympathy alone – think of what Thackeray, who had never been near a battlefield, manages to do with the aftermath of Waterloo. But here, even here amid the Holocaust, even here among the dying Jews, there is only the customarily cold, reptilian eye.

27 September 1991

Sick characters in search of an author

After the War FREDERIC RAPHAEL (Collins)

FREDERIC Raphael has been turning out stuff like *After the War* for a very long time, ever since his precocious 24-year-old fingers hammered *Obbligato* out on to the typewriter in 1956.

Whatever you might say about the impetus behind this waterfall of screenplays masquerading as novels – *The Glittering Prizes*, *Oxbridge Blues* – the formula obviously works. This new one hit the *Times* bestseller list at Number One and there are stray references on the jacket to the 'major 10-part drama series' (was there ever a *minor* 10-part drama series?) into which the book will slickly metamorphose.

Perhaps you don't know Frederic Raphael's work? If so, *After the War* is a good enough place to start as it's much like all the others: a riot of over-written chatter in which the usual cavalcade of bright young people comes down from Cambridge and marches confidently on through the sexual quadrille and the tackier end of showbusiness. Sounds familiar? Yes, it's exactly what happened in *The Glittering Prizes* and *Oxbridge Blues*.

But give Raphael his due. He knows he is above this sort of journeywork. And so *After the War* sets out to be an epic, 'a novel of great scope and vision', 'a sweeping portrait of the post-war years'. To be sure, there are a good many 'issues' bobbing up here and there among the simpering over film rights and other people's wives – issues like Israel and Suez, the end of the Empire and the Nazis. They're purely incidental. They are there in the same way that the classical tags are there, and the references to Kierkegaard: to show that Raphael is *au fait* and to glaze over the fact that *After the War* is simply a book about being clever, an exercise in conversational one-upmanship.

For, despite the knowledgeable discussions of Suez and the Jewish identity, despite the knowing eye cast over 1960s London, the world that Raphael conjures up is pure tinseltown. Perhaps, somewhere, there are people like Michael Jordan, his unlovable playwright-cum-film-director hero, or Barnaby Monk, Svengali of the *Daily Crusader*; but plausibility is not the distinguishing feature of Raphael's cast. For a start he can't do the names. His aristocrats tend to be called 'Claudia Terracini' or 'Jolyon Urquart', his loutish plebs 'Bernie Platt' or 'Vic Fidgin'. But, much more important than this, he can't do the dialogue.

It's actually rather incredible that 'the author of a succession of highly acclaimed novels', the winner of an Oscar, dammit, for *Darling*, can get away with this sort of tosh, these relentless, punning ripostes, these gaudy young heroes who answer the phone by saying: 'Hello, possibly.'

There's an exquisite moment when Samuel, Jordan's barrister father, meets a young American. 'I'm working for the Joint Palestine Appeal,' Buddy informs him. 'Not a joint to which I am greatly disposed to offer a slice,' Sam whips back. Yup, it has all the awful, stylized consistency of bad art, as does the arrival of a visitor to the Jordans' Greek island. 'This is paradise isn't it?' he enquires. 'Then you must be the snake,' Jordan tells him. 'The other parts are already cast.'

And on, and on. Through 500-plus pages the wisecracking continues. It continues when the characters make love, propose marriage or contemplate the death of their nearest and dearest. At the heart of it, you suppose, there is a self-conscious striving for 'insight' on the author's part. 'There's a kind of conceit in underestimating yourself the way you do, Michael,' one of Jordan's confreres remarks. 'Being a cog in someone else's machine gives one the illusion of commissioned irresponsibility,' says another. Think about those sentences. Think about them hard. They're supposed to be subtle, but all that's really there is a sort of flashy meretriciousness, an epigrammatic shorthand that replaces any examination of how real people think and act.

Raphael would argue – any novelist would argue – that these are his characters and that's the way they behave. It's not as simple as that. For in Raphael's books the *dramatis personae* simply exist in their author's shadow. Jordan, Monk and co. are puppets whose style and outlook, their cynical worldweariness, the awful smugness, are merely their creator's. In fact there are times when the author seems gleefully aware of this. 'Does everyone have to be clever all the time?' Mrs Jordan demands in desperation. *After the War* would have been a less awful book by a long way if everyone could have exercised a little restraint in this line.

13 May 1988

History as bunk

English Music PETER ACKROYD (Hamish Hamilton)

PETER Ackroyd has been very careful to identify himself with the great tradition of English literature. He aims high: his biographies of T.S.

Eliot and Dickens demonstrate that he isn't going to be overawed by anyone else's genius. (*Dickens* wasn't so much a biography as a process of self-identification.)

His fiction – *Hawksmoor*, about the 18th-century architect, or *Chatterton*, 'about' the 18th-century poet and *pasticheur* – show off his skills at imitation if nothing else, regurgitating the past so that we can think, when we're reading him, that we're cleverer than we actually are – and that Ackroyd is cleverer than he actually is.

Now, with *English Music*, Ackroyd tries to express the entire range of English aesthetic thought from the Middle Ages to the present day, and he is way out of his depth, so much so that you wonder how on earth it ever got published. He's always been a bit keen on the self-referential, post-modernist stuff: here, he doesn't so much gaze at his navel as disappear up his own bottom.

The story is a simple one. Timothy Harcombe is the son of a faith healer with intellectual pretensions. (He asks his child to look up the word 'palimpsest' early on, which is the kind of behaviour social services are on the look-out for these days.) His grandparents take him away and send him to school. He befriends a crippled boy called Campion. He goes back to his father and resumes his former life as his assistant. He works in an art gallery. He goes back to his father, who has since joined the circus as a magician – the job he had before Timothy was born. His father cures Campion and dies as a result. Timothy stays on in the circus until his grandparents die. The end.

This is unexceptional enough, not much worse than most of the pap we are asked to believe is good, contemporary fiction. But what makes the book so dismal are the visions that Timothy has in between chapters. These are cut-and-paste jobs of the history of Eng. Lit., with Timothy as the hero. He dreams he meets the cast of *Alice in Wonderland* and *The Pilgrim's Progress*. He dreams he meets Charles Dickens, and gives away the plot of *Great Expectations* to Pip. He meets Hogarth, William Byrd, Daniel Defoe, Yorick from *Tristram Shandy*. Every person he meets bangs on about 'English Music', the continuity of the English race and its thought.

We were warned something like this might happen in the acknowledgements. 'The scholarly reader,' he says, 'will soon realise that I have appropriated passages from Thomas Browne, Thomas Malory, William Hogarth, Thomas Morley, Lewis Carroll, Samuel Johnson, Daniel Defoe and many other English writers; the alert reader will understand why I have done so.'

The alert reader shouldn't have any problem working that one out. The alert reader will understand that Ackroyd has 'appropriated' the thought and prose of these writers because they read better than his.

There is a gloriously daft section in tin-eared blank verse pinched from Blake, in which he runs through the A-level syllabus and murders it. This is what he has Keats say: 'Beauty is truth, truth beauty,/The imagination is not a state, it is the shape of human existence./Nature has no outline but the imagination itself,/For language is eternity, issuing from the lips of Albion.'

The sad thing is that this is what passes for thought in *English Music*. For Ackroyd, literature is a collection of postures that he adopts towards his own daffy theories. All *English Music* says is 'I've read this, and this, and this. Aren't I clever?' You might wonder how Ackroyd, a master of the art of critical log-rolling and back-scratching, is going to get out of this one.

As if anticipating some unfriendly reviews, he has the Red Queen say, early on: 'Of course you can't read it. It's a looking-glass book. You're only meant to hold it and *look* as if you've read it. That is the meaning of criticism.' Oooh! If this is what Ackroyd really thinks, he should resign as the *Times*'s chief book reviewer.

22 May 1992

Out of the back passage

Tess EMMA TENNANT (HarperCollins)

*W*HAT is the averagely competent novelist to do in an age where the intelligent reading public has largely given up on contemporary fiction and the trains are full of commuters avidly rediscovering the joys of *War and Peace* and *Vanity Fair*?

One obvious response to the tribes of people who lament that 'they don't write novels like *x* anymore' is to compose sequels to all those evergreen classics – to *Gone with the Wind*, for example (done), *Rebecca* (about to be done by Susan Hill, reputedly for a million quid) and *Wuthering Heights* (two versions, apparently). The list is endless and most of the novelist's traditional brow-furrowers (who? where? how?) are happily cancelled out by the presence of a cast, a milieu and the beginnings of a plot.

Easy, isn't it? A slightly flashier stratagem is to write *variations* on great works of modern literature. This tendency has been in evidence for some time now, has intellectual respectability (borrowings from dead authors can be marked down as 'intertextuality') and the inestimable advantage of being ideologically OK. Any feminist tinkerings with luminous Victorians, for instance, can be justified on the grounds that the original is incorrigibly phallocentric and the writer is storming the citadels of a white, male literary establishment. Again, the list of potential rewrites is endless, and no doubt Martina Chuzzlewit and Edwina Drood are even now preparing to spring, untrammelled, from the autumn catalogues.

A glance at her back catalogue reveals that Emma Tennant has been mining this particular lode for some time (*The Adventures of Robina, Faustine*). Her update of *Tess of the d'Urbervilles*, consequently, conforms to a rather predictable pattern: set in the Dorset of the 1950s and 1960s, told by Liza-Lu, Tess's sister who currently has charge of the latter's baby granddaughter, with Alec as the local ton-up kid and Angel Clare a hippy rock musician. An agreeable twist sees Tess murdering her father (with mother's help) for abusing her child.

All in all, a thoroughly modern piece of buggering about with great literature. However, that's not the half of it, for Ms Tennant plainly has a much sturdier quarry in view. This is to establish *Tess* as merely another stopping point on the great, high feminist trajectory. Geology, it was, that began the 'myth of male superiority' – all the fault of protozoic atoms, apparently – after which we are washed away by a tidal wave of barmy, transcultural didacticism which brings together Great Goddesses, Indo-European Sky Fathers, Frigg, Balder, Penelope, Odysseus and St Augustine, all of them working through time to suppress women's sense of themselves.

Everything is connected, of course, and even the superior household appliances of the modern age are spiritual manacles: 'Just as much as all the nameless women and eyeless, vastly burgeoning fuck-goddesses of extreme antiquity; we were, despite all the machines, sacrifices on the altar of fertility.'

As a fairy-tale, Laura Ashley feminist, Emma Tennant is in a class of her own. The late Angela Carter was not more whimsical; Fay Weldon is not more cosily hectoring. Ms Tennant specializes, of course, in loopy mythological projections ('But the boys will inherit the sceptre of the kings'), in a high, tale-telling style laid low by jargon ('... like the earth before the balance was thrown away by the rise of the phallocentric culture, the stories we told were equally about the bravery, and the hardships, and the love and

151

growing up of female and male children alike') and, above all, in hilarious, self-conscious lectures. I mean, how do you write a sentence such as 'Even then, in the days of the druids, the end of the matrilineal age was in sight' or 'Now we must find the strength to convert – if necessary, to kill – the enemy of the natural balance of the Earth before it is too late' without bursting into laughter?

Allan Massie has been wheeled out on the jacket to suggest that Ms Tennant 'writes with wit, fully in control of her material and technique'. This is odd as the material in *Tess* sprawls all over the place, and the technique is simply a wide-eyed, jam-it-all-in-and-squat-on-the-lid inclusiveness. Even stranger is this overpowering wish to sit precariously athwart other (and better) writers' juggernauts.

Emma Tennant isn't a bad writer, not by any means, but the main effect of this piece of tweaking on the feminist literary thread is to send the reader back to Hardy, cursing all the while at these pale, prejudicial, modern imitations which, inevitably, are scant substitutes for the real thing.

7 May 1993

Hob knobbing

The Weather in Iceland DAVID PROFUMO (Picador)

*E*VERYBODY knows the English novel is ailing. But it still comes as a surprise to find it is quite as sick as this.

David Profumo is both brainy and posh. As a reviewer, he was once the great attraction of the *Literary Review*. Since then he has turned to writing nobby columns for the Saturday *Telegraph*, about fishing and fatherhood, both of which have become rather preening. A few years ago, he also published a fearfully refained little novella called *Sea Music*, about upper-class angling in the Hebrides.

This new novel is Profumo's big shot at *littrachar*. There seemed every reason to hope it might be really rather good. That it's such a horror is perhaps indicative of something more than just a personal lapse.

The Weather in Iceland aspires to be a state-of-the-nation novel. It's set in 1998. Richard Slide, the eighth and last Duke of London, looks back over his life, from exile in Switzerland. In Britain, there has been a military coup, after a gradual breakdown of law and order, and the royal family has been deposed. The greenhouse effect has set in sumfink dreadful, too.

The debt this scenario owes to Martin Amis's millennial fantasy, *London Fields*, is obvious; from the device of constantly referring to the apocalyptic weather, to all the little touches in the prose. When Profumo writes a phrase like 'my synapses jolt, the ganglia crackle and make strange arcs' you know who he's been conning.

More than this, Profumo has absorbed the Amis line that what makes writing good is constant stylistic excess. This novel is yet another one written by Humbert Humbert, all long words and dapper combinations. When the narrator feels happy after having sex for the first time, he says: 'Perhaps by some system of iatrohydraulics my cerebellum has been cleansed of accumulated jism . . .' When he sees his son and heir he exclaims about: 'The soft lunulae of his buttocks, the nectarine soles of his feet, the startled concentration with which he filled his first, amazing nappies with inky, neonatal scoria.'

Where Profumo differs from Amis is that he's high-born. He is the son of the Profumo of the Profumo affair (who, though he doesn't use it, has the title of Baron). In creating this character of the Duke of London (b. 1956), Profumo (b. 1955) has simply created a grandiose vehicle for fantasy about his own life. The Dook, as well as being a great toff, is portrayed as being dead clever too (first from Oxford, PhD from Cambridge). Hence he can be supposed to wield this tremendously hoity-toity prose style.

Dukie's life-story is wholly predictable. The great family house! The endearing eccentricities of the servants! Nanny's touching loyalty! Tough times at prep school, though! Then – Eton! Yes, bloody Eton. This is the most extended, devoted treatment of Eton seen for many years, perhaps since Cyril Connolly. Goodness, how it can mark a chap's life if he doesn't get into Pop! There's a splendid theme for the English novel, what?

Next, as for Profumo himself, comes Oxford (those dining clubs!), followed by dalliance with debs, marriage, fatherhood, and that's about it, apart from Dark Family Secrets and a lot of grumbling about the awful state of Britain these days. And of course there are a few little detached essays about intriguing subjects (remember Graham Swift and those eels?), such as the history of barbed wire and the lifecycle of the spider, to show that the outside world is jolly fascinating, too, when you really find out about it.

It is almost touching to discover that the aristocratic novel still exists, even in such a degenerate form. What really distinguishes *The Weather in Iceland*, though, is its amazing muckiness. Just as the Dook – or Profumo? – prides himself on his recherché vocab, so too he delights in esoteric sex.

It's not just word-play, either, though there's plenty of that. Sex is hunting fur pie, night baseball, shooting the yoghurt, parking the Tonka truck in a new garage. Masturbation? 'A couple of times a day I would take Rosy Palm and her five daughters on a trip to the eyelid movies, and every night without fail I would enjoy a handraised pork pie,' boasts the Duke, remembering his days at Eton, 'cleaving clenched Kleenex to marinated glans.' There's class!

There are also a number of choicely named variants fully described. The Judgement of Solomon, for example, as performed by an Icelandic air-hostess. 'She bent down and proved herself to be an even more skilled linguist than I had realized, for no sooner had I yelped into the myoclonic jolts of orgasm than she raised her mouth, leaned over my chest, and expelled a viscid stream of semen simultaneously from each of her nostrils.' Just fancy!

And then there's the Wolfbag, which involves a man putting his hand down his partner's throat to make her sick as he buggers her, possibly not such jolly fun for her as for him. 'I imagine it may be of Middle Eastern origin, a second cousin to the once popular practice of sodomizing a large goose and slamming its neck shut in a drawer at the *moment critique*, thus raising its body temperature and causing a similar constriction of the cloacal muscles around the root of the intruded member,' observes the Duke learnedly. He also reminds would-be practitioners of 'the need for proximate towels, especially if you have recently shared a Hawaiian prawn curry, Mimosa fried rice, and coconut ice-cream.'

Isn't it good to find our betters can still give us a lead on something? Plenty of scope for a third *Telegraph* column here, surely.

21 May 1993

The Indescribably-portentous

The First Church of the New Millennium BRYAN APPLEYARD
(Doubleday)

THERE never was a newspaper columnist who didn't aim higher. The ancient prejudice against penny-a-liners, Thackeray's gentlemen of the corporation of the goose-quill, endures, and if your average tabloid or broadsheet hack has an anxiety it is generally that he or she isn't being taken seriously enough.

Ambition, consequently, infects these hierarchies like a kind of distemper. The TV critic fancies himself as a political pundit; the political pundit fancies himself as a cultural commentator. At the very top of the heap comes the cultural commentator, who for some reason imagines he can write the novel that will make Proust's shade really sit up and pay attention, don't you know.

No one, at any rate, could accuse Bryan Appleyard – formerly the impresario of 'Bryan Appleyard's Sunday Forum' in the *Sunday Times*, since hired at some unimaginable salary by the *Independent* – of not taking himself seriously. *The First Church of the New Millennium* fairly bristles with beetle-browed intent.

No Hampstead adulteries or mimsy Tuscan chatter for this boy! Set in an England lurching on the cusp of the 21st century, it assembles most of the preoccupations familiar to Appleyard's readers – architecture, popular science, the machine age – into what some puzzled Doubleday publicist has marked down as 'a brilliant, painful and witty fable for our time'.

The problems facing Stephen Rix, Appleyard's architect hero, start when he walks into a field outside his country retreat and finds himself inside an enormous Gothic cathedral. An hallucination? A vision? A sign? Rix's statuesque wife thinks he's evading his responsibilities; his elfin mistress has her doubts; Orlando, his camp business partner, wishes he'd get back to the lucrative blocks of flats. Fortunately Hirtenstein, the manic property developer, is prepared to subsidize this folly – he sees it as a futuristic leisure centre – and after the local council has been bribed and persuaded into approval the project steams ahead.

All this comes interspersed with some prophetic stuff about virtual reality, space travel – Captain Dale McCluskey and his mission to Mars is a running motif – and end-of-century designer drugs. The whole, concluding at the cathedral's opening ceremony when Rix, paralysed from a car-smash, decides to destroy his baby, might just be read as a fable of consumerism ruining people's dreams, written by someone with a working knowledge of Golding's *The Spire*.

But while it was kind of Mr Appleyard to share his undoubtedly groovy thoughts about the future with us in this way, one or two teeny doubts remain. Anyone approaching the work of a first-time novelist has necessarily to ask one or two questions. Can he or she do the characterization? Or the plot? Or the dialogue? The answers in Mr Appleyard's case are: no, not really, and no *with emphasis*. What he really likes doing is descriptions, hulking two-page evocations of hairdressing salons, architecture, gymnasiums, and, just occasionally, the portentous flourish.

Some of these portentous flourishes are worth quoting at length. Of a shopping mall: 'Small bands of teenagers, tense and malodorous, swirled about each other like planetary systems, while edging nervously and self-consciously through the crowd, their eyes flicking warily to detect significant contact.' Of a clock: 'This clock had no depth, how could it tell the time? It would tell us what came after eleven thirteen, but only when it came. For the moment, however, its message fitted the likely facts.'

Of an encounter with his mistress: 'The words "no problem, no problem" whispered in my mind as I swam peacefully into her arms and moved into the controlling logic of her body.'

The foregoing is printed on hard, expensive paper, costs £14.99, and was presumably exclaimed over by the author, his family, his agent and the kind people at Doubleday. A false distinction, perhaps, but the amount of money Mr Appleyard received for it would probably keep a family of five in comfort for the best part of a year.

28 January 1994

6

GRAND OLD STAGERS

Snoozing on their laurels

Babbling Brookner

A Misalliance ANITA BROOKNER (Jonathan Cape)

*W*HEN Anita Brookner won the Booker Prize in 1984, Rupert Lancaster, Cape's publicity director, wrote a crowing article in the *Bookseller*. He wound up with the gallant remark: 'It's as if Hereford United had won the FA Cup.' Indeed *Hotel du Lac*, a 'Hereford United of a book', got a bigger boost from the Booker than any other winner before or since. Not being about Kafkaesque kaffirs or Antipodean bone-persons, it sold over 70,000 in hardback, and 221,072 in the first year of paperback publication. The paperback turned over no less than £431,090 in those 12 months.

Perhaps timid punters were charmed into buying by chairman-of-the-judges Richard Cobb's famous little witticism: 'In an operation of this kind one would not go for a Proust or a Joyce – not that I would know about that, never having read either.' The small-scale cosiness of Brookner's work subsequently caused controversy in the literary pages. What everyone seems to have missed is the fact that far from being amiable, romantic and cute, the Brookner novel, beneath its veneer of elegance, is downright nasty.

'The novel' because she's only written one. Six times now. Each time she promises she'll stop, saying it gives her a headache, but every autumn another one appears, the same length (190 pages) and the same story. Cape turn them out in a cutesy-pop format, literally smaller than any other novels they publish (LC8 – just 8" tall), with a fine art picture on the front to suggest the classiness of what's inside. With sales like that who can blame them? They're probably even pleased Dr Brookner maintains product continuity so efficiently.

In the Brookner novel a good, educated, selfless woman suffers at the hands of uneducated, selfish, bad women. The suffering consists of her not getting her man and his babies. There are no other points of interest, though for social range there is invariably a comically defective servant or two. *A Misalliance* is the most self-parodic edition of this little yarn yet. The preposterously named Blanche Vernon has been deserted by her husband for a low-class tart, contemptuously called Mousie. Blanche moons around in high-class clothes in her high-class flat, drinking high-class wine and preparing high-class food, occasionally venturing out to look at high-class paintings. Meanwhile she moans on and on about the low-class person her husband has gone off with and the low-class people she has met since. It is her having anything to do with the lower classes that constitutes the 'misalliance' of the title. And there is a laughable little twist in the tail. As a result of associating with low-grades at all, the saintly Blanche momentarily becomes herself ever so slightly less morally upmarket, by wanting to go on holiday. In a two-line ending she gets her husband back as a reward for putting her toe that far into the gutter of selfishness.

Brookner, through her transparent heroines, writes about what she offensively calls 'moral status'. She has it and the rest of the world doesn't. She has, she self-pityingly believes, been punished for it. Her unalterable virtue has cost her men and babies ('I only ever wanted children, six sons', she modestly announced in an interview). The novels amount to no more than an elaborately modulated squeal of 'it's not fair!' *A Misalliance* is one long (or so it feels) self-indulgent sermon about Blanche's 'honour', 'heroism' and 'innocence', relieved only by outbreaks of surging contempt for the 'dirty play' of the rest. Brookner writes, she has admitted, so as at least in imagination 'to control', 'to relegate', 'to ordain', and 'to dispose of' the carelessly happy. If that is the art of fiction then everybody else has been labouring under a radical misapprehension.

The funny thing is that beneath all the formal perfection what drives her books on is not fine morals at all but 'farmyard thinking', as she herself calls it – a conception of the relation between the sexes firmly on all fours with that purveyed by Mills & Boon.

Men are 'a prize' that women must capture by fair means or foul. Tragically for the naturally fair like Brookner – 'I would love to be dishonest,' she says – foul works best. This idiotic theory of life appeals to old-school masculinists, as indeed it is supposed to,

Notoriously Dr Brookner's invincible honesty does not extend to her own age. In 1984 *The Times* diary pointed out that the date of birth she has supplied to all the reference books, of July 1938, meant that when she graduated at London University in August 1949 she must have just had her eleventh birthday. She wrote in protesting against the 'churlishness' of printing any woman's age, girlishly insisting 'I am 46, and have been for some years past.'

5 September 1986

Temple of Gloom

The Temple STEPHEN SPENDER (Faber)

*A*PART from a handful of freaks and geniuses, there are two types of literary celebrity in England. The first dies young, leaving behind a few fragments of promise. The second goes on living for a very long time, is showered with honours and academic distinctions and becomes a grand old man of English letters.

Stephen Spender, Knight and Professor Emeritus, chose the second route to fame. Having failed to get himself killed in the Spanish Civil War, he simply went on living, writing, and – of far greater importance – getting himself written about. Now, pushing 80, when he decides to publish an autobiographical 'novel' dating back nearly 60 years, what is the result? Why, page after page of glowing testimonial, massed reviews and Philip Howard copying out blurbs as if his life depended on it. Unfortunately, no amount of puff from no matter how reputable a source can disguise the fact that *The Temple* is a bloody awful book.

As with many literary careers it is a question of motivation. When he first met T.S. Eliot, the youthful Spender confessed to a desire 'to be a poet'. Regrettably, this did not have quite the effect that he intended. 'I can understand your wanting to write poems,' Eliot replied, 'but I don't know what you mean by "being a poet".' Neither, if the truth were to be known, did Spender. He can't write, he really can't. Who is there who recalls a line of his poetry or remembers him as anything more than a hanger-on in the interminable literary politicking of the 1930s?

No, Sir Stephen's claim to fame is that he knew Auden and Isherwood. It is quite a good claim to fame and here, in this autobiographical account of what he got up to on the Rhine in 1929, it is paraded for the edification of a new generation of readers. *The Temple* is an artless *roman à clef* in which nearly everybody is somebody else: Spender is 'Paul Schoner', the youthful writer ('who carried his poems around with him as a traveller in a foreign country carries his identification papers'). Auden is the poet 'Simon Wilnot', who produces stuff like: 'After love, we saw/Wings dark on the skyline/"Buzzards" I heard you say'; Isherwood the novelist 'William Bradshaw', whose inspection of Paul's poems produces the judgement: 'I must say it struck me as among the most interesting writing I have seen by a young writer.'

Well, yes. Nominally an account of Paul's visit to Germany where he has a great deal of fun responding 'to the Weimar world of the bronzed young Germans of his own generation', *The Temple* is actually another attempt to demonstrate to the world the collective genius of Messrs Auden, Isherwood and Spender. It is an exercise in mutual admiration – Isherwood and Auden telling each other how frightfully talented they are, Spender taking pages to explain the meaning of 'In 1929' – in which the uncharitable may detect echoes of Evelyn Waugh's famous review of Spender's autobiography.

'What makes them unlike any writers in English history, except the early pre-Raphaelites', Waugh wrote of the Spender gang, 'was their chumminess. They clung together. They collaborated. It seemed always to take at least two of them to generate any literary work, however modest. They praised one another tirelessly ... And these young cards convinced half the reading public, not only that they were very clever fellows, but that they represented all that was noble and beautiful and unworldly, that they alone inherited the glories of the past, that the future was theirs alone and that anyone who differed from them was either a blackguard or a freak.'

The other clue to *The Temple*'s dramatic *longueurs* can be found in a sentence from that same autobiography: 'When I write prose I am impatient with that side of writing which consists in balancing a sentence, choosing the exact word, writing grammatically even.' From the critic's point of view it was jolly decent of Sir Stephen to admit to this. According to the blurb, *The Temple* has been 'entirely rewritten' since its pre-war genesis in Spender's notebooks. Really? The style is limp and pedestrian. 'Paul felt as though his hands were on levers of a machine fabricating happiness' is about Sir Stephen's idea of a literary flourish.

This is a foolish, self-regarding book, its characters stagy marionettes who might dance in Sir Stephen's memory but fail signally to do so on the page. Worse, it confirms what one always suspected about the 1930s literary mafia, with their graceless posing and relentless self-obsession – what terrible, terrible bores they were.

18 March 1988

Stale Bunns

Difficulties with Girls KINGSLEY AMIS (Hutchinson)

*T*HE new Kingsley Amis novel illuminates with startling accuracy two salient features of the modern book world: the old pals act that surrounds any production by a 'senior novelist'; and what happens to surly young iconoclasts when they grow old.

If any proof were needed of the dishonesty of the current reviewing establishment, it lies in the reception accorded to books by Grand Old Men of English Letters who keep on knocking it out. There has been quite a lot of stuff produced by these fluent, unwearied pens in the past few months and each time it is greeted by back-slapping and mutual admiration.

You might think that somebody would have seen through this cheery conspiracy by now, but along comes Kingsley ('Life in the old boy yet') Amis with his successor to *The Old Devils* (which won the Booker Prize) and the response is, yup, deferential profiles and long reviews in all the newspapers.

In the case of Kingsley Amis, the hype lavished on a book that is simply not worth the attention is tempered a little by the existence of some ghostly revenants. *Difficulties with Girls*, you see, performs the time-honoured trick of reintroducing characters from old books and having a look at them later on in life. But Patrick and Jenny Standish (née Bunn), who first turned up 28 years ago in *Take a Girl Like You* and are now lodged uneasily in the midst of the swinging 1960s, have worn almost as badly as their creator.

In any case, whatever may have happened to the Standishes – Patrick carried on womanizing, Jenny couldn't have babies – doesn't really matter. Although in the end Jenny conceives, this isn't a book about people. Still less is it a book about the changing social scene. It is a book about *prejudice*.

Prejudice. Thirty years ago, as a surly young iconoclast, Kingsley Amis had some pretty strong opinions as to what he did and didn't like, but these were mitigated by a chronically funny sense of humour and considerable literary artistry. Nowadays the old boy is a pundit, pure and simple. As *Difficulties with Girls* is set in the 1960s, the butt of so much oldster displeasure, this gives him quite a lot of scope: nearly all women, most men, gays, modern poetry and poets, educational methods, drugs, any form of behaviour that might remotely be labelled as 'permissive'. Taking place against the backdrop of Roy Jenkins' homosexuality law reforms and featuring a character called Tim whose 'difficulties' are ascribed by a crank psychologist to latent inversion, it is a fine old display of saloon bar philosophy.

None of this would matter, of course, if *Difficulties with Girls* were well written or funny, or read as if it hadn't been negligently dictated into a tape recorder. It isn't any of these things. Is this sentence a clue? 'She considered that as regards what you were born with she had a better deal than most, but she had been behind the door when they were doling out the knack of getting on with the booze. Those who could go through life half-cut were just not aware of how lucky they were.'

Apart from the drink, well to the fore is the persistent bogus anti-intellectualism that has dogged Amis since *Lucky Jim*. *Bogus?* Take the occasion when Patrick Standish is 'reminded with some force of the moment in the Powell novels when the narrator chap gets no change whatever out of his uncle on asking him if he has news of a former attachment of his who told fortunes with cards, Mrs Turdley or some such name.'

Now, Amis has read Anthony Powell's *A Dance to the Music of Time* and knows that the character is called Mrs Erdleigh. Standish, who is a clever bloke – a publisher, no less – would know this too. But it suits Amis's purpose to pretend that anything but cursory acquaintance with English literature is beyond them both. The younger Amis was like this too. In *Difficulties with Girls* you are again confronted with the uniquely dreary result of prejudice taken to excess: the clever man posing as a philistine.

30 September 1988

Rotten to the corr!

Blood of My Bone: The First Born of Egypt Vol. V, SIMON RAVEN
(Muller Century Hutchinson)

STILTON, Roquefort, Gorgonzola, Blue Vinny perhaps? But none so ripe and stinky as Simon Raven. We Raven fans have a reason for living: to see just how deep into putrefaction he can sink and still put pen to paper. These days he is far gone and the queasy hold their noses and gag. We connoisseurs of corruption, though, have never had it so good.

Raven has underway the longest *roman fleuve* ever composed. It began with the 10 volumes of *Alms for Oblivion*, which were published through the 1960s and 1970s. These were semi-realistic, with their characters notoriously based on real people Raven had known at school, such as James Prior and William Rees-Mogg. When the sequence finished there were sighs of relief all round.

Raven, however, has observed the advantages of the multi-volume novel. Once a publisher has taken it on he cannot very easily back out halfway. He immediately started another, or rather continued the same. *The First Born of Egypt* is merely *Alms for Oblivion* part two, with the dying old characters replaced by their worse offspring in an internal propagation system.

Anthony Blond, his first publisher, had gone bust perhaps in the effort of printing Raven but not before commissioning Raven's second lot. When Century Hutchinson took over Muller Blond it found itself with this overgrown incubus on board, gulping down advances. That is how a businesslike house comes to be backing such a monster.

Raven was sacked from Charterhouse for homosexuality after only four years, and then from Cambridge for idleness. Having been expelled from these paradises, they are the invariable scenes of his lubricious fantasies. In his novels he has simply created the world in which as a snobbish, bisexual public school cad, locked in emotional adolescence, he longs to live.

As he has aged, this world, ever more remote from reality, has become ever more perverse and his novels, instead of coming forward in time, have slipped back into never-never land. Only long-established Raven readers can appreciate him now: his people have become so bizarre that you need to know how they got so strange.

Poor Raven does his best to help with incessant footnotes of his earlier works, and long conversations in which the characters recall their previous exploits to each other, but, like truly high game, he remains an acquired taste.

Blood of My Bone is ostensibly about a fight between good and evil for the soul of a juicy schoolboy called Marius Stern. Evil is represented by a diabolical classics master, Raisley Conyngham (super-rich, cloak-wearing), and his hench-boy, Milo Hedley, a fresher at Trinity College, Cambridge. Good consists mainly of the people at the fictional Lancaster College, Cambridge: Carmilla Salinger, Balbo Blakeney, Piero Caspar, Greco Barra-clough, etc. A vast cast of stable-girls, peers and queers are betwixt and between. A ludicrous trip in a boat round the Mediterranean, recreating the last journey of Ulysses, provides what little there is of a plot, and the whole is dressed in camply high-faluting prose.

It is all a pretext for Raven's fabulous self-indulgence. In classic salacity such as this: 'Having with some difficulty found harbourage just north of Split, Jeremy and Fielding visited the Museum of Antiquities. Near the entrance was a Garden God with a colossal erection. "It feels so warm," said Fielding, "almost throbbing." "Have a care, dear. It might come all over you." "Yummy."' Or this: 'He has a huge, kind bottom, just like his huge kind face. I shall be very gentle with him. I shall ease my way up into him, and caress his penis at the same time. He has a large, long, rather flabby penis (so Milo Hedley tells me) which just at the last moment goes very stiff and comes very copiously. So when I feel that it is about to come, I shall cry out (even if I myself cannot come), "O Christ, Jeremy, I'm coming, O Jesus Christ", and he will cry out, "O Christ, Marius, Christ, I'm coming too, O Jesus, Jesus Christ" (or something of the sort), just as he begins to squirt and shudder and spurt into my hand . . ."'

In misogyny: 'Do you suppose that woman *can* have dropped that brat?' In sadism: a red-hot poker up the arse literally, 'Don't overdo it; just a little further in.'

In public school jargon, all petty absits, advent absits, quarters, Greens and Fives. In vicarious gluttony and luxury. In ludicrous names and titles: Sir Thomas Llewyllyn, Knt; Luffham of Whereham; the Honourable Grant-chester Fitz-Margrave Pough, Companion of Honour; Sir Jacquiz Helmutt; Marquess Canteloupe. In weird moralizing.

For, strangest of all, Raven thinks this elaborated absurdity to be a moral tale, about whether the schoolboy Marius is to have 'a life concluded with honour as well as success' or is to be seduced by the demonic schoolmaster into 'a career of stealthy attachment of power through moral and intellectual manipulation of the innocence and weaknesses of other human beings'.

Raven believes himself to be promulgating virtue. Or says he does. Perhaps it is just that Century Hutchinson asked for some explanation of why it should be paying out for such tosh (Raven painfully rubs their largesse in with a typically showy dateline: 'Walmer; Corfu; Castellonet de la Conquiata; Florence'). If so, it is a small irritation to bear to be allowed to carry on savouring his extraordinary stench. None so niffy, never.

3 March 1989

She devil . . .

The Cloning of Joanna May FAY WELDON (Collins)

*F*EW of us now believe that all our actions have lasting consequences. We don't think we face final judgement – or that the soul exists.

It's part of the reason our novels are so feeble. Most of our novelists have become incapable of taking their own stories and characters seriously. Some brainy men, such as Julian Barnes and Martin Amis, have reacted by making their novels bags of tricks about how life is a bag of tricks. And innumerable dopey women have simply bored on about themselves and their best friends and called it fiction when they've finished.

But Fay Weldon has done something a little different. She has become a first-rate bully. If the novel is no longer a serious business, why treat it with any respect? Weldon has pioneered the novel of contempt – contempt for the people she writes about and contempt for her readers.

Mistakenly she has been thought to be a feminist writer. Actually her abusive cruelty is widely distributed. She despises men and women both – if anything women the more, for being more easily victimized. If, as a survey has suggested, her novels have actually promoted discontent among women and occasional adultery, it is not because she has taught women to value themselves more, but less or not at all.

Arrogance shapes her work on every level, from the overall structure to the single sentence aside. Her writing sets people up to squash them flat, whether over the length of the book or just in a bracket. It is populated only with cut-outs, targets, numbered dummies for shooting down.

The Cloning of Joanna May is vacantly sadistic, even by her own standards. Carl May is a horrible, immensely rich industrialist, the owner of 'Britnuc', a nuclear power company. He has divorced his ageing wife, Joanna, after catching her *in flagrante*, and instead picked up a bimbo, Bethany.

Thirty years ago Carl ordered the 'cloning' of Joanna, and there are now four genetically identical 30-year-olds spread around the country, unaware of their kin. Carl hopes thus to supply himself with younger, more compliant women for the future. The novel expounds, rather than develops, this situation.

Weldon no doubt believes she has written an important first fiction about the possibilities opened up by genetic engineering. But the revolting truth is that Carl fascinates her because she has lent him all of her own contempt for other people, their weakness, the way they can be manipulated. She is interested in him because he is a successful megalomaniac. His 'cloning' is just what she herself practises in her fiction.

When Joanna, with typical Weldon malignancy, ponders on the people Carl can get created – 'all kinds ... Ugly, headless, always miserable, always in pain: five-legged, three-headed, double-spined: every leg with perpetual cramp, all heads schizophrenic and spina bifida twice over ...' – we can hear the voice of the author herself, relishing what she can do, what she can inflict, in her novel.

So we have these four minimally varied clones. The bulk of the book consists of rhapsodic, ritualized, snobbish abuse of them, one after the other – 'Jane, Julie, Gina, Alice' – chapter after chapter. Weldon's continual trouncing of her puppets becomes unbearable. Her prose consists of fatuous authorial triumphalism: 'How had it come about that Joanna Parsons, that English rose, had married Carl May, this upstart from a kennel? Why, because, she fell in love with him, of course ...'

Even her asides have intolerable spitefulness: 'Dr Parsons smoked a good deal, and coughed quite often, and presently was to die of lung cancer ...' What, do you suppose, is Weldon's idea of 'the mark of a properly finished office building'? It's when the first window cleaner has 'toppled to his death'.

The actual characters of the novel are casually killed off for effect too. Carl May ends up irradiated for fun. And Weldon likes gynaecological torture most of all. Her readers are mostly women and she dishes out punishment to them. The whole plot of this novel is a malevolent playing on women's fears – fears, for example that an aborted child may have been secretly kept alive and experimented on. Weldon's tasteless pressing on a woman's 'pulsing, gurgling, bloody redness inside the whole point of her being', as she calls it, is vilely exploitative. Clive Barker could teach her tact.

In 1987 Collins paid Weldon £450,000 for her next three novels, of which this is one. It is to be hoped they will not recover the money – and it seems unlikely. Weldon's novels are strictly unreadable; the only life they contain is that of her own conceit.

26 May 1989

Mummy drear

Moon over Minneapolis: or Why She Couldn't Stay FAY WELDON
(HarperCollins)

THERE are, God knows, few enough writers in these unlettered times with any claim to be considered a public figure, but Fay Weldon, sensible, no-nonsense, motherly Fay, is one of them.

For that depressed section of the populace that gets its political opinions from the *Guardian*, its interiors from Habitat and its clothing from Laura Ashley, she remains a potent icon, ceaselessly popping up whether the subject be poor Mr Rushdie (a good thing) or poor Mr Easton Ellis (not necessarily a bad thing) to advise us all on what to think.

But the *writing*, murmurs the respectful student of Eng. Lit., what about the *writing*? Well, the writing, on the evidence of this brief collection of short stories, lurches some way behind, back in the dusty rear of the Weldon cavalcade. A small matter of, on the one hand, the material and, on the other hand, the way in which the material gets worked out.

First, the material. *Moon over Minneapolis*, nominally about women, is by implication about men. Men, it seems clear from this bleak little assemblage of morality tales, are *absolute shits*, darling. Men slap you about (Oriole, in the opening number 'didn't mind ... It was the price, she reckoned, a woman paid for being successful'), men put you in hospital or in the bin, men have a distressing habit of sleeping with your best friend, though presumably it isn't her fault, poor dear, just a result of gender expectation.

Always the collective focus, you note. Very rarely in a Fay Weldon short story does an individual man misbehave himself, but *en masse* they're bastards, no question. 'Men in business had wives to live their lives for them ...'

'Men would take Romula's hand ...' The most cursory piece of scene-setting is the excuse for another sniper's bullet from the sex war ('Don't forget his wife', Weldon's narrator sternly advises, introducing a story set in Sarajevo where the assassination of Archduke Ferdinand precipitated World War I, 'everyone forgets his wife, the Archduchess'). Even when we come across the most right-on male specimen imaginable, it never works, does it, girls? Poor old Erin in 'A Visit from Johannesburg' marries a left-wing county councillor, but 'in fact he talked about his responses and his feelings so much, and how he could best make amends for the sins of his gender, that she sometimes fell asleep before he got round to sex'. Well, you can't have everything.

Chronic partisanship, though, is not quite as culpable as pointlessness. The main disability of Weldon's writing is that everything is rigged, each character in terminal thrall to the conceit around which the story revolves, each opposition cranked up in symmetry with its partner. The characters, consequently, frozen into figurative ice, exist only to act out the roles that the writer assigned to them.

Occasionally, in moments of extreme ghastliness, they even speak symbolically: 'We're heading for a crash', says the air-traffic controller who fears his marriage is coming to an end. A good example of this rigid fakery comes in 'Ind Aff: or Out of Love in Sarajevo' in which a girl student and her married professional lover holiday in Yugoslavia. 'It takes more than an assassination to start a war,' he lectures her. 'What happened was that the build-up of political and economic tension in the Balkans was such that it had to find some release.' Strait-jacketed by design, parallels established by whopping marker flags, the relationship limps on to its all too predictable bust-up.

Take away the cattleprod psychology and what remains? Really good writers tend to convey in their works a sense of the randomness of existence, how piecemeal and unfocused it all is. (*Discuss. Ed.*) Fay Weldon, you fear, merely possesses an exaggerated sense of order, a wish to make the world conform to whatever patterns she cares to impose upon it. This, of course, is all of a piece with her praiseworthy desire to sound off about Salman Rushdie or *in vitro* fertilization. She is Mummy, you see, and Mummy knows best.

9 June 1991

Mediocre is the message

The Message to the Planet IRIS MURDOCH (Chatto & Windus)

OVER the last month or so the gentle chatter of London literary society, the quiet susurrations about who's sleeping with whom and who on earth, my dear, is this James Kelman person, have been disturbed by a series of loud clacking noises: the sound of distinguished lady novelists and their reputations going down like ninepins.

It has been a sequential business. First we had Peter Kemp tearing Anita Brookner into tiny fragments in the *Sunday Times*. Then we had Margaret Drabble's *A Natural Curiosity* receiving such a scathing set of notices that her publishers, when they came to advertise it, were forced to do without reviewers' quotes altogether. This week's candidate for mass excoriation is the *grande dame* of English letters, Iris Murdoch.

The degree of hostility attracted by *The Message to the Planet* has been quite remarkable. '. . . lack of action, interminable breast-beating and unbelievable or all-too-believably boring characters,' thought Rhoda Koenig in the *Literary Review.* According to the *Sunday Correspondent*, it was 'hugely bad'. Even Jan Morris, a lifetime Murdoch fan, could be found ending her piece in the *Independent* with the suggestion that, really, it was about time that this particular genre was brought to a close.

Why this universal condemnation? And why now? It is not as if this Iris Murdoch, the 23rd, is especially different from the most recent of the preceding 22. For a start it is immensely long and, in its central situation, immensely familiar. Its chief character is a reclusive ex-mathematician and painter Marcus Vallar, whose friends are convinced that he has discovered the meaning of life. Their earnest conversations ('Marcus is beyond good and evil') seem to be confirmed by an incident in which Marcus appears to raise a fourth friend if not from the dead, then at any rate from his death throes.

The secret? No one is entirely sure, but 'what was necessary was a kind of deep thinking, which would involve new concepts, or perhaps no concepts at all, and which was not philosophy, or science, and was certainly not mythology or poetry . . . or morality'. Subsequently, Marcus is removed by his daughter to an expensive rest home in the country where he becomes a local guru and the cast assembles to look on, speculate and fall in love with each other.

This is not so much *an* Iris Murdoch novel as *the* Iris Murdoch novel. It has the silly names (hands up anyone who knows a 'Gildas' or a 'Marzillian'?), the overblown, italicized orations ('Happiness, Franca, happiness, we have it, we'll keep it, *you* must keep it'), the mad, gorgeous women who refer to their boyfriends as 'darling silly beast'. Above all, it is interminable.

The stories about Murdoch's refusal to be edited are well-known – and it is a fact that the contribution of her editor at Chatto is limited to correcting a shaky grasp of London topography – but any decent publisher's editor asked to read *The Message to the Planet* would spot immediately that it is just a mass of material, a formless sequence of events and conversation, demanding shortening, sharpening and compression. At its heart lies a tremendous sense of absorption. If only Murdoch could be persuaded to stand back from her work just for a moment, you feel, then there might be an end to these prolix grinds and a book that didn't give such an impression of bursting at the seams.

Meanwhile, why all the critical squawking noises? After all, like any Iris Murdoch novel, *The Message to the Planet* is full of elegant descriptive writing and deft set-pieces. Moreover, unlike most modern writers, its author isn't afraid to use melodrama to bring off a particular effect.

But these are trying times for the senior novelist. For years the Murdochs and the Drabbles could unload their offerings on the public with a fair chance that the reviewers would be polite enough to conceal their reservations. The treatment handed out to poor Dame Iris does no more than symbolize a great deal of accumulated resentment. Book-reviewing in this country is beginning to look like a blood sport again.

13 September 1989

Another Iris stew

The Green Knight IRIS MURDOCH (Chatto & Windus)

'Iris is the queen of Chatto. She isn't actually edited,' admitted her publisher, Carmen Callil, a few years ago.

When an attempt was once made to trim one of her novels of its redundancies and absurdities, Murdoch insisted that every word be put back before it was published. Quite right too. If you once began to cut the nonsense out of an Iris Murdoch novel, you'd never be able to stop, until there was nothing left at all, not a page, not a word. For her novels are nonsense through and through; the purest bilge; finest essence of tripe. They are so inimitably dreadful that they almost come out the other side into being good again. But not quite.

The Green Knight, her 25th, does, however, mark a new peak of self-parody. It's half a dozen Murdoch novels all casseroled into one great gungy mess. A satanic don called Lucas tries to kill his step-brother, an unsuccessful actor called Clement, in a park one night. But a millionaire Jewish Buddhist butcher called Peter Mir (which means both 'world' and 'peace' in Russian) intervenes and is instead killed himself. Or is he? After Lucas has been acquitted of his murder, on the basis of self-defence, Peter Mir comes back from the dead seeking justice. All sorts of spooky things happen, he symbolically stabs Lucas a little bit, and then he disappears back to being dead again.

This sublimely silly story is a modern retelling of the medieval poem 'Gawain and the Green Knight' (the Green Knight challenges Gawain to cut off his head with an axe, picks it up and walks off with it under his arm, and then returns a year later to have his own swing at Gawain, but merely nicks him, because he's such a good sort). Murdoch has made no attempt whatsoever to make this story plausible in contemporary terms. No explanation is given of how Peter Mir returns from the dead nor how he dies again at the end. Nobody's behaviour makes any sense at all, from start to finish – surely a bit of a drawback in a novel?

And that's only the start of the twerpishness. There's a boy called Harvey with a bad foot who is therefore the wounded Fisher King, or maybe Philoctetes. There are three weird sisters, including a poltergeist girl called Moy who has a great battle with a swan in the Thames, talks to stones, and later plunges into the sea in Cornwall to swim with the silkies. There's a 'distinguished' dog called Anax with marvellous blue eyes who plays a crucial role in the plot and at one point delivers a 10-page monologue. Angels keep appearing, people keep fainting. A hamster named Colin plays a small but significant role.

And at the end of the book most of the characters, having been secretly in love with others all along, suddenly pair off. In Murdoch's world that means that teenagers start talking like this: 'Oh Sefton, we're here, we've arrived, this is it – trip no further, pretty sweeting – I'm so happy, I'm crazy with happiness, the world is brilliant, it's shining . . . We are transformed, we are blazing with light, I tremble before you.' 'I tremble too,' his doxy doughtily ripostes, instead of running off at top speed.

Murdoch doesn't try to make her characters convincing for the reader. To her, they're real and that's enough. The effect is of overhearing her contentedly chattering away to herself, rather than being addressed. The style, as ever, is an adjectival morass, not only in the narrative – people are always feeling 'an anguished passionate need', or 'some sort of silent raging grief' – but in the dialogue too. The characters, being all her, all speak the same way. It's nothing for them to say 'I feel so senseless and contingent and unmade' twice before breakfast. In fact, it's *de rigueur*.

It is Murdoch's astonishing self-absorption that gives her those uniquely duff sentences that are her trademark. Years ago even Malcolm Bradbury was able to parody her in a phrase: 'Flavia says that Hugo tells her that Augustina is in love with Fred'.

Undeterred, Mudrock is still producing these conical formulas over and over again. 'When Bellamy later went up to find Emil, Louise suggested to Harvey that he might like to sit in Sefton's room, but he declined.' 'Clement, abandoning Bellamy, who was following Peter around, set out to look for Joan whom he had seen in the distance talking to Cora Brock.' 'Harvey, looking up at Moy, thought suddenly, Anax loves Bellamy, Moy loves Clement, I love Aleph.'

Since they're all ciphers, the reader can't give a toss which one's which, let alone who does what to whom or why, and which one's the dog. But to Dame Iris, they're obviously more substantial than the world itself.

In fact, there's no contest. There is no outside world in her writing. Murdoch is a donnish Daisy Ashford, Ashford grown up and gone a bit barmy, and she dwells in never-never land.

But just like Daisy Ashford, a funny little note of realism breaks in whenever she comes to comestibles. Murdoch likes her tuck. 'Sausages and cheese biscuits', 'lentil stew and curried cabbage', 'stilton and spinach pie', and, above all, sandwiches, are described with enthusiasm. Indeed, at the climax of the novel, when all is in turmoil, it is quite brilliantly said: 'In the kitchen the sandwiches had established some kind of momentary reality and rational calm.' It's a pity these sandwiches didn't write the book.

10 September 1993

Big and boaring

Shakespeare and the Goddess of Complete Being TED HUGHES (Faber)

TED Hughes was once described by Sylvia Plath as 'the only one huge enough for me'. He has certainly come out with a whopper this time. *Shakes and the Goddess of Complete Being* is a total explanation of

Shakespeare's complete works. According to Dead Huge, they're all based on a single 'myth', or 'Tragic Equation', which only he has discovered.

He has derived this potty myth from a combination of Shakespeare's early narrative poems, *Venus & Adonis* and *The Rape of Lucrece*. In the first, the divine power of female sexuality erupts when Adonis is unwise enough to reject the advances of Venus, the Great Goddess – a symbolic Boar charges him and kills him. In the second, Tarquin rapes Lucrece. According to Hughes this is because, this time, the Boar of sexuality has somehow become part of the hero, turning him into a madman.

Hughes has pasted these two stories together to make a mythic structure which he then hails as the real meaning of Shakespeare's plays. They're all about the different forms of the overthrow of the rational by the irrational, or, to put it another way, about the relation of the male heroes to the uncontrollable sexual power of the Goddess. Or, to put it another way, about the Boar.

Ted Hughes has always had a thing about fierce animals, such as hawks, pike and piggies. Here he has contrived to make all of Shakespeare about a sow (the Boar symbolizes the female, remember). That, by common consent, sows play a relatively minor role in Shakespeare's plays is neither here nor there. It's a *myth*, innit?

Hughes is just hugely over-excited about this saucy porker. 'Her combination of gross whiskery nakedness and riotous carnality is seized by the mythic imagination, evidently, as a sort of uterus on the loose – upholstered with breasts, not so much many-breasted as a mobile tub entirely made up of female sexual parts, a woman-sized, multiple udder on trotters,' he writes feverishly. 'Most alarming of all is that elephantine, lolling mouth under her great ear-flaps, like a Breughelesque nightmare vagina, baggy with over-production, famous for gobbling her piglets, magnified and shameless, exuberantly omnivorous and insatiable, swamping the senses.'

Phworr! No wonder, for a man, the Boar symbolizes 'everything about female sexuality that is awesome, alien, terrifying and "beyond" the reaches of his soul', and which can only be contained 'within ritual, "religious", quasi-magical procedures'. (And for woman?)

In writing his plays, Hughes explains, Shakespeare managed personally to assimilate the Boar, at least 'for a decade either side of the turn of the sixteenth and seventeenth centuries'. 'Elsewhere, in every other individual, the rejection continues to be made, the Boar charges, the madness erupts.' I'll say. Women, eh? Can't live with 'em, can't live without 'em.

In one sublime moment, outstanding even in a book studded like a plum pudding with memorable stupidities, Hughes hints at where Shakespeare might have acquired his supposed fascination with hogs: 'As a country boy, and the nephew of several farmers, Shakespeare enjoyed a familiarity with pigs that is not irrelevant to his myth.' (Not *too* familiar, let's hope – not the sweet Swan of Avon, puh*leeze.*)

Mostly, Hughes just ploughs on through the plays, looking for Adonis and Tarquin, the Goddess and the Boar – and always finding them, since all the mythic archetypes can assume any different aspect that Hughes cares to think of. If they're not one thing, they're another. The Goddess can be one character or split up into various different ones, for example. And if the Tragic Equation doesn't seem to be there at all? No matter. 'The mythic terminology appears in the finished work no more than the mathematics (without which they would have been unthinkable and impossible) appear in the nuclear reaction and flash of the bomb.' Fine, fine.

Shakespeare and the Goddess of Complete Being is a classic example of the work of an autodidact: energetic, ambitious and valueless because it has never been exposed to criticism or even self-doubt. He has the fearsome confidence of the true crank, predicting what he will find and rejoicing to 'find' it.

Hughes is writing the gospel of his own peculiar religion here. Myth, of course, needs no proof and is, by the same token, impervious to contradiction. But, like many a nutter before him, from L. Ron Hubbard to the bag-ladies, Hughes dresses up his fantasies in spurious scientific imagery. He keeps gabbling away about a 'mythic power circuit', force fields, double exposures, dial panels, polaroids, red giants and black dwarves, holograms, cyclotrons, 'the multiple helix of this particular pattern', and the like. He is particularly keen on the difference between the right and left brain, remarking that 'the Boar and Adonis meet, that is, in the corpus callosum'. Oh, I *see*.

At one choice moment, discussing *Hamlet*, he even uses this gambit to explain why it is virtuous of him never to mention anything discordant with this theory: 'Once again, I shall resolutely ignore everything, but the skeletal essentials of my theme. If the X-ray plate moves even slightly out of focus, everything will disappear in the mass of complications.' Even this sentence doesn't give him a moment's pause.

Shakespeare, claims Hughes, was a 'psycho-biological' type, 'a rare type, but a type' – a shaman. Once shamans were found in Siberia but now, we may infer, they are confined to a tiny area near Exeter.

10 April 1992

A man of lettuce

Paradise News DAVID LODGE (Secker & Warburg)

AFTER a long process of saturation extending back to the early 1960s – his first book, *The Picturegoers*, almost had him marked down as an angry young man – David Lodge, quondam Professor of English at the University of Birmingham, has reached the point at which he can safely be considered a grand literary panjandrum.

His novels sell in swathes – *Nice Work* did 300,000 in paperback – before proceeding to the small screen. The occasional abstruse work of literary criticism still emerges to quicken the pulse of the academic journals. There is even a 'fiction master-class' in weekly instalments for readers of the *Independent on Sunday*. In the critic/creator stakes Malcolm Bradbury seems only a faint, pursuing shadow.

At first glimpse *Paradise News*, in which a lapsed Catholic priest and his elderly father head off to Hawaii to visit the latter's dying sister, looked like quintessential Lodge – a titular resonance reminiscent of *Nice Work* or *Small World*, the usual lashings of sex and religion, the customarily joky despatches from the front line of popular culture. What it also displays is the first hint of freewheeling, that fatal downhill slide that tends to sweep away the middle-aged writer: a sort of creeping gigantism whereby each writerly characteristic becomes progressively more enlarged at the expense of the characters expressing it.

As a novelist, Lodge has two styles: the highbrow style and the middle-to-lowbrow style. The highbrow style is a matter of scholarly parodies, deconstructions of tourism and a running gag whereby characters are named after well-known academics (Knoepflmacher, Sheldrake) or notorious literary types ('John Walsh', the hero's father, is *a real side-splitter* by the way). The middle-to-lowbrow style is a matter of an extraordinarily unsophisticated sense of humour. What does David Lodge find funny? On the strength of *Paradise News*, I should say the way in which ordinary people speak, misheard conversation and leaving your passport in the duty-free shop, respectively.

Well, no doubt Proust sniggered over a banana skin once in a while. It has to be said though that there is a limited amount of fun to be got out of the tourist package deal, even more so when you come to consider the serious stuff that Lodge is wheeling in beneath the skirts of sunburn and bickering honeymooners: stuff like cancer, religious doubt, child abuse and mental handicap. The change in tone, when the action switches from mid-flight satiety to Aunt Ursula's approaching death, is more or less unsustainable.

In the past Lodge could pull this trick off. *How Far Can You Go?* for example, mixed tragedy and light relief in a convincing way. Nowadays the gaps – between the hero's wistfulness and his predictable sexual going-over, between sensibility and sentiment, between grim destiny and a forgotten share certificate that suddenly provides the dying woman with a windfall $300,000 – is just too great.

What to blame? Characterization, naturally. Alone among the thronging cast, Bernard the lapsed priest has authenticity: his emotional yearnings, spiritual uncertainty and dreary South London childhood are movingly inked in. But he marches alongside a collection of two-dimensional clowns. Perhaps in the end it's a question of not defining your audience. Like Lodge's two styles, there are two literary audiences these days: the highbrow and the middle-to-lowbrow. Occasionally, just occasionally mind, as with a novel like A.S. Byatt's *Possession*, the one can be bullied into buying the other. *Paradise News*, its seriousness invariably brought down by slapstick, is unlikely to achieve this cross-over status. 'Why do clerics always laugh at the simplest jokes?' Bernard wonders at one point. For 'clerics' read 'ex-academics'. Whatever the answer, the result reads like a cross between *A Question of Faith* and *The Benny Hill Show.*

11 October 1991

Raking in the Lolita

The Enchanter VLADIMIR NABOKOV (Picador)

THE English Nabokov cult began in the late 1950s when Lord Weidenfeld bought the rights to *Lolita*. In the anti-censorship climate of the time – in which the book was to become a *cause célèbre* – this was a shrewd move. Not only did it inflame the sensibilities of the dirty raincoat brigade but cartloads of respectable academics of the like of Lionel Trilling were wheeled in to pronounce on its moral value, delicate word-play and so forth.

Lolita sold hugely and throughout the 1960s publishers busied themselves in dusting down the lengthy backlist of books like *Pale Fire*, *Despair* and *Pnin* that Nabokov had accumulated since he began writing in the early 1920s. This process of disinterring the Nabokov archive, which continued after the author's death in 1977 with the publication of his labyrinthine literary lectures, grinds on with the arrival of *The Enchanter*.

Two points ought first to be made about this slim volume, described by Picador as Nabokov's 'long lost novel'. The first is that it is not long lost. Nabokov wrote the original version in 1939, put it on one side until the 1950s when it was offered to his American publishers, and did further work on it during the 1960s. It then went back on the shelf until a final 'rediscovery' three or four years ago.

The second point is that it is not a novel. In fact the original typescript, which measured only a bare 55 pages, is little more than a longish short story. However, Picador have managed to bulk it out with various introductory notes and a generous postscript by the translator, Nabokov's son. The result, still only a wafer-thin 127 pages, is printed in large type with very large spaces between the lines.

The slight interest of this carefully spun-out fragment lies in its early rehearsal of the *Lolita* theme, the story of a 40-year-old man's obsession with a 12-year-old girl whom he espies from his vantage point on a park bench. All the classic signs of the pre-pubescent Nabokov heroine are brought sharply into focus: 'the indistinct tenderness of her still narrow but already not quite flat chest, the slenderness and flow of her uneasy legs . . . her dress hung so closely in back that it outlined a small cleft'.

Delirious at the thought of all this approaching maturity – 'such warm-skinned, russet-sheened, open-lipped little girls got their periods early, and it was little more to them than a game, like cleaning up a dollhouse kitchen' – he decides to pursue her by marrying the sickly, widowed mother. Here there is a minor disadvantage in the form of occasional exposure to 'the repulsively listing conformation of her ponderous pelvis, not to mention the rancid emanations of her wilted skin' but fortunately death supervenes and our hero is left alone with his guileless nymphet.

The subsequent tampering, which takes place in a hotel bedroom, is coyly but extensively described. Having lulled his victim to sleep with judicious draughts of wine, the narrator can't wait to take advantage of 'the stillness, her naked clavicles, her hot armpits, her legs'. What follows is a gourmet guide to the pre-pubescent female anatomy, ranging from the neck ('he tasted, exerting almost no pressure, her hot silky neck') to the legs ('long, just slightly parted, faintly sticky'). Finally, with the aid of a great many genteel metaphors, the seduction gets under way as 'passing his magic wand above her body' our hero begins 'moulding himself to her, testing the fit ... nothing mattered now and, as the sweetness came to a boil between his wooly tufts and her hip, now joyously his life was emancipated and reduced to the simplicity of paradise ...'

Yes, it's coitus, yet *interruptus* alas, for the girl wakes up in mid-ejaculation and screams for help. 'Senselessly discharging molten wax, too late to stop or conceal it' her ravisher makes his escape out of the window, only to find nemesis lurking outside in the shape of a passing truck.

Predictably all this sententious smut has met with riotous acclaim not least from well-known Nabokov bores like Martin Amis. 'It is hard to imagine how any other book this year will give such sentence-by-sentence pleasure as this tale,' gushed Alan Jenkins in the *Times Literary Supplement*.

Unlike his admirers Nabokov himself had doubts about *The Enchanter's* quality. Time seems to have proved him right.

6 March 1987

Beast of Eden

The Garden of Eden ERNEST HEMINGWAY (Hamish Hamilton)

NABOKOV liked little girls. Forster felt for policemen. Joyce enjoyed juicy knickers. Proust tormented rats. But Hemingway, now Hemingway was into haircuts.

The Garden of Eden is not the first story in which haircuts are central to the plot. Samson was scissored by Delilah. Pope immortalized *The Rape of the Lock*. But surely it is the first novel ever to feature a wash and trim in almost every chapter. A short back and sides is the prelude to tragedy.

The novel is gloriously embarrassing. It tells of David, a young newly married writer, honeymooning in the South of France. All is going swimmingly until one day his wife Catherine decides to give him 'a wonderful dangerous surprise'. Yes, she gets a cut. 'Run your fingers up at the sides,' she says seductively. But haircuts will out. It doesn't do to meddle with such dark forces. Having got 'a true boy's haircut' (a short one) she starts acting the boy in bed. This, says Hemingway, is devil's work, corruption, damnation. It is the Fall.

Just what this 'dark magic of the change' involves is not easy to determine. One of the 'devil things' they do, post-haircut, seems to be girl on top. Davis is so taken aback by this that he says he can't tell who is who. From this they dizzily progress to deeds that are truly indescribable. No appliances are mentioned, so I'm afraid that in the end it probably all comes down to Bottoms, just like *Lady Chatterley's Lover*.

By page 44 Catherine, now chummily dubbed Devil, is offering him a further surprise. Yup. Another haircut. An Eton crop. ('Feel it.') On page 79 there is, believe it or not, another surprise. They both have their hair cut. And bleached. Things are hotting up. By now Catherine is wearing the trousers ('well cut' of course).

With them both down to stubble, Hemingway needs a new head of hair. Easily arranged. When they're sitting in a café a girl comes up to ask, what could be more natural, where they got their hair cut. Three pages later she turns up at their hotel with her own mussable trim. In no time a *ménage à trois coiffures* is on. She massages hers. He fondles theirs.

Cannily refraining from introducing a fourth mop, Hemingway gets a bit stuck here. Much play is made with sun-tan. It shows off one's hair so. By now Catherine has become the darkest white girl in the world, and the blondest.

It can't last. Baldness beckons. This maelstrom of barbering has taken its toll. Since according to Hemingway hair is just about the sole determinant of sexual identity, none of them know whether they are coming or going – though there is plenty of what must be one or the other. The marriage breaks up and David goes off with Haircut Three, also known as Heiress.

These hairy fantasies, composed in 1946, were understandably never released for publication by him. The Hemingway estate, however, has been steadily capitalizing on his remains in the last few years and has now exhumed this relic. In order to release it on the general market rather than the academic one, it has made silent, unattributed cuts and interpolations in the text, modestly described as 'routine copy-editing and corrections'. These have just been discovered to amount to a virtual editorial re-write. Everything has been tampered with – times, places, the lot. Whole characters have been eliminated; the book we have is about a third as long as the text Hemingway left.

Passing *The Garden of Eden* off as a proper Hemingway novel appears now to have been little more than a confidence trick. Hamish Hamilton were presumably aware of what had been done, but thought they were onto a good thing anyway. After all the book is not Hemingway's crowning glory. It has plenty of those simple declarative sentences that are such a happy resource to *Punch* humorists. It goes hunting and fishing, eating and drinking. It testifies once again to his belief that women are better seen than heard, indeed best seen asleep.

If nothing else then it should appeal to hair-buffs. *The Garden of Eden.* At a salon near you.

20 March 1987

Great Gores of today

Live from Golgotha GORE VIDAL (Deutsch)

*A*T first glance *Live from Golgotha,* a satire about modern time-travellers interfering with the events of the Crucifixion, seems an opportune assault on the current wave of loopy reinterpretations of the life of Jesus (cf. A.N. Wislon, etc.).

All such new versions of the gospel story reshape the life of Christ, and so the validity of the direction that Christianity has taken, not on the basis of evidence (there isn't any) but merely according to contemporary taste.

Thus a male American feminist bishop, haply called Spong, believes that the Virgin Birth was a wicked cover-up of the rape of Mary, and that Jesus was married to the sadly misunderstood Mary Magdalen (*Born of a Woman: A Bishop Rethinks the Birth of Jesus,* Harper). Barbara Thiering, an Australian ninny, has Jesus surviving the Crucifixion, going on to marry, fathering a family and retiring to the South of France, like Peter Mayle, to write His own gospels (*Jesus the Man,* Doubleday).

And here comes Gore Vidal with a witty parody of these grabby new gospels? No. Here comes Gore Vidal imposing his own set of well-worn prejudices, just like the rest.

The narrator is Timothy, the recipient of two of Paul's epistles, writing as Bishop of Thessalonika in 96 AD. Initially he recollects the creation of the Church with St Paul (a businessman nicknamed 'Saint'), who, for commercial reasons, has successfully presented Jesus as a Messiah for everyone, not just for the Jews. This being Vidal, Timothy and Saint are homosexual lovers, and Timothy opens by announcing: 'I have golden hyacinthine curls and cornflower-blue, forget-me-not eyes and the largest dick in our part of Asia Minor.' Foreskin jokes follow.

The plot is tedious and complicated: about rival time-travellers trying, retrospectively, to use Timothy to change the version of the story of Jesus that gets handed down over the centuries to our time. At the end of the twentieth century, a mysterious figure called the Hacker has started (somehow Vidal can't be bothered to explain) eliminating all records of the Jesus transmitted by Paul, so as to show Jesus to have been purely a Jewish messiah.

Later it emerges that the Hacker's name is Marvin Wasserstein ('thirty-something . . . a lot of acne scars, but otherwise he's a sort of Al Pacino type'). Later still, it emerges that Marvin is none other than Jesus Himself, then as now a Zionist fanatic, who escaped the Crucifixion (substituting fatboy Judas) and time-travelled forward to the end of the twentieth century.

Part of his plan is to get the crucifixion of ridiculous Judas videoed by a time-travelling camera crew, in order to destroy the basis of Paul's Christianity for everybody. As a messianic Zionist, what he plans now that Israel has been re-established, is a nuclear Judgement Day in the year 2001 ('After Damascus, Baghdad, and Cairo are ablaze, I shall take out Berlin, Warsaw, Moscow and Pasadena . . .').

Serious biblical scholarship of recent times (e.g. Geza Vermes, *Jesus the Jew*) has stressed that Jesus was in many ways a typical Jewish holy man of his time. Vidal has taken this perception and used it as a vehicle to caricature Zionism. They are terrorists now; so was Jesus then.

Timothy (a Greek, remember), having been made to realize this, comments: 'If Jesus was *not* a Christian, as Saint Paul had taught, but just another run-of-the-mill Zionist terrorist, then I was all for doing him in right now.' And he does. Aided by another visitor from the future, he travels back to 33 AD, and ensures that Jesus/Wasserstein does, after all, Himself die on the cross, so simultaneously averting Armageddon in 2001 and allowing Paul's beneficially falsified version of Christianity to survive down the centuries.

This is the Crucifixion that ends up being videoed – by the Japanese, the dreadful dominance of the yellow man being another of Vidal's tediously fixed ideas, along with the evil of the American empire, and the malignant effects of popular television.

The convoluted structure and silly camp jokes (the general effect is as if *Bill and Ted's Bogus Journey* had been scripted by Simon Raven at his worst) don't disguise the nastiness of the content. It's not that *Live from Golgotha* is blasphemous against Christianity – it has nothing to say about it. Like all recent rewritings of the Gospels it tells only about the writer's own self: in Vidal's case, a mixture of lubricity and affectation, prejudice and conceit.

9 October 1992

Sentenced to hard labia

Memories of the Ford Administration **JOHN UPDIKE (Hamish Hamilton)**

*W*ITH the first chill winds of spring comes Updike time once more – the TV profiles, the interviews, the glittering critiques. What is it about John Updike?

No home-grown talent ever gets treated with half the respect accorded to this fey old sexagenarian from Massachusetts: the page-long encomia in the *TLS*, the frequent use of words like 'fecundity' and 'genius', and the pictures of the man himself, posed before the New England bracken and looking like a particularly zestful pixie.

English critics love Updike, mostly because he seems to possess the qualities English writers so conspicuously lack. Barnes, Amis junior and Ackroyd – Updike is a three-year foreign holiday compared to these cautious domestic package tours, a ski-run of glissando prose and wide-eyed saunters into the great unknown.

On the one hand he manages to pull off the rare feat of acting as a social registrar, making sense of recent American history in a partial but horrifyingly plausible way. On the other, he can do the language; that is, write in that alert, confidential and hyper-imaginative style for chapters on end. This is quite an achievement. After all, when a writer like Ian McEwan essays a stylistic flourish the crowd stops talking and holds its breath. We're not used to relaxed brilliance, which is why, perhaps, we tend to overvalue it when we see it.

Memories of the Ford Administration is a rather typical Updike novel, a conflation of past, near-present, linguistic skywriting and the sort of sod-you middlebrow vocabulary ('dyad', 'chthonic', 'gynous') that requires frequent trips to the dictionary. Similarly, Alfred Clayton, its reminiscent narrator, is a fair specimen of Updike man: a professional historian – the book purports to be a contribution to an academic symposium – obsessed with a figure from the remoter past (Buchanan, the last pre-Civil War president), racked by dealings with wife, mistress and casual flings. Its themes might be summarized as the elusiveness of historical truth (*that* old one again), the frightfulness of bourgeois America under late capitalism, and, less immediately, female genitalia,

Updike's obsession with pudenda is well known. His interest in this spectral closet of the modern novelist's mansion was made evident as long ago as 1974 in a lengthy poem entitled *Cunts*, in which he suggested that 'we must assimilate cunts to our creed of beauty'. Well, indeedy-doody we must, Mr U. Lead right on in there and close the corral gate after you, sir.

The present opus simply thrums with this kind of thing: references to that 'puckering wave of flesh', elsewhere described as 'oysterish' and 'livid' – 'the *frilly* look of it' Updike interjects at one point. Ever keen to locate sexual detail in a social context, he notes that 'pussies were triangular in the Ford era, before high-sided swim suits compelled women to shave their groins of all but a vertical strip of natural adornment'.

Gosh. Well, it makes a change from the endless drafts of Clayton's unpublished biography of Buchanan, which are frankly pretty tedious. There is also the question of the language. Whole tribes of respectable critics have gone on record to confirm that Updike is a linguistic master, a writer who – miraculously – can describe things as they actually are, and thereby isolate the wonderful uniqueness of objects, situations and people. In fact, all Updike's overblown and clever-clever style manages to do is to interpose itself between the reader and the thing it affects to portray.

Thus Clayton maintains that his domestic scandal 'sat like a clammy great frog, smelling of the swamp of irrecoverable loss, in the bosom of our family'. He describes the house he inhabits with his wife as 'this hairy fringy nest she and I had together accumulated one twig at a time'. Later the kitchen sink discloses 'a shark's grin of washed silver'.

In each case the reader, beckoned towards a revealing description, ends up further away – washed silver looks nothing like a shark's grin – and annoyed by the fact that all he is being asked to admire is Updike's OK-ness as a writer. Good prose, Orwell famously remarked, is like a window-pane. Updike's, though, is nearer to stained glass – full of light and colour and extremely pretty, but in the end only obscuring the variety of scene and incident beyond.

12 March 1993

7

POETRY

Verse than you think

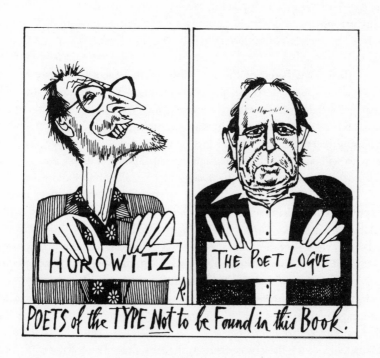

POETS of the TYPE <u>Not</u> to be Found in this Book.

Reed warblings

Nineties JEREMY REED (Jonathan Cape)

*M*Y *dears*! Barely a whisker into 1990 and already *la décadence* is upon us. Berkoff's *Salome* is playing to packed houses at the Phoenix theatre; Donald Sinden is creaking across the boards at the Playhouse impersonating Oscar; various quaintly dressed young people have appeared *ensemble* in the *Sunday Times* supposedly to epitomize the spirit of the new decade; and now, bang on time, comes pretty Mr Jeremy Reed with a thick volume of poems aptly titled *Nineties*.

There has been quite a lot about Jeremy Reed in the Sunday supplements recently: Jeremy Reed displaying his splendid cheekbones, making his fascinating *moues* and generally camping it up to tremendous effect. Cape has published his novels *The Lipstick Boys* (oh yes), *Blue Rock* and *Red Eclipse*. Last autumn he brought out a critical study with the engaging title *Madness: The Price of Poetry* (Mr Reed pictured on the jacket fervently pressing his lips against what appeared to be a piece of stonework). Amid all the silly newspaper articles and the talk about *fin de siècle*, the imputation is that if we are to have a 1990s which in any way resembles the 1890s, then it will be Mr Jeremy Reed, singing his sad little songs and twanging, coyly, his little lyre, who will emerge to become their principal poetical ornament.

The original decadent poets – Dowson, Le Gallienne, Symonds *et al.* – were, in case you didn't know, one of our less distinguished literary groupings. Their characteristics have been enumerated by Professor J.H. Buckley in his book *The Victorian Temper*: 'Sedulously ... they strove to proclaim by their very dress and speech and gesture, a full aesthetic autonomy ... As writers ... they struggled to make a highly personalised style the ultimate expression of their highly stylized personalities.' Well, Jeremy Reed certainly looks extremely decadent, and I think we can take it from the jacket photograph – anguished stare into mirror from beneath untidy fringe – that he has a highly stylized personality.

Decadent poetry itself was distinguished by several singular *motifs*: by a choice, exotic vocabulary, by a sensibility that looked not to nature but to art for its images, and by an obsession with sex built largely on sexual ambiguity. Jeremy Reed scores pretty highly on all these counts, what with the lines about 'calyx, the pistilled thread' and the 'thrush-speckled locket' (a strawberry, naturally), the children compared to Picasso drawings and the stanzas about bisexuality ('opposites reconciled by overreach'). In fact, each succeeding poem is not much more than a scoop into a bran-tub of Ninetyish gestures and preoccupations – poems about tarts, drugs, fetish and suicide, taking in venerable camp icons such as Baudelaire and Mallarmé, newer totems like Lou Reed and Bowie ('pantomorphic chameleon') and the usual dandy appurtenances of roses, lilies, cravats (a whole poem about neckties) and darkling hushes.

Somewhere among this recitation of sighs, pouts and arty nudges, Mr Reed suggests that 'one looks for a new poetry, something animated, a renaissance of imagery, a futuristic dynamic'. This is rather odd, as what he himself turns out is some very old poetry – and some very old attitudes – indeed. Ask what Mr Reed stands for (as one can ask all but the most *dégagé* poet) and the answer is: not very much at all, save for a rather generalized notion of 'art' and (by implication) the sound scheme that youngish men with dyed hair should be given sums of money sufficient to keep them producing these darling volumes for the public edification.

Mr Reed has passion, but without apparent conviction; is excited by words but has no obvious interest in what lies behind them. For the majority of his poems are not actually about anything. They are simply *descriptions* of scene, situation, incident and – in the case of the pieces about well-known painting – just chunks of art criticism chopped up into irregular lines of blank verse.

To do Mr Reed justice, there are one or two quite decent poems included here ('Mistletoe', 'After It Was Over') in which Lorca, Mallarmé and co. are temporarily dumped in favour of straightforward observation of the countryside. The rest is a quietly hysterical emotional splurge. According to the blurb, Mr Reed is 'reaching out to a new decade', in which case the implication is that 20th-century poetry will end – a phrase I owe to that distinguished critic Miss Julie Burchill – not with a bang but a simper.

2 February 1990

Verse . . . and verser

All You Who Sleep Tonight VIKRAM SETH (Faber)

*T*HERE are not many authentic national characteristics, but one of them, perhaps, is the pronounced English distaste for poetry. The English don't *like* poetry, they really don't. They used to, of course. But then in the post-Prufrock period, when the ancient comforts of rhyme and metre disappeared and nobody could work out what anything meant any more, they stopped.

Since then they have liked it occasionally but only if disguised in an unassuming, elegiac garment of Englishness (or what passes for Englishness) – unhistrionic and resolutely anti-intellectual. It is significant that the two most popular poets of the post-war era, Betjeman and Larkin, were really poets in spite of themselves, scared stiff lest anyone should accuse them of elevated thoughts and the elevated expression of them. After all, it's only *poetry*, isn't it?

'What's wrong with a poem that rhymes?' 'I'm sure it's very clever, dear, but what does it *mean*?' In these and other sniffish put-downs lie the conventional response to modern English poetry, a response which it is very difficult to fault – most contemporary verse is spineless in the extreme. Amid this atmosphere of indifference mixed with grinding resentment, Vikram Seth looks like the answer to a traditionalist's prayer. He has clarity. He writes love poems in rhyming couplets. And with no Martian overkill – no women knitting described as plaiting spaghetti, no cunnilingus depicted as feeding yourself ambergris à la Craig Raine – he produces very simple and not unmoving accounts of human emotion. 'Across these miles I wish you well/May nothing haunt your heart but sleep' goes a couplet in 'Across' – charming, quite charming.

All You Who Sleep Tonight comes four years after *The Golden Gate*, a hugely successful 'novel in verse' which made Vikram Seth's name. It is a varied collection taking in love, travel and longer narratives spoken by fugitive 'other voices'. In it, according to the jacket, Seth 'conveys his feelings with directness and clarity, and with the memorable use of rhyme and metre'. No problems with the directness and clarity, well, not for the moment, but 'memorable use of rhyme and metre'? Try these four lines:

> A glass of tea; the moon
> The frogs croak in the weeds
> A bat wriggles down across
> Gold disk to silver reeds

Taking a regular six-beat verse and then breaking its back in the third line ('wriggles') might just veer on the right side of imagination, but take this couplet:

> Like stars that rise when the other has set
> For years we two friends have not met

This is not 'memorable' use of metre so much as a *wrong* use. Read it to yourself and you'll find it so irregular that the underlying rhythm scarcely exists. Worse than this, perhaps, is the vagueness of the phrasing. 'Like stars that rise when the other has set'. What Seth means is: 'Like two stars, one of which rises when the other has set', but he can't be bothered to explain this. In fact, the charge of laziness hangs over the collection, detectable even in 'Soon', a moving and regularly rhymed poem about Aids whose continual degeneration into assonance – 'God' rhyming with 'good' and so on – suggests that the poet simply abandoned the attempt to find proper rhymes.

But it's perhaps the opening poem, 'Round and Round', that exposes the technical limitations. In it the poet imagines he sees an ex-girlfriend's bag in an airport carousel:

> After a long and wretched flight that stretched from daylight into night
> Where babies wept and tempers shattered
> And the plane lurched and whisky spattered . . .
>
> I knew that bag. It must be hers
> We hadn't met in seven years!

Several things conspire to destroy this: the banal rhymes within rhymes, that awful third line 'the' which undermines the rhythm, and most of all the 'hers/years' combination. Rather than reverting to a simple, chaste traditionalism – Betjeman, thou shouldst be living, etc. – Seth is actually aping the characteristics of a great deal of modern poetry, which is to say that he is rag-baggish, undisciplined and occasionally inept. Despite the odd evidences of charm, Auberon Waugh and the 'save English poetry from barbarism' cheerleaders will have to look elsewhere.

3 August 1990

From Bad to verse

Dancing the Dream: Poems and Reflections MICHAEL JACKSON (Doubleday)

POETRY is sissy stuff that rhymes. Usually, you can't give it away. But this little bundle of bosh is riding high in the bestseller charts, up there with *Diana* and the Michelin Guide to stuffing your face.

This phenomenon is the final confirmation of how insignificant books are now, in comparison to the music business. Pop is publishing's last hope. Publishers know that if you can get any fraction of a rock audience to consider buying a book, you're in the money.

'Course, it's not so easy, as a visit to the book section of any Virgin record shop soon shows. There you see them, the young, in all their glory, patiently holding books up to their ears, or doggedly trying to insert them into the slots of their CD-players. A few bright sparks have worked out that the things have to be opened, the pages turned, so as to be seen. These virtuosi stand gazing ecstatically, as picture after picture is revealed by this rewarding trick.

Your actual reading, your *reading* as such, however – you know, the grimy finger wobbling along the line of type, the cracked lips wonderingly forming vocables – is rather less in evidence. In fact, it is obviously only conscientiousness, and pride in craftsmanship, that makes publishers put words in books at all. Just for themselves, they like to feel they're there, although they know they'll never be used.

Such professionalism has its risks, however. For example, if anybody ever did manage to read this collection of his verses, Michael Jackson would stand revealed, irreversibly, undeniably, as completely barking, daffy as a duck, a very long way round the bend. Off the wall, like.

It's not just that his rhymes are duff. (Though they are, wonderfully so: 'I looked for you in hill and dale / I sought for you beyond the pale / I searched for you in every nook and cranny / My probing was at times uncanny...')

It's that these compositions give a comprehensive insight into his fantasy life. And Michael Jackson believes he is God. Really.

You can see how it happened, can't you? Celebrity on that scale from childhood onwards would make any of us think rather well of ourselves, after a while. Adulation is always easy to credit.

But Michael has gone the whole hog. He knows He's God, and no mistake. And that makes his book an interesting case-study.

All of these poems celebrate Himself, naturally. What else should He do? If Michael Jackson were God, you might think he was a decent sort of god. As he's just an albino popstar, they read a little oddly.

On the one hand, God is immortal ('Immortality's my game') and very important indeed ('I am the galaxy'). On the other, it is lonely work ('I get lonely sometimes, I get lonely'), because there isn't anybody else to talk to.

The only other human being appearing in these poems is the mother of God ('Eons of time I've been gestating / To take a form been hesitating / From the unmanifest this cosmic conception / On this earth a fantastic reception ... No matter where I go from here / You're in my heart, my mother dear.')

Only children and babies appear ('Children show me in their playful smiles the divine in everyone'). Jackson thinks of himself as a holy child. A poem records how he became aware of it: 'Magical child grew brave and bold / Diving deep into his soul / In exquisite ecstasy he discovered his role / In his Self was infinite scope / This mysterious force was mankind's hope.'

This revelation caused Him certain problems, inevitably, with the rougher types. 'He knew his power was the power of God / He was so sure, they considered him odd ... this perplexing creature / With the rest of the world he shared no feature.' Indeed not.

Yet it has the inestimable advantage of rendering him perpetually youthful (it's rubbish about the plastic surgery) and indeed immortal. 'I was born to never die,' he says, proudly. After all, can a star die? '"Oh no," a voice in my head says, "A star can never die. It just turns into a smile and melts back into the cosmic music, the dance of life." I like that thought, the last one I have before my eyes close. With a smile, I melt back into the music myself.'

Then, really, when you're God, nothing's alien to you, is it? Ostensibly describing His dancing, He lets us know how it feels: 'I become the stars and the moon. I become the lover and the beloved. I become the victor and the vanquished. I become the master and the slave. I become the singer and the song. I become the knower and the known. I keep on dancing, and then, it is the eternal dance of creation. The creator and the creation merge into one wholeness of joy.' Spiffy, eh?

The only problem is who you can share these splendours with, when you're God. There really isn't anybody suitable. Sure, He talks to His creation. '"Moon, I'm here!" I shout. "Good," she replies. "Now give us a little dance."' (He does, he does.)

And 'Planet Earth, gentle and blue / With all my heart, I love you,' he declares, generously, from the vacancies of interstellar space.

But it's not the same, is it? No, the only fit company for Michael is to be found in the mirror. 'I wanted to change the world, so I got up one morning and looked in the mirror,' begins one classic 'reflection'. In the mirror he found just his type. 'I touched the mirror with a grin. "Let's not be alone again. Will you be my partner? I heard a dance starting up. Come." That one in the mirror smiled shyly. He was realizing that we could be best friends. We could be more peaceful, more loving, more honest with each other every day. Would that change the world? I think it will ...' A racing certainty, surely.

'One thing I know: I never feel alone when I am earth's child,' says Mr Whacko, the world's first stone-washed human being. 'This sense of "the world in me" is how I always want to feel. That one in the mirror has his doubts sometimes. So I am tender with him. Every morning I touch the mirror and whisper, "Oh friend, I hear a dance. Will you be my partner? Come."'

You can bet he does it, too. *Spoooooky!* Thank God none of his fans can read.

31 July 1992

Rhyming cobblers

The Literary Review Anthology of Real Poetry Ed. Auberon Waugh
(Ashford, Buchan & Enright)

IF one wanted to settle on the date when British poetry split into two irreconcilable halves, a good candidate would be 1917, the year in which T.S. Eliot published *The Lovesong of J. Alfred Prufrock*.

All at once domestic literature, previously a mass of varied, seething forms, took on recognizably opposed shapes. On the one side were the modernists – it was at about this time that word 'highbrow' became a term of abuse – with their free verse, their cleverness and their wilful obscurity. On the other ... well, on the other were the defenders of 'real poetry', defined as traditional verse forms hymning conventional sentiments in a comprehensible way. On the one hand Eliot and Pound; on the other Larkin and Betjeman. With a few minor exceptions (where, for instance, do you put

194

Auden?) most British poetry of the past 70 years can be categorized by means of this convenient demarcation.

Perhaps Mr Waugh's most ingenious comic idea of the past few years – and there have been many – is the *Literary Review*'s monthly poetry competition in which members of the public are offered alluring sums of money to produce parodies of 'real poetry'. It is all the more ingenious in that the joke is relentlessly kept up, even here in the anthology, bringing together 130 of the 'best' of these submissions.

'Pastiche and parody are not eligible for the first prize, although even this rule has been waived on occasion,' Mr Waugh writes in his tongue-in-cheek introduction. It is, as the discerning reader will note, that 'on occasion' which gives the game away. In fact the rule has been waived on every occasion and it is this that gives the anthology its status as one of the decade's great exercises in literary subversion.

The result is a quite masterly debunking of the traditional in poetry: a series of bland, dull, derivative little poems tinkling away in the straitjackets of their rhyme schemes, heavily reminiscent of Betjeman, Barrie, Belloc and all those insipid light versifiers that most adult English men and women remember from their childhood. There is Angus Hill and his nods to Coleridge ('There is a special constable and he stoppeth one of three'); there is Bill Greenwell with his artful reproductions of Gilbertian patter songs; and there are poems about cats and giving birth to twins.

Plainly, it took considerable care to assemble a collection that was quite so comprehensive in its suggestion of the arid, deficient garden in which the seeds of 'real poetry' are sown and Mr Waugh ought to be congratulated on his determination.

Even more pleasing is the impish spirit of fun which attends Mr Waugh's conduct of the enterprise. If the reviewer is to be allowed two mild criticisms of this splendid jape, they are that the joke does not quite hold up for 118 pages and that two or three of the poems (for instance Adele Geras's *An Elegy for Miss Ratcliffe*) actually have some lurking merit about them: a minor blemish that will doubtless be rectified in the many future editions.

The lesson, however, is invaluable: we all read in the textbooks that modernism was an historical imperative, that it 'had to happen'; but it is nice to receive a practical demonstration of why.

9 November 1990

Tripe and onions

The Forward Book of Poetry 1994 (Forward Publishing)

*H*ERE's a turn-up. For years now the bright young sparks on the books pages have been saying that the current British novel is nbg. No memorable characters, no gripping stories, all that – whack, whack, whack, good fun really.

But it became a bit monotonous, knocking down these knackered novelists. To their surprise the reviewers found that it would be nice to have something to praise after all, if only to make the whackings look more selective. They hankered for the old-fashioned politesse of saying: 'What I mean is, your book's crap in comparison to *this* one.'

Then Harry Ritchie – the brave boy who became literary editor at the *Sunday Times* after everybody else, from Martin Amis to Normski, had turned it down – had an idea. He'd say that, yeah, the novel's bollocks but poetry is brilliant. This had the inestimable advantage that hardly anybody can bear to read modern poetry, so nobody would contradict him.

And they haven't. Every dork-brain now goes around saying, 'There's an exhilarating renaissance in contemporary British verse.' The *Independent* prints a 'Daily Poem' to make its remaining readers feel even more superior, and the *Guardian* has duly followed suit.

And poetry has got a prize too. A Medici wannabee called William Sieghart, who runs a company that produces in-house business magazines, saw an Opening. All he needed to do was set up a poetry prize and in no time people would be calling it 'the bardic Booker' (wordsmith: John Walsh).

It's worked a treat. Poetry is perfect for promotion because so little reading is required. The main difference nowadays between poetry and prose is that, dreadful though it is, poetry doesn't go on for nearly so long.

And is it cheap! Unlike articles by journalists, poems hardly cost a thing. Remember, many people actually *pay* to publish their poems.

So here we have the second great *Forward Book of Poetry*. Unlike the first, it has been competently edited. As well as the prize-winners (Carol Ann Duffy, £10,000 for best book; Don Paterson, £5,000 for best first book; Vicki Feaver, £1,000 for best single poem), there are 80 more poems, all previously published, selected from books and magazines by a panel of five judges. It really is a representative selection of contemporary poetry, a judiciously taken soil sample.

That's why it makes such painful reading. It would have been nice to have believed in a renaissance of *something* – macramé, treen, sherry trifles, it hardly matters what – but no luck. An hour with this book and you're disabused. These poems turn out to have that frightful silliness, that sprightly fatuity, which stops almost everybody but poets from reading poetry after adolescence.

To make a poem of the year, you need less wit than an alternative comedian, less invention than a mediocre hack. Carol Ann Duffy's 'Valentine' is a pretty good example. 'Not a red rose or a satin heart. / I bring you an onion' it begins.

Well, well, what a card, eh? An *onion*. Whatever next? Being a dogged poet, she tells us, laboriously working out the ways in which the jolly old onion makes a first-rate valentine. 'It will blind you with tears / like a lover', you see. Only if you chop it small, of course, but never mind. Then, should you proceed to snack on it raw, there's yet another way in which it makes a spiffy token of love. 'I will give you an onion. / Its fierce kiss will stay on your lips, / possessive and faithful / as we are, / for as long as we are.' Pooh! What's more it'll repeat on you something rotten too, I bet (but maybe that's not poetry?).

And at the end, this talented vegetable even supplies a little touch of melodrama. 'Lethal. / Its scent will cling to your fingers, / cling to your knife.' Knife, eh? A dark undertone there, if I'm not mistaken. Now that's poetry, that is.

Were some stand-up to deliver himself of this *jeu d'esprit*, or somebody you know to discourse thus on the romantic symbolism of root vegetables over the breakfast table, you would not, in all likelihood, be much impressed. But set it out as verse with only a few words per line and suddenly it's art.

Everything awful you remembered about poetry is richly represented here. There are those dreadful poems about being a poet ('I was my own poem,' says another of the Duffys). There's even one about being a poet who wins a poetry competition.

There are atrociously forced findings of significance (one nerd constructs a poem out of the resemblance between a kettle de-scaler, or 'de-furrer', and Adolf Hitler, 'Der Führer'). There are those poems that make up their own daft rules (one has only words of one syllable, another consists of lists of three things). There are those that are spoken by unconventional narrators, like photographs taken from unusual angles (one is spoken by an unhappy lettuce marooned in a fridge).

There are dreadfully winsome comparisons – 'You're numb as hair, as mute as cats, / as soft as lettuces . . .'. There are excruciating rhymes you can see coming from a mile away ('celery/salary', 'conkers/bonkers'). There are poncey words (falchion, mussitate, cordillera). There are preening poeticisms ('silvery plenitude', 'civil urgencies of sweet desire', 'grey visitant in fish-vigil' – that's a heron, by the way).

And then there are those crowning statements at the end of poems about the meaning of life, which poets having got thus far generally feel entitled to deliver to us. Perhaps the best here is by somebody called Mark Robinson. 'The world is hard but worth it,' he advises. It's certainly more than you can say of the *Forward Book of Poetry*.

3 December 1993

Rhyming couples

My Secret Planet **DENIS HEALEY** (Michael Joseph)
Seven Ages: Poetry for a Lifetime **Ed. David Owen** (Michael Joseph)

*T*HE age of the politician with literary interests is popularly supposed to have ended with the death of Churchill, but all around us tiny green shoots are protruding from what was assumed to be a mouldy and decaying bough.

Kenneth Baker has edited an anthology or two; Roy Hattersley has embarked on a sequence of jumbo-sized novels. Even Lady Thatcher, on the evidence of Philip Larkin's letters, has been known to recall (imperfectly) the odd line of poetry. The simultaneous publication of Denis Healey's saunter around his mental lumber room and David, or as I suppose we had better start calling him, *Lord* Owen's selection of his favourite poems is an alarming extension of this trend.

God knows what Michael Joseph thought it was doing in releasing these two within weeks of each other, though. Two recently ennobled former Labour cabinet ministers; two collections of 'writers who have influenced my life' (Owen confines himself to verse, but the cradle-to-grave format remains) – they were bound to get reviewed together. Equally, they were bound to attract comparisons of the most mutually injurious sort.

Lord Owen, unhappily enough, lets himself down in the second sentence of his brief introduction. 'I have picked these poems for the music of their language, the memories they evoke or for the way they complement each other, adding to the beauty of the whole.' A little later he writes: 'Poetry for me is the music of the spoken word.' These are exemplary sentiments. To them might be added the thought that the act of writing a poem is to unleash another star into the welcoming firmament.

Though Lord Owen's speculations on the form might sound like the worst sort of nursery-room whimsy, it is at least fairly easy to get the measure of his anthology. In fact the word 'generic' might have been invented to describe it. A good test is to think of any highly familiar poem you learned at school – MacNeice's *Bagpipe Music*, say, or Wilde's *The Ballad of Reading Gaol* or Larkin's *MCMLXIV* – they're all here. An even better, supplementary test is to ask an aged relative to think of any highly familiar poems he learned at school – Macaulay's *Lays of Ancient Rome*, say, or Coleridge's *Kubla Khan*, or Kipling's *If* – they're all here too. Set against this predictable company Wendy Cope seems like an outrageously modern ironist.

With Lord Healey, alternatively, we are immediately transported to what Ronald Firbank would call 'the heart of a brainy district'. The old bruiser's intellectual credentials are, of course, well established: double first in Lit. Hum., turned down a career as an Oxford don, introduced Iris Murdoch to the novels of Samuel Beckett. Scarcely has the second page of the 'Boyhood' chapter of this literary life been reached than Healey is ruminating about Thomas Traherne. Great gouts of Turgenev and Dostoevsky follow in the rear and the general effect is just a tiny bit exhausting.

The infuriating – or invigorating – thing about *My Secret Planet* is that it isn't a pose. The constant intellectual one-upmanship is quite unfeigned. After all, which other retired UK politician could give you his views on Kant without provoking eyebrow-raising incredulity? He and Owen might share a few favourites – Kipling, Hopkins and Dylan Thomas, for example – but the gulf between them gapes. To Lord Owen, you feel, 'literature' is a facial expression, something one picks up on appropriate occasions, like a Sunday suit or an old boys' tie; to Lord Healey it is a way of life. But even Lord Owen seems a literary colossus when compared to some of his youthful successors in the House of Commons. In a semi-literate age the idea that poetry is the music of the spoken word can even have a faint nobility about it.

20 November 1992

8

BIOGRAPHY

Lust for lives

Waugh Requiem

Evelyn Waugh: The Early Years 1903–1939 MARTIN STANNARD
(Dent)

S ECOND-division publishers J.M. Dent & Sons spent many years making a comfortable living out of the profits of the Everyman's Classics series of reprints.

When, in the early 1980s, a glut of rival editions caused this source of income to dry up they branched out along more contemporary lines, specifically modern novels and modish biography. *Evelyn Waugh: The Early Years*, by Martin Stannard of the University of Leicester, is the exemplar of this new buck-chasing approach.

Unfortunately the ground is already well trodden. Since Evelyn Waugh's death in 1966 there have been enough books about him to satisfy even the most leisured of his admirers: editions of the letters, diaries and journalism, memoirs of him as a schoolboy, a commando officer and a country neighbour, and a series of heavyweight studies with titles like *Masks, Modes and Morals: The Art of Evelyn Waugh*.

Such is this wealth of documentation that Martin Stannard occupies most of the preface to his own 500-page assessment (a second volume is threatened) in defending an endeavour that, as he admits, 'might cause the most avid Waugh fanatics to throw up their hands in despair'.

There are two aspects to this defence. The first is that Christopher Sykes's earlier biography was unnecessarily evasive ('a fastidious discretion which often needlessly veiled information that was even then common knowledge').

The second is that Stannard's book has something startlingly original to say about its subject, or, as he puts it, 'attempts something which no other biographical study of Waugh has done: to forge a relationship between the crucial events of Waugh's life and his developing aesthetic'.

While the first claim is defensible – and Sykes's discretion is soon remedied by some spirited grubbing about in Waugh's private life – the second is nonsense. All Stannard means by this critical smokescreen is that as Waugh grew older he and his books became more disillusioned, a highly unoriginal notion which appears for instance in a study called *The Will to Believe*, written by a don called Richard Johnstone in 1982.

One could forgive all this – it is the biographer's characteristic vice – if Stannard had any idea of how to marshall his material or write decent prose. But whereas Sykes was concise and lucid, the author of *The Early Years* is prolix and dull.

To do him justice Mr Stannard is painstaking, painstaking in his 30-page trek through Waugh's antecedents, painstaking on the manuscript emendations, and when it comes to the foreign trips of the 1930s, quite interminable. Like many modern biographies it is not so much a work of themes or structures as a compilation, the result of diligent fossicking around in other books with which most readers are already over-familiar; a notable example here being *Messengers of Day*, the second volume of Anthony Powell's memoirs.

This recasting of second-hand opinion becomes all the more evident when we get to the critical judgements. Waugh's interest in cinematic technique, reflected in the swift exchange of scenes and the snappy dialogue of *Decline and Fall* and *Vile Bodies*, was originally noted by Sykes, while a discussion of the benign influence of Firbank is remarkably similar to David Lodge's essay 'The Fugitive Art of Letters' which appeared in a long remaindered volume called *Evelyn Waugh and His World*.

Stannard's other irritating characteristic is a tendency to overdramatize what actually happened. For someone who is at pains to deflate much of the fantasy of Waugh's diaries, he is extraordinarily keen to take quite ordinary events or descriptions and doctor them in a suggestive or misleading way.

Waugh's arrival at his first teaching job, with a number of small boys in tow, is elaborately built up – 'he sat gloomily amongst the rabble ... The children had realised the vulnerability of the new master' – culminating in a ruse whereby a humiliated Waugh is persuaded to transport their luggage to the school in a taxi.

The *Diaries'* description of this incident is a little more laconic: 'A tiny taxi took me and 200 handbags to the house.' Similarly, Waugh's mention of increasing forgetfulness is enough for Stannard to deduce 'clear signs of strain, possibly of mental aberration'.

Stalking his quarry through thickets of lifeless prose, through stale Catholic controversies, through the reiteration of all those worldly letters ('there were little Arab girls of 15 and 16 for ten francs ... so I bought one but didn't enjoy her much'), Stannard rarely comes close to laying a hand on his shoulder.

Assessments of Waugh's character emerge through the construction of elaborate Aunt Sallies which are simply not worth stoning. 'The popular impression of Waugh today,' Stannard writes, 'would seem to be that he was, if not a signed-up member of the British Union of Fascists, then a man whose political tendencies were perfectly in keeping with their policies.'

Julian Symons thinks that Stannard's laboured odyssey is likely to become the standard work. Even Waugh *fils* describes it as 'well-mannered'.

The Early Years is actually a book that combines minimal new information and maximal prolixity. Sykes was gay and witty; Mr Stannard is dogged and humourless. It is a sad comment on the author's abilities that his funniest revelation comes in the bibliography, where among a list of monographs on Waugh's writings can be found *Le Jeu de l'absurde dans l'opéra d'Evelyn Waugh*, written by a man named Tosser.

Christmas 1986

The Hundred Years Waugh

The Brideshead Generation: Evelyn Waugh and His Friends
HUMPHREY CARPENTER (Weidenfeld & Nicolson)

OH God, the autumn bookshop browser will cry as he catches sight of the powder-blue covers glistening on the table in Waterstone's and notices the jacket photograph (the Oxford University Railway Club in 1925) *not them, not again*. But it is them again, all of them.

That tedious collection of upper-class bores and minor literary figures – Acton, Howard, Byron, Betjeman, Connolly – all those people you thought had been decently laid to rest in a series of unnecessarily long and respectful memoirs, here they all are again, corralled and marshalled under the brooding figure of Evelyn Waugh. *Oh God*, the reader cries, *not them again. Aren't there more interesting things to write books about?*

A bit too much has been written about the Waugh circle in the past 20 years, quite a bit too much: innumerable fat biographies and studies, reminiscences by the most marginal of his hangers-on. At this stage in the proceedings everything about him, every anecdote, every speculation has that grey dusty air of *déjà vu* and *The Brideshead Generation*, in which

Humphrey Carpenter 'comes to some disturbing conclusions about Waugh the artist and Waugh the man' is a famously lame assemblage, full of familiar memories.

Harold Acton queens it round the quadrangles of Christchurch for the umpteenth time. The elderly relative of Waugh's second wife – his first wife's cousin – makes perhaps her tenth appearance in print to remark that 'I thought we'd seen the last of that young man.' You see, you read this book before. You read it in Anthony Powell's autobiography, in oh so many dim volumes of recycled gossip. You saw the illustrations before, all of them, in Christopher Sykes's biography, in *Evelyn Waugh and His World* . . .

Carpenter doesn't provide any footnotes to this enterprise, which is perhaps a good idea as there isn't a paragraph in the book that doesn't have its genesis in a work by somebody else. In fact, aside from its analyses of Waugh's novels, *The Brideshead Generation* is simply a series of rambling recapitulations. Part One, which describes Acton and Brian Howard at Eton, is a straight lift from a book by Marie-Jacqueline Lancaster called *Brian Howard: Portrait of a Failure*. Later on there are some bold thefts from Anthony Powell's *Messengers of Day*, from all the Waugh letters and diary entries that have appeared countless times elsewhere. Each aspect of Waugh's career, each point on the trajectory has its well-documented source which Carpenter gaily appropriates.

None of this would matter, perhaps, if Carpenter didn't so unquestioningly accept his characters' (and their biographers') estimates of their own seriousness. Reading the accounts of Waugh and his coevals at Oxford, you might be deluded into thinking that what we have here is a group of frivolous young drunks whose university careers lasted only as long as it took for them to obtain thirds or get kicked off the premises for idleness. But oh dear me, no, these are serious young people, don't you know.

When John Betjeman chooses to prance around carrying a teddy bear named Archie it's 'an implicit comment on the immaturity of the English upper classes' (I'd have thought it was an explicit comment on the immaturity of John Betjeman, but there you are). Throughout, Carpenter invests his subjects with a greater seriousness than they actually possessed: five second-hand pages, for instance, on Maurice Bowra – surely one of the most tedious men to stalk 1920s Oxford – with his side-splitting 'I'm a man more dined against than dining' sallies.

There is ulterior motive here, of a sort: the connection between Waugh and his chums in their careers and personal lives and the influence he might have been supposed to exert on them. But the links are tenuous. Waugh might just have helped the break-up of the Betjeman marriage by luring Lady Penelope off to Rome and it might just have been the stimulus of *Brideshead Revisited* that inspired Powell to write *A Dance to the Music of Time* in the first person, but the shared assumptions about father figures, country houses and nostalgia seldom amount to anything, or indeed are worked out with any conviction.

Carpenter is on much surer ground in his dissection of Waugh's novels – good on the borrowings from Firbank, good on some of the implications of *Brideshead*, even if, again, his search for seriousness leads him to describe the mass seasickness on the Channel crossing which opens *Vile Bodies* as 'a metaphor for the despair engendered by modern society'. In fact this could have been quite a good short critical book. Unfortunately short critical books on Waugh don't sell. The books that do sell are the ones aimed at the *Brideshead* snobs and the devotees of horrible Victorian architecture: all that 'reactionary chic' for which Carpenter in his conclusion tries to make Waugh responsible. Marking Waugh down as a prototype young fogey is only the last of the borrowings (it comes from Peter York's *Style Wars*) in this overblown and unnecessary compilation.

15 September 1989

Greene with ennui

The Life of Graham Greene, Volume I, 1904–1939 NORMAN SHERRY
(Cape)

*L*ITERARY biography is all the rage these days. Holroyd on Shaw; Wilson on Tolstoy; Brome on Priestley – the last couple of years have brought a rash of these fat, best-selling books which take up an unconscionable amount of bookshop space, get serialized in Sunday newspapers and are crawled over by respectful reviewers.

It is a growth industry in which no one cares if the ground is already well-trodden. You might think that we have heard all we could possibly want to hear about the late Evelyn Waugh but no – Martin Stannard is busy labouring away on Volume II of his colossal opus (volume one weighed in at 500 pages) with Lady Selina Hastings, her own study lately commissioned by Weidenfeld, panting rather forlornly in the rear.

Although critics habitually defer to these gross slabs of summarized lives and recapitulated plots, the standard of literary biography in this country is pitifully low. To take only the books listed above, Holroyd on Shaw was interminable; Wilson on Tolstoy told you rather more about Wilson's own prejudices than the genius of his subject; Brome on Priestley was a check-list of other books by or about the sage of Bradford. In fact most modern literary biography is little more than compilation – an assemblage of everything known about or written by the subject with a few valueless generalizations of the 'was now in love for the first time in his life' sort thrown in as a substitute for analysis.

It has to be said that the first volume of Norman Sherry's life of Graham Greene, 15 years in the making and the product of an epic quest in which Professor Sherry tracked Greene's spoor over various remote parts of the globe and nearly went blind in the process, is a better book than any of these undistinguished forebears. It is interesting, well written (there was a time, of course, when one *expected* books to be well written) and it pursues the connection between Greene's life and art with a certain amount of exactitude. given the fact that its subject is a cantankerous and litigious old party – as a rival, unauthorized biographer found recently to his cost – it is surprisingly revealing of all the wild-eyed, boredom-killing morbidity with which Green has cossetted his days.

No, *The Life of Graham Green Vol I* isn't over-discreet or too heavily invested with the biographer's own personality, it is simply on the one hand far too long and on the other quite unable to discriminate between what is and isn't relevant. For Sherry, like many biographers, has no idea that some pieces of information might be more interesting to the reader or more revealing about the subject than others. Consequently he puts in everything. He puts in Greene's change of address cards; he puts in the announcement of his wedding. He puts in the letters he received informing him of the death of various of Greene's friends he had tried to contact.

There are virtues, of course, in saturation. You can justify – up to a point – the torrent of mawkish love letters written by Greene to his first wife on the grounds that they disclose both the depth of his feeling and the more sentimental side of his character. It is a little less easy to justify the favourite Sherry trick of accumulating vast amounts of excess detail on events and subjects with which the youthful Greene had no connection. The rowdy Armistice Night celebrations at Berkhamsted School in 1918 get a couple of pages: Greene, alas, didn't attend them. Waugh, Acton and the Hypocrites

Club in 1920s Oxford are similarly described: Greene, Sherry reveals, 'was not a member'.

Even more tedious are the footnotes, in which no subject is too insignificant, no bit-partner too dull, to receive the dogged quota of explication.

The problem, of course, and the explanation for this excess of leaden marginalia, is that Professor Sherry is obsessed. Such is his fixation with Greene and Greene alone that no one else gets a look in; not Vivienne, his first wife (whose reaction to the tide of sentiment would be interesting to hear); or J.B. Priestley (only the Greene side of the row over *Stamboul Train* gets reported).

Something of this obsession surfaced in Sherry's recent *Independent* interview where Anthony Mockler, the rival biographer, was summarily trashed as a 'charlatan', merely because his book had taken three years rather than 15 to produce. Whatever the defects of Mockler's book, it will at any rate be shorter. There is a good chance that it might even be a little more discriminating.

28 April 1989

Trivial Hirsute

Bernard Shaw 1: The Search for Love MICHAEL HOLROYD
(Chatto & Windus)

*T*HIS, you may know, was rather an expensive item for its publishers. With two volumes, the notes and sources, and an abbreviated paperback edition to come, the British rights to this book cost Chatto, let's say it again, £625,000. The most paid before for a literary biography was £90,000 – for Ellman's *Oscar Wilde*.

It works out at a pound a word. Perhaps not such a lot, after all – about the same as a British Telecom 'Telemessage' – yet still a puzzling outlay. For this book is so painfully dull that this pound a word would hardly be incentive enough to read it.

Bearded-man biographies are not easy reading at best. Holroyd's two previous essays in the genre did have something going for them – Lytton

Strachey was a frantic bitch and Augustus John a frenzied bonker. But Shaw was and is a bore, simply. Nobody wants to know any more about this monster of self-importance and clever stupidities – not at all, let alone three volumes' worth. So how come?

The plain answer is that Carmen Callil, who bought the book for Chatto, had her own reasons for splashing out. Holroyd may now be married to Hampstead's Margaret Drabble but, before that, one of the innumerable literature fans he communed with was the appealing Carmen. Moreover Holroyd notoriously lives apart from Drabble – he in Notting Hill Gate, she in NW3. What can Drabble offer that's as good as Carmen? An impartial entry in her *Oxford Dictionary of English Literature* hailing her husband as the greatest living biographer. And then?

The complex answer has to do with Holroyd's conceit about biography as a genre, not with what the book is actually like – boring and badly written. It makes a horribly jerky progress through Shaw's early career and never does succeed in bringing him to life. No great discoveries are made, and the whole thing is mounted on a primitive psychoanalytic scaffolding. This comes in two parts. Firstly, the child Shaw was called 'Sonny' and, don't you know, 'Sonny' was a part of himself that Shaw damagingly lost contact with when he transformed himself into 'GBS'. Secondly, his parents lived in a curious *ménage à trois* with a music teacher, Vandeleur Lee, and Shaw, do you believe?, ever after tried to recreate this situation both in his life and in his work. And that's it for theory.

Holroyd's own style is a mixture of PC Plod reports ('On 16 August he ... Two days later ... On August 20, a Sunday ... The following Tuesday Shaw noted in his diary ... On the Saturday he went down to stay with the Webbs ... The following morning he was off along the Monmouth road ... On 30 August he announced ...' – all in one paragraph) and silly showings-off. Holroyd loves to demonstrate how clever he is by such witticisms as 'he could not absent himself from her infelicity' and 'it took one to make a quarrel'. Prime among these imbecilities is his opening sentence: 'Bernard Shaw died on 2 November 1950 aged one week, three months and ninety-four years.' Bet you can't count backwards.

This is the prose that Holroyd's agent Hilary Rubinstein describes as 'like the best chocolate truffle from the best chocolatier – it just melts in the mouth'. It is supposed to be the reason for anyone to read the book. Because what Holroyd has pioneered as a biographer is the book about a subject whom the reader has no interest in beforehand nor greater respect for afterwards. So you can slurp away on the life without any of the bother of thinking about the work. Who the subject is hardly matters, so long as the man has a beard. It could have been Rolf Harris. It may yet be.

The justification, much proffered by Holroyd, is that biography is as much literature as the novel, or more so, and is not dependent on anything as adventitious as who it is about. And his presumption goes a step further. He believes that his life of Shaw is also *Shaw*'s last book – and his best. Holroyd has taken over Shaw, thinks himself Shaw, and intends that his biography should be the form in which Shaw survives, as his lives of Strachey and John are for them. In some ways this is an original literary project to have undertaken. But this time the megalomania has come unstuck. For the book is just as dislikeable as Shaw himself. Holroyd never convinces you that even he himself can take any pleasure in Shaw.

The publishers remark that 'subject and author are perfectly matched'. Sure. Shaw 'made himself a publicity phenomenon', says Holroyd. He should know. It has become almost impossible to find a paper without an interview with the leading biographer, complete with a portrait of him soulfully contemplating his subsidiary rights. You will be pleased to hear that, not content with having done a 'work in progress' programme a few years ago, the *South Bank Show* is shortly to show a second special on Holroyd, and doubtless a third, covering the second volume, is now in the planning stage. All the review pages will lead with this 'Book of the Year'. Yet not one in twenty buyers will wade through to the end. What we really need now from Holroyd is a guide to how it's done. That and *Sex Tips for the Older Man*. In one slim volume.

16 September 1988

The Bungle Book

Rudyard Kipling MARTIN SEYMOUR-SMITH (Macdonald/Queen Anne Press)

MARTIN Seymour-Smith is no stranger to controversy, or at any rate to the factitious, self-regarding controversy that passes for literary debate in this country. About a quarter of a century ago he brought out a book which suggested, among other things, that Shakespeare was a homosexual.

Now, ever impenitent, amid a welter of publicity and some excited squeaks about 'cover-ups', he has written another one alleging that Kipling was bent as well.

Well, it's an original notion. What next, you wonder? Jane Austen as a lickerish lesbian (after all, she never married)? E.M. Forster as a Bloomsbury stud? One sometimes gets the feeling these days that a serious radical biography would suggest that Dickens was a family man who devoted himself to his wife or that John Lennon never took drugs and gave most of his money to charity.

Martin Seymour-Smith's contribution to the find-a-theory-and-make-the-facts-fit school of biography gives the game away in the very first sentence of the first chapter. 'Kipling's ambivalence about women,' he writes, '. . . may have stemmed from an early emotional reservation about his mother.' Note that use of the word 'may'. It's a word that turns up quite a lot in the 373 rambling pages of *Rudyard Kipling* (along with 'might', 'could have' and 'I should think') and its tireless reiteration is enough to certify that what we have here is a grandly suggestive edifice of speculation fashioned out of remote possibilities.

'I should think.' Martin Seymour-Smith thinks quite a lot of things. He thinks that Kipling at school in England in the 1870s 'might' have been shown Swinburne's notorious poems about flagellation. He also thinks that an early schoolmaster might have suspected him of 'homosexual behaviour'. He is more or less certain that when the 17-year-old Kipling considers himself engaged to a girl named Florence Garrard, 'Rudyard was "in love" simply as a protective exercise . . . He was able to keep fiercely aloof from the nature of his own sexuality, even perhaps to avoid self-questioning.'

You see the trick? You begin with a faintly ridiculous suggestion, transform it by dint of a little judicious prodding into a marginally plausible hypothesis and end up by treating it as an established fact. By the time he gets his subject to India in the 1880s Seymour-Smith is tossing about phrases like 'Kipling's homosexuality' with unwavering conviction, chucking in airy prognoses about his 'submissiveness' and even suggesting at one point that 'he was, I should think [*I should think!*], the "woman" in any idealised homosexual fantasies which he may have allowed himself'.

Golly! All this of moustachioed, grim-visaged Mr Kipling with his manly stuff about the thin red line and the white man's burden! The drawback is that there isn't a line of proof, not a whisker. The only mildly shocking thing to emerge from this spirited grubbing around in the bran-tub of Kipling's psychology, the positing of a love affair with somebody called Wolcott Balestier, is the fraudulence of Seymour-Smith's method.

Take this as an example. In India the 20-year-old Kipling fancies himself enamoured of the daughter of a neighbouring vicar and consequently drives five miles each Sunday to church for a glimpse of her. His father writes amusingly about this to a friend, describing it as 'a most wholesome sign that he is growing to his proper boyhood'. What is this? Nothing more than a Victorian paterfamilias acknowledging his son's arrival at maturity, but for Seymour-Smith it's certain proof of inversion. After all, 'what was it that his mother and his father were so worried about that they should speak of "wholesomeness"?'

This is ridiculous. But then, this is a ridiculous book. Somewhere in it Seymour-Smith describes himself as a 'critical biographer', which is equally ridiculous. *Rudyard Kipling* isn't a biography. It's a rambling discursive shuffle around various aspects of Kipling's personality. There are no notes so you can't check anything. In fact, there's hardly any documentary evidence at all – most of it is simply Seymour-Smith leafing through what other biographers and critics have said and wondering whether he agrees. It is also surprisingly badly written, a book in which women are 'raven-haired'.

The genteel tone says it all. For at heart this is a very old-fashioned exercise, an attempt to *épater les bourgeois*. But there are not many *bourgeois* left these days, certainly not enough to be shocked by this tremulous piece of nonsense.

17 February 1989

Sylvia Cringe

Bitter Fame: A Life of Sylvia Plath ANNE STEVENSON (Viking)

ANNE Stevenson prefaces *Bitter Fame* with a curious disclaimer: 'This biography is the result of a three-year dialogue between the author and Olwyn Hughes, agent to the Plath Estate. Ms Hughes has contributed so liberally to the text that this is in effect a work of joint authorship.' Olwyn Hughes got Stevenson to expand what had started as one of Penguin's much slighter *Lives of Modern Women* into this megalithic-seeming 430-page Plath–

Hughes bible. It presents a 1,000 per cent sanitized view of Olwyn's brother, the Poet Laureate Ted Hughes (whose agent she also remains), and a commensurately unsanitary view of his ex-wife Sylvia.

Sylvia met Ted and married him in 1956. In the summer of 1962 the marriage broke up, and in the freezing February of 1963 she was found with her head in the gas oven, dead at 30. She had published only two major works, the *Colossus* poems and her autobiographical novel *The Bell Jar*, but her posthumous publications have been legion, as has the secondary literature about her.

Though women's lib only really got going a decade later, the confessional poetry of Plath's last year is what guarantees her enduring halo atop the pantheons of mid-20th century literature and feminism alike. *Bitter Fame*'s own goal is that, though avowedly designed to dispel the image of its subject as a bitch-goddess, devil-mother and symbolic mentor to monstrous regiments of loony wimmin, it goes to notably far-fetched lengths to characterize her as one of the looniest ever.

The reasons are not hard to find. Both Sylvia and Olwyn are on record as to the paucity of love lost between them. Anne Stevenson is on record as taking a dim view of extremist and confessional writing in general, and people who contemplate (let alone commit) suicide in particular. The co-authors' shared concern seems to be, to a near-obsessive degree, the complete whitewashing of Ted Hughes from any responsibility for his wife's sad fate.

The way this is attempted is ludicrously crude. Sylvia is thwacked resoundingly over and over for alleged destructions of Ted's literary properties. Yet the information Hughes himself revealed in his introduction to Plath's published *Journals*, that he'd destroyed an entire volume and that another notebook had 'disappeared', is confined to a brief footnote in *Fame*.

Again, while Ted bothered to write telling a previous biographer that the idea of Sylvia resenting his acclaim as a poet was 'a major misjudgment of her character', the gospel according to Anne 'n' Olwyn implies just this. And though, on the other hand, the biographers do give Plath credit for organizing her husband's career early on, typing and sending out manuscripts and so on, they more often ascribe the basest of motives to her.

Thus, when Ted has gone for good and she muses on inviting her mother to move to Devon from America, it can only be because 'Clearly Sylvia, with her long-term future as a writer in mind, was angling for a babysitter as well as a supportive mother (and typist) who would live close at hand.'

This does serve, however, to remind us that though Sylvia's mother is still

alive, as are her brother and widower, none of these, whom one might reasonably expect to be 'supportive', has been interviewed for this would-be definitive authorised Life. Instead we get, at best, the gossipy conjectures of old mates
of Ted's such as Lucas Myers, who confides: 'I had expected Ted to preserve his
freedom from everything to poetry and, if he were eventually to get married, to
marry someone close to nature, a daughter of the English countryside.'

But Myers is as Boswell compared to the specially commissioned
'Appendix' from Plath's obvious enemy Dido Merwin, whose 25 pages of
unadulterated vitriol read as though composed to order for some Ghoul's
Treasury of Longer Vilifications. Even so, Merwin's is only one of several
chronic cases of bitter jealousy unleashed.

The message most plainly conveyed by this disgraceful misuse of pseudo-
academic knitting needles is that if Sylvia Plath were alive today, she'd have
got herself another agent long ago.

10 November 1989

An American in Paris

Simone de Beauvoir DEIRDRE BAIR (Cape)

A N American visitor once approached James Joyce in Paris saying he
wanted to kiss the hand that had written *Ulysses*. 'Please yourself,' replied
the novelist, 'but remember it's done a lot of other things besides.' The
exchange typifies the gulf between the hordes of American culture-vultures
who have traditionally descended on Paris and their recalcitrant heroes.

Most literary tourists, however, come only to gawp. Ms Bair, in contrast,
comes to write biographical doorstops. Her first target was that celebrated
Francophile, Sam Beckett. Now she has focused her attentions on Simone
de Beauvoir, aka Mrs Jean-Paul Sartre (Monty Python), 'France's No 2
Existentialist' (*Newsweek*) or simply *La Grande Sartreuse*.

For the Beckett biography, Bair had the nearest thing to cooperation
anyone was likely to get from that fastidious old crow. Sam said that he would
neither help nor hinder, and he was as good as his word. Beauvoir, in
contrast, was much more forthcoming and gave freely of her time from 1982
up to her death in 1986.

Why? The question is particularly pertinent given that the subject had already revealed a great deal about her life in a remarkable four-volume autobiography. Why should this formidable dame help a young American to plough the same furrows – especially since she must have known that doing so would undermine the image so artfully fostered in the autobiography?

Bair's explanation is that Beauvoir welcomed the chance to talk about her life 'because no one before me had proposed to write about *all* her work'. Most people were interested in her only as an appendage to Sartre or a feminist precursor. 'This was very important to her, of course, but she did so want people to remember her as a writer of many different genres.'

A close reading of Bair's enormous (718-page) tome, however, suggests that Beauvoir may also have had other motives. One is that she wished to combat the unflattering (and unfair?) image of her propagated by her critics – not to mention the jealous harpies and groupies who had hijacked Sartre in his dotage (and who now control his literary estate). Another motive may have stemmed from the perception that cooperation represented a strategy for damage-limitation: Beauvoir must have realized that Bair's version of her life would expose significant lacunae in her own autobiographical account. The effect of such exposures might be mitigated if they were achieved with her help rather than having to be wrung from documents and the testimony of others.

Bair was a risky accomplice for such a subtle task because she seems to know little about Sartre's philosophical work – and, by implication, about Beauvoir's – and because she is one of those writers who must Tell All. Though her basic sympathy is never in doubt, in the end her portrait of Beauvoir is more devastating than anything essayed by the lady's enemies. Simone comes over as pathetically dependent on Sartre. She appears always in supporting roles – some of them indescribably menial – an amanuensis, *hausfrau*, nursemaid, *confidante*, fixer and pimp for a male who never seems to have progressed much beyond infantilism in his emotional life. Her relationship with Sartre – the famous 'open marriage' in which both were supposed to be free to undertake 'contingent relationships' – is portrayed by Bair as an emotional prison in which he played the field while she was always held back by the need to maintain her place in the queue of accommodating young women who jostled for a turn in his bed.

This unedifying tale is told in a breathless prose style which is by *Newsweek* out of Barbara Cartland. Bair has a compulsive need to pretend that she was *there* – from birth to death. Baby Simone's eyes, for example, 'were dazzling from the moment of birth. She was a lusty, healthy baby of decided temperament who set about the business of living with a concentration that was unnerving in one so tiny.' Likewise, Bair always knows what her subject is thinking. Thus Beauvoir 'lay in her sickbed, poised on the verge of adulthood with no satisfactory answers. Her formal education would end in a few months, and she had to make all kinds of decisions about her future life. How tempting it was to think of finding herself suddenly the other half of a couple, with someone who would take care of her and see to all her physical needs.' And so on, apparently *ad infinitum* and certainly *ad nauseum* in a chronicle that tells one everything about Beauvoir except what we really wanted to know, namely why Sartre always regarded her as his intellectual equal.

6 July 1990

Our Mutual Funds

Dickens PETER ACKROYD (Sinclair-Stevenson)

(Dickens, Eliot, Wilde – an imaginary conversation)

DICKENS: Well gentlemen, I think we are all assembled, we that have so much in common.

WILDE: I spent a lifetime convinced of my singularity, but let that pass.

ELIOT: And yet our gathering is not complete. Where is Mr Ackroyd?

DICKENS: He will be here presently. He is being interviewed by A.N. Wilson for the *Daily Telegraph*.

WILDE: That is a definition of celebrity.

DICKENS: Hush, let us get to the matter in hand. The matter of myself. Or rather the matter of ourselves. For we have all, these seven years since, marched and fretted on the stage of Mr Ackroyd's imagination.

ELIOT: And yet the connection is not so very strong. You and I have made stout biographies. Mr Wilde here was the subject of a novel.

WILDE: Then I have the advantage of you. My life was ever a work of fiction.

DICKENS: Stop. There is someone coming.

(Ackroyd enters. He winks at Wilde, smiles quizzically at Eliot and finally regards Dickens with unfeigned admiration.)

DICKENS: And so, sir, we meet at last.

ACKROYD: On the contrary, we have met several times. Once in a room in London. Another time on an underground train in Essex. You had a white beard and seemed preoccupied.

DICKENS: This is preposterous!

WILDE: Not preposterous, merely poetic. But Mr Eliot has a question.

ELIOT: I do not understand the biographer's art. It is beyond my experience. But it seemed to me that, among your critics, Professor Carey's was the response of a man who dislikes what he reads but cannot bring himself to say so.

WILDE: That is a definition of a *Sunday Times* reviewer ... But I too have a question for Mr Ackroyd. There are ourselves. There was poor Chatterton. Even your last novel reminded one of dear Mr Hardy. One might almost say that your imagination was entirely vicarious.

ACKROYD: It is of no consequence.

WILDE: Gracious! You sound like Mr Toots in *Dombey.* I see that both your sense of flattery and your sense of discretion do you credit. That is a criticism of your book, by the by ... But we are evading the greater issue. Mr Dickens?

DICKENS: It is a very long book.

ACKROYD: It was a very long life.

ELIOT *(sharply)*: That is not a justification. If nothing else, the artist must discriminate.

WILDE: While Mr Ackroyd gushes? I take your point *entirely.*

DICKENS: I am impressed by your confidence. I am startled by your style. So many sharp, singular words: Dust. Water. Birds in flight. Birds caged. The wind. Light. I do not understand it.

ELIOT: That is odd. You were one of the earliest English impressionists.

ACKROYD: I must go. I have an appointment with William Blake.

WILDE *(laughs)*: *Another* visionary?

DICKENS *(thoughtful)*: Do you think that you have succeeded, where so many have failed?

ELIOT: Mr Raine thinks not.

WILDE: Mr Raine, of course, would know.

ACKROYD: At the time of writing I certainly did. Immediately after the book was finished I thought I did. Now I'm not so sure. Only the bank manager has the answer.

14 September 1990

HG Sauce

The Invisible Man: The Life and Liberties of H.G. Wells
MICHAEL COREN (Bloomsbury)

A COMMON biographer's trick in these publicity-conscious times is to take some reasonably well-known fact about his or her subject and convert it, by means of agitated squeaks about conspiracies and cover-ups, into the blinding revelation of 'truth'.

Shortly before Christmas, for example, W.J. West published *The Larger Evils*, a highly tendentious study of George Orwell which, while purporting to reveal the 'truth' behind the composition of *1984*, in fact disclosed only the paucity of Mr West's background reading. The targets, sad to relate, had been brought down years before, and by more agile pens.

Michael Coren's life of H.G. Wells, the shock waves of whose advance publicity have been resonating around literary London for weeks, falls into a similar category. It is one of those 'controversial' biographies, don't you know, which seek to convict a famous man of all manner of hitherto unsuspected depravity.

Something of its intent can be deduced from the sweet reasonableness with which Mr Coren sets out his stall. 'I prefer sympathy with the truth,' he announces demurely, 'and if in pursuit of such I lose sympathy for my subject, it does not in any way tarnish or lessen my motives or sense of empathy.' Two hundred and forty pages of industrious dirt-digging later, we are left with what an excitable Bloomsbury publicist has called 'one of those iconoclastic biographies that change our perception of their subjects for ever'.

Really? The reader, sifting through this slim and notably overpriced volume, which, despite its brevity, seems to have taken its author more than three years to write, might be forgiven for thinking that he has missed something. The dirt is there all right: by the time of Wells's death in 1946 he stands convicted of a politically incorrect attitude to women, rampant anti-Semitism, a belief in the value of eugenics as a solution to the world's population problems and a diverting collection of personal failings.

The slight drawback is that none of this can really be said to fall into the category of blinding revelation. There are some stern noises about H.G. being previously 'untouched by charges of anti-semitism', but those accusations were made by Orwell (and others) about half a century ago.

Wells's views on eugenics were given an airing in John Carey's *The Intellectuals and the Masses*, published last year, and if Coren had wanted an exposition of Wells's opinions of women, which might be summarized as 'I support your demand for liberty, now take your clothes off', he need only have looked at Peter Kemp's invaluable study *H. G. Wells and the Culminating Ape*, which is about 10 years old.

Paper tigers, then, tiptoeing through the long grass and trying to look fierce in the company of impressionable reviewers, and about as novel, at this stage in the proceedings, as the suggestion that Byron slept with his half-sister or that John Lennon took drugs. What, you might wonder, is the point of this debunking?

Like all those books about Dickens's mistreatment of his wife, *The Invisible Man* is written with the not quite deliberate assumption that bad behaviour on the part of the artist somehow extinguishes the value of his or her art. Mr Coren does not actually say in so many words that because H.G. Wells had disgusting views on the Jewish question his books are worthless, but the conviction lurks beneath all the pious references to the 'stain on his writing and his character that is indelible'.

This is a depressingly common assumption in current literary criticism. We had it recently with Philip Larkin, and now it seems we have to have it again with Wells. But it ought to be possible to acknowledge that a man can be a great novelist while simultaneously holding opinions that are anathema to the majority of civilized people. We may not like him for it, but they no more invalidate his work than, as Orwell put it, the second-best bed invalidates *Hamlet*.

Another clue to Coren's intentions comes in the book's queerly lopsided feel. The point about H.G. Wells is that he was the author of four or five of the finest social comedies in the language, a topic to which Mr Green devotes about three pages. As a political and social pundit – Coren's chief area of inquiry – he stops being interesting in about 1914. But it suits Mr Coren's purpose to ignore this. The result is a massively prejudicial work which, inevitably enough, adds hardly anything to our understanding of Wells or his achievement.

15 January 1993

Harpers and queenery

Serious Pleasures: The Life of Stephen Tennant **PHILIP HOARE**
(Hamish Hamilton)

THE Hon. Stephen Tennant – aesthete, recluse, dandy, homosexual and socialite – died at his home Wilsford Manor near Salisbury, early in 1987. Opened up and auctioned off, the house, which its owner had scarcely left during the previous decade, disclosed a 60-year-old timewarp, a treasure-trove of exquisite decoration, rococo artifice and gilded splendour. The cameras popped, the journalists chattered and at last, in death rather than in life, the Hon. Stephen found himself briefly famous.

He was that sort of man. It was, as Philip Hoare demonstrates in this long and meticulously researched biography, that sort of life. The Hon. Stephen was born in 1906, a scion of the fabulously wealthy Tennant family. His mother, who dressed him as a girl until the age of eight and referred to him as 'Steenie', detected evidence of his precocity in an early excursion to the garden. 'Oh,' said the four-year-old, catching sight of a burgeoning pansy, 'something's looking.' A bit later the Tennant children were lined up in front of their father, Lord Glenconner, and asked about their ambitions. 'I want to be a great beauty, sir,' the infant replied.

And after that, needless to relate, it was downhill all the way. Encouraged by his doting mamma, Steenie embraced artistic ambition and hypochondria in his early teens. At 14 he was eyeing up soldiers from the local army base. At 18 he was the most effulgent of the British Young Things. In his 20s, Lady Pamela having died suddenly, he inherited £15,000 a year and acquired Wilsford.

Already at this early stage the principal stanchions of his character were firmly in place: vanity (make-up, peroxide and long hours in front of the mirror); sloth (he started spending large parts of his life in bed in the late 1920s and never really broke the habit); and the ability to inspire affection in the wackier sort of period manhunter. 'I would gladly die for him,' remarked his most famous inamorato, Siegfried Sassoon (who later penned the memorable affirmation 'Oh Steenie I would promise to serve you to the end').

In characteristic fashion Sassoon was soon given the elbow. The ability to discard painlessly remained one of Steenie's most enduring talents: many years later he rewarded Hugo Vickers, who had contrived a reprint of his one commercially published work, by never communicating with him again.

The last 50 years of his baroque existence were spent in travel, in cultivating literary acquaintances, in writing an unfinished novel entitled *Lascar,* and in sleep. It would be satisfying to think that Philip Hoare has written a bad book about this saucy old heartbreaker, but in fact he has written a very good one, consulted all the right source material and brought in all manner of elegant period detail. And yet if ever a biography cried out not to be written it is this voluminous recitation of pouting, prancing and dressing up, all of it lavished on a subject who, as Lady Caroline Blackwood judiciously opines, 'was just an eccentric gay who didn't really do anything'.

Brian Howard. Cecil Beaton. Steenie ... We are fascinated by these people, these boys who should have been girls, these gilded triflers, these mincing social freaks, and the result is that our recent literary history – the literary history of the inter-war period – is nothing more than this spineless gossip, this magnification of non-existent talent.

The humblest coal miner who ever tried to write a sonnet is of more intrinsic literary – and social – interest than Steenie Tennant, but alas the toff hagiography strain of English letters endures. Like Vickers's life of Beaton this is a *Harpers* biography, in which the ability to design a pair of pyjamas somehow compensates for the want of any deeper human values.

It is not, perhaps, the Hon. Stephen's fault, and in fact you end up feeling rather sorry for someone who plainly never stood a chance. After all, to lie in bed for 60 years fingering your bibelots and indulging your vanity is your own affair. It is the 400-page biographies about you, the fawning *Tatler* articles and the elevation of this pansy posturing into something significant, that strikes the authentic note of moral disgust.

22 June 1990

Morgan grinder

Edwina Mountbatten: A Life of Her Own JANET MORGAN
(HarperCollins)

I N the relentless publicity of the past few weeks Janet Morgan has been speaking movingly, to anyone who'll listen, about the new man in her life,

Robert Bruce, Lord Balfour of Burleigh, a crossbench peer, 18 years her senior.

She chirruped away to *Harpers* that she has 'acquired a domestic life'. To Angela Lambert of *The Independent* she was more forthcoming. She does all her own and Robert's laundry and they have 'crisp sweet-smelling' fresh linen sheets on the bed everyday. A glance at page 154 of the biography reveals that Edwina Mountbatten too liked to sleep in linen sheets – 'a nightmare to launder' – though hers were also decorated with pink silk bows.

What Morgan appears to have omitted to tell anyone is that Lord Balfour has a wife, and that the revelations of the laundry cupboard are just another episode in her ceaseless campaign to embarrass and taunt the long-suffering Lady Balfour.

It certainly breathes new life into the old saying about washing your dirty linen in public. Publicizing your book is one thing, using your book to publicize your personal life is quite another. And therein lies the problem.

A biographer who identifies too closely with his or her subject is liable to produce a book that is self-promoting and awash with adulatory gush. Morgan is guilty on both counts in her official biography of Edwina Mountbatten. She tells you a great deal about the mad social whirl of the Bright Young Things of the Mountbatten set in the 1920s and 1930s, but remarkably little of any interest about the woman who became the last Vicereine of India in 1947.

When Morgan was asked to write about Edwina, she was apparently less than thrilled. As she confessed to Sally O'Sullivan (OBN) at *Harpers*, her first thoughts were whether she really wanted to spend 'valuable years' unravelling the life of a 'pleasure-loving socialite'. It comes as a considerable surprise therefore to find Morgan so intoxicated by high society that she can hardly bear to drag herself away from chronicling the antics of Edwina, husband Dickie, and their assorted friends, Bunny, Fruity, Poppy, Lola, Laddie.

The first half of this interminable read is little more than a blow-by-blow account of Edwina's social calendar with mind-fogging details of parties, royal tours, polo matches, interior decor, infidelities and wedding presents. The whole sticky confection is relayed in prose that owes something to the stylistic excesses of Elinor Glyn mixed with the slangy bravado of an Angela Brazil heroine (time simply 'whizzes' by, Edwina's 'a goody-goody', and Dickie's 'happy as a lark').

Morgan's *Agatha Christie* (1984), her only other biography, is similarly clogged with superfluous detail. But at least she forced herself to get to grips with the compelling mystery at the centre of Christie's life, her 10-day disappearance in 1926. Here she conveniently sidesteps the controversial issues. The famous allegations accusing Edwina of having had an affair with Paul Robeson are rebutted with the word 'piffle' and the not very convincing argument that we must take on trust Edwina's statement in her diary that she'd never met him. Yet Edwina was a proven liar – in her diary and elsewhere – and the other sources which suggest rather the reverse should at least receive a proper airing (as they did in Duberman's recent life of Robeson).

Just as telling is Morgan's handling of the friendship between Edwina and Jawaharlal Nehru, on which so much of the hype surrounding the book has centred. The strong likelihood is that she is correct in her assumption that the relationship was platonic. But her failure even to examine any of the evidence to the contrary (for instance that of Russi Mody, son of the governor of Uttar Pradesh, who once came upon them in passionate embrace) leads one to question her standards of impartiality.

She makes the fatal error of taking Edwina almost entirely at her own estimation, and rarely attempts to see her from any perspective other than her own. Nor does she bring any interpretative skills to bear on her mass of material. This becomes glaringly obvious in the second half of the book when, without explanation from Morgan, Edwina suddenly metamorphoses from pleasure-loving socialite into a nun-like figure worthy of canonization, endlessly visiting troops and hospitals.

The nagging question which remains after finishing this book is how anyone capable of producing it could have risen to the dizzy heights that Morgan has achieved. She has been, among other things, a Visiting Fellow of All Souls, a member of the policy review staff at the Cabinet Office, and a special adviser to the director-general of the BBC.

Morgan's impressive qualifications clearly recommended her to Edwina's daughters, though they may now be wringing their hands over the anodyne portrait of their mother she has produced. Alternatively, that may be precisely what they wanted.

5 July 1991

Toadying the line

Margaret Thatcher: The First Ten Years LADY OLGA MAITLAND
(Sidgwick & Jackson)
Margaret Thatcher: The Woman Within ANDREW THOMSON
(W H Allen)

YOU might think there were already enough hagiographies of the PM to be going on with – those by Tricia Murray, George Gardiner, Russell Lewis and Penny Junor to name but four. Does even the most adoring disciple want to read more?

Yes, according to Messrs Snipcock & Tweed. And so here is the fragrant doyenne herself, Lady Olga Maitland, to help us celebrate the great anniversary. 'On 4 May 1989,' according to her breathless introduction, 'flowers, congratulations and tributes flowed into No 10 Downing Street. All day the famous shiny black door of No 10 opened and shut to well-wishers celebrating a decade of Mrs Margaret Thatcher's premiership.' Not bad going for a book that was already printed and despatched to the shops by 4 May 1989.

Prediction is a risky business; but in Lady Olga's case it is no more hazardous than writing accurately about the past. Chapter One of her slim volume transports us back a decade to a dinner on 3 May 1979, the eve of the general election. 'Mrs Thatcher was told that the latest poll placed her one point behind Neil Kinnock. There was a pregnant pause before she said, "I don't believe that."' As well she might, since the leader of the Labour Party at the time was Jim Callaghan.

Facts are stupid things, as Lady Olga's great friend Ronald Reagan once put it. (Incidentally, her dust-jacket biog. reveals that 'she is one of the only British, non-political figures to hold an audience with both President Reagan at the White House and the Pope'. It adds that she stood in 1987 as Conservative candidate for Bethnal Green – in a non-political spirit, presumably.) Facts are also tiresome things, since ladies of a certain rank cannot be expected to do their own research and it's so difficult to get staff these days.

Thus Margaret Thatcher became leader of the Conservative Party on 'a fateful day in 1974'. (Only one year out: a good effort.) In 1989 Carol Thatcher is 'now 27'. (Nine years out: rather a wild stab.) Mrs Thatcher said 'Rejoice!' after the recapture of Port Stanley. (South Georgia actually; still, right side of the world.) Mark Thatcher is 'handsome'. (Come off it.) And then there is this charmingly unintentional destruction of the official account of the Gibraltar killings: 'The terrorists were stopped in their tracks. The opposition cried that they should have been simply arrested – why kill them? The Government response was that in essence these people had been shooting to kill innocent people for years. They had to be judged and dealt with in their own manner.' Er, not quite.

And then there is her ladyship's own brief appearance in the pageant of history, reported with customary accuracy: 'One-sided nuclear disarmament was such an affront to the sensibilities of the average Englishman that it was hardly surprising that when I set up the Women for Defence (later to be known as Families for Defence) it was swept along on a tide of nationwide support.'

But for most of the book the doyenne is modestly prepared to step back and let Margaret take the credit for saving Britain. 'The nation has almost become a wider extension of her family,' we learn. 'Margaret Thatcher has always taken the time to confront issues, whether they be personal or national. A thought is spared for anything that affects people – for people make up a nation. She has extended a hand across the nation for one reason alone – she cares.' Kleenex, anyone?

But, just when Olga seems to have won the Order of the Brown Nose outright, here comes a late challenger ... Andrew Thomson was Thatcher's constituency agent in Finchley in the early 1980s. Now he has decided to tell all.

'Margaret Thatcher is blessed with an exceptional level of brain-power,' he daringly reveals. She is also 'a living example of the neighbourly and charitable ideal which she urges on the nation.' Few people know this, however, because 'she shuns publicity for her charitable work'. She is oddly shy of publicizing other virtues, too. Although her childhood teddy has appeared in exhibitions, according to Thomson, 'what is not so well known is her affection for small, cuddly and live animals. Only once has she been publicly photographed with a dog.' Thomson found this modesty deeply frustrating. 'Clearly, I wanted everyone in the constituency to see their MP as the warm-hearted woman she can be and not as the heartless virago some sections of the media had made her.' But she wouldn't let him.

12 May 1989

Ape shit

The Passion of John Aspinall BRIAN MASTERS (Cape)

> The Tiger, on the other hand, is kittenish and mild,
> He makes a pretty playfellow for any little child;
> And mothers of large families (who claim to common sense)
> Will find a Tiger well repays the trouble and expense.
> (Hilaire Belloc, Cautionary Verses)

Aggressive people have aggressive pets. Your average urban thug keeps a brace of Alsatians. John Aspinall, being more than averagely thuggish and having plenty of acres at his disposal, maintains a large menagerie of tigers, wolves and gorillas.

His thuggery is largely philosophical. He believes that humans are 'vermin'. He favours a policy of 'beneficial genocide'. He wants the population of Britain reduced from 58 million to 18 million. He also advocates 'a right-wing counter-revolution, Franco-esque in spirit and determination'.

'Aspers' has certainly done his bit for population control. In August 1980, one of his staff, Brian Stocks, was killed by a tiger. A month later another employee met the same fate. In 1984 yet another young keeper died in action on the Aspinall estate; this time the culprit was a bull elephant. Only 39,999,997 to go.

There have been plenty of close shaves. A gorilla bit into a vet's arm, piercing an artery. A wolf leapt at the throat of Aspinall's mother. Robin Birley had part of his face bitten off by a tiger in 1970; he was disfigured for life. A year earlier, a 19-year-old model called Merilyn Lamb had her right arm torn to shreds by one of Aspinall's tigers.

Aspinall's whole theory of zoo-keeping is that tigers and other wild animals are really kittenish and mild. No matter how many people are killed or maimed, he goes on believing it. To quote Brian Masters: 'The confirmation of the belief that the terrifying tiger and the fierce, intractable gorilla were nothing of the sort, that their decency could be relied upon, and that he could commune with them on a level which was hitherto inconceivable, touched reserves of tenderness and humility in John Aspinall which, one suspects, are a latent part of human character rarely called upon in lives divorced from contact with other primates.'

As this passage suggests, Masters is a graduate of the Arslikhan school of biography. In his preface he claims that, though he is an admirer of Aspers, he has shunned hagiography and summoned a 'degree of objectivity'. Only a few pages later, however, he tells us that even as a child Aspinall's super-human qualities were evident. When a swarm of wasps descended on a family picnic, everyone fled – except for young John, who 'remained, unperturbed and fearless, as the wasps whizzed and buzzed around him, some even settling upon him. They did him no harm.' While he was still a youth Aspers was seen 'lifting a huge trunk of ancient wood which three men together could not budge'.

And so it continues, for more than 350 pages. Unpleasant facts are lightly skipped over or ignored altogether. There is no mention of his outstanding meanness to his ex-wife Jane, mother of his first two children. Many of his seedier friends – such as Greek gambler Taki – are omitted from the story. Those who can't be neglected entirely are treated with great discretion. Jimmy Goldsmith, for instance, 'wants to improve society and seeks to do so with financial strength' – which is one way of putting it.

What of Lord Lucan? Masters is predictably incurious. 'Aspinall behaved throughout the investigation like one of his great Zulu heroes, discreet, honourable, firm and unyielding,' Masters writes. 'The rest he would consider to be nobody's business but Lucan's.' It is certainly not Masters' business. But the faithful amanuensis does let slip one revelation, perhaps accidentally. Some weeks before the murder, Lucan had told Aspinall's mother that he wanted to kill his wife. 'She had replied to the effect that he must do whatever he thought was right.' Jolly big of her.

But Masters makes nothing of this. Instead he spends most of the book on his knees. Aspinall's generosity, his tenderness, his humility are all hymned at length. And his absurd book, *The Best of Friends*, is treated as the masterpiece of our age, displaying 'the elegance and sophistication of Bertrand Russell, without his paralysing inhibitions'.

To prove the point Masters quotes one sentence from Aspinall's book: 'The thongs of affection that bind the gorilla are hidden in his fur.' Here is Masters' verdict on this little *aperçu*: 'The subtle alliteration and metric balance of this sentence give it power and poetry. There are many such. This is the language of a man who is still in awe.' Pseuds' Corner here we come.

27 May 1988

Sick characters who found their author

The Shrine of Jeffrey Dahmer BRIAN MASTERS (Hodder)

'IT's just a sick, pathetic, wretched, miserable life story, that's all it is. How it can help anyone, I've no idea.' So Jeffrey Dahmer, the Milwaukee mass-murderer, said about himself after he'd been caught.

Brian Masters begs to differ. He just loves Dahmer's story – loves it to bits. As a dupe of that crank Colin Wilson, Masters believes that Dahmer, like other murderers, has much to teach us. He believes, in fact, that Dahmer – murderer, necrophile and cannibal – could show the rest of us a few things. 'Dahmer's crimes permitted him to act, for a moment, at a higher level of intensity than is given to ordinary folk with ordinary joys,' he says admiringly on the one hand, patronizingly on the other.

The Shrine of Jeffrey Dahmer is an interesting book, although not quite in the way Masters intended it. For what we have here is not so much an analysis of a pathology, as a collision between two pathologies – Masters', as well as Dahmer's. The text that has resulted is best viewed as itself an exhibit, the product of warped thinking by its author as well as its subject, a sort of long-range *folie-à-deux*.

Ghoulish accounts of murder have always been popular, of course. There's no mystery about it. Heads turn eagerly as people drive slowly by the site of a car wreck or a plane crash. But Masters doesn't accept that he is part of that gross trade.

As a howling snob, he used to write books about duchesses (literally), you see. Then along came Dennis Nilsen. Masters pathetically says that what first attracted him to Nilsen was that, when he was sent for trial, he seemed to be carrying a copy of the complete works of Shakespeare. A Hintellectual! Well worth a biography, then.

'I treated it just as I treated the Duchess of Devonshire,' he has claimed, 'as just another job of work.' Actually what had attracted him was the nature of Nilsen's crimes. Masters showed startling empathy with Nilsen's feelings, as he kept corpses of his victims for 'company'. Had Nilsen murdered girls, rather than boys, he would doubtless not have been so fascinated. It's to Masters' credit that *Killing for Company* is nonetheless a relatively restrained and balanced production.

Masters' own muddled preoccupations came to light when, five years later, he published a painful little memoir called *Gary*, about his own attempt to keep a boy with him. He had adopted a 13-year-old delinquent he had met in the street, with charitable intentions but also for his own satisfaction, 'taking on the exquisite exhilarating enchantment of responsibility for a young life without having worked for it'. The relationship came to grief.

No analogy between this benevolent enterprise and Nilsen's ghastly crimes seems to have occurred to him, even though he quotes himself saying pompously to some suspicious education inspectors: 'Were there no homosexual element in my emotional furniture it is doubtful that I would have noticed the boy at all. I invite you to consider that you might be glad to acknowledge the unheralded benefits of a homophilic trait . . .'

Were there no homosexual element in Masters' emotional furniture, it is doubtful he would have noticed Jeffrey Dahmer at all. As it is, he has written here an account of his life and deeds that is systematically biased in Dahmer's favour and against everybody else: his parents, the police, judges, lawyers, psychiatrists. Again and again, his words betray his real sympathies, his deep identification with Dahmer. It's a cacophony of wrong notes.

When Dahmer had already committed his first murder and a day or two later masturbates over the victim's severed head, Masters writes lyrically: 'As he stood there, moving his hand towards the artificial restoration of peace, the boy of 18 in a solitary house in the quiet Ohio countryside took his first step towards madness.' When Dahmer does disgusting things, Masters takes care to describe them as favourably as possible. 'Dismemberment was unpleasant and messy, but it was the only practical option open to him.' That's all right then! When Dahmer molests a corpse, Masters calls it a 'cuddle'. When Dahmer describes himself as 'thoroughly corrupt and evil', Masters protests. 'Perhaps the tiniest chink of light still danced upon his soul from time to time,' he suggests winsomely.

Masters' expressions of horror are reserved for Dahmer's prosecutors. After conviction, American law allowed one relative of each man to express his or her feelings to the judge in open court before sentence was passed. Masters is repelled by this, as he has never been by Dahmer's atrocities. 'Barbaric,' he calls it, a 'rough medieval spectacle', 'this hurtful charade', 'this distasteful exercise', 'it is surprising that it should be tolerated,' he chides.

Throughout he has relied on Dahmer's own version, as though he were trustworthy, and omitted much that is unflattering. A glance at one of the downmarket versions of the story, *Jeffrey Dahmer* by Dr Joel Norris (Constable), shows that Dahmer was a vicious racist, which may have something to do with the fact that nearly all his victims were black. But there's no mention of this in Masters, just as he edits out Dahmer's most repulsive deeds, murmuring 'the reader will be spared relentless repetition of these increasingly tragic events'.

Trying to reassure himself, Masters repeatedly maintains that the predilection Dahmer and Nilsen shared for dead bodies is not so abnormal. It's all a matter of differences of degree, not of kind, he insists. 'The desire to behave in a necrophilic manner is far more widespread than most people will care to admit,' he believes. 'There are brothels in Paris wherein the whore will obligingly make herself up to look corpse-like and lie in a coffin waiting to be ravaged; such places do not want for customers,' he reports knowledgeably. 'Less overt is the man who asks his wife to "play dead" and keep quiet while he performs the act of love without her assistance; I know some happily married women who are pleased to gratify their spouses in this way and simply be "taken".'

Speak for yourself, Brian. But then, you have, haven't you?

26 February 1993

9

MEMOIRS

A bouquet of forget-me-nots

Roald Rat

Going Solo ROALD DAHL (Jonathan Cape)

*I*N gratitude for the heaps of money he has made them, publishers have been pulling out the publicity stops for the 70th birthday and 26th book of Roald Dahl. Like some monstrous Merlin, kept alive by bees' jelly, the gaunt old misanthrope has peered at us from full-page ads, colour supplements and TV screens. Perhaps he will never die.

Few would deny that inside this balding head lies the most revolting imagination at work in literature today. Dahl's stories appeal to the instincts that draw a crowd at traffic accidents, and even his books for children have an unpleasant streak. Fat people, ugly people, smelly people, old or cross or boring people come to gruesome ends. All peculiarities are mocked with the cruelty of the school playground. Dahl encourages the skinhead inside every child yet his books are blatant propaganda for his own banal middle-class preferences. It is not a pretty mixture.

Consider the fate of the four unlucky children in *Charlie and the Chocolate Factory* (2 million copies sold). Augustus eats too much, Veruca is spoiled by her wealthy parents, Violet chews American gum, Mike Teavee watches too much TV. All of them get their comeuppance, whereas Charlie, the son of a poor industrial worker, inherits the Wonka sweet factory. Although called Oompa-loompas, the dwarfish slaves from the land of the cacao bean have been given white skins by the illustrator, which leaves the average SDP mother with only one correction to make. 'Goodnight, darling. Just don't forget sweets are bad for your teeth. That's something Mr Dahl forgot to mention.'

What kind of man is this author? What past has shaped such a mind? One approaches his autobiography with something like fright. Perhaps, when you poke inside him, Roald Dahl will disintegrate into palpitating gore like the humanoid robots now rampant in the cinema.

But the truth is sadder than that. *Going Solo* is a very good read. In this second volume of his memoirs Dahl covers his early manhood in Kenya and his exploits as a fighter pilot during the war. The book is short, vivid and powerful. Every page is gripping. His encounters with snakes in Africa, his near-fatal crash in the Western Desert, the desperate aerial dogfights in Greece – all this is brilliantly told.

Brilliantly, but not movingly: that's the peculiar thing. The book takes a while to shake off the nudge-nudge, exaggerated style he uses when talking to children. The colonial types on his ship are mocked with post-imperial hindsight, and there is a goody-goody note in his guilt about the killing of Germans, which doesn't stop him dwelling on the details: 'It was a horrible sight. His head seemed to splash open and little soft bits of grey stuff flew out in all directions . . .'

But these faults are left behind as the air war rises in his memory. From then on we get the true Dahl, talking straight. In an honest endeavour to record the most searing experiences of his life he tells us about Mary Welland, the nurse who cared for him after his crash, and about David Coke, the brave man who flew at his side in Greece. This is where we should be moved. But we're not. These good people never come to life. Dahl's account, although vivid, is strangely short of warmth, laughter, pity or companionship. One is left with the clear impression of a courageous man but a cold one.

Did he change at that time, or was he always the same? Hard to say. But the war, it seems, left a hole in Roald Dahl's head which was never filled up again with ordinary human emotions. Only nightmares float into that vacuum; only children escape his disgust. Like other good commercial products, the master of horror was made in Germany.

19 September 1986

Arts Council rant

Giving It Away: Memoirs of an Uncivil Servant CHARLES OSBORNE
(Secker & Warburg)

O z-BORN he was, in 1927, but his memoirs have it that real life only began on arrival in this country, after 25 years of sexlessly roaming the gay bars of Brisbane and Melbourne. Over the next four years he was repeatedly sacked from stints as life-class model, chorus boy, bookshop assistant, cinema commissionaire and Meridian underwear rep, till his glad eye lit on a windowcard: BOY REQD – GIVE ASS ONLY. Oz burst in to find himself in the fur-lined HQ of the *London Magazine*, being eyed in turn by the last of the Bloomsbury groupies, John Lehmann (pronounced *Layman*), who took him on instantly.

When Alan Ross bought the *LM* in 1961, Osborne was retained as his role escalated from Ed. Ass. to Ass. Ed. Then in 1966, at the first of many long free lunches subscribed by unwitting taxpayers, Oz was engaged as Ass. Director to the nation's Literature Dept. And after serving three years of lunch in this capacity, it was over another that he was appointed full-time Director.

Osborne's account of his Arts Council decades is like the Watergate tapes edited by Nixon, an impression reinforced by smarmy mug-shots of himself with cronies and aides, and a Checkers-like one with a glum-looking dog captioned: *Charles & Asta at home.*

It's certainly been a dog's life for the literary community in this charlie's reign. He coyly admits the main service rendered by the department under his thumb was to himself and his chums – Ross, Karl Miller, Ian Hamilton, C. James. *London Mag* enjoyed no Arts Council backing till Oz left it to join the Arts Council – since when it's had £309,080. Miller's *London Review of Books* has had £203,500, Hammerhead's *New Review* £193,438. All the co-editors of these journals played musical chairs on Ozborne's 'Advisory Panels' and regularly voted themselves the lion's shares.

Despite eroding far more public money than all other magazines they have continued to bomb hopelessly on the open market. *New Review* threw in the towel after four years of proving incapable of giving itself away. Oz blames its demise on the *Eye*'s alleged campaign 'to club the review to death'. The truth is that no mag was ever writ down but by itself. The reading public wanted no truck with such a load of old pseudery. Osborne calls himself a poet but finds 'something sordid in adopting poetry as a profession'. Odd, considering that his pretension to the slightest literary repute hangs on the coat-tails of Auden, the superpro poet of the century, a version of whose life Oz cooked up as soon as he'd died.

He calls Auden his friend, though the old boy made it quite clear that he'd consider anyone attempting a biography his sworn worst enemy. Equally oddly, he's also invoked in Ozborne's *Letter to W.H. Auden* as telling the author to 'take it from your old mother' – who is herself quoted to the effect that her brat's verse is 'a dreadful curse: / As a poet you're a failure'. Oz proceeds to rhyme this Clive Jamsily with 'I'm gunna hail yer', indicating how kind Gavin Ewart was being when he called such doggerel 'Pretty Terrible'.

Osborne blusters and snaps about how absurd it's been for poets whose work doesn't sell to expect AC subsidy, and how thrifty he's been to block travel and book applications from hundreds of writers. He wrote in *The Listener* (12 April 1984) 'I have always assumed I was the one author who could never obtain a grant from the Council' – yet this avowed non-professional's slim volume was one of the few whose appearance (from Calder, a month or two after this confidence) was blessed with the statutory flyleaf ta-very-much for being 'subsidised by the ACGB'. He was, likewise, one of the few constantly sent on poetry and speaking tours, courtesy the self-same sources.

Oz cites Lehmann's observation that he 'never made a move that was not precisely calculated well in advance', and we can now see, with hindsight, how artfully he engineered the removal of his own ill-tended beds from the monetarist Glories of the Garden. The 'weedkiller' resolution of 1984, that literature no longer needed a full-time staff, was a transparent cover-up to save the faces of Osborne and the Council, albeit at the expense of his entire department.

Sacking him would have admitted what a bummer they'd had in the saddle, so a ludicrous phasing out of literature as barely fundable was the bureaucratic premise by which this director's 20 years' militant inertia could be smoothed into retirement at last.

Osborne's career and this account of it are a triumph of civil defence. He doesn't mention that when he first took office the allocation for literature stood at 1% of the AC budget. He's left it at less than 0.4% – £500,000 out of £135,000,000! – but made sure he left with a golden handshake of at least £20,000.

His ultimate failure is the uncivility and disservice to real vocation, initiative and imagination. He's been civil to a few pals, given little away and taken a whole lot home.

His book keeps telling the reader what a great wag he is, but what Oz seems to think both astute and hilarious are would-be 'civilized' *aperçus* such as, 'If two-thirds of the poets now writing dropped dead, the loss to literature would not be great.' It's unlikely that his nibs could identify 0.4% of working poets. Nevertheless, he clearly considers himself a literary antique to be preserved at all costs. The recent overpraise of these heavily retouched reminiscences by the incestuous literary establishment will no doubt help.

23 January 1987

Redgrave digging

A Family & Its Fortunes RACHEL KEMPSON, LADY REDGRAVE
(Duckworth)

THE blurb, fatuously, declares that the author 'shows here that she is a born writer'. What the book shows is that Messrs Duckworth lack a proof-reader and an editor who knows anything about the theatre. The mystery is who persuaded Rachel Kempson to write this strangely self-deprecatory autobiography, and what the motive was.

The names that are dropped in theatrical memoirs clang in on cue: Noel, Binkie, Larry, Peggy, the lot. There's also the occasional writer: 'Another guest was Evelyn Waugh, whom I found it interesting to meet as I had read many of his books.'

The problem is that, in spite of the artlessness of her prose, Lady Redgrave comes across as a rather good person with a genuine talent who utterly lacks belief in herself. Her family and friends are lucky in her, but it is not certain whether she is lucky in them.

In 1934, her second season at Stratford, Rachel Kempson played Ariel, Olivia, the Princess of France, Titania, Hero and Juliet. She was in her early 20s, and had played the last two the previous season as well. A year later she found herself acting opposite the handsome Michael Redgrave in Liverpool, and soon they were married.

His family, however, thought her an indifferent actress, and a friend opined woundingly that Edith Evans should play Juliet opposite Mike instead. Redgrave didn't demur, and Rachel wondered, as well she might have done, about the future of the marriage, before they'd even reached the altar.

It wasn't long before Redgrave had a far from clandestine affair with Edith Evans, Rachel being the last to realize. Still, there's no business like show business and Edith became great friends with her ex-lover's wife.

The two actresses were soon walking the Redgrave's eldest daughter, Vanessa, aged 18 months, in her pram together. At one point the future Workers' Revolutionary Party member had what her mother describes as a 'black rage'. 'Wallop her, Rachel,' said Edith Evans, 'wallop her and I'll stand by and witness you only did it in kindness.' As in most memoirs in which she appears, Dame Edith comes across as an appalling harridan.

Before they were married, Redgrave had qualms about marrying her too. 'He said that there were difficulties in his nature and that he felt he ought not to marry.'

The truth is that bisexuality is the natural condition of a lot of actors, and the more good-looking the thespian is, the more he's prone to it. Lady Redgrave tactfully doesn't name any of Mike's male lovers, instead concentrating on her own amours: a brief affair with actor Leo Genn, and a long-standing one with another actor, 'Tom', presumably still alive, married and thus not to be named.

Her parents' marriage was a miserable affair (her father was headmaster of Dartmouth College) and so was hers. Daughter Vanessa's marriage to Tony Richardson didn't last.

Later Vanessa declined to marry Franco Nero, the father of one of her children. Corin and his wife Deirdre (who has published a book on life with the Redgraves) split up when Corin joined the Workers' Revolutionary Party.

The family clearly has little fortune in love though plenty in the business. The children grew up in the 1950s and 1960s and rapidly established theatrical careers of their own, whilst Rachel was a founder member of the English Stage Company, and returned memorably to the Court in 1972 in John Osborne's *A Sense of Detachment* when she was howled at by the audience for taking her knickers off and reading out pornography.

Michael Redgrave died in 1985 of Parkinson's Disease, and Rachel became a national figure as Lady Manners in *The Jewel in the Crown*.

Meanwhile she became a grandmother ten times over and the dynasty seems set to continue.

Vanessa's daughter Natasha Richardson has just been acclaimed a star for her performance in *High Society*, and her sister Joely is about to have her first London season with the RSC. Jemma, Corin's eldest child, has already left LAMDA.

It will be depressing if they emerge in as peculiar a light as their relatives do in this odd autobiography.

3 April 1987

Jim slips

Time and Chance JAMES CALLAGHAN (Collins)

*F*LEET Street literary editors are not an imaginative bunch. One could predict with total accuracy whom they would choose to review the Stoker's memoirs.

Sure enough, every clapped-out social democrat of yesteryear has been wheeled out to praise Jim as the last of the Great Ones. It has been like listening to the speeches at a retirement dinner. Even the Queen has lent a hand by timing his knighthood to coincide with publication.

Callaghan expects nothing less. He is used to having a respectful audience for his every dunderheaded utterance. After all, as we are continually reminded, Jimbo was the first person to occupy the four great offices of state – Chancellor, Home Secretary, Foreign Secretary and Prime Minister.

What tends to be forgotten is that in each of these jobs he was a miserable failure.

He spent his period as Chancellor, 1964–67, pointlessly and damagingly resisting devaluation. Between 1967 and 1970 he made a strong attempt to outdo even Henry Brooke as the most nasty and brutish Home Secretary in living memory. As Foreign Secretary, from 1974 to 1976, he was unable to do anything that might not please his adored Henry Kissinger. (*Vide* his catastrophic inaction over the American-backed Cyprus coup in 1974.)

With this dismal record behind him, he was a fitting successor to Harold Wilson as Prime Minister. For three years he staggered from crisis to crisis, ludicrously chanting 'steady as she goes'. The electorate, eventually given the chance to ditch him, seized it.

So what has he got to say in his defence? 'Memory is a capricious companion,' he babbles in the first sentence of his autobiography, *Time and Chance*, a book that is as achingly dull as the title promises. 'Like the wind of St John's Gospel, "It bloweth where it listeth, and thou hearest the sound thereof, but cannot tell whence it cometh."' (*Get on with it – Ed.*)

What this means is that he has chosen to omit – or 'forget' – rather a lot. He doesn't mention his controversial involvement with Julian Hodge's Commercial Bank of Wales (see 1970s *Eyes passim*) and the Italian International Bank. He doesn't mention that in 1969 he caused parliamentary uproar and gave the English language a new word – 'Callamandering' – by delaying boundary changes until after the general election. He doesn't mention that as Foreign Secretary he had to fly to Kampala and abase himself before Idi Amin. Strangely, he doesn't even mention that until the age of about 30 he was called Len rather than Jim.

Even with the events that he does mention, his version is shamelessly, bottomlessly, memory-bogglingly incomplete and dishonest. One can amuse oneself by filling in the gaps. For instance, Callaghan's account of a ministerial colleague at the Foreign Office states simply: 'I asked Harold for

Joan Lester, a great-hearted soul with a following on the left of the party, who would never fail to be my conscience ... It was a good team. Later, to my regret, Joan resigned.'

The mis-spelling of Lestor's surname is the least of his inaccuracies. Her role as his 'conscience' looks rather different when you remember Callaghan's sneering comment to a group of civil servants just after her appointment (although, needless to say, you won't find this in the book): 'Miss Lestor's to be our conscience in this department. And we all know what we do with our consciences, don't we?'

His onion-induced tears at Lestor's 'resignation' are even more ridiculous. She did not resign: she was transferred to the Department of Education and Science, *at Callaghan's instigation*. When she asked why she was being given the push, Jim told her: 'You see, my dear, the trouble is that I like to have people around me who are *friends* of mine.'

Indeed. And luckily for him they have all been asked to review his wretched book.

1 May 1987

Pain in the artz

One in Four MICHAEL KUSTOW (Chatto & Windus)

HERE at last we have what we have so long wanted: a worthy sequel to that classic of British letters, *Sir Peter Hall's Hot Dinners 1972–1980*. Yes, *One in Four*, Pooterishly subtitled 'A Year in the Life of a Channel Four Commissioning Editor', is another Artz Administrator's Diary. And it's a killer.

A moment's reflection will warn that anyone treating the world to their recent journal is unlikely to be doing so as an exercise in humility. But nothing prepares the reader for Kustow.

He has wisely not attempted to compete with Sir Peter on the ingestion front. Though meals are recorded – occurring quite correctly in such places as Le Caprice, L'Escargot, La Coupole, the Groucho Club, and 'a restaurant on 43rd and Broadway that tries to ape *La Coupole*' – he barely mentions what he ate. Nor has he tried to outdo Hall on conferences, congresses and impressive trips abroad, clocking up just the decent minimum over the year: New York, Paris, Brussels, Paris again, Venice, Tel Aviv, New York again, Salzburg, Paris again, Lucca, Paris again, Berlin, New York again, Paris again, Stockholm.

Instead he has wisely concentrated his energies on the one area where he knows himself to be in with a chance: simple conceit. Speaking well of himself is what he does best. Not many people have the nerve to describe themselves as 'tigerish', do they? And he's been tremendously disciplined about it. Not much else gets in here at all.

Kustow is the Channel Four Artz Editor, the man responsible for bringing you such delectable *bonnes bouches* as dancer Michael Clark's bare bottom and poet Tony Harrison's bad language. He it was who saw that Dante had messed up by making the *Divine Comedy* a poem, when it should so obviously have been a cartoon video in 34 parts. From the Channel's first days, he has most doughtily done his part in 'keeping the door open to the third world, women, gays, structuralist film-makers, late Jean-Luc Godard, miners, neighbourhood oral history'.

The route to greatness was direct: after Golders Green and Oxford, the RSC, the ICA, the NT, and finally recruitment by Jeremy Isaacs. The dates are what matter. It was in 1967 that he became director of the ICA. Kustow is 1960s Man in its purest surviving strain (with beard). Everything he has produced at C4 testifies to this and the immaculate decade is invoked on every page of this book. Artz persons get no higher praise from Kustow than that he knows them from the 1960s – unless it is that he knows them from the inner sanctum, the very holy of holies, the calendar year 1968.

As he puts it, with rich period illiteracy: '1968 in its broadest meaning was more than politics in the traditional sense'. It was when people like Buckminster ('Bucky') Fuller explained that 'most of the world's political, social and cultural problems could be solved by better design and information-sharing'. In other words, by Channel Four.

Others may have forgotten this great truth, but not Kustow. And if people don't want what's good for them, why that, as he explains again and again, is only because people have 'latent needs', needs that they don't even know they have until they are told about them – the need, for example, for a nine-hour stage version of the Sanskrit epic poem *The Mahabharata*. 'Let's try to wrong-foot people into illumination,' he wages.

Kustow would, of course, be awfully disappointed if people did know what they needed, because then he wouldn't know better, would he? And he does, you see. I mean, it's still a counter-culture, isn't it? And he and his friends are embattled worker-heroes, aren't they? 'Street people against the clubmen.'

Lunching with Melvyn Barg, he remarks on how they're both outsiders: 'He a northerner, me a Jew – together at the same Oxford college.' So there you are. Never mind that the entire TV arts establishment consists of such people now, a bunch of cronies going round and round like goldfish – from Mr Michael what-I-think-you're-trying-to-say-is Ignatieff with his talk of 'thrusts, insights, passions', and Ms Marina Warner with her 'women's symbolic inheritance' dinner party, to the magnificent Farrukh Dhondy who tellingly remarks that Britain is '*essentially* democratic, man – not just bourgeois democracy. Look at the way our secretaries shout at us!'

These are the people who would share the anguish caused by a nightmare Kustow describes. In the dreams he has arranged to meet a few friends – you know, Sam Shepard, Harold Pinter, and their wives – at the Groucho Club. But when they get there it is in South London and 'instead of looking like a chic Italian hotel' it looks like the Athenaeum.

But, incredible as it sounds, I'm afraid that, just as this book was published, Mr Kustow woke up in the middle of something even worse. Channel Four has been taken over by Michael Grade (without beard). This long and revolting CV will avail him nothing. If Grade takes the trouble to read it carefully it will rather speed Kustow on his way, for it is the testament of a man who, despite all the trendy artworks he has sat through, is quite without taste – as is shown by the idiotic way he has written one chapter backwards 'like a rewinding video' and another in dialogue 'like a script'. In fact his only real appreciation of the artz is as a means of self-projection.

He describes a Picasso self-portrait: 'He produces his hand from where his nose should be, hooks his palette round what might just as well be a big toe as a thumb, and hangs his prick from God knows where.' His comment? 'It's just the way I feel.'

Fair enough, eh?

11 December 1987

The braying fields of Eton

Eton Voices DANNY DANZIGER (Viking)

*V*OICES we don't get, of course. What we have is a book of transcripts. Danziger has taped 42 Etonians talking about Eton and done his best to make their ramblings readable. He has not had much luck.

Edited transcripts of tapes can be made works of art. There are two masters of this craft: Studs Terkel and Tony Parker. What they produce stands comparison with any fiction, calling upon comparable skills. The interviewer both has to conduct the interview without his presence distorting what the interviewee says, and then to edit the mess of speech into the formality of the page. This is not as easy as you'd think; certainly not as easy as Danziger thinks.

Danziger's previous effort in this field was called *All in a Day's Work*. That consisted of 50 people (including a prostitute, you bet) banging on about their jobs. It was like being cornered by 50 bores at the same time, quite apart from being a rip-off of a good book called *Working* by Studs Terkel.

Now he has got Etonians to reminisce. Not too difficult, you might think, rather like buying an alcoholic a drink; and a good way to get a book written (or at least dictated) for you by other people – people more famous than you are – at no cost. All you need to do is take aim and jab your finger at your Sony. If you hit the red button, you're there.

So the colour mags – whence Danziger emerged – believe. It's why we get all those back pages in which people tell you how they walk the dog before breakfast, which then consists of two rather than three pieces of toast. It's cheap copy, the tiny difficulty being that it's also unreadable.

For the written word does somehow tend to be better written than the spoken word transcribed. Assuming, that is, you can write. Danziger can't.

His sole contribution to this volume is a brief introduction, more than half of which consists of reprinted quotes from the rest of the book. The little that remains goes like this: 'There's a sense of England about Eton ... At the same time there is something very un-English about Eton ...' Marvellous.

His final thought on the justice or not of the school's existence is that 'children of all backgrounds' should be equipped with Etonian values: 'Why should optimism and self-confidence be the preserve of the wealthy or well-connected?' Why? Why? Now there's a hard one, eh? Worthy of the SDP in its heyday.

As for the Etonians themselves, they are dismally predictable, for Danziger can't edit either. They all say it's the best school; they dream about it; there was homosexuality. Moreover they talk about things in the same order, beginning with why they went there ('genetically this was correct ... my family have been going to Eton, every male member, since 1745,' says the Hon. Nicholas Monson) and ending with what it did to them ('the only thing Eton left me with was that I rather like boyish women now, and I rather like bums,' says Derek Malcolm) and whether they would send their own children there (yes).

Plainly Danziger was ticking set questions off a card. Though these questions are never given, his half of the conversation is readily inferred from the inanity of the answers. Even Etonians – who are distinguished from the rest of us mainly by the importance they attribute to Eton – must balk at reading through this lot, even Nicholas Coleridge, the shiny-head editor of *Harpers & Queen*, who says he is ten times more interested in Etonians than in anyone else.

He puts it like this: 'There are certain people who weren't there, and I do admit that in some strange way I think, "Now, why weren't they?" And I know that in some awful way it counts against them slightly.'

And you don't even get enough filth for your money, though Anthony Blond does say of corporal punishment: 'It's only charm is sexual' (remembering that Sir Peter Swinnerton-Dyer screamed and screamed like a pig). Martin Llewellyn recalls 'a Burmese cane with insulating tape tied round the end in a blob'.

Lord Longford boasts that he 'never masturbated at Eton'; Lord Hailsham was 'bitten on the leg by the present Duke of Montrose'. Lord Brocket says there were some odd people in the house – 'one black chap who was Nigerian, with very Nigerian features, you know, big lips' and another who had 'much finer, more Ethiopian-type features'. And a contemporary of Derek Malcolm, now a famous solicitor, ran 'a regime of terror which involved us actually eating cold cream mixed with shit, human shit'.

Unpleasant certainly, but no worse than the self-importance and self-satisfaction that unites the Etonians. Eton is the *only* school, they agree – like the Catholic Church, Longford explains helpfully. Etonians are best. 'The average height of Etonians must be higher than in any other school,' asserts one. The OE tie is 'the only tie in the whole world you can wear with a black or blue suit,' declares another. 'Etonians are beyond social climbing,' they chorus. 'There's no higher you can go socially.'

Thus the famous Eton self-confidence which they all so complacently talk about and exhibit, however vestigial their abilities. The only sympathetic speaker is the Rt Revd Simon Barrington-Ward, Bishop of Coventry. He says: 'I think I would say that it still seems rather incredible that somebody like Douglas [Hurd] is a Cabinet Minister, or that Tony Lloyd is a judge, or that I am a bishop, for that matter ...' So would we, your reverence. 'It was almost as if everything was part of the school, or the school had become part of everything.' Don't we know it.

Danziger brilliantly misquotes Robert Birley, former head of Eton, as saying that an Eton education is 'an anaesthetic experience'. Would that it were. Bring back Naim Attallah's *Women*, we say.

10 June 1988

Thomas the Wank Engine

Memories and Hallucinations D.M. THOMAS (Gollancz)

A NUMBER of critics have quite a high opinion of D.M. Thomas. Here is Malcolm Bradbury: 'Thomas's is an unusual order of imagination, rare in Britain, Russianised, dense, an imagination that possesses the powers both of pastiche and genuine innovation.' Not bad, eh? However, it's to be doubted whether any opinion of D.M. Thomas is quite as high as that held by the man himself.

Thomas the novelist, poet and translator knew he was made as a writer from the moment the *Sunday Express* assured its readers that the rude bits of *The White Hotel* were vital to the book's artistic unity and should be read without a blush.

The author, lately sacked from his job at a defunct college of further education and enmeshed in his usual emotional entanglements, could scarcely believe his luck: a popular newspaper actually commending all that oozing pudibunda! The rest is well documented: celebrity (*The White Hotel* sold hugely on both sides of the Atlantic), sky-high advances and a series of follow-up novels, each more inferior than the last.

Several reviewers of *Memories and Hallucinations* have already made its author a luckless victim of their asperity. It is easy. There is the 'borrowing'. There is the attitude to women. There is the epic selfishness. There is the fact that Thomas is so obviously wrong – innocently or wilfully – in so many of his utterances. But curiously no one has yet pointed out the conspicuous merit in this feverish autobiography, which is to document in an extensive and salutary fashion an awful moral tale from the world of books: what happens when you take a competent, unsuccessful novelist, give him a lot of money and kid him that he's a genius.

For *Memories and Hallucinations*, despite lookbacks to a Cornish childhood and undergraduate Oxford, is a series of dispatches from the life of the internationally successful writer: dispatches from the aeroplane, the conference chamber and the analyst's couch. It demonstrates with alarming success the consequences of literary celebrity. The first thing to go is your prose style. 'I have become terrified of art. It is the fatal Oedipal crossroads where dreams, love and death meet' is Thomas's opening sentence. 'We are all mysteries. *The heart is a dark forest* in Turgenev's phrase,' he writes a little later.

But there are more worrying drawbacks than this. Gradually your books get harder to write, possibly because you can't think what to put in them. You behave even more badly to the people who might try to interpose themselves between you and the page. 'Well make your plans,' Thomas tells his first wife, on the announcement of her re-marriage, 'but just don't tell me. I've got to finish my novel and I need calm.'

Worst of all, forced to fill all those gaping crannies of time, you resort to all the traditional expedients of the rich and idle: you submit yourself to analysis ('It seems you had entered a very conformist phase. You'd had this turbulent, emotionally rich adolescence, then suddenly you – conformed. Yet you say you were happy'); you sit earnestly through all the jigaboo nonsense of clairvoyance, and – of course – you spend long periods of time thinking you are ill.

Much of the most entertaining chapter consists of Thomas's attempt to discover what's wrong with him. Tests are negative. Numberless medics assure him that the malaise is a psychosomatic delusion. And finally Thomas convinces himself that it was a psychosomatic delusion ('You're right ... it *is* mental'). Then he finds out that he has had glandular fever.

What figure emerges from this chaos of self-indulgence? Well, a man with almost nothing to say, a man who can come out with stuff like '. . . since ultimately I believe God is stronger than viruses, I must think sex is good. And it *can* be as good with a stranger as with someone you love. Though of course, when there is love as well, then you can occasionally reach a mountain peak.'

Inevitably this sort of self-preoccupation puts you in mind of another notorious Cornish autodidact, A.L. Rowse. In fact, Thomas's excoriation of his 'hostile critics' – there must be a few of them by now – bears a marked resemblance to the man who alleged that people who found him third-rate only demonstrated their own third-rateness by doing so. The air of smug invincibility is characteristic and quite impenetrable.

24 June 1988

Bad Day at the office?

Grand Inquisitor: Memoirs SIR ROBIN DAY (Weidenfeld & Nicolson)

*W*E must tread carefully here; Sir Robin Day is a litigious old buzzard. He has just issued a libel writ against the *Evening Standard* for calling him 'libidinous' – a description that we accept has no truth in it whatsoever. No doubt he will also be dispatching a writ to his old friend Ludovic Kennedy, who broke ranks in the *Sunday Telegraph* the other day to reveal something of the Grand Inquisitor's approach to the fairer sex.

'To a woman whom he finds sitting next to him at a dinner party,' Ludo reported, 'he may well inquire as to whether she prefers intercourse at night or in the morning . . . Many a letter has had to be despatched in the morning to those whom he has unwittingly bruised the night before.'

This disclosure may have come as a rude shock to the viewing millions, but it was no surprise to those who have observed the off-screen Day. His public image may be that of the People's Friend, a witty and charming servant of democracy who is fearless in calling politicians to account; in reality he is a Garrick Club bore of the worst sort, pompous and insufferably conceited (his photograph on the cover of this immodestly titled book catches him in mid-smirk). He is also, as a failed politician himself, in awe of the establishment: his instincts are those of a minister rather than a journalist.

Thus he approves of the BBC governors' capitulation to Leon Brittan in banning *Real Lives* and is furious that they then reversed the ban; he condemns the corporation's refusal to show Ian Curteis's feeble Falklands play. On all the broadcasting controversies of recent years – Zircon, *Maggie's Militant Tendency, Death on the Rock*, etc. etc. – he sides with the Government. Anything that annoys politicians – from the 'deplorable' *That Was The Week That Was* through *Yesterday's Men* to *Spitting Image* – is, in Day's view, a disgrace. Parliament, he adds, should never be mocked, even in newspapers. So much for the People's Friend.

The rot set in at the BBC, he argues, with *TW3* and the liberal reign of Sir Hugh Greene in the early 1960s. It was Greene who said that, though the BBC should be neutral between left and right, there were some questions on which it could not be impartial – between truth and lies, for instance.

Day, at his most pompous, is scathing about this 'dubious reinterpretation of the BBC's duty of impartiality'. It is not the BBC's job to be in favour of truth or freedom or justice, he thunders: that would be 'contrary to its constitutional obligations'. Yet a hundred pages later he flatly contradicts himself, supporting the idea of a broadcasting ban on Sinn Fein on the grounds that the BBC can't 'fly the flag of moral neutrality' in the struggle between good and evil. 'Television,' he declaims in the book's final sentence, 'should be biased in favour of reason.'

Most people might imagine that the BBC had been pretty good to Robin Day. It has given him many plum jobs – presenting *Panorama, The World at One, Question Time* and countless other programmes, not to mention his general-election extravaganzas – and has rewarded him handsomely. It threw a huge banquet in his honour in 1980 to celebrate his 25 years in television. It has even helped him to plug his book, allowing him a half-hour of prime time with Ludovic Kennedy a couple of weeks ago.

In return he is quite breathtakingly ungrateful. His 'memoirs' are really an extended whinge at how terribly he's been treated by the corporation – seldom offered any work, never appreciated enough, sneered at by pinkoes, and so on. What little evidence he produces for this implausible claim is laughably petty and proves only his vanity rather than the Beeb's perfidy.

He seems to think, for instance, that *Question Time* should have been called *Day*, by analogy with *Wogan* and *Parkinson*, and grumbles that 'the BBC has never shown much enthusiasm for putting my name in a programme title'. (Apart from *Daytime, News Day, Talk-in to Day* and

Conference Day, that is.) 'As the programme has advanced in years, the newspapers have christened it Sir Robin Day's Question Time,' he adds modestly. 'But that was not taken up by the BBC.' Poor little diddums. Still, at least he got his knighthood.

27 October 1989

Barbie droll

Weep No More BARBARA SKELTON (Hamish Hamilton)

D IMLY in the distance, like conversation rising from a crowded room, can be heard the chatter of Barbara Skelton's reviewers: 'Dear old Barbara, what a girl eh? ... Poor old Cyril, what a scream eh? ... Weidenfeld's hairy backside, ha ha ha ... What a girl, didn't give a damn eh? ... Litigation ... Alimony ... Dear old Barbara, what a girl eh?'

Weep No More, the second volume of Barbara Skelton's memoirs, has been extensively reviewed by the dozen or so people on whom reminiscences of the late Cyril Connolly cast such an enduring spell. It turned up in the *Spectator*'s 'Books of the Year' selection, where Francis King confessed himself 'greatly entertained' by its 'devastating truthfulness'. Auberon Waugh wrote an admiring article in the *Independent*, cheekily suggesting that Lord Weidenfeld – the subject of some indiscreet revelations – might like to reprint it in paperback along with its predecessor. At the same time Duncan Fallowell concluded that the first book, *Tears Before Bedtime*, was 'a little masterpiece'. What's it all about, you wonder? What on earth is it that she did?

Not a lot, actually. Barbara Skelton's chief claim to fame – one hesitates to use so judgemental a word as 'notoriety' – is the number of mildly celebrated people she managed to sleep with during the course of a long and illustrious career as a sort of literary good-time girl. Some of these – Connolly, Weidenfeld – she ended up marrying. Others – the French writer Bernard Frank – she shared with somebody else. A third contingent furnished relationships of a less tumultuous order but presumably fulfilled the valuable service of allowing Miss Skelton to keep her hand in. Memorialized in remembered conversations, old letters and diary entries from the 1940s and 1950s, the figures in this sad procession have only one shared characteristic:

their foibles are all unerringly exposed – Cyril Connolly lying in bed murmuring to himself 'Poor Cyril, poor Cyril'; Weidenfeld, with whom she subsequently takes up, alternating desperate love-letters ('believe that my pleas are sincere and not made lightly') with no-nonsense demands of the 'Suppose I should want another woman?' sort. The millionaire physician Derek Jackson, husband number three, distinguishes himself by his stinginess ('First I was taken to see his lawyer in Switzerland and asked to sign a document whereby I relinquished all claims on my future husband's millions').

Or perhaps, on reflection, he was simply being circumspect. A feature of Miss Skelton's attitude is that marriage should mean something. Weidenfeld, divorce papers having been filed, looks good for £2,000. However, a solicitor's letter ('Our client instructs us he will pay Peter Jones' account for £13.2s.6d and the account of Phelps Beddard for £19.1s.3d' and the phone bill) soon demolishes this brave dream. Jackson, though, has to part with a house in Provence, where his ex-wife spends lonely days broken only by the arrival of Frank (like Connolly 'immensely talented and witty') who, when not scribbling, will occasionally deign to throw plates at her or beat her up.

And so it goes on. Lists of people she saw at parties. The amusing dedications inscribed in her copies of Cyril's books. Cyril's witty remarks (when asked how he will feel if she marries Weidenfeld, he replies: 'Like someone who has missed a close putt on the last green of a championship'). Connolly appears, by the by, as the only half-way likeable person in the book and certainly not up to either of his opponents' fighting weight.

None of this explains why Miss Skelton's slight memoir should have achieved such universal *réclame*. Or perhaps it does. For *Weep No More* is an exercise in gossip. The vitally important role played by gossip in English literary history is well-known. In fact it could be said that whereas other countries have literary history, its English equivalent consists largely of these injurious remarks about other people's private lives.

For some reason our literary masters, the sort of people who scream with rage whenever a serious novel looks as if it might win a prize, find the anecdotes of Lord Weidenfeld being mistaken for an escaped baboon while out jogging naked in the Provençal woods wildly diverting. It is the old drawback of the English literary life. One wants, occasionally, a little seriousness and one gets instead Miss Skelton's revelations about Weidenfeld's hairy backside. Somehow it seems a poor sort of exchange.

8 December 1989

Bang to rights

Nothing to Declare: Prison Memoirs TAKI (Viking)

*W*HAT's prison for, then? Reform, restraint or retribution? It's an 'ard one, innit? Nobody knows.

Many fine minds have wrestled with the problem. The great novelist Michael Ignatieff began his career with a book called *A Just Measure of Pain: The Penitentiary in the Industrial Revolution 1750–1850*. Iggy studied the history of Pentonville prison, which was founded in the belief that crime was caused by environmental factors, rather than simple wickedness, and that by controlling a criminal's environment, he could be reformed. This questionable notion survived 'because it spoke to a heartfelt middle-class desire for a social order based on deferential reconciliation'. Got that?

On 14 December 1984 Taki Theodoracopulos, a rich Greek 'playboy', was sent to Pentonville for four months for importing cocaine. He was let out early, on 28 February 1985. So what are Taki's thoughts on the purpose of imprisonment?

'My prison experience has brought me to consider a number of questions about our penal system and our current social attitudes,' he writes, 'but so far, not one of these questions has led me to a single answer I can stand on.' (Let alone a leg.) 'The problem, of course, is complex to the point of absurdity. How do we rehabilitate people who can't read and write? Who are addicted to drugs? Who can make a living only by hurting other people? Do we lock them up and throw the key away? Yes, of course, what else is there to do? No, of course not, how inhumane! What's the right answer? I haven't a clue.'

Taki isn't being modest. *Nothing to Declare* woefully demonstrates that the man is far more closely confined by his own stupidity than he ever was by prison bars.

As an account of life inside it is banal. The cells are small. Slopping out is horrid. Everything's filthy and there's a nasty smell. The other prisoners are a bad lot. Most of the warders are OK, though one or two are unpleasant. The food is poor. Time drags.

As a tour round Taki's mind, *Nothing to Declare* is far more alarming. Woven into the prison diary is the story of his life. It's a chronicle of wasted time. He's spent a lot of money, played sports, fucked around and induced snob magazines such as the *Spectator* and *Vanity Fair* to run columns by him about this 'high life'.

Somehow he has persuaded himself that they've shown him to be a fearless critic of the idle rich. 'I've often found myself attacking the rich and powerful in my various columns simply because they are rich and powerful,' he writes. He fails to understand that editors use him as an exhibit, not a critic.

The style of *Nothing to Declare* is the product of an unquestioning belief in the importance of his exclusive world. The suicide of another convict is described as 'very depressing'. Only the accidents that befall the rich are 'tragic'. 'A tragedy occurred that put a damper on polo for the year. Elie de Rothschild, a leading member of French polo and a scion of the banking family, was struck by a ball during a particularly lively practice match and lost his eye ...' 'All three have since died tragically: Chandon, the champagne heir, while racing a car, the two Crawley brothers while flying their private plane ...' And so drearily forth.

Everything in Taki's circle is the biggest, the best, the most. His publisher, Tom Stacey, has 'the best-looking secretaries in the whole of England'; John Aspinall is 'England's greatest gambler and poshest party-giver'; Taki's yacht was 'the most beautiful sailing boat in the world ...' By such reiterations, the futile rich seek to reassure themselves that they matter.

The only other stylistic flourish Taki can manage is laboriously ironic comparison of ordinary life with this high life. Thick snow? 'The kind Gstaad sees all too seldom.' Prison hygiene? 'Bathing in prison, needless to say, is not exactly like bathing in Marienbad.' A new mop? It's 'the cleanest mop this side of the Carlyle Hotel'.

Taki learns nothing from prison. He's incorrigible, because he hasn't got enough brain cells to take correction. He believes otherwise, of course. For a few days he is made to sew buttons on army uniforms. 'Time drags as never before. I think of the millions of women who have to do this type of work in order to live, and for the first time I understand the inhumanity of the Industrial Revolution,' he bleats.

With *Nothing to Declare*, Taki has pioneered a new literary genre: the prison memoir in which the reader feels no sympathy whatsoever with the author. On the contrary, you're soon so annoyed by the self-important little shit that you're delighted he's banged up. 'Deferential reconciliation', my arse. They should never have let him out.

15 March 1991

Better dead than read

Blood on the Walls: Memoirs of an Anti-Royalist WILLIE HAMILTON
(Bloomsbury)

*A*MID the recriminations and post-mortems that are accompanying
Labour's fourth election defeat, the value of this little book in helping
to determine How It All Went Wrong has been mysteriously overlooked.

Blood on the Walls, the memoirs of a Durham miner's son who went on
to achieve lasting notoriety for being rude about the royal family, is a
revealing examination of the mentality of the old-style Labour Party, the
party of smoke-filled rooms and trade union muscle. It is also – the two are
connected – one of the most wretched political autobiographies ever put
between hard covers.

Why is Willie Hamilton's account of his life and opinions so very dreadful? Is
it because of the arch refusal to go into details whenever things turn mildly
interesting (no serious names are named politically and 'there were exciting
moments' is all Hamilton will say about the proximity of a female establishment
to his teacher training college)? Is it because of the hempen homespun angle
which tends to convert ordinary people into, you guessed it, 'folk'? Is it because
of the banal conclusions about the parliamentary life ('the price of being an MP
is paid by his wife and children') which we have read in every other political
memoir since the dawn of time, or the lumpen Scotch saws ('the best laid
schemes of mice and men gang aft agley')?

No, the wretchedness is almost solely attributable to 1) self-righteousness;
and 2) conceit.

There never was a politician unconvinced of his own rectitude or his
fitness for the position to which God – and Hamilton, a staunch Roman
Catholic, is fond of invoking the deity – called him, but this conceit is of a
very special sort. He quotes the statistics of his election victories. He quotes
approving press comment. He mentions, *en passant*, the terrific sales of his
previous book *The Queen and I*. All this one can forgive. It is a little less easy
to forgive the overweening confidence in his personal judgment. For
Hamilton, it appears, was always right – right about the time-servers on the
Labour front bench, right about the Tory bastards (his hatred of Conservative
politicians is almost pathological) and, superabundantly, right about the
parasites in Buck House.

Such is Hamilton's unswerving adherence to his own line that the inconsistencies of his position simply fail to strike him. He inveighs against toff landlords and their noble lordships only to salute one couple who had him to stay for 'treating their lodgers like gentlemen'. Bakeries full of cake are had and eaten simultaneously. Thus in the 1960s rising parliamentary salaries allow the MP and his family to move to a 'much better house in leafy Beckenham'. Unfortunately 'it was a Tory area and my children had to go to *their* schools'. Willie has a tremendous time harrying the local education authority without ever pausing to wonder whether Beckenham might not have been the best area to move to in the first place.

The same bloody-mindedness invests his political career. After much manoeuvring he gets Harold Wilson to give him the chairmanship of the Public Estimates Committee, a post he seems to have coveted. Hamilton's final judgement? 'A monumental waste of time'.

What makes *Blood on the Walls* even sadder is the depth of genuine feeling that underlies it. Born into a penurious childhood in a Durham miner's row, beset by family tragedy, hamstrung by his convictions – signing up as a conscientious objector in 1939 must have taken courage – Hamilton was clearly angered by the suffering and inequality he saw around him and determined to do something about it.

What, you might ask, was the result? At one point he has the cheek to mark Harold Wilson down as a creature of the establishment, but who, for all his stereotyped resentment of the royals, was more of the Labour establishment, who proceeded more dutifully through the lobbies at the whips' behest, than Willie Hamilton?

For all the good intentions, the ingrained surliness – what he calls, hilariously, his 'anarchical views' – end up only a whisker away from personal score settling. This was old-style 'socialism'. Incredibly, there are still people who mourn its passing.

24 April 1992

Moll flounders

Moll: The Making of Molly Parkin: An Autobiography MOLLY PARKIN
(Gollancz)

THE 'clinging to the wreckage' school of autobiography has always been a fail-safe way to pay the rent. Can't take the juice any more? Talent gone? Grey matter dissolving in a mulch of amphetamine sulphate? Well, put it down in writing, lad.

Just as Jeffrey Bernard has spent 20 years conducting a career on the back of his inability to obey doctors' orders, so along comes Molly Parkin, determined to milk a decent livelihood out of the – one scrabbles for the right non-judgemental word – er, *difficulties* that have attended her shaky progress through life.

These days, of course, Molly Parkin – born plain Molly Thomas in South Wales a shade over six decades ago – looks simply like a creature from a vanished age. The 1960s are gone, darling, and who but a fool would want them back? But most people in their early 30s will retain some faint memory of the days in which she strayed into the margins of their consciousness: the smutty novels in which one used lubriciously to browse, the delicate *Sun* columns about how her husband fancied Elsie Tanner but she didn't mind. Even then, apparently, her great days as a fashion journo were already gone, gone along with half-a-dozen jobs and the faintest vestiges of sobriety, but miraculously she hung on, beat the drugs, the drink and the angst, and now emerges more or less unrepentant to tell us all about it.

Moll fills in some of the gaps in this shambling transit. Very predictable gaps they are too. The Welsh childhood, the sex – Messalina in her prime would have been hard pressed to keep up with Ms Parkin when the mood was upon her; the drink (a quarter-century on the bottle); the husbands. If anything so disjointed could be said to have a dynamic – though for someone who was so often out of her head she has an uncanny ability to remember decades-old conversation – it lies in a confident estimation of her talents.

Ms Parkin's books were plainly the dandiest productions on the block, and she suggests that she was 'highly regarded as an intuitive interviewer'. Or perhaps the secret lay in coat-tail chasing. Some of the funniest bits come when she attempts to insinuate herself into the company of the rich and famous, accosting Woody Allen in a restaurant, brown-nosing Bette Midler ('she saw by my appearance that I wasn't the average run-of-the-mill journalist'). A fine clue to the general tone of the book can be found in the picture of Moll in her finery captioned 'look for Zandra Rhodes and Fenella Fielding'. No doubt the woman in the extreme top corner is indeed Miss Fielding, but you would be hard pressed to confirm it on the strength of the two eyes and a fringe vouchsafed to view.

And so on, through the whole vista of sexual encounters with everyone you've ever heard of – James Robertson Justice, John Mortimer, a whole rugby XV once – champagne for breakfast and waking up in last night's vomit. Casting my eye down the blurb I had a pretty good idea of what I might find, and, yes, there it was, a reference to the author's 'total honesty'. Memoirs of this sort are always 'honest'. But does taking out the back catalogue of your extravagances in public and simpering over them really count as sincerity?

Looking back on a lifetime's dissipation from the vantage point of a newly acquired spiritual peace, Ms Parkin's tone is horribly uneven: half regretful, half coy, as if she can't quite make up her mind whether to applaud, giggle or condemn. This uncertainty is a pity, because it undermines the much more revealing early part of the book – an account of a tough valley childhood, brutal father and adolescence in the blitz. All this ought to have the capacity to move, but if we can't take the Vamp in the Hat routine seriously, what are we to make of the remarks about her grandparents – 'I would sleep in many beds, with many bodies, known and unknown, later in life, but these two are the ones I still recall with the most tenderness.' Much as you appreciate the sentiment, the temptation to mark it all down as just another part of the pose is all but irresistible.

Curiously, in the end one can live with the gang-bangs and the gleeful indiscretions. Less easy to live with, though, is the degree of indulgence extended by a charitable media. One of the features of the publishing world at the moment, what with cutbacks and list-pruning, is the inability of a great many quite decent writers – people one has actually heard of – to get their books published.

All around us, while talent dies on the vine and the Bloomsbury air hums with the sound of scratching pens as publishers write famous authors' books for them, the likes of Molly Parkin continue to blossom confidently into print. It is this, rather than the tales of what James Robertson Justice did to her with a lightbulb, that stick in one's throat.

30 July 1993

Vacuum gleaner

An Autobiography: Part One: From Congregations to Audiences
DAVID FROST (HarperCollins)

D AVID Frost, said Kitty Muggeridge brilliantly, is the man who rose without a trace. Frost's autobiography aims to prove her wrong. More than 500 pages thick, it tracks every detail of his rise up to the year 1970. Pitifully, all it demonstrates is how right she was.

It seems hardly possible that even a ghosted autobiography of this size could offer no insight whatsoever into its author. Always, willy nilly, some personal touch or stylistic slip reveals the character of the writer beneath the platitudes. But not here. It's null; it's a void.

Frost may always have seemed rather a hollow man, but this book confirms that it's worse than that: he is not just empty, he is a vacuum. There isn't a human being there at all. David Frost is a one-man *Stepford Wives*.

The format of this autobiography suggests that he may even suspect as much himself. Its dogged setting down, plink plonk plunk, of every stage of his career is prompted by something more than the realization that sooner or later afflicts everybody who works in television – that even the greatest success in this medium is ephemeral. Nabokov mockingly called the first version of his memoirs *Conclusive Evidence* – evidence, that is, that he had existed. Frost is genuinely in search of such evidence.

He obviously feels he exists only when he is being broadcast. This must be why most of his autobiography consists of transcripts of long forgotten programmes, even when they consist of material he didn't write and interviews in which he only asked the questions. Equally numbing extracts from his more favourable newspaper cuttings about these programmes are used to join up these fat slabs of tedium. It's Frost's attempt to prove that he wasn't just a bad dream. In hell, the only reading matter allowed is showbiz memoirs like this.

So how did David Frost attain the disastrous success that has been his career?

Strangely, for those who know him now as the archetypal celebrity lickspittle, he began as a satirist. Born in 1939, the son of a Methodist minister, Frost went to Gillingham and Wellingborough grammar schools and then to Cambridge, and immediately began the career of push and shove that has continued to this day.

He is sadly typical of a generation of Butler Education Act grammar school boys who began as radicals but then joined with the establishment as fast as they could, becoming more deferential than any insider. He defends the class system ('something of an emotional safety net'), boasts that Harold Wilson came to a champagne breakfast he gave at the Connaught in 1966, and announces on the sleeve that he is married to 'the former Lady Carina Fitzalan Howard'. This leading light of *That Was The Week That Was* now feels honoured to peer *Through the Keyhole*.

Frost himself doesn't have a clue what it was all about: all those programmes, all that frantic transatlantic commuting, the founding of LWT. In his preface, he says peculiarly: 'While this book is indeed, as its title indicates, the first part of my autobiography, it is also an autobiography of the sixties. I hope, therefore, that I have managed to go easy on the extraneous personal details, and where there was a choice between a sixties anecdote and a personal anecdote with equal claims to inclusion, I have always tried to choose the former.' Autobiography of the 1960s! Extraneous personal details! Frost obviously hopes that if he's not a person, at least he's an era.

Accordingly, he tries to offer some thoughts on the decade. 'Were the sixties vital and dynamic, or flawed and phoney? Real and progressive, or superficial and self-destructive? Answer: all of the above.' Well, thanks David.

Frost stands for nothing but his own celebrity. He is the perfect television man. One of the best remarks in the book comes from the former leader of the Hitler Youth, Baldur von Schirach, whom Frost once interviewed. Von Schirach told Frost: 'At the age of 23, you did your first programme on television. At the age of 23, I was made head of the Hitler Youth. So you see, Mr Frost, we have a great deal in common . . .' Quite so.

In search of his missing soul, Frost makes some ludicrous claims that his revolting career has somehow been a perfect fulfilment of his father's Methodism. 'My belief in the intelligence and integrity of members of the public, and their ability to make up their own minds when their democracy supplied them with the necessary raw materials, sprang directly from the attitude of the religious figure I knew best, my father. His appreciation of the value of each individual life and its propensity for good, and his total lack of condescension or pretension made a subliminal impression and set an indelible example that was every bit as valuable in the studio as it would have been in a pulpit.' Oh yeah? Join us as we go *throooough the keyhole*! Amen.

One unfortunate side effect of printing transcripts of so many interviews is that it reveals how mechanically repetitive is his questioning. Frost obsessively asks all his interviewees, from Moshe Dayan to Noel Coward: 'How would you like to be remembered by future generations?'

There's no point in asking him this. He won't be remembered at all – unless it's as an explanatory footnote to Kitty Muggeridge's *bon mot*.

13 August 1993

Rumpy-pumpy of the Bailey

About Time Too: 1940–1978 PENELOPE MORTIMER
(Weidenfeld & Nicolson)

PENELOPE Mortimer was married to John Mortimer from 1949 to 1971. This is her memoir of those years, plus a bit more afore and aft. It's been seized on by the papers purely because it's supposed to contain some juicy bits about porky old Rumpole.

And sure enough, it does. When he first met her, she was still married to her first husband. But this did not deter the 24-year-old Mortimer from saying in a car one day: 'What about a quick fuck and then home?' To judge from the rest of the book, Mr Mortimer has carried on saying much the same to any woman who will listen ever since. 'His barrister's uniform smelled of sweat, semen and cologne,' says Mrs Mortimer genially.

Her account of their marriage is chiefly an account of a sequence of infidelities. His 'flirtations – infatuations, whatever they were' became 'an almost constant part of my life', she says. It wasn't the sex she minded, so much as the 'implausible excuses, furtive muttering on the 'phone, a flowering of Carnaby Street shirts and medallions'.

When she became pregnant for the eighth time, he talked her into an abortion and sterilization on the basis, she says, that it was essential for their happy future together. Later, she discovered he was carrying on another affair at the time. 'There were bitter quarrels, savage recriminations. His invective was more brutal than he intended – why didn't I just get out, go, I was useless to everyone, I was hideous, why didn't I *die*?'

Not quite an *ideal* husband, then, old Rumpy. They finally divorced when the woman who became his second wife discovered that she in turn was pregnant. After the divorce, they continued to wrangle about money. 'His attitude was simple: "Why should I support you when you're not there to cook my dinner?"' she remarks sweetly. He had, she derisively notes, become 'obsessed by food', a passion she disdains. One of her deftest, most wounding strokes is carefully to describe the young Mortimer as 'thin' and even 'skinny' (honest).

However, if this book is intended as a settling of accounts, it fails. Far from winning the reader over to her side, Penelope Mortimer proves an intolerably annoying narrator herself.

The manner is deadpan. Things just keep happening to her. She doesn't know why, she can't even remember what happened or who was there. It's not her fault.

'Let what happens seems fortuitous, change inexplicable – that's how it is when you're living it,' she proclaims. And indeed, it appears that she really has lived her life as a succession of meaningless affairs, unplanned pregnancies and haphazard moves. But as a style for looking back, it's arch, disingenuous and inadequate. Every time she says she can't remember something or doesn't know why she did it, the reader simply thinks: then why on earth am I paying you to say so?

Never has an autobiographer offered so many disclaimers. The war? 'I remember nothing about it except the serene barrage balloons and the fine network of their tethers.' What happened when she told her first husband she was pregnant by another man? 'I have an impression of weeping, and don't think that it was mine' is her complete recollection. The friends she and Fatso had during the first years of their marriage? 'I try to recall those friends, but few of them have names, let alone faces.' Her greatest literary success with *The Pumpkin Eater*? 'Lacking any urge to join in or get together or be organized I didn't understand what it was for, and I still don't.'

She's particularly forgetful about her own promiscuities. At one point, she brilliantly remarks: 'I think Jeffrey and I must have been to bed together by then, but the event or events were so unmemorable that I can't be sure.' Later she starts dealing with them in batches. 'I had a number of brief, unmemorable affairs,' she tells us. Well, thanks.

Her attempts to offer some little analysis of this life are singularly crappy. 'I lived most of my life as if I were triplets,' she offers in a 'Prologue' – a neat trick in its way, always somebody else to blame! Why did she make 'great efforts to be sexually attractive and none whatever to be lovable'? 'Like many other paradoxes in my life, I find this perplexing,' she says blankly. Oh come *on*.

It's because you become so irritated, just as a reader, by her systematic refusal to take responsibility for her actions that sympathy stirs even for her ex. It's merely a disguise for extreme egotism, after all. When Mortimer first told her about his adulteries, she says: 'All my life I had been used to absolute power, exclusive attention. Who was I, if I wasn't unique?' It's the one moment when her guard is down – and it's still, albeit in fractured form, the assumption behind this book.

A horrible man called Auberon Waugh, Mortimer records, said of one of her books: 'Psychiatrists expect to be paid twelve guineas an hour for pretending to listen to this sort of ego-maniac drivel.' It'd be a lot more than that now. Best forget it?

5 November 1993

10

SEX

Laughing all the way to the bonk

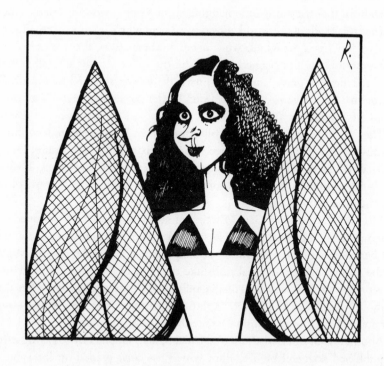

Blue job

The Faber Book of Blue Verse Ed. John Whitworth (Faber & Faber)

JOHN Whitworth originally solicited contributions for an anthology of *coarse* verse – a conception that seems to have been aborted by Faber's Craig Raine, something of an expert at cannibalizing big names from the past and lacing them with trendy but vastly inferior poetasters of the present. The end-product, unmistakably wrapped up by Raine rather than Whitworth, is an indigestible fudge of the familiar, the feeble and the indiscriminately filthy.

Eskimo Nell, The Ball of Kirriemuir, Diamond Lily of Piccadilly and other gems from the camp fire and changing-room choirs, working-men's clubs and lavatory walls of the world, are coupled here with the student-rag visions of Wendy Cope's Strugnell, who 'needs a woman/who'll come across on half a pint of beer'; of Raine himself – 'in the valley of your arse/all flesh is grass, all flesh is grass'; and of Whitworth, whose similar lust for ribald rhymes has similarly infected his reason: 'If after 20 years of screw/Your nose drops off, it's balls to you.'

The genuine balls of this collection have been squeezed without permission from the time-honoured register of bawdy poets: Catullus, Ovid, Martial, Chaucer, Villon, Rochester, Burns, Verlaine, Cavety *et al.* They'd surely be appalled to find their work pressed into the service of some of its latter-day bedfellows here.

After 60 years of blue, Gavin Ewart's mucky brain has clearly dropped off down a drain: 'The small buttocks of men that excite the women/but ah? the beautiful feminine broadness!' Yes folks, that's the whole 'poem'. Much of the contemporary material reads like the sorts of filler and dirty-picture caption favoured by any run-of-the-mill 'adult' publication: 'Here lies the body of Patrick who Served Aphrodite delightedly/Even when quite geriatric/He still raised a nightie excitedly' (P. O'Shaughnessy).

Another nadir of the bathetic and banal is, alas, supplied by some hitherto unpublished doggerel by T.S. Eliot which has been snarled up for Faber's proudest boast, as strengthening the book's 'judicious scattering of the best limericks'. Eliot would obviously have published it himself had he thought it merited it. On reading it now you'll understand why he didn't.

T.S. E's lines on the predatory assignation 'at the violet hour' between 'the young man carbuncular' and a bored typist in *The Waste Land* would have made a far worthier representation. But then Eliot's true poetry of the brass tacks of 'birth, copulation and death' would provide more reality than this cynical labour of sexploitation could bear. A typical opportunity missed is the absence of the bluest verse ever penned by a some-time Faber poet, W.H. Auden's *The Platonic Blow,* also known as *The Gobble Poem.* According to Humphrey Carpenter this was composed to show a college professor 'exactly what sort of a person Auden was', with admissions like 'I rocked at the shock of his cock' working up to a shamelessly joyous performance of fellatio. Instead of this, Faber pushes two brief, tame sparks of formalist word-play at us with a *Psst* as examples of Auden 'writing at his most frank'.

The elevations of would-be clever-dickery and simpering under-grad. smut above so much authentic sex poetry typifies the overall hypocritical debasement. There's next to nothing beyond a few modish gestures by or for women. Selima Hill can only be in because, unlike Sappho or Bessie Smith, she's a fashionable hypee of the day. The vignette recalling her Gran saying 'Ah, bless your little cotton socks!' is sheer sewing-circle genteel – about as blue as Pam Ayres on *Blue Peter.*

Fleur Adcock – whose *Faber Book of Women's Poetry* was also re-edited by Raine – contributes an earnest ode to wanking: 'Five minutes are enough to fill/that gap between the Sunday papers and lunch.' It evokes the most likely functions for this perfumed farrago of pseudo-intellectual porn in the rest-rooms of loveless yuppies.

26 October 1990

Not so cunning stunts

The Literary Companion to Sex, Ed. Fiona Pitt-Kethley
(Sinclair-Stevenson)

HERE, for St Valentine's Day, is something atrociously British. We are perhaps the only nation in Europe still prudish enough to find the mere idea of a woman talking dirty irresistibly exciting.

Fiona Pitt-Kethley's career has been based entirely on the fact that, though a woman, she can be as smutty as a man. Otherwise her writing is devoid of interest: flat-footed and cloth-eared. If her scrawls about blow-jobs were signed by a man, they would never have been published more extensively than on a lavatory door.

But there are still men who thrill to simple proof that *women do it too*. Philip Roth caught this adolescent emotion nicely in *Portnoy's Complaint*: 'Amazing! Astonishing! Still can't get over the fantastic idea that when you are looking at a girl, you are looking at somebody who is guaranteed to have on her – a cunt! *They all have cunts!* Right under their dresses! Cunts – for fucking!'

This is exactly the level on which Fiona Pitt-Kethley's works are enjoyed, by those who enjoy them – notably her great patron, Karl Miller. Famously, Fiona Pitt-Kethley received 85 rejection slips before she managed to get a poem published. Her career was eventually founded on repeated appearances in the academic magazine, the *London Review of Books*. Its editor, Karl Miller, was so excited by the idea that a woman could talk as basely about sex as a man (Amazing! Astonishing! etc.) that all other criteria were abandoned. Week after week, reviews about anthropology or jurisprudence were studded with little anecdotes about sex worthy of Bernard Manning or 2 Live Crew.

Pitt-Kethley none-the-less pretends to believe that her sexual explicitness has held her back. 'Yes, I've always been treated unfairly because of my frankness,' she said recently. 'Women have always talked dirty – to each other. Some men feel it slightly threatening when they see it in print.'

And she has the gall to maintain that she's generally been done down in her career because she's a woman.

But – ironee! – her sex is certainly the sole reason she's ever hit print. In *Manifesto of a Female Casanova*, she announced 'Sex is a constant pleasure. As with anything else, experience makes you more skilled,' and 'I'm exceptionally discriminating. I only have it off with good-looking partners. I'm not cheap, I'm free.' These exciting remarks were thought deserving of the front page of the *Independent*'s Saturday review. But imagine them coming from a man – they wouldn't even earn a laugh in a pub. Yet Pitt-Kethley, poet, sails on. The *Guardian* has recently given her a column – 'Ars Amatoria' – for further felicities of this order.

And here we have her personal anthology of mucky bits ('Every book and every poem has its orgasm or high point . . . What I have tried to do is collect together all these orgasms to make one long orgiastic read.')

Originally commissioned by Hamish Hamilton, it was rejected when delivered. Why? According to Fiona, it was because it featured too many perversions – in other words, it was too exciting. So it's been issued instead by Sinclair-Stevenson, the embarrassing independent publisher recently taken over by Reed International. And the real reason's clear; it's too boring and badly done.

The choice of passages manages to include much that's over-obvious (*To His Coy Mistress*, *Lady Chatterley's Lover*) yet excludes both the great (Keats, Tennyson, Browning, Pope, Joyce) and the contemporary (Heller, Mailer, Beckett, Auden, Larkin, Martin Amis). Instead, there are wretched anecdotes about a Chinese man peeing in a girl's mouth, three poems by the awful Jeremy Reed, and verse of this order: 'I am a penis,/the masculine totem./My base is a bag/that is known as the scrotum ... I am a penis,/a bit of a card,/ mostly quite soft/but at times rather hard.' A snip at 18 quid, eh?

Fiona has translated many of the classics represented herself, or handed them over to her mum, Olive Pitt-Kethley, thus reducing these to the true Pitt-Kethley note ('Why don't I kiss you? You're bald as a coot/Why don't I kiss you? You're bright red to boot/Why don't I kiss you? You've only one eye/Kissing you'd just be a blow job, that's why' – Martial, don't you know.)

As sexiness goes, this ain't much, but in Britain it'll do. The reason people here sit glued to their televisions, watching adaptations of Melvyn Bragg or Fay Weldon, is solely in the patient hope of seeing a little sex. Everybody knows this, few admit it. Just dress sex up as culture and you can sell it to us. Even in the form of Fiona Pitt-Kethley. We're *desperate*.

14 February 1992

Second helpings of coq

The New Joy of Sex ALEX COMFORT (Mitchell Beazley)

HERE's a triumph of the book-packager's art. No artefact was ever more embarrassingly redolent of its period than *The Joy of Sex*. Yet here it is, slightly tarted up and more than trebled in price, back on the bestseller list nearly 20 years after it was first published.

Alex Comfort wrote this instruction manual in two weeks in 1972. It sold more than eight million copies and founded the fortunes of Naim Attallah's Quartet Books – largely on account of the many scratchy drawings of a hideous long-haired brute with a beard and a dopey expression, industriously poking away in various postures at an equally blissed-out bint with a beehive. These were the first such illustrations to be respectable, perhaps because it was obvious that nobody could possibly look at them for pleasure.

Comfort's other artful dodge was to disguise his book as a bistro. He presented the information in the form of a menu, with 'starters', 'main courses' and, repulsively, 'sauces and pickles'. Lots of crappy French words were thrown in to make you feel you'd had a real night out: *cassolette, cuissade, flanquette, feuille de rose, pattes d'araignée, coq au vin,* and the like.

At a stroke or two, Alex Comfort became the Robert Carrier of bonking; the middle class's guide to the rich dishes of the continent, or how to follow *soixante-neuf* with *blanquette de veau.* He hardly needed to argue the case for more sexual experimentation: by choosing these metaphors he had side-stepped the forces of repression, instantly taking sex out of the context of ethics into the realm of treats you really ought to try.

You don't hear so much of Robert Carrier now, most people having realized that it's not good for you to tip too much cream into your casserole. The same obscurity should by rights have descended on Alex Comfort, for the same reason.

In the first edition, Comfort was blithely saying that 'venereal diseases could be stamped out altogether in our generation if people stopped treating them as a special case, and if nobody had a vested interest in them as a deterrent'. Perversion, other than 'digging up corpses or committing lust murder', wasn't a useful category then, except to describe puritans. Anal intercourse was worth a try ('there are lovers who vastly enjoy it') as were 'foursomes and moresomes' ('we see no earthly reason why pairs of friends shouldn't make love together ... the bisexual element is an important turn-on in all swapping ...').

All this has gone, willy-nilly. The publishing director responsible for the new edition hopefully maintains, however, that far from being 'The New Joy of Celibacy', 'the book is as wild and funny as it ever was', and the pictures illustrate 'more fancy positions than ever'.

Indeed, it has been ingeniously touched up. For the first time there is a set of artily baffling black-and-white photos, of a pair feigning rapture. There are new drawings (in colour now to do the red bits proud) of a new couple. He is blond, muscular, clean-shaven, a lot more intent; she has masses more hair and a great big smirk.

There have been many surreptitious little adjustments. The book no longer bears the wondrously naff subtitle, 'A Gourmet Guide to Love-making'. Instead in tiny type, among the publishing information, there is a warning about Aids which amounts to a legal disclaimer of the whole thing: 'The advice and/or information included in this book should be considered in the light of present understanding of such health risks. The reader is advised to consult a physician about these risks.'

All the sections have been quietly rearranged. 'Starters' are now called 'appetizers', perhaps in recognition that appetites are flagging; 'Sauces' now arrive without pickles, for weaker stomachs. 'Fidelity' which used to come at the end among the 'Problems', is now at the beginning, among the 'Ingredients'. 'Anal Intercourse', meanwhile, has been moved from 'Sauces & Pickles' to 'Health and Other Issues'. The list of opening topics has altered from 'Beds, Birdsong at Morning, Birth Control, Clothes, Come Again . . .' to 'Love, Fidelity, Safe Sex, Tenderness . . .'

Some indefensibles have been silently dropped altogether, such as 'Buttered bun', the yucky, though still culinary name offered for 'a woman who has recently had relations with another man'. Comfort's remark on condoms – 'many people dislike the feeling of no contact' – has disappeared too, whether or not it remains true. Even alcohol is out these days. 'If you're serious about sex, stay with Perrier water.'

In a page on 'The Implications of AIDS', Comfort puts the best face on it all. 'There is no occasion for panic, or for losing out on the joy of sex – simply for informed caution. A crimp on the candy-store exploitation of sexual freedom may give us time and motive to redevelop its affectionate side. Now read on.' It's a piece of fantastic hypocrisy. No author did more to encourage the candy-store view of sex than Comfort himself, in this very book – and this edition is full of the same recipes, however reshuffled. Only now some of the candy is poisonous.

22 November 1991

Fleet Street muffia

Ambition JULIE BURCHILL (The Bodley Head)

THIS novel is dedicated somewhat mysteriously 'To SD my BF.' The 'SD' is a reference to Susan Douglas, associate editor (features) of the *Daily Mail*, who first commissioned La Burchill to write a column for the *Mail on Sunday*. Ms Douglas also happened to be in a Brighton hotel room with *MoS* editor Stewart Steven when he had a heart attack, a scene that appears to form the model for the novel's opening. 'BF' is more ambiguous, with 'Best Friend' unlikely after Susan Douglas has read through the antics of the heroine Susan Street. Perhaps 'F' is for something more typically Burchillian.

Nothing, however, can explain why Random House paid Burchill £175,000 for the UK hardback rights to two novels, this being the first offering.

It is a long-awaited and over-reviewed Shopping and Fucking novel with the single-word title characteristic of the genre – *Lace*, *Destiny*, *Pearls*, etc. What is it this time? Oh yes, the 'A' word: Ambition. La Burchill's novel is a hymn to the self-assertion of the career girl, in this case Susan Street, whose ambition is to edit the *Sunday Best*, a tabloid with teeth.

Ambition is what once used to be called a bodice-ripper, from The Bodley Head – which once used to be called a great publishing house but which has recently been relegated to the status of a mere designer label by its owners Random House. The book contains a certain amount of shopping: in Rio de Janeiro (page 51), and New York (pages 171–2), and tedious lists of designer labels and shop names. There is also a disposition to substitute designer labels for adjectives describing clothing and other objects, and although Ms Burchill probably intended this as a joke subversive of the genre, it only irritates and confuses.

When she refers to Susan Street's briefcase later in the narrative merely as a briefcase, are we to assume it is the 'Etienne Augier briefcase' we have encountered on pages 45–6, or the 'dark green leather envelope briefcase from Victor Hugo' mentioned on page 71, or is Susan Street perhaps a three-briefcase career girl? So much for the shopping. There is, however, plenty of 'eating out' – which doesn't mean consuming food in restaurants.

The fucking element is less confusing but no less tedious. It is in novels such as this that pagination really comes into its own, because if you're lucky an assiduous reviewer will tell you what you really want to know – where to find the dirty bits while fingering the single copy on the shelf at Hay Hill. Mindful of public duty, therefore, here is a ready reference: pages 55–62 – orgy in Rio de Janeiro at which six whores, male and female, put Susan Street through her paces ('That's not an orgy, that's a dinner party', reflects one of the characters); pages 102–6 – two black men slurp Krug from Ms Street's quim; page 130 – heterosexual coupling in alley beside Kremlin Club and afterwards he wipes his cock on her £250 tights from Fogal of New Bond Street; pages 172–6 – orgy in S&M dyke club in New York; page 231 – orgy in Bangkok nightclub.

Don't get Burchill wrong; career girls are taken seriously but they are also taken by masterful men. As David Weiss tells Susan on page 111: 'Get over that toilet.'

Ambition follows the usual excrescences of the Burchill prose style: the relentless, puny puns ('condemned to birth in', 'the son-in-law also rises', 'analysis-retentive'), the banal aphorisms ('Cunnilingus is the waiting-room of sex'; 'a career girl's refuge is her bathroom'), the meaningless figures of speech ('telephones that squatted smugly on her desk'), and the conjunctions to end sentences elegantly with. Characters such as Tobias X. Pope, media-baron-cum-pervert-cum-philosopher 'with a reputation somewhere between Rupert Murdoch, G. Gordon Liddy and the Marquis de Sade' hardly convince, even as caricatures. The plot doesn't add up to much either since Ms Burchill (who is happily married, incidentally) is determined to have her muff and eat it.

Her heroine gets the job and gets her man, who just happens to have an enormous penis ('like a cosh wrapped in plush pink velvet'). Not only that, but he actually proposes to her in the end. Soon it will be time for Susan to watch *Thirtysomething* and shop for designer maternity wear.

7 July 1989

Long Tale Sally

Destiny SALLY BEAUMAN (Bantam Press)

THE smart magazines have had a little titter about *Destiny*, the romantic blockbuster by Sally Beauman, but no one else has said very much.

Because Sally is cute and went to Cambridge and lives in Hampstead and knows everyone, she is not going to get done over in the literary pages, which are largely written by people like herself. Nor even in the popular press. The result is that no word of warning has got out. Millions of innocent women are going to buy this book in the expectation of a nice clean swoon. They will read it with growing dismay, until they get to page 97, at which point they will throw up.

Destiny isn't romance, it is filth. There are scenes in it so revolting – far nastier, for instance, than *Fear of Flying*, and without any saving glimmer of humour – that they cannot be described in a family magazine like *Private Eye*. But those with the stomach to carry out a consumer test should try pages 40–5, 97–9, 158–60, 217–20 and 346–9. That should do for the sick-bag.

The book is also colossally boring. Even in the clean bits, it is written so deliberately to a formula that it has a dead, mechanical air. Sally Beauman, who learned her trade at Mills & Boon, knows how to write a book by numbers, and in going for the epic romance (archetype: *Gone with the Wind*) she has thrown in all the right ingredients: strong-willed heroine, available ordinary man, elusive glamorous man, rags to riches, war and peace, ancestral mansion, dynastic feuds. She has also not neglected the triple-S factor – Sex, Snobbery, Shopping – required in contemporary versions of the genre (archetype: *Scruples* by Judith Krantz). Between the ubiquitous couplings is the regulation scatter of brand-names and fashion labels, marquesses and movie stars.

When written with passion, the epic romance can provide a great popular triumph like *The Thorn Birds*. But *Destiny* lacks the necessary throb of sincerity. It has been put together by a clever girl from Girton who has studied the form and sold out.

The funny thing is she has botched it. Not only has she overdone the sex, she has made the drastic mistake of Americanizing her heroine. All British writers, even the good ones, come unstuck when they try to do an American, and here is no exception. The American scenes in *Destiny* are comically unconvincing.

She has also gone on too long: 400,000 words is twice too many, for a novel of any sort. From the mind of Sally Beauman such a length is unreadable.

Not that the author need worry. She has already pocketed the swag and run. The laugh is on her agent, Pat Kavanagh of A.D. Peters, who has been boasting about her own part in this great commercial event, claiming responsibility for the book's American scenes and for the destruction of an earlier draft as 'too slow and too quiet'.

But the real guffaw can be saved for Bantam Press, which bought the book in the UK and USA at a price driven through the roof by auction ($1.6 million total). This side of the water the fall-guy is Bantam's MD, Mark Barty-King, a sweet and handsome man known in the trade as Captain Marvel. Having been muscled out of Granada by Collins, Barty-King was in need of a coup at Bantam. He will probably last another 18 months.

Sally Beauman may well have wrecked her publisher. The better news is she has probably wrecked the whole market for SSS epic romance. Carol Smith, the best agent in the field, believes that *Destiny* is the last of its breed. 'You can open a book like this and predict everything that's going to happen in it. The trade is bored, the public is bored, I'm bored. It's time to get back to real writing.'

Rosemary Cheetham of Century, who dropped out of the bidding for *Destiny*, agrees that the genre is over. Having thrown away the latest Judith Krantz on a plane, half-finished, she is wondering what to do with her life.

For the rest of us, the immediate responsibility is to warn as many people as possible not to give *Destiny* to their mothers.

17 April 1987

Bear essentials

Triangles ANDREA NEWMAN (Michael Joseph)

'A CHICKEN,' say the Russians, 'is not a bird and a woman is not a human being.' It seems rather a strong line to take. But perhaps they've been reading Andrea Newman.

Triangles is a collection of short stories published to capitalize on the success of *A Sense of Guilt* on television. These stories were first published in such magazines as *Cosmopolitan*, *Woman's Own*, *Woman* and *Woman's Realm*. You guessed it, they are aimed at women, and they are about women and men.

To be more accurate, they are about women and men and a third party to make up the triangle. Normally this third party is another woman or man, though once it is a city and once a child. They are stories of jealousy and infidelity, Newman's stock in trade.

The view they offer of the relation between the sexes is strikingly repulsive. Marriage is death; deceit is life. The men women want belong to other women, the women men want belong to other women. (One cheery twist on this theme; in the final story a woman is picked up by a strange man in a supermarket and they instantly cavort in a caravan in the car park. Then you're told it's husband and wife playing at being strangers. Laugh!)

It's a reductive outlook reduced further by the fact that these stories are short and there are 15 of them. Seductions, betrayals, writhings and bereavements – all happen one after the other in grotesque double-quick time, like the Keystone Cops on a chase.

Andrea Newman is able to inject just enough nasty little observations into her calumnies to make them stick like tar and make you feel mucky. Men don't do well in this world, the creeps, but women, creepers to the creeps, do worse.

What these women want in men! Hair, for example, sprouting like cress. 'A few dark hairs curling out of a leather jacket' lead on over the page to a superb crop. Promise fulfilled: 'His whole body was covered with black fur and his cock was the right length for her and wonderfully thic . . .' Whoops! Family newspaper.

This deep pile, it's about all a man needs. Another plush one walks into a room: 'He had . . . dark hair escaping from his collar and cuffs, suggesting it must be all over his body. She fell instantly in love, or was it lust? She didn't care' (about all the discrimination Andrea Newman is ever able to bring to bear on that distinction). Over the page: 'She was in bed with a large furry animal and they were giving each other every sort of pleasure.'

Such 'comforting warm fur' is also to be found on a cat, the reader shudders to learn. Rightly shudders. Over the page: 'Afterwards the cat came to join them, purring and sniffing the sheets . . .'

Not that it's cats that men should most strive to imitate to please Andrea and her readers. They should rather practise being trees, and bears. 'He was a great bear of a man . . .' rhapsodizes one ursomaniac.

'She longed to have him fill her up, to feel him on top of her, heavy like a fallen tree,' thinks a dendrophile, daintily. Sure enough, Andrea not being in the business of disappointing the readers, she does. 'She was crushed by his weight, under her fallen tree at long last.'

Or they could aspire to be tree and bear simultaneously. ('It was like hugging a tree or a bear,' gasps an enthusiast, a little confusedly.)

What they should not do is fall asleep, congress achieved. Many sore complaints are entered about this. But sympathy can be felt for these men, worn out as they are, aiming to please: hairy, beary, confused trees. Not much can be felt for the chickens. Never so many, never so headless.

Suddenly it all comes clear. Andrea Newman must be Kingsley Amis in disguise. And look at the book jacket. It wasn't a very *expensive* disguise.

16 February 1990

Penis mightier than the sword

Dirty Faxes ANDREW DAVIES (Methuen)

*T*HAT spent, twilit world that exists where writing stops and television starts has heard quite a bit from Andrew Davies in the three years since he gave up his lecturing job at the University of Warwick and set up as a freelance. Plays. Novels. *A Very Peculiar Practice*. Current Davies scriptwriting credits include Michael Dobbs's serendipitous *House of Cards* and (prospectively) the 'adult' version of *Pride and Prejudice*, replete with Mr Darcy in his bath and bouts of heaving sexual frustration.

Ah yes, sexual frustration. In this complex post-modern age, of course, writers specialize: angst, Mrs Thatcher or the middle classes. Andrew Davies' field of expertise is sex. For sex, don't you know, is *very important*. Sex is, well, sex is the glue that binds us all together.

Dirty Faxes, his new collection of stories, is all about sex. An academic worries, on grounds of snobbery, about falling for his cleaning lady ('au pairs have a long, well established and respectable tradition as persons into whom it is OK, even *de rigeur*, to dip the seigniorial wick. But cleaning ladies ...') A writer gets sent a string of smutty electronic messages ('How would you like to sit on my tits and flap those big balls in my face?') A Broadway production assistant has an affair with the down-beat English dramatist.

Or rather, not completely about sex. Look back at that list of characters and what do they have in common? Answer, they are all writers. As a general rule the protagonists in Davies' stories do two things. They write, and they think about, speculate on, or experience, sex.

Sex. The thing about sex in fiction, as Mr Davies and the rest of the slick smut plus contemporary tricksiness brigade seldom grasp (and *Dirty Faxes* is 'unmistakeably a book for the high-tech nineties', don't you know?) is that sex is only interesting if it has a moral element. Give it proscription, give it codes, boundaries and transgressions and there is some point to it. The best sex in novels happens off stage, or is merely hypothetical. *Vanity Fair* is a sexy book. *Pride and Prejudice* is a sexy book (and there Mr Davies has a point). *Dirty Faxes* isn't. Take out the moral element, let people do it whenever they feel like, with whomever they feel like it and all you are describing are technicalities with the occasional schoolboy giggle about sitting on my tits thrown in.

There is something uniquely grey and chauvinistic about all this. The women in it are mostly objects. The thrills are of the cheapest imaginable variety, sheer cattleprod, as in 'Coming Mince', where a girl who has answered a lonely hearts ad goes to bed with – you guessed it – a famous writer who ejaculates meat all over her. Look for some humanity, the sense of observed life, and all you find is the image of the writer hunched over his typewriter writing about writers and sex, as if it were a sort of easily decodable computer game. The stories in *Dirty Faxes* strike the authentic, amoral voyeur's note. As you might expect, numbers of them first appeared in that beacon of sexual enlightenment, *Cosmopolitan*.

7 December 1990

Completely bonkers

A Time to Dance MELVYN BRAGG (Hodder)

MELVYN Bragg has always felt warmly about Cumbria. But last year he really came to the boil.

'The summer of '89 was one of the hottest in memory. I had thought about the Lake District in various ways – as an escape, as a hobby, as the natural phenomenon on my doorstep, as a deep geological and literary mine, as a perfect walking space and, most mysteriously, as somewhere in which, very occasionally, I could "lose" myself, go into a rich neutral of the mind and after some time re-emerge fortified. Until then I never saw that the Lake District lived and breathed sex.

'But it did. The soft round fells were breasts, the broad valleys cleavages, the deep cuts vaginas, the warm cropped turf lay back in the sun like your bare pelt waiting to be disturbed. The trees, the tresses ... To make love here was the condition of being alive. The land was there for nothing else.'

'Course this erotomane ain't Melv personally, it's just the hero of his *novel*, a retired Cumbrian bank manager. Not the same at all. For example, the bank manager's 54 and Melv's only 50 – though it is true that the bank manager has kept his figure, what with clambering up and down those soft round jobs.

'I was wiry and all the fell-walking over the years had kept things tuned up. Never have the results of fell-walking been put to such good use!'

By this little jest the bank manager means straightforwardly that, old as he is, he can keep it up for hours – 'a couple of hours' at a time, he specifies, dauntingly, and then again the same night, and then again in the morning ('The third act and, in many ways, the most powerful ... Usually at about six, I would wake up huge.') A goer, then.

The book is one long, bragging contact ad. It's a book by a man about how right women are to adore him, with all its come-on's and look-at-me's artfully arranged into a romantic sob story.

The bank manager (bit of a literary gent on the side, he is) puts it all in a letter to his love. He has fallen for a pretty 18-year-old girl of low birth, Bernadette. The first time he treated her to a bit of swordsmanship it was on an anorak, up on them fells, don't you know.

And Bernadette's not just well pleased, she *loves* him. Floreat hanky panky! For him: 'Erect nipples grazing on my hungry skin', and plenty of 'reaching into the melting fluid rubbered silk' (*reaching*?). And by 'eck, for her too. 'Sometimes we were doing so much to each other I thought I would explode.'

But – problems! – the bank manager turns out to be already married, to ailing 60-year-old Angela. In the book's greatest bad-taste out-break, Angela gets to write a letter herself to hubby, telling him she loves him ever so. He's just so lovable! So lovable that she gives him permission to fell-walk away to his heart's content. Then she gets cancer and dies. Handy, that.

But this lovable man tastefully left off his pioneering in Bernadette's broad valleys and deep cuts while his wife was expiring in hospital. And now Bernie's moved, so he has some little difficulty getting hold of her again. Sad! Happily, at the end, after the exchange of mawkish letters, they seem set to embark upon more three-act bonanzas.

The reader, Bragg evidently hopes, will be rooting for them and their rootlings. For what this account of *amour fou* is really saying is that it's not so *fou* so long as you've kept yourself fit.

A Time to Dance is a grotesque rewrite of *Lolita*. Literally. Vladimir Nabokov: 'Lolita, light of my life, fire of my loins ... Lo-lee-ta; the tip of the tongue taking a trip of three steps down the palate to tap, at three, on the teeth. Lo. Lee. Ta.' Melvyn Bragg: 'The three syllables, softly clacking my tongue against my palate. Bern – how urgent, how hot! A – the pause, a sigh the fulcrum of anticipation; dette – the stab, the claim.'

Somehow Bragg has missed the point that *Lolita* is about a lunatic committing paedophilia. He has adjusted the lovers' ages into legality. More to the point, perhaps, he has laboured to make the coupling of youth and age not just plausible, but appealing. Four more years, Melv, four more years!

The title and epigraph, by the way, come from *Ecclesiastes*. 'A time to weep, and a time to laugh; a time to mourn, and a time to dance ...' Which is where we also find this: 'The beginning of the words of his mouth is foolishness; and the end of his talk is mischievous madness.'

8 June 1990

Nothing to brag about

Rules of Desire – Sex in Britain: World War I to the Present CATE HASTE
(Chatto)
Crystal Rooms MELVYN BRAGG (Hodder)

HERE'S a fine pair. Cate Haste is, it says nowhere on her book, married to Melvyn Bragg. They've both just published shoddy books about sex. They make an illuminating comparison.

Cate Haste has written a leaden survey of changing mores. You can't make sex boring? Oh yes you can, you know, if your sentences are boring enough. Hers certainly are.

This is an exhausted plod through all the previous histories of sexual behaviour in modern times, with a couple of pages painfully ground out of every obvious milestone on the way. Havelock Ellis, Marie Stopes, Bertrand Russell, Radclyffe Hall, Vita Sackville-West, the invasion of the GIs, the Kinsey Report, the Lady Chatterley trial, *Fanny Hill*, the Profumo Affair, Mary Whitehouse, the 1967 acts, *Oz*, Cynthia Payne, Cecil Parkinson, Jeffrey Archer, Clause 28, James Anderton, *A Time to Dance* . . . here they all come again. Or nearly all. Hubby's own small contribution to prime-time pornography is passed over by Ms Haste in silence – nose compressed between finger and thumb, eyes averted, probably.

She thanks one of her friends for inspiring her 'to concentrate on the personal'. It was good advice and might have made for a more entertaining book, but she was not able to follow it. Indeed, with the help of lots of daft statistics ('One survey found that petting increased from 7 per cent among those born before 1904 to 22 per cent among those born 1904–1914 . . .'), she has, rather remarkably, succeeded in removing all sense of human agency whatsoever.

Describing the current situation, she writes: 'As the individual's obligation to conform to externally imposed concepts of moral duty has declined, a sense of moral duty towards self, which may or may not coincide with the community's interest, has increased.'

Oh right. Sounds just like you, doesn't it? Or anybody else? This style of sub-academic writing effectively suppresses the human reality of what is described, shielding the writer, appearing much grander, more remote and authoritative than it actually is (to anyone who can stay conscious while trying to read such stuff, anyway). Knock as long as you like: nobody's home.

Melvyn, of course, is not so shy. He's been writing novels for 25 years now. But he first hit the big time with the sexed-up *The Maid of Buttermere* in 1987 ('the slow tidal wave of sex . . . he woke from a feigned sleep and moved once more inside her to feel the silk and flesh quick sway of this magically alert oblivion where two bodies were one body . . .' etc.).

Then came the fantastic embarrassment of *A Time to Dance* ('Eyes closed, fingers inside you, reaching into the melting fluid rubbered silk – a relief map of mysteries – the eager clitoris, reeking of you, our tongues imitating the fingers . . .' – *Christ!*). And there was the TV version, finally granting us what we have so long wanted, a view of Ronald Pickup's parts.

Was Bragg abashed? On the contrary. He interpreted the catcalls as acclaim. In interviews he explained that Hardy, Lawrence, Updike, Henry Miller, Nabokov and other top-class scribblers had met just the same reception when their erotic masterpieces were published. Hint, hint.

277

Rather impressively, Bragg's new novel, *Crystal Balls*, is even worse than its predecessor. But you wouldn't know it from most of the reviews. Bragg is still the central figure joining the arts and the media. No one wants to offend. In the *Times* Victoria Glendinning gave it half a page of soft soap: '. . . the pressure to communicate, like the lavishness, is appealing. There is material for three novels in *Crystal Rooms*.' Other papers covered themselves differently. Despite the book's obvious newsworthiness, the *Telegraph* and the *Independent on Sunday* ran only oblique short pieces. The craven *Independent* and *Guardian* have somehow avoided reviewing it at all. No matter. It's in the bestseller lists now.

It shouldn't be. It's a mess, equally inept at the level of the single sentence and the whole plot, no less thoroughly sentimental than it is crass.

Because it is non-existence as art, Bragg's own gross tastes come through the more clearly: for Sancerre and other comforts of a lush London life in the media, for taking television seriously – and for icky sexual explicitness. Here we go again: 'He bent over her and kissed her face, stroked her face, kissed her neck, her breasts, with his right hand opened her moist vagina and slipped fingers rapidly into it, working them sensuously round the contours and dark opening flesh which yielded and undulated very slightly . . . Jen reached up and took his hard penis in her hand. Moving gently so as not to excite him too much too soon, but enough for it to swell and gorge to a bruised helmet, she began to graze on him and he on her . . .'

Melvyn likes to keep his hand in, doesn't he? And this sex is supposed to be admirable too, lyrical like. The passages describing the sexual exploits of the fat, sozzled, cynical hack who is not Lynn Barber are aimed straightforwardly at degrading the woman as much as possible. She masturbates drunkenly at work. 'Now she sat contemplating the cheap bog door in that most unbecoming posture – knickers round the ankles, gnocchi-filled stomach straining at the belt, thighs folding over the green stocking tops, skirt exposing too much, oh much too much tile-white bum already glued to the cheap pink plastic seat, and she was left with what had already become an increasingly regular alternative.'

Although married, she goes to bed with a great fat Maxwell lookalike. 'She gorged herself on it . . . Having tied him up, she took one of his hands and guided it, accompanied by her own, into her vagina. "Christ! It's bloody enormous," said Rudolf . . .'

This is the work of a dirty little boy and nothing more. There's a fair distance between this and the laborious, neutralized formulations of Cate Haste. Summarizing the Annan Report, she writes: 'More open portrayal of sexual themes might sometimes prove gratuitous but it could also advance understanding. The pursuit of artistic excellence might involve shock which was not necessarily a bad thing. There was a delicate balance . . .'

Perhaps. But rubbered silk and bruised helmets? No thanks.

3 July 1992

Porn crackers

Pictures at an Exhibition D.M. THOMAS (Bloomsbury)

*F*OR once, the blurb says it all. *Pictures at an Exhibition*, D.M. Thomas's tenth novel, is apparently 'a return to the dark and provocative themes of *The White Hotel*'.

Anyone remember *The White Hotel*? Well, it sold several hundred thousand copies and was translated into 20 languages, and if by 'provocative' you mean exploiting human misery for artistic and commercial gain, then, yes, this too is a provocative book.

The holocaust, Auschwitz and the gas chambers are, of course, exquisitely trendy subjects, the final frontier of the acceptably unacceptable. Madonna will be coming on in swastikas soon, no doubt; but it is all art, isn't it darlings, and terribly *serious*, so we can all gawp with the clearest conscience in the world.

William Styron in *Sophie's Choice* actually surmounted some of these barriers, and we can charitably extend the benefit of the doubt to Martin Amis. But no one up until now, I think, has ever suggested that Auschwitz, grinning skeletons and simmering Jewish fat had any redemptive qualities.

D.M. Thomas in the guise of his various narrative voices appears to take a different view. *Pictures at an Exhibition* kicks off with the memoirs of Dr Chaim Galewski, a Czech Jew whose attendance at the ovens is interspersed with Freudian attempts to repair the damaged psyche of his superior, Dr Lorenz. Everybody, inevitably enough, is convinced that what they are doing is for the best: the whole death camp panorama, consequently, is conveyed with frightening laconicism, all incidentals and throwaway detail.

Galewski records that the train ride to Auschwitz was accompanied by 'the usual overcrowding and starvation, resulting in hundreds of deaths'.

Later on as a prison trusty 'the work was terrible, but we could steal food from the clothes of the victims'. Excavating some mangled corpses in search of plunder, he reveals that 'the bodies were in a pretty filthy state, smeared with shit and even menstrual blood in one case'. All this comes interleaved with some lively set-pieces, including a Jewish girl forced to fellate her former abuser as he hangs garotted, and a 'psycho-sexual experiment' in which the victims are compelled to refrain from orgasm on penalty of death.

While the tone of this opening section – half gloating, half detached – might be difficult to take, what follows is somehow even more depressing. Succeeding chapters home in on a collection of more or less contemporary Londoners – the time is late 1990 – linked by their relation to an elderly Jewish psychologist named Jacobson, their drearily adulterous private lives, and, however marginally, their connection with the lurid Nazi past.

Never mind the frailty of the attachment – all done with dreams, snippets of Freud, amazing coincidences and sado-masochistic jollies; what Thomas seems to be insinuating is that Auschwitz is a common experience, touching us all (there is, predictably, an inane attempt to add Mrs Thatcher to a line of tyrants that takes in Lenin and Hitler). Finally, numbers of people are bloodily knocked off by the psychologist's crazed wife, who believes 'that there was more sense of spirituality in Auschwitz than there is in modern London'.

What is Thomas trying to do? Either he seriously believes that the death camps were some sort of apocalyptic artistic happening, fenced round with kinky sex and symbolism, in which case God help him; or he thinks that you can somehow cope with these horrors by demythologizing them, reducing them to the matter-of-factness of Lorenz and Galewski's fireside chats. But the point about evil is that it isn't assimilable in this way, and to knit a tea cosy of sexy detachment around suffering is simply unforgivable.

Whatever Thomas's motives, the rest is everything the reader of his novels would expect: the cleverness (Thomas's ploy of cannibalizing real life for the purposes of art is mimicked by one of his characters), the pop-eyed sex, the appropriation of historical texts (in this case an account of starving Jewish children reduced to eating mortar from the walls of the house in which they are confined), and the slack formulations of 'devastating blows', 'humiliating events' and 'sensitive adolescents'.

'I dislike the voyeurism of it,' Dr Lorenz observes to Galewski, apropos one of the sex experiments. 'So do I,' Galewski replies. So would anyone. This is a disgusting and repellent piece of work. The only appropriate response to it would be to compel Thomas to visit one of the death camp museums in Eastern Europe and make him watch tapes of piled corpses – real people, you know, who *actually died* – until he was physically sick.

Forget about Red Hot Dutch and the titillations of the top shelf. This is *real* pornography.

12 February 1993

Cock and ball story

While England Sleeps DAVID LEAVITT (Viking)

SIR Stephen Spender – now in his mid-80s – has spent the last half century or so defending his reputation from hostile or mischievous attacks.

Last year's culprit was Hugh David's spectacularly inaccurate *Portrait with Background*, subsequently found to harbour more than 100 errors of fact. Misguided celebrations can be equally unsettling, though, and Sir Stephen's latest recourse to his lawyers has been prompted by an apparent star billing in David Leavitt's current opus about the 1930s, Spain and hot young left-wing breath.

Spender, here masquerading as a writer named Brian Botsford, who conducts a relationship with a likely lad who works on the Underground, looks to have won, as complainants in the world of publishing generally do. At any rate Viking has responded to his displeasure by taking all copies of *While England Sleeps* off the shelves.

Leaving aside questions of identification – and Botsford, with his quivering sexuality, his self-absorption and his journal keeping seems pretty near to the youthful Spender – you can see the litigant's point. Nobody minds appearing in a work of genius, and, as Evelyn Waugh once remarked, you can say what you like about anybody provided you make him attractive to women (not something that applies here, alas), but *this* dainty little amalgam of sententiousness and sodomy? The badness of *While England Sleeps* is surprising, for David Leavitt's previous books – two novels and a brace of short story collections – were excellent: explorations of gay America which succeeded by showing that their protagonists were ordinary people (not a heterosexual's put-down, by the way – most homosexual heroes are either champion satyromaniacs or neurotics).

Stick Leavitt down in pre-war England, though, drench him in the whole Spender/Auden/Isherwood perfumery of arty chat, lefty politics and earnest buggery and he falls to pieces. Why is this?

Apart from the hackneyed theme – upper-class writer meets working-class boy, who breaks his heart and then dies on the way back from Spain – the fault can be laid at the door of the novel's obsessions. These are various – they include communism and the London Underground – but rising effortlessly to dominate them in a single fixation: penises.

In fact Botsford's interest in the male sexual organ is the novel's distinguishing feature. As early as page 20 he is remembering the 'long, disinterested cock' of an old college friend. A bit later, considering a school chum re-encountered as a left-wing activist, he recalls that 'his cock was enormous'.

Fortunately Botsford's own genitalia are a source of equal fascination to others. 'Got quite a big one, have you?' the plebeian Edward suggests on the occasion of their first date. 'Like to see it?' Brian enquires. 'Quite a big one,' a casual pick-up found in a urinal somewhere confirms. 'Want me to take care of it?'

Was it for this, one wonders, that the trailblazers of the gay novel, Firbank, Forster *et al.*, laboured for so long? It will have become clear by now that Leavitt can't do the dialogue. Neither, unhappily, can he shake off a kind of sub-romantic breathlessness that renders most of his rapt descriptions faintly ridiculous.

Never mind the 'long, disinterested cock'; a bit later we come across a 'zealous erection', not to mention some sleeping children who 'exhaled long, ragged ribbons of breath'. All this is interspersed with some serious chatter about communism and some terrible aphorisms of the 'Who touches the body, however fleetingly, also touches the soul' sort.

More interesting, perhaps, is the question of provenance. If Botsford is Spender, then *While England Sleeps* bears an uncanny resemblance to *The Temple* (1988), Spender's fictionalized account of what he got up to in late 1920s Berlin. There is the same self-importance, the same prosy reflection on life and art, the same excitable style. On second thoughts, perhaps we should really be congratulating Leavitt for producing a scintillating exercise in ventriloquism.

Whatever Leavitt's intentions, one wonders why Sir Stephen is so assiduously blocking off a thoroughfare down which he himself has so lately travelled. *While England Sleeps* might be a silly dramatization of the early life and opinions of Sir Stephen Spender, but it is no sillier than some of Spender's own efforts in the same direction.

19 November 1993

11

THE BIG ISSUES

*Freedom, feminism, Fergie,
flying saucers . . .*

Out to lunch

Choose Freedom ROY HATTERSLEY (Michael Joseph)

*W*E know Roy Hattersley the bantamweight politician, the light essayist, the not-so-light luncher. Now meet a new persona: Roy the heavyweight philosopher.

To prepare his public for this implausible role, the fatboy has tried to dump some of his old images. In a recent interview with Daniel Farson (*Sunday Today*, 1 February), Roy spluttered crossly about cartoons showing him 'with double chins and a huge belly', and even more crossly about 'rumours of those damned lunches. I only have three a week and they're business lunches and not always much fun.'

So now we know. What of 'Roy Hattersley' the legendary trencherman, tucking into cherry soup and smoked goose at the Gay Hussar with lamb chops at the Reform Club for afters? An imposter, apparently. The real Roy has no time for more than a cold samosa: he is too busy constructing 'a clear and philosophical basis' for the Labour Party.

The unwary reader may be lured into taking Hatterjee at his own estimation. He writes literately, sometimes even elegantly. He argues with seductive confidence. But if you pause for a moment to consider what he is really saying it turns out to be blithering, blubbery babble. Half the book states the obvious, at great length; the other half is largely nonsense.

For evidence of the former, look no further than the risible title. Or the quote from Tony Crosland which he takes as his text: 'Socialism is about the pursuit of equality and the protection of freedom in the knowledge that until we are truly equal we will not be truly free.' Roy describes this as a 'self-evident truth' – yet proceeds to spend many of his 250 pages repeating it.

When he strays from the 'self-evident', Hatter's intellectual pretensions collapse altogether. He tells us that there are some subjects about which there is no intrinsically 'socialist' position. 'There is, for example, no such thing as a socialist defence or foreign policy – save only for the support of liberty in both the Soviet Union and South Africa.'

Come again? Is there no 'socialist' policy on colonialism, or overseas aid, or the arms race? Why are South Africa and the Soviet Union the only exceptions? Where, for the purposes of Hatterjee's ludicrous argument, does home policy end and foreign policy begin?

Roy is silent on this, as on anything that might be difficult for him. Instead he jabs his pudgy finger at von Hayek, von Mises and other right-wing thinkers: scarcely an original or controversial enterprise for a socialist.

What would be far more interesting would be to know what Slobberchops thinks of the Wilson and Callaghan governments: were they not the embodiment of Hattersism, full of ample-girthed chaps who could quote Tawney and Crosland as easily as Roy does? Where, if anywhere, does he think they went wrong? To answer questions like that, Roy might have to get his hands dirty. So he ignores them.

Roy prefers, daring fellow that he is, to denounce Mrs Thatcher. And, of course, to bang on in the most general way about freedom. He gets himself in a terrible muddle with this. Freedom, he says again and again, is 'the ultimate objective of socialism'; equality is merely a means to that end. Yet he claims that socialism is a commitment to ensure 'the greatest sum of freedom ... and, in consequence, the most human happiness'. So freedom is not an end after all, but a means; the end is now happiness.

Fattersley thus seems to minimize the gap between himself and the frightful Thatcher – a peculiar thing for a *soi disant* 'socialist' to want to do.

She, too, would say that she strives for happiness, freedom and equality. The only difference is in their vision of equality, but since Roy relegates this to a subsidiary position it doesn't seem to matter that much anyway. For what it's worth, Thatcher desires 'equality of opportunity', the modern version of the old line that the Ritz Hotel is open to all. Hatters wants the old Tawneyite idea of 'equality of outcome', a world in which everyone doesn't merely have the right to dine at the Ritz but actually gets to dine there. Unless they'd rather go to the Gay Hussar, of course. The debrecni sausage is delicious.

20 February 1987

Roger's Thesaurus

Untimely Tracts ROGER SCRUTON (Macmillan)

ROGER Scruton is an anomaly: a conservative intellectual. In the past, few Tories have felt a need to theorize and few have been able to write or enunciate clearly. Even now most Tory utterances are pleasantly uncomplicated: the faithful barking of Paul Johnson, say, or the appreciative gargling of Auberon Waugh.

But this will not do for Professor Scruton. He wants his arguments; he has to have his reasons. Of course, to well-brought-up Tories this simply shows him up as a grammar school bug, too keen by half. Scruton knows that intellectuals are a bit off, but he just can't help himself. He is a philosopher, through and through. For the social solidarity which stiffens most reactionaries, he seeks to substitute a flow of 'hences' and 'therefores'.

It is hard work. Not, of course, that conservatism is out of fashion. It was a superb piece of effrontery to call this book *Untimely Tracts*. But even so, trying to find an incontrovertible argument for every little taste, or distaste, is a task no Tory in his right mind would ever set himself. Roger, however, has not been daunted.

Untimely Tracts collects his articles written for the sizzling new *Times*, from 1983 to 1986.

Certain of these pieces simply rehearse the political positions which we all now – do we not? – accept. We should do murderers the courtesy of topping them. Scargill should be tried for sedition. It is no use talking to the Soviet Union. NATO should get chemical weapons. Oxfam and War on Want are not charities. Most teachers are themselves 'diseducated'. Brown-skin people should be taught to speak the Queen's English, not 'creole or pidgin'. School fees should be charged against income tax. It is *deplorable* that MPs 'are no longer drawn from a class which feels no need to use the Commons for the purpose of social gain'. Hereditary peerages are essential to economic stability. 'Hereditary monarchy is, in a sense, the most representative form of government.' We must 'restore to the religious orders the land which our most oppressive monarch once stole from them'.

Well, yes, of course. The joy of the book, however, its distinctive achievement, lies in those more personal and emphatic passages in which Professor Scruton shows us why his aesthetic preferences are not only morally distinguished but also politically necessary.

Take that horrid decimal coinage: 'The dozen, which can be divided by two, three, four and six, had to give way to the decade, which can be divided only by two and five, *and which is therefore resistant to the natural impulse of human generosity.*' No more thruppeny bits to distribute to the deserving and grateful poor, you see.

What are the important institutions in the country? Obviously Peterhouse of Cambridge, the Aldeburgh Festival, and Berry Bros and Rudd, wine merchants of St James. 'Those who do not know it are probably suffering from some moral deficiency...'

What should our apprentice New Right man, ethically, drink? White burgundy, of course, 'this vital component to our culture'. For fine wine is far more educational than anything provided in our degenerate state schools. 'What could better engage the learning of the classicist than the rival claims of Chateau Ausone and Mercurey, the one named from the estate of a Roman poet, the other from the temple of a Roman god? What could stir the English speaker's sense of history more effectively than Chateau Talbot, named from the great Earl of Shrewsbury ... What could more poignantly remind us of the voice of poetry than the great names of Burgundy – Vougeot, Chambertin, Meursault, Chambolle-Musigny les Amoureuses?'

What should the devoted Scrutonian, morally, eat with his *premier crus*? The message is straightforward. 'Eat animals – as many animals as you possibly can – so as to fulfil your duty to the great chain of being.' What should he smoke afterwards? Cigars, non-Cuban, as sold in abundance by JR Cigars of New York; because the choice available is 'a justification of the market economy far stronger than any mentioned in the works of Freidman or Hayek'.

What should he listen to? 'The C Major melody of the Mastersingers, which represents the achievements of bourgeois culture.' What, finally, should he dance – the minuet?

Yes, the minuet. All Scruton's politics are actually aesthetics, aimed ruthlessly at obtaining for himself Batard-Montrachet and ballroom dancing.

These days, he complains, 'what passes for dancing is in fact a lonely parody of the sexual act, a formless vibrating of the body accompanied by vacant expressions and wild movements of the hands and arms'. The minuet, by contrast, is 'exclusive of political fulfilment'. If you do not understand the minuet, he asserts, then you can never understand politics. Mrs Thatcher has got it all wrong. Tipsy twinkletoes rule. OK?

2 October 1987

Cock and bull

Intellectuals PAUL JOHNSON (Weidenfeld & Nicolson)

*T*HE New Right has surprised us with many intriguing new thoughts over the past decade – mostly along the lines that the young, the old, the sick and the poor had best learn to look out for themselves.

However, one of its real corkers has gone unnoticed: the proposition that it is indecent and un-Tory to think too much. Roger Scruton put it nicely in *The Meaning of Conservatism* in 1980: 'Conservatism is characteristically inarticulate . . . Conservatism becomes conscious only when forced to be so . . .' Conservatives should not be ashamed of acting on instinct and prejudice, he specified. They should be glad to be stupid. And of course they have been.

Eight years on, here comes Paul Johnson, having deduced that there's a book in it. Over time his thinking has developed thus: 1) Clever people are bad. 2) Often they're socialists. 3) They deserve to be done over. Bingo, and round to Lord Weidenfeld's for a stupid cheque.

Paul Johnson is the Luca Brassi of the Tory press. Slow on the uptake but effective when he gets going, he ranks now as the chief Tory popularizer, the monarch of the *Mail* opinion pages. Knowing the truth about everything that ever happened, he is not bashful about his competence to pronounce. His credits include *A History of Christianity, A History of the Modern World, A History of the English People* and *A History of the Jews.* All you need to know in one easy volume in each case.

So here we are with *Intellectuals,* otherwise *Great Cock-ups of the Clever Dicks.* This sticks loyally to the technique of his previous triumphs: fillet other people's books and bung in your own sermon. In *Intellectuals* the lesson goes like this: it's these clever lefties that cause all the trouble in the world, they all lead filthy lives themselves, so what right have they got to preach to the rest of us?

Occasionally, however, the argument becomes less sophisticated. One of Mr Johnson's recurrent tactics in this book is to diagnose penis trouble at the root of radicalism. His first intellectual is Rousseau. Why was Rousseau so chippy? Answer: he had a dodgy dick, 'a deformity of the penis in which the urethra opens somewhere on the ventral surface'.

Soon it turns out that almost all of these malcontents had pitiful private parts. Marx? He had a boil on it. Ibsen? He was so embarrassed by what he'd got that 'he would not expose his sexual organs even for the purpose of medical examination'. And Victor Gollancz believed he would lose the thing entirely if he didn't keep his eye on it. 'He would constantly take it out to inspect it, to discover whether it showed signs of VD or indeed if it was still there at all.'

According to his own theory, we can only conclude that Mr Johnson, himself so far to the right, so strongly wishing to conserve things as they are, must be most unusually graced in this department.

In addition to this recital of the clever dicks' dicky dicks, we hear much about their failure, one after another, to wash properly: 'Sartre was notorious for never taking a bath and being disgustingly dirty.' Eggheads also borrow money and don't return it. They're egotistical. And they drink too, you know. Why, Johnson himself once saw Hemingway drink six martinis at a bar in Paris.

Johnson professes to believe that penis health, spruceness and sobriety constitute 'the moral and judgmental credentials of intellectuals to tell mankind how to conduct itself'. The truth is that he hates intellectuals simply for being intellectuals, and any stick is good enough to beat them with. Come to that, any intellectual will do for a beating.

At first it is difficult to grasp the principle of selection that makes Shelley, Hemingway, Sartre, Victor Gollancz, Lillian Hellman, Cyril Connolly, Kenneth Tynan and Rainer Werner Fassbinder important and typical intellectuals. Then light dawns. They've had readable recent biographies or memoirs published, thus saving Johnson from doing any irksome original research.

Not that who they are matters, since Johnson insists they're all the same. As he reviews each 'case', as he calls it, he introduces every slur with a *Mail*-think generalization: 'Like most intellectuals he preferred ideas to people ... As with so many famous intellectuals, people – and that included children and wives – tended to become servants of his ideas ... He was by now, like so many leading intellectuals before him, an expert in the art of self-promotion ... As with most intellectuals, there came a time in his life when he felt the need to identify himself with "the workers".' And so crashingly on.

Unfortunately, although he so convincingly establishes that brains are bad, Johnson fails to tell us, on the positive side, whether or not it is possible to have too much of a good thing. Is there, in his view, an optimum level of cretinization? Has Prince Philip exceeded it?

And where does he place himself? He is of course renowned for his fragrance, his sobriety, his chastity and sweet moderation. No problem there. But brainwise? When he says that 'a dozen people picked at random on the street are at least as likely to offer sensible views on moral and political matters as a cross-section of the intelligentsia', he appears to be allying himself with them. But actually, grotesquely, he is suffering from the classic ailment of ageing columnists. He believes himself to be *Dr* Johnson. Not only is Dr Johnson used to deliver crushing blows at various points in the Johnson narrative but, in case you missed the point, the book is dedicated to 'My first grandchild, Samuel Johnson'.

Reactionary thoughtlessness is a bizarre development for the *New Statesman* firebrand of the 1960s. (The publishers, by the way, are so incredulous to find that Johnson should once have edited the *New Statesman* that they compensate by claiming on the sleeve that he has also edited the *Spectator*, which he has not.) But it makes sense. Johnson once thought for himself. No longer. It is precisely because he has given it up and surrendered the whole question of what to think to the Church and the Conservative Party that he has acquired such facility as a popularizer and propagandist. The move has spared him much of the work that most writers face: a Faustian bargain. This book's mugging of those who have used 'their own unaided intellects' is a form of self-censorship too. Robert Frost was wiser:

> I never dared to be radical when young
> For fear it would make me conservative when old.

14 October 1988

Scrambled Mogg

Picnics on Vesuvius: Steps Towards the Millennium
WILLIAM REES-MOGG (Sidgwick & Jackson)

JUST before Christmas, William Rees-Mogg wrote his last column for the *Independent*. Some bolshie sub gave it the derisive headline: 'Is this the end of life as I know it?' Henceforth his compositions will be appearing in the *Times*.

Senior staff at the *Independent* are heartbroken. From the launch of the paper, they have found him such a dependable guide to the meaning of life, the universe and everything. All you need to do, they discovered, is read

Rees-Mogg's columns carefully and then believe exactly the opposite. It never failed, they say, tearfully. Now they don't know what to think.

At least Rees-Mogg has left behind this treasury of past triumphs, so we can look back and admire the almost supernatural accuracy of his forecasting. On 22 January 1992, for example, looking into Fergie's tea-leaves, Rees-Mogg wrote: 'Nor do I believe for a moment that the duchess's antics, innocent as they seem to be, are doing any damage to the monarchy. The question of the future of the crown is a non-question; it is all got up by the press.' Put a few 'nots' in there, in the right places, and this was an almost uncannily far-sighted assessment.

Or again, on 11 March 1991, when base rates were 13 per cent, Rees-Mogg warned 'any further reduction in interest rates is likely to restart a major house boom'. Indeed! Or rather – *not!* For those lucky few sharing the secret of how to interpret Rees-Mogg, this was priceless information.

No less inspired was his evaluation of Robert Maxwell on 11 November 1991, concluding: 'I am glad he was buried yesterday on the Mount of Olives, which is a place of grace. I shall remember him with affection ...' To the initiated, there could hardly have been a more savage condemnation.

Yet it is not just for his power of prediction that we must revere Rees-Mogg. Rather, it is for the sheer grandeur of his style, the way he sweeps so impressively from the tiniest detail of his own life to the great questions of history, with scarcely a pause – in fact, let's admit, with never a pause – between.

Who else would dare begin an article ('Landmarks in a Life Which Has Seen the Shadow of War Lifted') like this: 'On my tenth birthday, 14 July 1938, I was given an ice-cream cake with a cricket-bat and ball on top; it was big enough to be shared with the 30 boys in my house at school. Four months before, Hitler had invaded Austria ... Two months after my birthday, Neville Chamberlain flew to Munich'?

At the time, Rees-Mogg was probably alone in realizing which was the critical date of the three. Now we are all privileged to share that thrilling perspective – and there are many such moments here.

Truly, he is a man of destiny. 'Destiny has a way of making itself,' he says here in passing of his own marriage. She may have been his secretary, but it was meant.

It is this sublime confidence in himself, as a Mogg and a Wessex man, that permits him to take such long views, not just from year to year, but from century to century, millennium to millennium, into eternity indeed. For Rees-Mogg, it just all joins up.

So what does the great seer foresee? Good news! He foresees *dooooom.*

Yup, things are going to be OK! Who would have thought it?

According to Rees-Mogg, the world is facing imminent economic and social collapse, what with the slitty eyes beavering away, mugging getting out of hand, overpopulation, nuclear proliferation, Aids and all.

On Aids, says Rees-Mogg with a touch of justifiable pride, he has done 'special work'. There's a whole section about it here, and his conclusion is, as ever, that only religion can save us: 'Christian morality is a strategy for survival', you see. Condoms are useless. 'The "unzip a condom" approach to the HIV epidemic reminds me of the filter-tip response to the issue of cigarette smoking and cancer,' he says scornfully.

There may be those who will say that this remark shows that Rees-Mogg, for all his wisdom, is a little out of touch with modern life. After all, they might observe, most condoms these days use the more comfortable button-fastening; zips are hardly ever seen.

But this is petty quibbling. Of the basic truth, that only becoming a Catholic right away can avert the end of the world, there can be no doubt. The millennium is coming, you see. 'By the year 2000' is Rees-Mogg's favourite way of beginning a sentence. 'As we approach 2000 years after Christ, this ancient human fear of some final calamity is not as unthinkable as it would have seemed 50 years ago,' he says.

Only a 'worldwide spiritual revolution' can help. Only the Pope can resist Islam. Only saints, and sages from Somerset, can lead us now.

Travelling the country, he met some black people once. 'I was particularly touched by the young black boy, with the scars of handcuffs on his wrists, who said to me: "It must be grand to be a lord".'

What he seems not to realize is that we all feel like this about him. Our gratitude is bottomless. For as he says, 'saints are so important in the spread of religious belief. They profess their faith, but their conduct is the real evidence of its truth.' Yes, indeed.

'I am certain that we are all eternal spirits, with an eternal purpose,' Rees-Mogg tells us. 'We are all like eggshells filled with spiritual realities we cannot begin to understand, filled indeed with the whole glory of Heaven.'

Some of us are hardboiled, some soft, others poached, and a few are scrambled, but we all can, if we choose, enter the new year and eventually the next millennium, hand in hand with Lord Rees-Mogg.

1 January 1993

Psi's Corner

The Hidden Power BRIAN INGLIS (Jonathan Cape)

As every publisher knows, the public has an unquenchable thirst for bilge about the supernatural. Any sort of half-witted tosh about Bermuda Quadrangles, Abominable Snowmen and UFOs is guaranteed to go down a treat, especially if it presents a theory linking them all (Yeti Space Pirates). Most propaganda for astral projection, ley-lines, henges and poltergeists has been published by small businesses called 'Aquarian Press' or 'Arkana', but recently the big boys have moved in, led by Cape, and they have not been offering essays in scepticism. Who wants to read about weird things *not* happening?

In 1982 Cape's made a packet with a ludicrous book commissioned by Tom Maschler. *The Holy Blood and the Holy Grail*, which claimed that Jesus had it off with Mary Magdalene, produced a number of children including Barrabas, was not crucified and founded a dynasty in France, looked after ever since by a secret society led at various times by Botticelli, Leonardo da Vinci, Isaac Newton, Victor Hugo, Debussy, Cocteau and Uncle Tom Cobbley. Nice one. In their autumn list they have announced an even more gripping follow-up, *The Messianic Legacy*: 'Was there more than one Christ? Was Christ the founder of Christianity? Were the disciples as peace-loving as is traditionally believed? What do the Nuremberg rallies and rock concerts have in common? What links York Minster with *Star Wars*? Drawing on a vast range of disciplines, the authors provide a fascinating discussion of politics, advertising, marriage, art, Jung, royalty and consumerism to assess the present climate of opinion.'

It can hardly miss. And having scored once, Cape are now going the whole hog. September will see another Maschler special, *The Geller Effect*, 224 pages of self-applause by the Israeli charlatan, dictated to Guy Lyon Playfair, author of such hard-hitting studies as *The Cycles of Heaven: Cosmic Forces and What They Are Doing to You*, and *This House is Haunted: An Investigation of the Enfield Poltergeist*. Meanwhile, with *The Hidden Power* they are attempting to make the market they are exploiting respectable.

The author Brian Inglis is, after all, a man with a notable career behind him, his accomplishments have included editing the *Spectator* and creating such TV programmes as *All Our Yesterdays*. It is only in his twilight years that his talents have been applied in the rather less estimable job, so dramatically abandoned by his friend, Arthur Koestler, of fronting for ghoulies.

Inglis is not, of course, unique in his admiration for flying saucers, spoon-benders and things that go bump in the night. Many of our greatest thinkers, such as Bernard Levin, who describes the book as an 'extraordinarily important and valuable work', are equally devoted to the Hidden Power or 'Psi' as Inglis defines the mysterious force that lies behind such disparate phenomena as spoon-bending, venus fly-traps and the migration of birds.

Much of this book consists of abuse of scientists for being trapped in a materialist and rationalist view of the world. He seems unaware that his incessant combat with 'scientism' is not only self-imposed but also essentially a struggle with himself, with his own habits of thought. Those of religious conviction will not find some of his 'psi phenomena' particularly surprising – only not important or spiritually significant. Typically it is those who have had their faith shattered by science who attempt to recover it by the ridiculous means of telepathy tests and the controlled levitation of ping-pong balls: hoping that science will thus give them back the sense of mystery that science took away. Inglis admits as much. Although from leprechaun country, he was schooled at Shrewsbury and 'brought up to regard science as a religion'. He has never escaped this influence, succeeding only in turning heretic within it. Just as the *Holy Blarney* authors say 'From our investigations emerges a living and plausible Jesus – a Jesus whose life is both meaningful and comprehensible to modern man,' so Inglis makes the cretinous remark that psychical research can 'restore a measure of credibility to religions'.

The intellectual degradation parapsychology enthusiasts are prepared to undergo reflects the importance of the hopes and fears they have invested in it. Inglis produces some nifty applications for 'psi', including dowsing for lost car keys and 'remote viewing one's car and intuiting dangerous mechanical defects', but he dreams of greater things. Although he denies any 'longing to believe', when he sees Uri Geller fiddling with a fork he hopes somehow, if this inexplicable thing can happen, maybe death is not the end.

11 July 1986

Milking the saucer

Alien Liaison: The Ultimate Secret TIMOTHY GOOD (Century)

*A*s the millennium approaches, nutters will multiply. It's a rule. Wait and see.

Here, for example, we have a millennial bestseller. Its publisher, Century, describes it as 'a story which will completely overturn our understanding of our place in the Universe. It is the ultimate secret.' If Century really believed this, it might justly be disappointed that the book is only number five in the bestseller list, lagging behind Delia Smith's *Complete Illustrated Cookery Course* and *Toujours Provence*. As it is, Century executives must be hugging themselves.

Timothy Good's previous book, *Above Top Secret*, published in 1987, claimed that flying saucers are constantly flitting all about us, but that the governments of the world choose to suppress the evidence, which otherwise would be plentiful and incontrovertible. With its beautifully calculated appeal to paranoia, this argument pre-empted all possible objection. So there's no proof of the existence of UFOs? Yes, *ample* proof. It's just that none of us is allowed access to it by the world's secret services. Naturally, under the circumstances, any rumour that escapes their monitoring must be given maximum credit.

Alien Liaison goes a step further. It's a fantastic jumble of stories about UFOs and aliens. 'In the last few years alone,' says Good, 'the massive scale of bewildering sightings, landings, contacts and abductions might convey the impression that Earth has become a kind of cosmic Clapham Junction.' And Good's a cosmic train-spotter.

The US has been test-flying captured UFOs in the Nevada desert. A retired US air force security guard socialized with aliens over a long period on his ranch in Colorado. An alien was captured alive in New Mexico in 1947 and kept for a few years at Los Alamos. Other extra-terrestrial beings have been the guests of the US government at various times since. Aliens have been industriously mutilating cattle in Arizona, concentrating on the sexual parts. A Brazilian man called Antonio had sex with an alien, twice, on a spacecraft, in October 1957.

She was 4½ feet tall, blonde, with a pointy chin, thin lips, 'high well-separated breasts, thin waist and small stomach, wide hips and large thighs' plus 'very red' pubic hair. Fantastic, eh? But even so, Antonio wouldn't swap our women for alien tarts. 'I like a woman with whom you can talk and converse and make yourself understood, which wasn't the case here. Furthermore, some of the grunts that I heard coming from that woman's mouth at certain moments nearly spoiled everything, giving the disagreeable impression that I was with an animal.' And besides, records Good, the Brazilian afterwards 'began to suffer from what can only be described as a type of cosmic "clap": severe headaches, burning and watering of the eyes, then excessive sleepiness followed by the appearance of various lesions on the body'. Use a condom next time, eh Toni?

None of Good's stories is usefully documented. That 'Colorado Break-through'? 'As a prerequisite to relating their experiences, the witnesses insisted on anonymity and requested that the precise location of their ranch in Colorado should not be divulged.' And so it goes.

'Suffice it to say, for the time being, that even if the entire MJ-12 document turns out to be fraudulent, I am convinced that the information contained therein, at least, is *essentially* factual.' The most frequently cited reference is back to Good's own previous books, as if they could be used to legitimate this one at the same time as they are themselves endorsed as a valid source. In this way, fictions gain the appearance of fact.

Nothing can give Good pause. And he has a wonderful way with inconsistencies. They're further proof! What about the fact that all these eyewitness descriptions of aliens are inconsistent? Some are eight feet tall, some four; some are green, some grey. A poser, no? No. It's because at least nine different species have been visiting Earth recently.

Obvious, really. And what about the fact that some UFOs turn out, on closer inspection, to be helicopters or planes. It's because the cunning little beasties *are disguising* their spacecraft as helicopters, of course. 'The idea is not as absurd as it seems,' says Good, wrongly. 'Mysterious unmarked aircraft have long been associated with the UFO phenomenon ... and it seems to me entirely feasible that aliens might disguise their vehicles or even produce facsimile aircraft ... as well as render their craft and themselves invisible, in order to keep us in a perpetual state of confusion.' So even planes and helicopters are further proof of saucers!

Like all believers in the paranormal, Good has faith. And he's not alone. There's a pugnacious introduction to this book by its dedicatee, the former Admiral of the Fleet and current clown, Lord Hill-Norton. He says he finds Good's 'astounding revelations' impossible to dismiss. 'The plain fact is that either what he reports here is true, or it isn't.' And he intends to treat it as true until it is 'equally publicly disproved'.

But as the expression of an internal need, rather than the product of external events, such faith is quite invulnerable to contradiction, let alone discouragement by any paucity of evidence. The need to believe doesn't go away when reasons for belief are lacking. If anything, it is exacerbated.

As an ingenious way of writing science fiction, *Alien Liaison* would be amusing enough. We all love spooky stories. But that's not what it's about. Good (formerly a violinist) is looking to UFOs for *salvation*. 'We may owe our very survival to some of these beings from elsewhere, since it is claimed that on several occasions they have intervened to prevent nuclear catastrophe. In addition to being motivated by compassion, they may also have a vested interest in the survival of our planet and its species,' he concludes, piously, pathetically.

This is to feed a deep human hunger with garbage. And that ain't funny, it's a sin.

16 August 1991

Wither the C of E?

The New Archbishop Speaks GEORGE CAREY (Lion)
Free to Believe DAVID JENKINS & REBECCA JENKINS (BBC Books)

IN the beginning was the Word? Not with these two it wasn't, not by a long chalk. Both their books are shocking – not because of the opinions they express, but because of the dullness and ineptitude with which they are written.

To anyone unused to reading the publications of Church of England men, it comes as a revelation – the wrong kind of revelation. Suddenly you see why Anglicanism is in such decline. George Carey is a suitable leader of this church; his book presenting 'the heart of his thinking on key issues of faith and life' consists of short chapters on the obvious topics, organized in four parts – *What Does It Mean To Be Human? What Is The Gospel? How Do We Live Human Lives? How Can We Understand The Bible?* – all salvaged from previous publications by Carey, and now decked out with a new introduction and epilogue. 'With all the rush of preparation,' says Carey, 'I would not have had time to write a new book' – nor the wit.

Doctrinally there's nothing new here. 'Although these chapters describe the core of my thinking,' he says, 'they do not represent its leading edge.' Sure, he's keen on 'gifts of the Spirit' such as speaking in tongues, and on evangelism or 'sharing good news', but he still keeps to the great C of E rule that one can be too extreme on either side, and that it's always safer to drive down the middle of the road.

What *is* new is the amazing bathos generated by his attempts to be homely. So what are these here Christian sacraments, George? 'When a football team score the winning goal in a cup final, the fervent supporters cheer their heads off, throw their caps in the air, jump up and down and yell, "We've won the cup!" ... The ritual, or action, gives expression to what is said. This is what Christians mean when they talk about sacraments.'

Oh right. But wot about this mind and body business? 'The biggest mistake is to think of ourselves as owning a soul as we would a suitcase or an umbrella. This was the way the ancient Greeks thought.' Coo! Was it? Learn something new every day. And this *conversion*, wot's that, boss? 'In Britain, during the change from coal gas to natural gas, people spoke about being "converted" to natural gas. When used of the Christian life it is associated with moving from one way of living to another ...' Sort of a valve change, is it? And faith, wot's faith? 'You buy a present for your husband's birthday, a watch perhaps, believing the maker's guarantee that it is reliable. That is faith.' Nah, that's just a guarantee, that is, George, take it from me.

Every one of Carey's terms of value is used thoughtlessly. He's a classic sucker for 'relevant' and 'authentic', sometimes in the same sentence. 'What is important is that our worship should be relevant to the congregation and its culture – otherwise it will not be authentic.'

'You have to understand,' Carey says, 'that I have always been a deeply-thinking person.' Few will be up to such a leap of faith.

The Bishop of Durham is a lot brighter, well up to civil servant level, and therefore one of the greatest brains the Church of England has had this century. However, he still couldn't write his own book. Although in the first person throughout, *Free to Believe* was composed by another, his daughter Rebecca, 'ordering and weaving together either what the Bishop of Durham has specifically written, or the content of his thought and argument, distilled and put into other words'.

This is a scandal: it reduces a serious book to the level of a ghosted celeb-biog. It means one has no idea how much weight to put on its words. Nor apparently does Jenkins. In the proof copy was the sentence, 'David Jenkins is personally prepared to stand by, and be identified with, every sentence written.' In the finished copy it had been cut. Understandably – this book too is horribly written, full of 'interfaces', 'wavelengths' and phrases like 'the current availability of God'.

Jenkins (or whoever) is attempting here to decide what kind of God could conceivably be worth worshipping. It's an honest endeavour and a necessary one for any Christian – but it doesn't come well from a 65-year-old bishop appointed to lead a flock.

Anyway, most of Jenkins's findings are negative. He keeps saying: if God's like that, sod Him. 'If God cannot cope with secularisation and contemporaneity then he is no god and we should have none of him.' 'If God knows everything in a computer-like way – including all the things that are going to happen – it is very difficult to believe in God at all.' 'If . . . God in the end is to reveal His true nature by delivering sinners to the Beast, while sitting back in Heaven with the righteous few to watch the fun, then surely it is the duty of all decent men and woman to be atheists. Such a god must be an idol, a tribal deity, a human fantasy and projection.' And so on. It is these vehement rejections of a God he personally finds unacceptable that have made him a media figure.

Where Jenkins is more positive is politics. Paragraph after paragraph resemble *New Statesman* editorials. The accounting system of the health service is wrong. The poll tax is hard for the poor to pay. The Metro Shopping and Leisure Centre near Gateshead may have too high a percentage of service industries and shops to continue to flourish in the long term. 'Anyone trying to get round London in a taxi these days has plenty of time to reflect on the destructive effects of affluence as we now understand it . . .'

Yet he knows (or they know) perfectly well that 'history demonstrates that it is not possible to arrange human society so as to neutralise the effects of sin' – or even to avoid traffic jams.

In so openly trying to find a religion and a God that are acceptable to him, Jenkins proves, more devastatingly than any external critic could, that Anglicanism has nothing left to offer (except jobs). It has no identity; it stands for nothing. If, finally, Jenkins does find such a religion, he'll have to found it too.

26 April 1991

Porn cocktail

Recipes from Le Manoir aux Quat' Saisons RAYMOND BLANC
(Guild Publishing/Macdonald Orbis)

*W*E live in a country where for several weeks now this has been the bestselling 'hardback manual'. Goodbye to the joy of sex; hello to the ecstasy of stuffing your face. Who needs *postillionage* when you can have *nage de homard au cumin*?

Raymond Blanc runs one of the most expensive but most highly acclaimed restaurants in the country, a few miles outside Oxford. A meal there for two tends to cost just a wee tidge more than the average weekly wage. To our leading dainty feeders, he is the living God, top gun, monarch of the glen, queen of the night, artiste of genius.

In a preface to this book, Egon Ronay says his platefuls are 'lyrical and akin to poesy'. As for his recipes: 'Like pearls from oysters, they result from lonely, struggling effort, and also from intelligence and quite exceptional intuition.' Well, in his line of business you do meet a better class of oyster.

Raymond is not shy of commending his own efforts either, hailing himself as 'kissed by the Muse of Flambe'. And food comes first in his view of the world, explaining even international affairs: 'Might a terrible dinner lead to war and a wonderful meal bring world peace, no less?'

Even what gets cooked has reason to be grateful, he thinks. He recalls 'the wonder of a fat capon studded with black truffles, surrounded by a ballet of the brightest red freshwater crayfish. Never could this capon have looked so good, even at the greatest and proudest moment of its life.' It probably couldn't believe its luck.

Of course Raymond is right. He's the master. He speaks the truth. When he says 'never be reticent – you deserve the best', it is no more than what I've been telling myself for years. He has quite the correct attitude to British tradesmen: 'Do not feel shy about asking a butcher to prepare a cut to your requirements ... if he seems surprised or reluctant at first, remember that you are helping him rediscover his craft.' Absolutely.

I'm sure he would agree with Lewis Carroll, who wrote to a child that if she got poor service in a shop she should stick a pin into the laggard's hand and say 'look sharp, stupid'. I expect Raymond would specify a 9-in Sabatier Professional.

Then there is his commitment to innovation. Sir Epicure Mammon resolved to eat 'the tongues of carps, dormice, and camel's heels ... the beards of barbels served instead of salads . . . the swelling unctuous paps of a fat pregnant sow, newly cut off, dressed with an exquisite and poignant sauce'. Raymond would think him a timid ascetic.

He has recipes here for 'terrine of fillets of venison, teal, pigeons and pheasant, wrapped in a mousse of their own livers, studded with wild mushrooms and hazelnuts', and 'pig's trotters filled with sweetbreads, garnished with veal tongue, kidneys and foie gras, served with the braising juices spiked with morels'. Just the thing for elevenses.

Squeamish he is not. Snail eggs? 'Quite delicious.' His instructions on sweetbreads go like this: 'There are two types, the long dangly ones from the throat, and the oval round ones from the heart; always use the latter.' He protests about not being allowed in this country to force-feed his own ducks and geese for foie gras, and tells us when buying to 'take hold of the top of one of the lobes (at room temperature) and pull apart; the foie gras should stretch slightly, with little resistance, then crack open'. Truly he is a man who would eat his own toes if the right recipe occurred to him.

So, a hero. But, alas, his book is not so straightforwardly admirable. Raymond asserts that his cooking is practical, derived from his rural French upbringing ('enchanted nights hunting for frogs') and from the ways of his mother, grandmother and food-loving ancestors. But this is not the selling point.

His admirers, such as Hugh Johnson, prefer to believe that 'he uses cookery as an artist uses light: to reveal his own vision of the world . . .' A crime then to *eat* the stuff: better put in it an art-book, which is what has been done here. Once upon a time cookery books consisted of written instructions meant for use; *Recipes from Le Manoir aux Quat' Saisons* is a manual only in the sense that it is equipment for a culinary hand-job.

Beautifully produced (colour separation in Milan), large and pricey, it is for drooling over only. It is a triumph of the designer 1980s; the type is elegantly grey, the paper slick; there are cute rustic engravings everywhere; and the pictures by 'top food photographer Michael Boys' are unbelievable.

These are not meals. 'Roast fillet of new season's lamb served with a crab flan masked with a curry sabayon' takes its ease in the garden, resting on a moss-covered step, while daffodils nod in obeisance all round. It is as if the food itself were having the picnic.

It's culinary porn, of course; and drooling foodies won't have long to wait for their next slice. These elevated adult mags are highly lucrative.

The frankly named *Dining in Grand Style* is already out, and Ebury Press had advertised for May a series called 'Flights of Fancy', promising 'unforgettable meals, stunning settings, food to fire the imagination ... Every title in this magnificent new series is lavishly illustrated in colour with over forty photographs shot on location to bring each menu to life', they say.

Eat the document. We're all Epicure Mammons now.

1 April 1988

Bum deal

Rosemary Conley's Complete Hip and Thigh Diet (Arrow)
Callanetics CALLAN PINCKNEY with SALLY BATSON (Arrow)
The BBC Diet DR BARRY LYNCH (BBC Books)

THESE three books are among the four bestselling paperbacks in the country, joined at the top only by the Comic Relief package. Since this is the time of year when people begin to fantasize about looking halfway fuckable on their holidays while simultaneously pigging themselves on Easter eggs, the sales are going to go on growing too. Fat tracts make fat profits.

The success of *The BBC Diet* book must be a tribute to the power of television, for it is honest and dull. Dr Lynch awkwardly insists on painful truths: 'If you take in more energy (calories) in your food than your body needs for your particular lifestyle, then your body will lay down that surplus energy as fat. The *only* way to lose weight is to take in less energy and expend more.'

There are no magic diets. He even says: 'You may have to accept the fact, even when you're down to your ideal weight and have toned your muscles up by regular exercise, that you still may not be happy with the shape of your body.'

Arrow books lead the publishing field in deluding the lardy. They specialize in books offering magic solutions, garnished with uplift, and have evidently got the package right. *The BBC Diet* has a plain cover showing a tape measure. The other two show a similar portion of slim stomach, bum and thighs of a young girl springing up against a blue background, with bright yellow lettering: good times on your sunny Med hols, you see.

Both Arrow writers claim to work miracles. *Callanetics* (famously practised by moundy Fergie) professes to tell you 'How to Look 10 Years Younger in 10 Hours'. It is no coincidence that like a religion, the discipline is named after its founder. What is offered here is salvation through discipleship. Callan Pinckney has more in common with L. Ron Hubbard or the 'Revd' Moon than with boring Dr Lynch. It is all evangelism: 'I too was lost and now am found.' Callanetics is a classic American degeneration of the religion impulse.

The actual recommendation is not to diet or lose weight at all, but to 'tighten up' with specialized exercises, concentrating especially on the bum. 'You can have a round, firm, peach-shaped behind, just like the little suntanned girl in the Coppertone sun oil ads,' she whispers. 'When you walk, you feel as if puppet strings are pulling your buttocks into the air' – apparently this sensation is to be considered agreeable. Americans, it becomes clear, think more of, if not with, their buttocks than their brains. Reagan explained.

Ms Pinckney is as shameless as Cellini in self-praise. 'New students, meeting me for the first time, often exclaim, "You have the tightest, most beautiful body I've ever seen."' She climaxes in triple adjective clusters: 'A fabulous, tight, fit figure'; 'a high, round, firm behind'. However, she has a little unwisely illustrated her book with horrific pictures of her students in their underwear, before and after, looking hardly any different.

But faith has never been vulnerable to fact, and what she is flogging here is a cure for mortality. 'Old age really *is* a state of mind,' she insists. You can become young again almost at once. 'The movements I teach produce results in *hours* not days, weeks, or months.' No wonder tyrannized women with 'thunder thighs', 'whale tails' and 'tree stump ankles' are queuing up to be told that 'dieting is not necessary for most people'.

Rosemary Conley has two paperbacks among the top ten best-sellers, *Rosemary Conley's Hip and Thigh Diet*, and *Rosemary Conley's Complete Hip and Thigh Diet*. The second contains all the recipes in the first filled out with readers' letters, charts of their slimming, and blank pages headed 'My Favourite Starter Menus'. An artist then; British with it.

To give her her due, she is not a disguised religious maniac but an overt Born Again Christian. Again the message is change your life and be saved. Again there is confession: the bulk of this book consists of letters from readers proclaiming that they have been beatified by the previous book. On every page Conley describes her diet as 'wonderful', a 'miracle eating plan'.

This plan is actually a bog-standard, wholly unoriginal low-fat diet. If adhered to it would help overall weight loss. But it is presented as somehow, mysteriously, specially targeted on the dreadful bum and thigh again, where women's fears converge. There is no factual basis for this, but then what is offered is a creed. (Her description of binge eating is nothing but an evangelical's account of sin: 'it's a nasty, deceptive, slippery slope'.)

Ms Conley operates in a weird world of faith and unbelief: 'To me there is absolutely no doubt whatsoever that cellulite exists.' She even ends up in a grotesque parody of the Creed itself: 'I also believe that Hip and Thigh massage creams did help improve the appearance of my own thighs . . .'

Both these Arrow books are addressed exclusively to women – exclusively to women's bums, in fact. They play, sometimes cruelly, on fears that their lives will be empty without a peachy rear. With a better behind is promised salvation and fulfilment.

Ms Conley reduces the whole problem of human life to firming the gluteus maximus. More complex faiths cannot compete.

1 April 1989

Bouquet of Barbied dolls

The Beauty Myth NAOMI WOLF (Chatto)

PUBLISHERS – why else would they be publishers? – lack information. To them a new book is only ever comprehensible as another version of an old book. So you get 'in the tradition of . . .' – as it might be, James Bond, Iris Murdoch, Wicked Willie.

Chatto came up with a corker for *The Beauty Myth*: 'The direct descendant of *The Second Sex* and *The Female Eunuch*, this book is a cultural hand grenade for the Nineties.' It's a perfect sentence, the second half unexpectedly matching the wondrous fatuity of the first.

This, Chatto says, is 'the book which will, finally, change women's lives'. Perhaps by finally sickening them with such books. For *The Beauty Myth* is just a mess – a cultural spongebag for the 1990, they might have said.

It slops pitifully around a painful and unresolvable subject: the importance of appearances. Any real thought about this subject would involve thought about what it is to be at once body and soul, to have life on the condition of death, to live in time – thorny problems which numerous brainy characters have pondered inconclusively, problems not likely suddenly to be cleared up for good by a brightly packaged item from Chatto.

There is *no* thought here, only agitation. Naomi Wolf believes that women, having won the freedoms fought for by an earlier generation of feminists, are putting themselves back in chains by preoccupation with slenderness and beauty – a new phenomenon, according to her.

She's hysterical. Sample: 'The experience of living in an anorexic body, even if that body is housed in an affluent suburb, is the experience of a body living in Bergen-Belsen ...' Dieting, she thinks, is 'more bizarre than cannibalism'.

Her final chapter, on going 'Beyond the Beauty Myth', is a bouquet of imperious idiocies. 'We must see that it does not matter what women look like so long as they feel beautiful' – and why not let's see that the Iraqis lie down the with Israelis, while we're about it?

Women must be nicer to other women. 'Older women can look at a young woman struggling at something familiar and take her out for coffee.' They *can*?

We arrive at the end of the world. 'It is also in men's interest to undo the myth because' – wait for it – 'the survival of the planet depends on it.' For the usual reasons.

There is one interesting section which explains the rest. Naomi Wolf had a miserable year as an anorexic teenager, and self-importantly she is still looking for someone else to blame. 'Who is obliged to make reparations to me ...? Who owes me ...? There is certainly a charge of guilt to be made, long overdue. But it doesn't belong to me. It belongs somewhere, and to something else.' That's as near as she gets to nailing the guilty men, or women, or images, or, ooh heck, *anything*. Her prose consequently has a severe problem with *agency*.

Who's doing all these bad things? She ain't got the foggiest. Women go shopping, she says, because 'somehow, somewhere, someone must have figured out that they will buy more things if they are kept in the self-hating, ever-failing, hungry and sexually insecure state of being aspiring "beauties"'. Let's go get 'em! Her sentences fudge away. 'The beauty myth was perfected to checkmate power at every level in individual women's lives' – perfected by whom? 'If this society really cared about women's health, it would ease up on the beauty myth' – and it'd come over for tea more often too.

'How might women act beyond the myth?' she asks on the last page.

We're agog. Weary, but agog. Suddenly, she becomes decisive. She writes: 'Who can say.' No question mark. It's a confession that might usefully have come a little earlier. On the jacket, for example.

28 September 1990

Lost in the male

Iron John ROBERT BLY (Element)

*M*UCH the best of the recent batch of books about Mr Major, this intriguing study claims that, under his deceptively mild exterior, the Prime Minister really does have a will of iron . . . No, you're right. Not really. Let's try again.

Iron John is a self-help manual for bashful men. It has been at the top of the American bestseller list all year. In Britain, however, it is published by Element Books, an obscure huddle of cranks in Shaftesbury who pump out garbage about Gurdjieff, aromatherapy, King Arthur, shamanism and foot massage.

The disparity confirms that this is a book of almost exclusively American interest. If it tells you little about men in general, it reveals an embarrassing amount about the hapless US male, reeling from feminism and still traumatized by Vietnam.

Though Bly's a poet, it's an ill-formed and laborious harangue. He takes a short Grimm fairy tale and repetitiously expounds its meaning, paragraph by paragraph, in the manner of the late Bruno Bettelheim.

A king's son leaves home and goes into the woods with 'Iron John', a hairy 'wild man' whom he has released from captivity. The incognito prince becomes a servant in another court. As he gets older, he is secretly aided by his mentor, Iron John, to become a great knight. Finally, he marries the king's daughter and forthwith Iron John is released from the spell which had kept him a 'wild man'.

Bly reads the story as an idealized image of masculinity. True manhood is attained only through initiation by an older man; it also involves getting in touch with 'the warrior' within.

We need to learn this again, says Bly, because under the assault of feminism

American men have become ashamed of masculinity itself. He wants men to be proud of being men. This involves no direct attack on feminism. Rather, Bly artfully praises feminists for expressing women's pain, rousing their pride, and cultivating sisterly solidarity. Then he borrows their techniques to do exactly the same for men. It's masculinism, feminism for men, and like feminism it's a separatist movement.

Iron John has already become the male equivalent of *The Female Eunuch*. It is even less coherent, but no matter. American men are plainly in desperate need for any book saying what this book says. They *must* be. How else could such tripe triumph so?

For Bly's made a bollocks of it. He has presented his arguments not as rational arguments, but in the form of an instant holy book of myths. In this, again, he has imitated radical feminism, with its awful nonsense about the Great Mother and all that.

Not content merely to make the Iron John story into a gospel text, Bly tries to create a comprehensive old testament too. Ancient myths are blenderized into Bly's myth-soup, ancient societies lightly chucked in as thickening.

'I would estimate,' Bly says, pretending to be careful, 'that people in the West lost their ability to think mythologically around the year 1000.'

Unfortunately, Bly himself still has it in spades. He graciously introduces us to 'the eternal realm'. 'Dionysus is still alive there, Freya, Odin, and Thor, the Virgin Mary, Kali, Buddha, Zeus, and Allah, Athena and Artemis and Sophia.' All getting on famously together, no doubt. What a wonderful apotheosis of the American way! Cultural relativism in the next world too.

Bly has the knack, essential to the composition of American self-help books, of arbitrarily giving names to concepts and then treating them with the utmost seriousness, as if they really existed. There's such a thing he decrees, as 'soul water'. 'The upper fifty feet or so of water in the male soul is, as we all know, very roiled and turbid these days.' The 'or so' is brassier even than the 'as we all know'.

'We can deduce then,' he remarks, 'that every man on earth will experience a Destructive Brutal Warrior as well as a Constructive Warrior, and a Dark Trickster as well as a Playful Trickster.'

Oh we can, can we? Bly deploys this coercive 'we', and those spuriously logical conjunctions ('so', 'therefore', 'thus', 'because'), non-stop, to cudgel the reader's brains into submission. No doubt many lame Harrys, limp Dicks and poor Johns in the States do need to be helped to stand up for themselves. But do they *really* need to be helped to be *hairy*?

Yes, yes, says Bly. Because 'powerful sociological and religious forces have acted in the West to favour the trimmed, the sleek, the cerebral, the non-instinctive, and the bald'. Oh dear. What we need now, you see, is 'a religious figure but a hairy one', 'a sort of hairy Christ'.

And where do we find him? Within! 'When a contemporary man looks down into his psyche, he may, if conditions are right, find under the water of his soul, lying in an area no one has visited for a long time, an ancient hairy man ... every modern male has, lying at the bottom of his psyche, a large, primitive being covered with hair down to his feet.' So there.

13 September 1991

Fathering about . . .

Fatherhood: Men Write About Fathering Ed. Sean French (Virago)

CLEVER Virago! Commissioning this book was an act of genius. Most feminist publishing houses would never dream of publishing a book written entirely by men. Why give men more space, when they already have so much?

But at Virago they knew better. Give men enough rope and they'll hang themselves. And, sure enough, *Fathering* is a spectacular mass suicide. It's one great hubbub of pompous old gits and bratty young twirps all shouting to be heard. Look at my rope! It's bigger than your rope!

No incensed polemicist or wily satirist could have come up with a more devastating portrayal of male vanity than these men have themselves unwittingly supplied in this little collection of essays. It'll serve as a feminist coconut-shy for years to come.

If one had any criticism of this masterpiece, it would surely be that at 120 pages, it's too short. It's hard to imagine what difficulties the editor, Sean French, could possibly have faced in gathering contributions. For quite a few men are fathers. Many of us know one.

And then it turns out the contributors haven't really understood the title anyway, since half of them choose to maunder on about their own fathers – that is, about being *sons*. If that's the definition, then most men – one might almost say all – have had a father of some kind or other.

Sean French could have chosen almost anybody. But instead – in pursuit no doubt of a more concentrated effect – he has chosen to use only his pals and ex-work mates from the jobbing litterateurs of North London, perked up with a little ethnic spice.

For brief though the book is, French has gathered here at least one classic example of every kind of male self-importance. He sets the pace himself by launching, in the very first paragraph of his introduction, into his own genealogy (his great-great-grandmother and his great-great-great-grandmother indeed), a subject of no interest whatsoever to anybody save himself.

Then there is Alan Brien's fascinating family reminiscences. What an old pro he is. Nobody does the experienced bon viveur better: 'There seems to be something about that cheesy, beany, cassoulet-smell of the infant shit, the ammoniac whiff of infant piss somewhere between a very sour white wine and a concentrated paint stripper, that is too overwhelmingly intimate for the virgin nose of the pre-paternal male.' Ah yes, such a superb bouquet is really best reserved for the mature connoisseur.

With a masterly change of tack, we have a contribution from a fabulously uncouth Canadian prat who works at Radio 3, Noah Richler, about his novelist dad. 'I remember the shadow of his enormous dick to the left of my eye,' he writes, with that precision which marks the true stylist. 'Man, the business of parenting is something,' he concludes wisely.

Then we have the academics, with Roger Scruton taking a philosophical look at the matter. He believes fathers have been quite mistakenly 'dethroned', and we are all regretting it now. 'The feminist call for equality, while seeming like a final demand for the abolition of fatherhood, conceals an even more passionate need for its resurrection.' Quite right, Roger, we're secretly begging for it. You begin to see the cunning stunt Virago have pulled off in getting this stuff into print.

At the heart of the book are the New Men. And the prize exhibit here is none other than – Jocelyn Targett, the gifted arts editor of the *Guardian*. It's a princely work of posing. 'I turn the pages of these baby books and tickle the chins of cute pictures. I look at pushchaired couples and yearn,' he says of himself, revoltingly.

And there is a dramatic plot here. Will having a baby make Jocelyn less great? He has been domesticated by it, you see. He's even done some DIY: 'I bought my first power drill the other day. It was something I'd never thought about until it happened, down at Do-It-All one Sunday evening. I found it an oddly moving experience.' So do we all, Jocelyn, especially if it's a Black and Decker with a hammer action and a sanding attachment.

Does all this home maintenance mean that Jocelyn may miss the Nobel

Prize? Pray not! 'Will I be sad if my baby costs me some of my aspirations? I think I will, and I think Baby is bound to. Having a child, I'm sure, presents the ambitious parent with a few inequitable would-you-rathers: would I rather work late or feed the tot leads ultimately to, would I rather achieve greatness or be loved overwhelmingly by my child for ever more, and I'd choose the love of my baby every time . . .'

Happily, of course we know that he has already achieved greatness, so this fascinating dilemma does not arise. But what a noble heart to choose thus! What a *man*.

6 November 1992

Sexual boreplay

Not Guilty: In Defence of the Modern Man DAVID THOMAS
(Weidenfeld & Nicolson/Orion)

'*E*RE! Fancy buying the autobiography of that mediocre hack who was editor of *Punch* when it closed? No? Even an ex-editor of *Punch* can work that one out. Best pretend it's something else, then. That Neil Lyndon made a bit of a splash with his wee bollocks, *No More Sex War* or something, wasn't it? Why not me too?

So here we have David Thomas's memoirs, cross-dressed as 'a meticulous account of the genetic, psychological and social roots of masculinity'. On the cover is a huge endorsement from P.J. O'Rourke ('whose work I had the great pleasure of publishing in *Punch*,' fawns Thomas). 'A splendid book – a Charge of the Light Brigade against the batteries of current wisdom,' says O'Rourke. It seems about right: some hideous blunder, quite pointless, and all that.

The message of this book is easily disposed of. Thomas thinks Feminism Has Gone Too Far, and men are now oppressed by women. This contention is put forward with the help of a ragbag of worthless statistics and tripey quotes. Thomas has no grasp whatsoever of what constitutes argument or proof. To show that men are unfairly treated at work, he offers 'a pile of newspaper cuttings collected over the past two weeks'.

Then he really gets down to the nitty-gritty. Feminists say that it's not fair that male tennis stars can win more than the women. But clever old Dave shows that the men play more games per match, and so they deserve it. Now there's an important point made.

What he's trying to prove, you see, is that 'men and women are the same ... but different'. And he puts his literary talent to work to achieve it. For example, he tells us that 'one way of looking at the male and female brains might be to imagine that they are two different types of computer – an IBM and a Macintosh, for example'. As a master stylist, he picks up this image and runs with it. 'The basic principles that govern them are the same. The actual writing, however, is different. Nor can they read one another's software without a great deal of trouble.' Explains a lot, don't it?

It's all scientific, like. 'The corpus callosum – the bundle of nerves that links the left and right halves [of the brain], much like a cable links the units of a hi-fi – may be as much as 23 per cent thicker in women than in men.' Coo! It's why they're all so bloody mad. 'As a result, women may be able to "access" much more of their brain at any one time ... This might account for feminine intuition and also for the traditional female trait of adding an emotional element to problems which men believe are purely rational.' Can't live with 'em, can't live without 'em, innit?

At one point, Thomas has a little outbreak of shame while describing the difference between men and women. 'I am both simplifying and exaggerating,' he admits. If only he had continued 'and being generally stupid', he might have had the beginnings of wisdom.

But if the arguments are crap, the autobiography is creepily interesting. There's the usual bragging about his time at Eton – 'a system that was designed to bring the best out of boys, intellectually, creatively, and on the sports field. It was certainly a world away from the non-achieving atmosphere that has been prevalent throughout much of English state school education over the last twenty years', arf, arf – and King's College, Cambridge, where he 'ran a student nightclub', the card.

Then comes the glittering career, lightly dropped into the research thus: 'In all my years as a journalist, including several spent as a senior executive on a number of publications, I am not aware that any of my female colleagues has ever been sexually harassed by me or anyone else.' Then there's the crowning glory, *Punch*. 'People who visited the office would remark upon the sexual energy that seemed to be fizzing about the place ... Jokes winged back and forth between the men and the women.' It's a wonder none of them ever crash-landed on the magazine.

Like Lyndon, Thomas turns out to be animated by a specific resentment against one woman – in his case, when he was an adolescent, a girlfriend dropped him and later refused to sleep with him because it wouldn't be fair to her new boyfriend. Thomas says it took him five years and 'a fair amount of analysis' to get over this, and he hints that her behaviour was as bad as that which gets men convicted of rape. 'There is ... no equivalent protection given to men against the manipulation of their feelings or sexuality,' he complains. Diddums.

Some of his outbursts display still uncontrolled hatred. 'However erect a man may be when he goes in, by the time he comes out he is flaccid and spent ... feminism chooses to think of the phallus as the source of all threat, but in the battle between cock and cunt, the cock always comes out the loser,' he remarks, charmingly. Divorcing husbands must be careful not 'to consent to sex' with their wives, he advises. 'Because if you do, she won't be the only one who's fucked.' Nice.

His own sexuality is evidently daffy. He's obsessed with transvestism and transsexualism – not just Jan Morris's, his own. He excitedly describes how at a Cambridge party he once got 'the studs of the university, the hard-drinking, red-blooded heroes' into frocks with him, and how, more recently, he got dolled up again, 'tucking my private parts into the cache-sex ... strapping on a vast, barmaid's bra stuffed with rubber titties ...' It's no surprise when he names as his 'modern heroes' Stephen Hawking, Sean Connery, Gary Lineker – and Quentin Crisp. 'Here is a limp-wristed, mauve-dyed, rouged and mascara'd, effeminate homosexual ... and yet he has lived the life he wanted to live.' Thomas envies him.

There are valid points that can be made on behalf of men: retirement ages aren't equal, nor is child access; men's health receives less attention than women's although they die earlier; women are perfectly capable of violence in the home ... But Thomas's advocacy serves only to discredit them: a gift to the feminists he most loathes. Back to the dressing-table, Dave.

29 January 1993

Born twee

The English Gentlewoman FLORA FRASER (Barrie & Jenkins)

THIS is one of those 'sumptuous' picture-books that will find itself stuffed into the Christmas stockings of maiden aunts and the bright offspring of the well-to-do all over the country. It is elegantly got up, reeks of culture – the sanitized, genteel culture that middle-class folk love to read about – and its author, if not famous, is at least the daughter of somebody famous.

Flora Fraser's first book, yet another biography of Lady Hamilton, came out last year and turned out to be an excuse for the customary fawning profiles of Lady Antonia, Grandpa Frank and all the other pen-wielding Longfords. There were flattering comparisons with mother – mother's literary accomplishments, naturally, also mother's looks (a glance at the jacket confirms this frightening similarity).

The English Gentlewoman, a star item in the catalogue of the newly revived firm of Barrie & Jenkins, is Flora's second excursion into print. Billed as 'a charming and original perspective on our past', it is more alarmingly described as 'a widely researched and entertaining text'. It is actually neither of these things.

When applied to these pallid ventures in historical chat, 'widely researched' is a polite way of saying that the author read a lot of books. In Ms Fraser's case that means a *lot* of books. To track her pursuit of the upper-class female through five centuries or so of English history is to uncover a word devoid of theme or pattern, consisting rather obviously of jottings from the various volumes she happened to read along the way.

The result is a sort of cursory recapitulation of source material which renders most of the subsequent generalizations entirely arbitrary. Take the chapter on the 19th century for instance. Flora has read Mrs Gaskell's letters and Queen Victoria's journals, so we get some rollicking paragraphs about Mr Gaskell's absence from the family hearth, and how Albert liked to hold hands on the sofa. However, she doesn't appear to have read Trollope or Thackeray or any of the lady novelists who seriously discuss the position of women in society, so her conclusions are simply a series of anecdotes. In much the same way, the 17th-century chapter ends up as a string of digressions, a discussion of the effects of the Civil War, going on to embrace pie-making and the prospects for adultery in a few hastily linked sentences.

So much for research. What about the 'entertaining text'? Now, Ms Fraser is supposed to be able to write and was paraded to readers of the *Bookseller* as 'one of our most promising young authors'. In fact, her style is a listless amble through pathways of seemly cliché, twee ('regardless of this masculine concern, gentlewomen continued to entrust the little swaddled bundles which were their infants to wet-nurses') and curiously cumbrous ('there was, then, a large number of gentlemen skilled in draughtsmanship and poor of pocket available, when it became the rage of young ladies to make sketches and water-colour paintings of the countryside').

Its distinguishing feature is a dogged, clumsy syntax. Try this sentence: 'Not through use of the needle and tambour but by reading and conversation, ladies made their minds elegant, and could now discuss a wealth of ideas and subjects with their male relatives.' Not only is it the wrong way round but you get a peculiar extra sub-clause tacked on at the end.

The English Gentlewoman is a meretricious and unoriginal work masquerading as social history, full of facts filched from other books, its insights consisting of spicy gossip about amorous nuns and the sex life of the Victorians. Thanks to the lustre and éclat of the Longfords and some determined literary log-rolling it has been reviewed all over the place and will be bought in swathes by the tribe of bookbuyers who like their history to have pretty pictures, wide margins and a whiff of gentility.

The illustrations aren't bad.

27 November 1987

This Lady's not for reading

Boadicea's Chariot ANTONIA FRASER (Weidenfeld & Nicolson)

*A*s a literary type – and no one could be more of a literary type than this diligent, gentlewomanly author – Lady Antonia Fraser belongs to a distinctly old-fashioned genre.

Sidle into any secondhand bookshop and you can see her Victorian predecessors lining the wall. They have names like Mrs Craik and Mrs Oliphant, homely pseudonyms like 'Aunt Selina'. What distinguished these ladies, who wrote mostly on historical subjects, was not their skill but their industry, their fluent if facile pens. Not to put too fine a point on it, they could knock the stuff out. Trollope parodied them in the shape of Lady Carbury, a character in *The Way We Live Now,* who manages after much negligent research to produce a lacklustre chronicle called 'Criminal Queens'.

Lady Antonia Fraser is our Lady Carbury. *Boadicea's Chariot* – a sprightly canter through a list of 'Warrior Queens' from Boadicea to Catherine the Great and on to Mrs Thatcher – is uncannily reminiscent of these prolix

Victorian compilations. Despite the footnotes, it's not a work of scholarship (although a lot of other people's scholarship is referred to here and there). No, it's another of those middlebrow historical gift-books, full of bogus themes, spurious categorizations and materials lifted from elsewhere.

Lady Antonia's first big problem is that not very much is known about some of her protagonists. Consequently, great summaries of Celtic mythology get hustled in as padding, not to mention chunks of Tacitus and dense reworkings of the latest archaeological research. Slightly less difficult is forging the links between this array of dissimilar female hoodlums, for of course every one fits into one or other of Lady Antonia's catch-all categories ('Amazon', 'Warrior Queen', 'Warrior Maid') or daft syndromes ('The Tomboy Syndrome', 'The Appendage Syndrome'). When this gets desperate there are always nebulous abstracts like 'courage', which links Zenobia of the Palmyres to Boadicea, although Zenobia's 'ambition (and her instinct for survival) set her apart'.

Judging by the fuss that attended the recent pronouncements of the June 20 group on politics and whatnot, you might assume that Lady Antonia is, well, a serious literary figure. However, try this sentence describing Boadicea's statue by the Thames: 'Lest for a moment we forget her ... she stands aloft in her chariot, knives sprouting from its wheels, and it is in fact these murderous knives which stamp our perception of her indelibly. Hers is a gallant – and a savage – story.' 'Lest', 'aloft', 'murderous', 'gallant' – it's the gentlewomanly high style, a procession of archaic clichés in which people don't get angry but 'wax indignant', don't show their emotions but 'give vent' to them.

'The existence of these spirited and respected individuals represents a state of affairs which is a far cry from the dream of true matriarchy and matrilineal succession,' she writes at one point in a horrible conjunction of old and new redundancies. Is this a joke? Does anyone seriously think that they can write like this and get away with it?

Judging from the volley of respectful reviews, apparently yes. *Boadicea's Chariot* is a workmanlike book, which in case you didn't know is critics' shorthand for bloody awful.

28 October 1988

Parvenue for the coarse . . .

Modern Manners: The Essential Guide to Living in the '90s DRUSILLA BEYFUS (Hamlyn)

*I*T'S a tough one, innit? I mean, you see somebody coming up to you. What you gonna say? Gotta get it right, haven't you? It can be a right bastard, can't it?

Well, now, for just 17 quid too, your problems are over. This sabre-toothed tart called Drusilla has gone public with the hard stuff. She knows and she tells. Brilliant.

'"Hello" is one of many informal greetings. Mentioning the time of day, "Good morning" or "Good evening", has its advocates, especially in casual encounters. Parting expressions include "Goodbye" or more chattily "Bye" as well as a whole range of colloquialisms such as "See you" or "Take care".'

Oh *hello*. Bye! Wonderful. It's a whole new world out there for me from now on. And Drusy doesn't stop with that either. No, she really knows her stuff: 'In courtship and love affairs, paying attention is of the essence.' Too right! You have to pretend to listen to the little darlings too, don't I know it. 'Getting to know the other person remains one of the principal aims of courtship' – yeah, if not the only one, know what I mean?

Apparently, another thing you have to do is conversation. 'Conversation offers boundless opportunities to make a good impression.' Well, maybe; but it sounds dodgy to me. 'The ability to communicate ideas whether in speech or writing is an enviable grace which enhances life all round.' Separates us from the animals, too, I shouldn't wonder, but I think I'll leave it out, personally.

But old Drusilla really levels with you, you got to give her that. Like on funerals. 'Convention does not allow you to address the dead except in memorials.' It's a complete waste of time asking them if they'd like a drink too, take it from me. And on parties. 'It is distinctly unwise to assume that the characteristics of our so called "plural society" in which colour, creed and class rub shoulders can necessarily be contained within the small world of private entertaining.' Too right! No way will I share my crisps with a nig-nog.

And on sex and that. 'Physical intimacy can perplex and even alarm very private people, even in today's climate of rude awareness.' Well, that's right innit, you got to ask first, it's the law. 'Nor should a lover feel offended if asked to use a contraceptive or give an account of their sexual health. Women carry condoms out of commonsense. It is the moment at which she produces the contraceptive that calls for sensitivity on her part' – like, in the upper classes she only gets one out after you've done the whole 'hello' bit, I imagine. That's manners, if you like.

Food too, she tells you the lot. 'Holding a knife and fork', for example. It's not that I haven't tried it. I have. But I couldn't get the hang of it. But I'm definitely gonna give it another go now, now she's told me how. And I know what to try it on too – potatoes. 'Potatoes baked in their jackets come halved or whole on the plate, or in a big dish from which you lift one or two. You may eat every morsel of both skin and flesh, or scoop out the white potato inside, leaving the jacket. It is a matter of personal taste. Use a knife and fork or fork alone.' Well, ta, I'll just see how it goes, eh?

And she's well up to date too. Like, it's not all ballroom dancing nowadays, far from it. 'Jiving and disco dancing breaks many accepted barriers – men and women dance solo or may cavort with their own sex to the rhythm of the beat.' I'll say. And she even tells you how posh people turn down drugs politely. 'It could be that they had a bad trip last time, or that they don't smoke, or that if substances are being sold they cannot afford them.' That's really nice, that is. Myself, it's usually just 'Cheers, but I'm still rat-arsed from last night.'

So I reckon this old boiler's book is really good. 'Course one of me mates has been snotty about it. 'Etiquette books,' this git said, 'only come into existence where people are trying to ape the manners of their betters. They play cruelly on class insecurity, pretending that manners are universal, when they are necessarily the product of exclusive social groups. This one is merely a Victorian guide for *parvenus* lightly modernized, compounded equally of insulting banalities and patronizing absurdities. The mere fact of its publication is a signal instance of the new snobbery, filtering down to the duped lower middle classes.'

Well, bollocks to that, say I. I never saw the use of books before, but this one's for me, definite. BYE!

5 June 1992

Nob value

The Field Book of Country Houses and their Owners: Family Seats of the British Isles HUGH MONTGOMERY-MASSINGBERD (Webb & Bower/Michael Joseph)

*H*UGH Montgomery-Massingberd has one great qualification for his line of work. When the toffs he writes about – Cruwys of Cruwys Morchard, Dymoke of Scrivelsby, Fetherstonehaugh-Frampton of Moreton, Houison Craufurd of Craufurdland, Foljambe of Osberton, Steuart Fothringham of Murthly – hear that he is on his way, they must feel pleasantly reassured. For Montgomery-Massivesnob is the only hack in the business with a name as ludicrous as theirs.

It has been the making of him. Massivesnob is no detached architecture critic or social historian. He is himself of the class he portrays: his articles are themselves exhibits in the show, if not the main turn. It is useless to wonder whether or not he realizes that this is why the *Telegraph* employs him. So much reflection is not in the nature of a nob.

Massivesnob writes a column in the *Torygraph* called 'Heritage'. This is the persuasive sales word of our time, signifying anything old and agreeable which might form the basis of a day trip. We have even been encouraged to think that there is such a thing as, contradiction in terms, a 'national heritage'. Somehow we have accepted that being herded around big houses, behind ropes, by self-important matrons means that we are ourselves the true legatees of the aristocracy.

Massivesnob, quite rightly, has no time for this confidence trick. When he says 'heritage' he means it: the inheritance of a name and of a house together, by a private family. He has conducted a long campaign to disabuse us of our belief in a 'national heritage' and to reassert the rights of the squirearchy. (His insistence on this has, doubtless, been a reaction to his own family house having been made over to the National Trust before his birth.) And he is admirably purist. These reprinted articles from the pre-lifestyle *Field* are not about great houses – or interesting people. True squires, they have no other distinction than their success at transmission.

That Massivesnob is now in demand to write similar pieces as a 'Heritage' column in a national newspaper says something about the times. For years he snuffled away at family trees as the editor of *Burke's Peerage*, scribbling too for the country magazines. He joined the *Torygraph* as obituaries editor. But now his pieces have become more than antiquarian. Hymns to private property are apropos. The landed are richer than they have ever been in their lives – and even council-house buyers are beginning to feel happier about family seats.

Not that any of this is made explicit. Massivesnob's appearances in print are winningly slapstick. His own ancestors invariably feature – usually his feminist great-grandmother, who tragically turned the family pub, the Massingberd Arms, into a temperance house. And his 'robust digestion' also stars, as he caps each visit by putting himself outside 'a couple of jumbo cold bangers and a glass of iced lemon tea', or a large helping of treacle tart. The words 'ravishing', 'luscious', 'exquisite' and 'engagingly feudal' exhaust his adjectival resource. Two obsessions recur: Lincolnshire, 'the still undiscovered Lincolnshire', and cricket, as played between the big house and the village.

The appearance of this buffoon must be entrancing to the proprietors of what he enthusiastically calls 'the dimmer sort of seat'. Here is someone who sincerely thinks nothing in the world so fine as 'the proud distinction of being, say, Fulford of Fulford, Fursdon of Fursdon, Kelly of Kelly or Spurway of Spurway', who, quite fantastically, is as gratified as they are themselves by their own existence.

Any further qualities are beside the point, though squirearchical accomplishments are loyally applauded. Burrell of Knepp Castle's appointments 'have included the chairmanship of the North West Sussex Water Board'; Staunton of Staunton is 'an enthusiastic beagler'; Sir Anthony Milbank of Barningham is 'an enthusiastic Gun and enjoys fishing'; while Robert Scrymsoure Steuart Fothringham of Pourie and Murthly is a wizard with a bow and arrow.

Clearly the social system that supports such accomplishments must be maintained. As Cookson of Meldon, owner of a measly 5,000 acres, somewhat laboriously explains: 'If the people of this country wish houses such as Meldon to continue to exist as part of the heritage – especially when the occupants are of the family for whom the house was originally built – then more consideration must be paid to them financially to help keep the system in being.'

Absolutely. And it will be, partly because the National Trust, ostensibly a democratic movement, has transformed public perception of what big estates represent. The houses were the pretty part of the whole social organization; they are the only part now on view; the system itself is thus glamorized by them. For himself, Massivesnob is quite unembarrassed to state that the fortunes of the Hobhouses of Hadspen were founded on slavery.

Conveniently for the National Trust, those who traipse round the houses, or buy picture-books like this, do so in order to fantasize about themselves as owners, not as scullions. Massivesnob, more lucidly, responded to the 'euphoria' of the budget earlier this year with an article looking forward to the return of servants, jovially reminiscing about the days when drunken gamekeepers could be shot.

The 'heritage' mania has softened us up for a return to inherited wealth. Hugh Montgomery-Massingberd may be a richly Wodehousian figure, but his book, lauding the privately owned, is symptomatic. It is the correlative to Peregrine Worsthorne's recent articles about the desirability of large inheritances and the return of a rentier class: the desirability in short of 'a social restoration'. Come the day, of course, Massivesnob knows where he will be – in his seat again. But the fans of his snufflings seem curiously unaware of where that leaves them: which is sat upon.

25 November 1988

Tit & Blum

Wallis & Edward: Letters 1931–1937 – The Intimate Correspondence of the Duke and Duchess of Windsor (Weidenfeld & Nicolson)

*T*HESE embarrassing letters, which have destroyed what little reputation the Windsors had left, are published, Lord Weidenfeld tells us, 'at the express wish of the late Duchess and authorised by her many years ago'.

The reality is rather different. The Duchess, a cabbage for the last eight years of her life, never authorized the publication of any of her letters, nor those penned by her lovesick prince. She was mentally incapable of giving any such authorization, and, far from 'requesting' publication, never knew of the plan to release the letters.

At the centre of the charade, stand the venerable crone, Maitre Suzanne Blum, the Duchess's 87-year-old Paris attorney, and Blum's sensitive minion, Michael Bloch, who affects the ultra-refined accent of a British aristocrat but is in reality the son of a Marks & Spencer linen salesman.

Rather strangely in view of the pro-Nazi anti-Semitic views of her royal clients, Blum is a Jewess with a fearsome reputation at the Paris bar, who for years has succeeded in striking terror into the hearts of British publishers and newspaper lawyers. To unravel her role in the letters saga, we must study the mournful chronology of the Duchess's disintegrating health.

When she came to London for the Duke of Windsor's funeral in 1972, Wallis was already in an advanced stage of arteriosclerosis, an illness which prevents the supply of blood to the brain. To the intense embarrassment of the royal family, she talked such gibberish that even close friends had to be kept at a safe distance from her.

In 1974, when Frances Donaldson's highly critical biography, *Edward VIII*, was published, Wallis was incapable of reading it. Blum *did* read it, however, and complained in the fiercest terms on behalf of her client to the publishers – who, ironically, were Weidenfeld and Nicolson.

In 1978, when Thames Television screened *Edward and Mrs Simpson* for the first time, the £1 million seven-part series based on Lady Donaldson's book, Blum denounced it as 'this dreadful thing. I can't tell you how upset the Duchess is'.

Far from being upset, Wallis never saw the series and remained unaware that it had ever been made – as Blum in fact admitted only three months later in an incautious interview with David Pryce-Jones. By that time, however, Blum had already announced to the world her intention of publishing the Windsor love letters, because, in *Edward and Mrs Simpson*, 'such a bad image is given of the Duchess that it could not be left unanswered'.

Meanwhile she cast around for a tame apologist to whitewash the Windsors. That winter of 1979–80, she took as her law pupil in Paris a 26-year-old Cambridge graduate, Michael Anthony Bloch. He was given access to the Windsor archives and two years later dutifully produced a classic whitewash, *The Duke of Windsor's War*, grovellingly dedicated 'To Maitre Suzanne Blum, guide, pupil, master, and friend', and according the now gaga Duchess the title of her royal highness, which she was officially denied. (Bloch never met Wallis. He glimpsed her only once from the door of her bedroom, propped up against her pillows.)

Blum and Bloch now began using their combined clout to try to censor any published criticism of the Windsors. In 1982, Macmillan's gave in to pressure and took Stephen Birmingham's book, *Duchess*, off the presses, before substantially amending it.

In 1985, however, the same tactics came badly unstuck in the case of Michael Thornton's *Royal Feud: The Queen Mother and the Duchess of Windsor*. Refused sight of the manuscript, Bloch surreptitiously obtained a proof copy and found to his horror that Thornton was not only highly critical of both the Windsors, not to mention Blum and Bloch, but had quoted extensively, without permission, from the Duke and Duchess's letters.

At Curtis Brown, who represented both authors, embarrassment was rife. Bloch's agent, Andrew Best, had only just negotiated a £500,000 advance from the New York publishers, Simon & Schuster, for publication of the Windsor love letters, to be edited by Bloch. Thornton's book would obviously scoop the market.

Bloch hurriedly sent the proof copy to Paris, from where Blum, outraged, cabled the London publishers, Michael Joseph: 'Have just seen proof *Royal Feud* which is libellous of myself and grossly infringes rights my client Duchess of Windsor – stop. Further publication at your peril: Suzanne Blum.'

Thornton cabled straight back in what were described as 'terms of succinct obscenity'. The precise wording is unknown, but shortly after receiving it, Blum reportedly suffered a minor stroke from which she has never fully recovered.

Bloch then retained the services of Oswald Hickson, Collier & Co., and, claiming to be 'exclusive licensee' of the Windsor letters, threatened an injunction against Thornton for breach of copyright and plagiarism.

Thornton, a hardened hack with years of Fleet Street warfare behind him, retained Peter Carter-Ruck & Partners, and insisted that he preferred to go to court, chiefly in order to subpoena Maitre Blum and also to demand sight of the Duchess of Windsor's written permission for the publication of her letters. His solicitor, David Hooper, also questioned the validity of Blum's power of attorney, by which the love letters were being released for publication. According to French law, a power of attorney is only valid while the person on whose behalf it is held remains in full command of their faculties.

Faced with Thornton's defiance, Blum and Bloch backed down. No injunction was sought and no writ issued. *Royal Feud* was published in London and New York without one word altered.

With the massive American advance from Summit Books, British publication by Weidenfeld and a reputed fee of £400,000 for serialization in the *Daily Mail*, the *Wallis & Edward Letters 1931–1937* are liable to earn well over £1 million. Where is all the loot going? Certainly not to the Duchess of Windsor, who is no longer here to enjoy it.

30 May 1986

The Young Fergie Handbook

Debrett's Book of the Royal Engagement (Debrett)
The Royal Wedding Official Souvenir (The Royal Jubilee Trust)

DEBRETT's splendidly banal attempt to cash in on the 23 July royal wedding is little more than a collection of photographs padded out with a fistful of news clippings from Fleet Street.

Describing themselves as 'the oldest and most authoritative source of genealogical reference on British aristocracy and Royal Family', Debrett's broach the delicate matter of 27-year-old Miss Sarah Ferguson's previous romantic arrangements, in particular the one involving ferret-faced 48-year-old widower Mr Paddy McNally, who is evidently some kind of Swiss-based motor mechanic: 'Sarah and McNally were involved for about three years, but their relationship ended in 1985 when Sarah realized that McNally had no intention of re-marrying – however much he admired her,' we are told.

We are also introduced to a Mr Kim Smith-Bingham, an Old Etonian who sold skiing trousers in Verbier and was Miss Ferguson's 'first real boyfriend', which I take to mean first lover. He, too, failed to pick Miss Ferguson when the time came to marry. He is quoted here as saying, 'we never lived together as the papers said but we did spend a lot of time together. When we split up it was just a question of starting to live different lifestyles.'

Neither Mr McNally nor Mr Smith-Bingham feature in the toadying official souvenir, which tries its hardest to play up Fergie's working career in galleries, PR consultancies and publishers – 'All jobs in which the highest skill of all, that of human relations, is the essential qualification.' This is presumably to compensate for other qualifications but the souvenir rather ruins it by telling us: 'An early employer complained not unkindly of her spending too much time on the telephone but he found her exceedingly keen and very hardworking.' The picture of a jolly Sloane on the phone comes unmistakably through the heavy grovelling.

Perhaps this is perfect for Andrew, who may need cheering up.

There is a gentle sadness about Debrett's awful book, and I think it has to do with primogeniture. Prince Andrew's most glittering prospect now is to become Duke of York. He is considered more handsome than his older brother Charles, has more 'pulling power' with the women and became a Falklands War hero by flying helicopters in action. But he is now merely fourth in line to the throne. On the day the heir's first son, William, was born, Andrew was in the South Atlantic. 'When he heard Prince William was born Andrew yelled with excitement and ordered drinks all round. A friend asked why he was so delighted since the new Prince had demoted him to third in line of succession. Andrew roared with laughter. "That's exactly why," he said, "Now I'll be able to have more privacy."'

I doubt it. Debrett's put in plenty of pictures from Prince Andrew's past, Koo Stark, Vicki Hodge, Katie Rabett – was there ever a *galerie* of such exotic sounding royal paramours? Miss Stark is credited with introducing Andrew to the joys of photography, and she was once invited to Balmoral by the Queen. But she was disapproved of, say Debrett's, 'because, when she was seventeen she appeared in a soft porn film, "Emily", which included a nude shower scene'. She was 'visibly upset' when her relationship with Andrew came to an end.

There's a picture of bikini-clad 1960s ex-model Vicki Hodge running along a beach and a reminder of the holiday in which Andy frolicked in the company of the experienced Miss Hodge and two younger women who disported themselves 'in and out of their swimming costumes'. But is this all in the past, with photography being the sole legacy from these interesting times? Fleet Street is desperately hinting about the Botham factor, and in Miss Ferguson's case making innuendos about the 'snow' in Verbier (where Mr McNally hangs out). Debrett's experts tread discreetly amid the discarded bikini bottoms and roll-your-own cigarettes, wisely not annoying the Queen more than they do by calling her son 'Randy Andy' and hailing his bride-to-be as the former paramour of an elderly motor mechanic.

With this in mind their managing director, Mr Robert Jarman, writes in a horribly fawning preface to the book: 'The delight amongst the Royal Family at Prince Andrew's choice is plain to see, and this delight appears to be echoed through the nation.'

The official souvenir guide, however, narrowly wins on sheer toadiness and also for confirming on page 16 the scoop story of Miss Ferguson's gold necklace with the mysterious letters 'GB'.

13 June 1986

Penny Dreadful

Charles PENNY JUNOR (Sidgwick & Jackson)

*B*IG ears aren't the only problem: 'His shoulders slope too much, his hips are too wide, his legs too short.' Send him back to the shop.

Penny Junor shows signs of exasperation. Here she is, who probably walks in beauty like the night, who surely is as wise as she is comely, reduced to earning her crust by reciting the wretched exploits of a man whose 'protruding ears and weak chin' frame a stuff-and-nonsense-filled head. No wonder she gets cross.

Besides, Big Ears didn't give her the goods. Miss Junor was granted only one interview with the Ugly Prince, despite the heroism of her previous trek over 20 years of stony ground, *Diana, Princess of Wales* (1982), in which, through gritted (though pearl-like) teeth, she managed to say that her subject was 'far from stupid'.

She bravely leads off with that meeting, writing it up in the manner of a psychiatrist's case report: 'He sat behind his desk, touching his signet ring, fingering his tie, playing with his fountain pen [gosh, who wouldn't, in the provoking proximity of Miss Junor?] and pulling out a large, crisply laundered handkerchief from time to time to blow his nose' (distraught, I expect, fighting for self-control, knowing that his misshapen advances would only be unwelcome).

But obviously they struck up a rapport, despite the cruel physical disparities. 'When he turns his attention on you, and smiles, it is as though for that moment there is nothing more important in his life,' she confesses.

Artfully, she 'applauded the work he had done for young people in the inner cities'. Winningly, she admired his sketches. 'I asked if I might see some more of his work and his face lit up with enthusiasm. Would I *really* like to?' You bet. Soon he was offering to show her his garden at Highgrove in the course of a further *entretien*. Who can say what would have happened next? Duchess of Auchtermuchty? Good Queen Penny? A second Abdication Crisis loomed.

But it was not to be. Miss Junor had suggested to Big Ears that she might 'usefully talk to Sir Laurens van der Post'. He had agreed. She then rang the great sage up but although he too, the saucy beast, was 'charming' on the telephone, he would not talk about the Prince. 'He does not, I discovered later, believe in biographies of people still living. Not long afterwards I had a letter from the Prince's office. He was sorry, but he had had a change of mind. There would be no further meeting. It appeared that, on reflection, he did not think biographies of living people were appropriate.'

Nipped in the bud, Miss Junor choked back her tears. Condemned to long and lonely days in the cuttings room, she struggled on. Hell hath no fury like a woman scorned, it is said, but Penny is made of finer stuff.

Admittedly a few notes of gentle disparagement do creep in from time to time. 'He is quite unremarkable to look at', of course. Well, he 'has to keep a close eye on his weight' to start with, and anyway, 'One thing Charles has never been noted for is sartorial elegance or a sense of fashion.' But it makes no difference. Power is a potent aphrodisiac – look at Henry Kissinger, she says – 'and there is no power quite so potent as that of the Prince of Wales'. She should know.

Pining as she may be, she marks up his report card with admirable detachment. 'He can be selfish and spoilt'; he 'enjoys his luxury'; he is 'altogether too sensitive' and 'was never much good' at team sport ('the wrong build and the wrong temperament'). 'Although he is keen to play the role of the common man when getting to grips with the inner cities, for example, he is not at all amused if he is treated as such.' Maybe he has a sense of humour 'but that, like the rest of him, is slightly anachronistic'.

The outlook for the next school year is grim. 'Unless Charles manages to conquer his own lack of self-confidence . . . he could be led astray'. He is lost without her, 'one of the saddest people I have ever encountered . . . He is more confused than ever about where he is going and what his life is all about.' He throws himself into working for wild flowers, 'live' cheeses and young thugs, but all to no end. 'The Prince of Wales has a pitifully low opinion of himself and a debilitating lack of confidence in his own worth.' Oh dear oh dear.

One closes this book feeling positively sobered. Willie Hamilton is right. What sense can there be in a system that has a man of 38 in 'the prime of life', weeping into his pillow every night? And, more importantly the fairest flower of Auchtermuchty reduced to turning out rubbish like this?

26 June 1987

Anecdotage

The *Oxford Book of Royal Anecdotes* Ed. Elizabeth Longford (Oxford)

A NTHOLOGIES are a publisher's delight. Writers don't have to write them, readers don't read them.

No other sort of book trades so profitably on the publisher's own name. Oxford and Faber have done well from anthologies because the punters dimly reckon that their productions must be reputable. Whether they are or not is irrelevant. What they do is take writing out of context and turn it into a bar snack. Anthologies are a characteristic produce of the short-attention-span era: the channel-hopping of literature.

As they flourish, they grow increasingly absurd in topic. Oxford, having done over the centuries of verse, turned to Local Verses, Travel Verses and Sea Songs. 'Short Poems' were obtained by the simple expedient of taking little bits out of long ones. Then they discovered the Big Theme. They've done Ages, Dreams and Death. Why stop there? Why not Birth? Copulation? Not to say excretion. Probably already commissioned . . .

Faber have gone through Political Verse, Popular Verse, Religious Verse, Reflective Verse, Useful Verse, and arrived at last at Kenneth Baker's disgusting classic, the *Faber Book of English History in Verse*. Taking stock, they have since headed straight for the dirty bits. The idiotic *Faber Book of Seductions* was relatively polite, but their new collection of 'sensual writing by women' is such a filth-packet that they have lost their nerve and ended up titling it simply *Deep Down*, instead of the *Faber Book of*, well you know.

Oxford have been smarter. Realizing that prose tends to be long and joined up, unlike lyric poetry, they have cast about for a suitable term to excuse breaking it up into bite-sized portions and come up with the valuable word 'anecdote'. Think once of *The Oxford Book of Something Anecdotes* and the years open out ahead of you, all ease, prosperity and long lunches.

Legal Anecdotes. Political Anecdotes. Military Anecdotes. Agricultural Anecdotes. Accountancy Anecdotes. Agronomy Anecdotes. And should you somehow get stuck, just stick a country in front and go for the export market. Thus we have recently had the captivating *Oxford Book of Canadian Political Anecdotes* (sedulously reviewed in the *Sunday Telegraph*, prop. Canadian Conrad Black). Can the *Oxford Book of Nigerian Political Anecdotes* be far behind? It could only be more entertaining.

All you need is a hack, preferably a famous one, a Longford for preference – they have none of them any talent, but plenty of application and self-importance – and, since the battier the better, Lady Longford herself best of all. Oxford plus royalty, serviced by Lady Longford? A winner.

Her whole introduction is a delight. She points out that the anecdotes are 'a whole series of small amulets hanging from one powerful arm', because, don't you know, 'these kings and queens are descended from one another and their story hangs together in a special sense. It is impossible to think of William and Mary without thinking of James II and Queen Anne, strung above and below on the same arm.' Absolutely.

Her toff's twaddle has that confident asininity of those who have never been interrupted, let alone edited. 'Every anecdote should have a touch of something that is either "funny/ha ha" or "funny/peculiar",' she confides. But 'because royal anecdotes are so closely allied to history they may also be informative'. Thanks. The unspoken message throughout is that Lady Longford is queenly herself and can give us yobs a few pointers.

Her thumbnail sketches of the different monarchs are alone worth the price of the book, priceless quality. She rates kings primarily by their physique. William the Conqueror? 'Powerfully built and of medium height, he grew fat and lost his front hair.' Henry VIII? 'His youthful beauty and mature corpulence were alike extreme.' Charles I? 'After a feeble start he grew into an athletic young man.' And so on. Only Prince Philip merits better. He is 'intellectually gifted'. Cannily she doesn't say with what.

The early anecdotes are familiar (no drawbacks in anthologizing) and dull.

Better are the illustrations of Prince Philip's giftedness. It is laboriously explained that when he and Princess Elizabeth visited Greece in 1950, 'she sailed in the more comfortable HMS *Surprise*, the C-in-C's Despatch Vessel, while Philip escorted her as commander of *Magpie*. Signals of great gaiety passed between the ships. Some were in clear. *Surprise* to *Magpie*, "Princess full of beans": *Magpie* to *Surprise*, "Is that the best you can give her for breakfast?"' Full story.

Philip has, of course, 'handed on to their son and heir a capacity for original thought'. You can see that in quoted *Sayings*. 'On his marriage: "Diana will certainly help to keep me young." On becoming aware of his inheritance: "I didn't wake up in my pram one day and say 'Yippee . . .' you know. But I think it just dawns on you, slowly, that people are interested in one . . .""

Funny/ha ha or funny/peculiar? Either way the fact that she thought it worthy of inclusion will certainly feature in my own forthcoming, impatiently awaited, sure to be profitable *Oxford Book of Longford Anecdotes*.

14 April 1989

12

CELEBRITY AUTHORS

The rise of the non-book

On the rubbish dump(ster)

Heiress NIGEL DEMPSTER (Weidenfeld & Nicolson)

*T*HE first thing to realize is that this is not so much a book as a deal, and the genius behind it is none other than that Mephistopheles among literary agents, Ed Victor. The second thing to realize is that this is not by Nigel Dempster, but by Nigel Dempster and Peter Evans.

In 1986 Jonathan Cape had published a book called *Ari: The Life and Times of Aristotle Socrates Onassis* by Peter Evans, a journalist who had been befriended by Onassis in the late 1960s. Ed Victor brought Evans together with Dempster, 'the world's best-known gossip columnist', and pre-sold various rights to this biography of Christina Onassis for sums totalling approximately £200,000. Dempster went to South America to dig up new material, then closeted himself in a small room with a computer at the *Daily Mail*'s old offices in Northcliffe House. The manuscript was ready in a couple of months. When it came to selling the serialization rights, the deputy editor of Dempster's own paper, 'Jonty' Holborow, turned the book down, but Brian MacArthur at the *Sunday Times* picked it up instead for about £50,000.

In a prefatory note to the book, Dempster acknowledges the invaluable assistance of Peter Evans who – he does not acknowledge – is receiving 50 per cent of the royalties. Dempster confesses that he has 'shamelessly' used Evans's notes and transcripts from his previous book throughout *Heiress*. 'Indeed,' Dempster writes coyly, 'every word in this book has in one way or another been influenced by him.' Perhaps this explains why there are so many sentences that have been virtually lifted from Evans's earlier book.

Given that so much of the material in *Heiress* is recycled, it is understandable that Dempster has gone to great lengths to ensure that rival gossip hacks don't steal his thunder over his few pieces of original research. In the September edition of *New Woman*, there is a decent, workmanlike profile of Christina Onassis by Tim Satchell. When Dempster saw a copy of the magazine, he went berserk. His solicitor Michael Rubinstein sent a letter to *New Woman* editor Frankie McGowan threatening to seek an injunction. The letter suggested that Satchell had stolen chunks from Dempster's book and demanded that all copies of the magazine be recalled and pulped.

Dempster told Satchell in a phone conversation that he had deliberately planted a couple of fabricated stories in his own book as a ruse to catch plagiarists and copyright infringers, though when pressed to identify one of these bogus stories, he demurred. Frankie McGowan claimed that Satchell's material had come from available, non-copyright sources. Anyway, *New Woman* belongs to Murdoch Magazines and since Victor had sold the serialization rights of *Heiress* to the *Sunday Times*, another Murdoch title, the magazine had little cause to fear Dempster's petulant threats.

Almost the only original material of any interest about Christina Onassis in this book comes form Luis Basualdo, the polo-playing Argentinian playboy. Dempster interviewed Basualdo earlier this year, paying him for his information, and was peeved when he discovered that Neil Mackwood, a gossip hack on the *Daily Express*'s Ross Benson column, had flown to New York at the end of August to interview Basualdo for a spoiling piece that was to appear in the *Sunday Express Magazine*.

Dempster rang Mackwood in his New York hotel, claiming to be in New York himself (it later transpired that he had been phoning from London) and asking him what he was up to. Mackwood told him that he was going to interview Basualdo and a friendly Dempster advised him that Basualdo wouldn't talk unless he saw the colour of money. Mackwood gave Basualdo $4,000 in travellers' cheques and interviewed him for several hours across three days.

Once he had returned to London, Mackwood received a curious message from Basualdo on his home answering machine to the effect that he, Basualdo, definitely had no contract with Dempster and that Dempster was talking 'rubbish'. Mackwood rang him back the next day and again Basualdo said emphatically that he had no contract with Dempster. All became clear when Dempster's solicitor sought and obtained an injunction against Express Newspapers on the grounds that his client had obtained an exclusive verbal contract from Basualdo.

Aside from the unlikelihood of the notion that an author would neglect to tie up a key source in an exclusive written contract if there were to be any contract at all, Basualdo then disappeared back to the Argentinian pampas, thus putting him beyond the reach of the *Express* lawyers who were seeking an affidavit. The injunction was allowed and the matter is due to go for a full trial at a later date.

Unfortunately all this is much more interesting than anything in Dempster's book, the contents of which need not concern our readers.

29 September 1989

Frank Delusion

The Celts FRANK DELANEY (Hodder & Stoughton)

THERE is a story told about the former book-jockey Frank Delaney which has him discussing the drawings of Palladio. 'But you know what I really like about Palladio,' he tells his interlocutor, raising a massive eyebrow, 'His buildings ... And you know what my favourite Palladio is,' he continues impressively, 'The Customs House in Dublin.'

In crossing the Irish Channel, Delaney has come quite a long way to become valet to the literary classes. The son of a Tipperary teacher and the youngest of eight, he remembers apparently walking from the station at the tender age of 18 to be interviewed at All Souls, Oxford (the college that does not take undergraduates). This is quite an achievement. However, he spent 11 years back in Ireland as a bank clerk and then, after doing numerous interviews with Radio Eireann, he joined the BBC, came to London and in 1978 launched the radio programme *Bookshelf* leaving behind in the Emerald Isle a wife and three children.

Some men have a passion for women, others a passion for wine but the chairman of the Ruislip Literary Society ('I took over from John Betjeman') has a self-confessed passion for words. These words – or 'worruds' – are delivered in a voice that has been likened to an elocution lesson in a convent. Certainly Delaney's fortune lies in his voice rather than his face which, since he fell off *Bookshelf*, has squinted gnomically from our screens.

While his way with worruds would not merit any attention in an Englishman, opening remarks to men like Berger, Borges and Burgess are, critically speaking, on the level of 'Naive question, but why do you write?' while Sian Phillips once enjoyed the variant 'Why are you so beautiful?' Delaney's classless brogue sends Ruislip's blue-rinsers into a flat spin. An easy retirement awaits him opening new libraries, majestically dressed in fedora and cape.

Delaney's great talent, however, is to reduce literature to palatable pellets of anecdote. Follow Leopold Bloom's wander through Dublin on a map, he urges, and you find him pacing the shape of a question mark. Genuine and amiable enthusiasm smooths over the potholes and lacunae in his own intellect. His deepest knowledge of literature probably lies in what people are earning from it. His deepest suspicion is reserved for an imagined literary mafia and members of his own 'murphia', like fellow ex-bank clerk Terry Wogan, whom Delaney believes has sold out for money: 'I could have gone that route, the money route – I was asked to do *The Parkinson Show* – but I was too interested in writing.'

To date his own writing consists of two works of popular literature – on Joyce's Dublin and Betjeman – and an unpublished novel that was 'too powerful' to be entered for the Booker Prize in the year he was a judge. After honing it for five years he was, according to a recent interview, aghast to discover that Peter Ackroyd had scooped him with *Hawksmoor*, a novel 'with an identical plot and eerie similarities'. His own will remain unpublished. But Delaney fans need not fear. From next week they will be able to watch him marching through the bogs of time in a six-part series on the Celts. And if they so insist, they can read the book that 'originated alongside' this BBC extravaganza.

Stumbling through the frothy, sub-Walter Pater rhetoric ('Where does the fact end, where does the myth begin, which is which') one is reminded of a student with an essay to write by dawn. Considerably helped by Caesar (one of Delaney's plans is a new translation of *De Bello Gallico*) and men like Cassius Dio Cocceianus, Delaney pads out his squint at the Celts – an illiterate, brilliant people of the oral tradition – with reheated legends.

Delaney's partiality for abbreviation – 'sudden ferocity: the Vikings struck' – is second only to his love of irony. ('An irony bubbles . . . the irony congeals . . . sweet paradox . . . one of the most potent forces in all the paradox of the Celtic tradition came to the aid of the revolutionaries – death.')

Ironically, he rounds on the two men who did most to popularize the Celtic revival: James Macpherson, whose Ossianic forgeries hoaxed many literati; and Iolo Morganwg whose invented Gorsedd prompted today's ludicrously romantic view of druids. Squelching in their footsteps, even Delaney, the best chairman the National Book League ever had (as he told its treasurer), is finally forced to admit that 'the search for a Celtic heritage is spurious'.

17 October 1986

Anglo-Saxon platitudes

Domesday: A Search for the Roots of England **MICHAEL WOOD**
(BBC Publications)

*F*ROM being a self-conscious and heavily subsidized sop to those critics who alleged the essentially corrosive nature of television, BBC Publications has blossomed over the years into a highly efficient commercial publishing house with an expanding turnover.

While most of this money comes from Rabbi Blue and exotic cookery books, the firm also keeps up a list of profitable 'serious' books: *Domesday: A Search for the Roots of England*, which sold over 20,000 copies in the run-up to Christmas, is typical of this successful combination of cash and cachet.

Domesday is the third of Michael Wood's historical investigations to be worked up into book form and the formula is by now fairly well established. *In Search of the Trojan War* had him cruising blithely through the Aegean. *In Search of the Dark Ages* found him – eager and tousle-haired – descending from a helicopter onto ploughed fields which might have concealed the site of some seventh-century skirmish.

The most recent series to grace our screens goes a step further. Taking the Domesday Book as its axis, it is historical enquiry on a grand scale, an attempt to show that 'some of the fundamental forces, such as attitudes to marriage, property and inheritance that have come to generate what has come to be understood as "English individualism" were already present in 1086'.

It is also, according to the blurb, an historical quest to which the author brings his usual 'erudition and enthusiasm'; two qualities which will bring an uneasy smile to the face of any professional historian who might chance upon the book. That this erudition is mostly other people's, in particular that of Dr Alan Macfarlane who once wrote a treatise called *The Origins of English Individualism* (Blackwell, 1978), is a venial transgression: after all, nobody minds the simplification for a mass audience of a complex and abstruse data. More worrying, though, is the use that Wood's much-vaunted 'enthusiasm' makes of all this second-hand information.

For a start, his basic premise – that the Domesday Book provides a sort of pivot on which the whole of English history turns – is a doubtful one. Wood insists that Domesday is nothing less than a comprehensive handbook to 11th-century social life, whose eccentricities are a fine means of proclaiming 'English individualism' at the expense of old notions of a collective 'feudal' society.

You would find no hint anywhere in *A Search for the Roots of England* that Domesday was actually a highly selective document, concerned only with ownership, whose major omission was those very feudal duties on which the whole basis of Anglo-Norman society rested.

Equally culpable is the Wood style of historical analysis, which weaves together a series of casual speculations into a skein of misleading hypothesis. A neat example of this comes in his attempt to establish the continuity of custom and occupation in a Cotswold village. Each sentence receives its shaky qualification: 'It seems likely that . . .' – but Wood emerges triumphant from this tangle of guesswork to conclude that the village is 'a model of how the lives of ordinary people could have gone on' during the 600 years of Dark Age tumult.

This sort of assertion might be given the benefit of the doubt. However, on several occasions the facts are so dim that Wood has to resort to more imaginative methods of recreation. 'English', 'individual', 'set apart' from the rest of Europe our ancestors may have been but this doesn't prevent their anatomist dashing off to remote parts of Europe for the purposes of irrelevant comparison. Dorsetshire farm-holdings 'can be imagined' by reference to census records from fourth-century Greece. Why? Because 'there is no reason to doubt that the basic patterns would be repeated'.

All this is complemented by some delightful illustrations, many of which have nothing to do with England at all, and a text in which *Daily Mail* prose is brought to bear on Anglo-Saxon resettlement programmes ('massive'), the rewards of Dark Age fighting men ('astronomical') and the splendours of Iron Age culture ('extraordinary').

Finally, having established beyond doubt this continuity of 'crucial aspects of our culture', Wood furnishes an apocalyptic conclusion in which four centuries of recent English history are subsumed into a single paragraph, full of drab generalizations which are not absolutely wrong but could not be refined without recourse to subtleties which their author is incapable of formulating. Stuart historians for example will be interested to find that in the 17th century 'the new middle class with its landed and moneyed interests overthrew the now out-dated monarchy'. If only, alas, it were as simple as that!

'The real past is difficult to recover' Wood decides at one point, an odd moment of uncertainty in a book characterized elsewhere by the cocksure tone of *Blue Peter* history that knows it is on to a good thing.

9 January 1987

Russell Harty's Grand Bore

Mr Harty's Grand Tour RUSSELL HARTY (Century)

POOR old Russell. What did he do wrong? Not only is he stricken with hepatitis, possibly picked up on his grand tour, but his book of that tour provides the most humiliating exposure of his shortcomings that could ever have been devised.

Suppose you wanted to torture a pretentious television personality. Could you have thought of anything quite as good as this: filming him on a trip to countries he knows nothing about, whose languages he doesn't speak, and then comparing his progress with that of the aristocrats of the 18th century? And would you then have had the nerve to issue his helpless spumings as a book with the title *Mr Harty's Grand Tour*? And then see to it that the jacket bears the claim that 'One of Britain's most perspicacious writers turns his oblique and witty eye on twentieth-century Europe.' Of course not. One can only throw up one's hands in defeated admiration.

What's the most embarrassing, stupid thing one can do on one's holidays? Get sunburned on the first day. Russell goes one better. He gets sunburned on the ferry. 'My hands swell and my face explodes and I become tetchy and depressed and irritated and miserable ... I lay in bed with two wet towels wrapped around two hot pieces of roast pork, formerly my hands, and listened to BBC Radio 4, and wished I'd been sensible and stayed at home.'

Suppose you knew your victim to be a fantastic bore about his North Country upbringing? How best to make the most of this? The answer is that you take him to the best places in Europe and let him notice no more about them than that which reminds him of home.

In Munich he thinks of 'the Pleasure Beach at Blackpool'. In Umbria he locates someone with whom he is able to 'hum a little of "Ilkley Moor Bah t'at"'. In Assisi he interviews the senior monk and, as they sit on the walls and listen to Vespers, his first question is: 'What about Moss Side?' The entire history of Germany he interprets through a pronouncement made by granny Harty 'when the Germans came over Blackburn in 1941'.

Then there is the appeal to your dupe's snobbery. Ideally you get him to admit to it straightaway ('Any passing psychiatrist would have little difficulty in noting that I am, in many ways a snob', page 17), but then nonetheless go on to grovel to unsavoury and disdainful toffs throughout the rest of the book.

Sadly lacking here is the delectable incident of Russell being flatly snubbed by the Nazi, Lady Diana Mosley, which was relished up and down the country in the first episode of the TV programmes. But on the other hand we do have him shaking hands with the Pope, which they were not allowed to film.

Even Russell observes that the Pope somehow managed to contain his excitement at meeting one of Britain's most perspicacious writers: 'The conversation was stilted. We talked of tourists of whom, I understood, he had seen quite enough that morning, thank you.'

Harty's equally frustrated attempts at coming to grips with cultural eminences seem, however, a mite under-exploited. There is his glorious art historical commentary in a Belgian gallery ('Nothing in man's nature has changed radically in the last half-millennium. If you've got it, flaunt it') and occasional *bonnes bouches* along the lines of 'I don't know whether Schiaparelli was a he or a she.' But what a treat is missed when he goes to see Leonardo's *Last Supper* in Milan and finds it shut for the day. Are we never to have his thoughts on this? Worth a TV special, surely?

Yet after these disappointments the great brain behind the project springs back with a master-stroke. Russell needs guides. One of these, escorting our hero around Zurich, is none other than Frank could-you-spell-that-please Delaney. No doubt Russell pleaded to be tarred and feathered rather than be publicly guided by Frank Delaney – but no deal.

There appears to be a cruel and iron hand behind all this. Why, one wonders, has Harty submitted so comprehensively to it? His only explanation is that, when the phone rings with 'someone in a position of power or privilege calling to say that they quite like the idea of a "Grand Tour"' he can only accede, because, he blushingly, self-deprecates, 'it is not my job to eschew the twentieth century and live in a cultivated limbo'.

For us, of course, the book is a bore. Given his head, as it were, Harty can be amusing. Here he does intermittently squeal about things being 'ghastly', 'awful' or 'horrid', and he does go for a gigantic facial. But otherwise, all duty, he holds himself back heroically. Think what *Dame Edna's Grand Tour* would have been and weep. Harty weeps himself at the end, and no wonder.

But where is the real Harty in all this? Is there perhaps one plaintive little cry of personal protest in his 'private portrait' of Mad King Ludwig of Bavaria?

'One large part of Ludwig's life was arid, empty, unfulfilled,' Harty writes. 'He was not the marrying kind. He preferred the company of men, and young and handsome men at that ... there was no one to share the private moments, no one to applaud a secret act of generosity . . . It is not a peculiar or unique or even rare situation that he endured. And it is certainly not made clear, by any existing record, whether this isolation sprang from his regal opposition, or from a vicious mole of nature.'

Even the hardest hearts would be wrung, you'd think. But not those of his masters, apparently. Pages 94–5 (should you be in a bookshop) consist of a sarcastic drawing of Mad King Ludwig posing in his robes – looking, beneath the beard, remarkably like poor Harty himself, mocked again.

Is it any wonder that Harty landed up in Airedale General Hospital feeling jaundiced?

15 April 1988

Levin on a jet plane

A Walk Up Fifth Avenue BERNARD LEVIN (Jonathan Cape)

I AM,' Bernard Levin casually admits on page 225 of his new offering, 'a very unobservant man.' The sentence ought to be inscribed on the title page, to save unwary readers the trouble of having to learn its truth for themselves as they chew their way through the stodgy pudding that is *A Walk Up Fifth Avenue*. It also begs a question: if he's so bloody unobservant why is he wasting our time and his by writing travel books?

The answer is rather sad, and necessitates a brief recap of some of Barmy Bernie's life-story.

For many years, Levin's main occupation has been to write a column in *The Times*. It has some admirers – not least himself. He has boasted that he is a 'maverick' and 'gadfly' who likes to go 'against the grain' in his *Times* pieces, but in fact the range is narrow and the view of the world is desperately conformist: tirades against Stalinist Russia, the Loony Left and the North Thames Gas Board; hymns of praise to Richard Wagner and Margaret Thatcher. Nothing very maverick there.

With such a limited repertoire it was inevitable that he would eventually grow restless. Sure enough, by the end of the 1970s Bernie began to feel that there must be more to life than churning out the same old hits and trousering the loot.

And thus, like the Beatles before him, he turned to the mystic east in search of fakirs. After visiting the ashram run by the Bhagwan Shree Rajneesh at Poona, Levin wrote several toe-curling articles in *The Times* announcing that he had discovered the secrets of the universe. The Bagwash, he revealed, was a living saint.

Worse was to come. Back in London, he and his chaperone Arianna Stassinopoulos – who were fast becoming Fleet Street's answer to John and Yoko – threw themselves into a cult named Insight. In October 1979, Levin told a large invited audience at the Café Royal that people could be 'changed' if they would only cough up £150 for an 'Insight training course'. One of those who did enrol on the five-day course, the playwright Snoo Wilson, found himself standing near an ungainly fellow dressed in a blond wig and a pink tutu, who was dancing like a sugar-plum fairy. After staring at the apparition for a moment or two he suddenly realized that it was Bernard Levin himself.

Somewhere, somehow – it has never been quite clear why – Bernie and Ari drifted away from their New Age lotus-eating. Then Ari drifted away from Bernie, in spite of the gallant dedication of his book *Enthusiasms* in 1983 ('To Arianna, with much more than enthusiasm'). Tired of waiting for him to pop the question, she took herself off to America, married a millionaire and became a Society Queen.

Having lost his religion and his girlfriend, where was our hero to find succour? Like so many jilted souls before him, he went a-wandering; and, being the man he is, he took with him on his travels a generous advance from Jonathan Cape and a clanking camera crew from Channel Four. The TV series, the book of the series, the articles from the book of the series – the scope for self-publicizing was endless. First there was *Hannibal's Footsteps*, then *To the End of the Rhine*, and now his stroll through New York as seen on television every Saturday night this month.

There is little to be said about this Fifth Avenue promenade, except that Levin is indeed very unobservant. He unerringly repeats every cliché about New York City: the cab-drivers speak no English and can never find their way around; the Empire State Building is tall; the Sunday edition of the *New York Times* has many pages; the city's politicians are sometimes corrupt; quite a few black people live in Harlem; joggers can often be seen in Central Park. And, er, that's it, more or less. On the rare occasion when he does stray into unfamiliar territory, his bafflement is as pompously laboured as that of a High Court judge who's never heard of Mick Jagger. Here, for instance, is the start of his fact-finding visit to a rap club in Harlem: 'Naturally, I had first to discover what a rap club is, and how it is different from, say, the Athenaeum. It is very different from the Athenaeum. A rap club is a club for dancing and all that goes with it, but with a difference. Its entertainment, though it includes singers and comedians, is based mainly on rap.' You don't say.

As that passage suggests, Levin's prose is as flatulent as ever. Older readers may recall his book about the 1960s, *The Pendulum Years*, which was full of such thoughtful remarks as 'The Sixties faced the future and the past at once ... forwards or backwards? Up or down? Modernisation or preservation? The future or the past? And which was which anyway?' Twenty years on, he is still using the same old rhetorical flourishes to disguise the emptiness of his thoughts. For sheer unembarrassed drivelling it would be hard to beat the conclusion that the gadfly draws from his journey up and down Fifth Avenue. 'The truth about New York today,' he declares ringingly, 'is as elusive as ever; but that is the truth about New York.'

Eh?

22 December 1989

Bye bye, Blackburn

The Very Best of Tony Blackburn (Lennard Books)

*T*HE rehabilitation of Tony Blackburn has been a long, and for everybody watching, painful process. His tale, after all, is a well-known one. Wanted to be a disc jockey, started on the pirate ships, played the first record on Radio 1, became very famous, told dreadful 'jokes', married Tessa Wyatt, ceased to be married to Tessa Wyatt, talked about it incessantly on air, was fired, was rediscovered by trendies on Radio London playing soul music, now employed by Capital's oldies station, still telling dreadful 'jokes', 25 years a disc jockey, grand old man of radio, etc., etc.

For many commentators on popular culture, though, he remains an enigma. Is what you hear all there is? Are there hidden depths to the man? Is that haircut for real? No one has ever found out.

Until now, that is. For with the publication of *The Very Best of Tony Blackburn*, a book marketed as a collection of his numerous and notorious 'jokes', this mysterious figure is finally revealed in his true colours – as an avant-garde novelist of the highest order, to be spoken of in the same breath as Gabriel Josipovici and the late B.S. Johnson.

Blackburn's public persona, such as it is, can now be seen not merely as that of a blank, facile, sex-mad disc jockey obsessed by 1960s soul music, but as a finely wrought fictional edifice, brilliantly conceived and flawlessly executed, a searing satirical sideswipe at all our received opinions of 'pop' music and its purveyors. The much-publicized failure of his marriage – Blackburn blubbed on air in between playing songs with titles like 'We've Thrown It All Away' and 'World Without Love' – now emerges not as the embarrassing self-indulgence we took it for at the time, but as vital research for a chapter in this most intriguingly innovative of modern novels. Blackburn has gone further beyond the recognized bounds of fiction than any writer now operating – his life is the novel, its publication a mere transcription.

There is no indication in the book of the author's true intentions. Without explanation, he divides his 'jokes' into seemingly arbitrary categories that are then arranged in alphabetical order. The longest of all the sections, entitled 'Marriage', runs to seven pages, in which Blackburn effortlessly portrays the bitterness and rancour he feels towards Ms Wyatt (who ran off with the co-star of her TV series *Robin's Nest*).

'Isn't life funny? I mean for a good 20 years my ex-wife and I were very happy – then we met . . .' And later, 'Do you know that more wives leave home than husbands? My theory is that husbands just aren't very good at packing suitcases.' The terse, tragic baldness of the prose style marks out Blackburn as perhaps the most original fictional voice to have emerged in decades.

The 'Life' section is equally revealing. Few writers would dare to sum up 3,000 years of human thought and achievement in eight jokes, but Blackburn is nothing if not daring. 'Life is like a shower: one wrong turn and you're in hot water.' Or, as he goes on to say, 'Don't forget, in two days' time, tomorrow will be yesterday.'

The issues Blackburn deals with range from evolution ('Wouldn't it be great if we had two heads? Then we could talk in stereo . . .') to economics ('My uncle owns a newspaper. Mind you, it only cost him 20p'). Perhaps the most revealing section, which indisputably forms the heart of the novel, is the section on 'Myself': 'I was a war baby – my parents took one look at me and started fighting.' 'I went to a christening last Sunday. It was funny – everyone said the baby looked like me – then the parents turned him the right way up.' 'The walls in my house are so thin, every time I peel an onion the people next door start to cry . . .'

Collected together, these 'jokes' provide a harrowing portrait of a character adrift from the real world, lost in the recesses of his own ego. It's a remarkable achievement.

So much so that some notable literary figures are already beginning to question the whole issue of Blackburn's identity. Is he really a clapped-out disc jockey playing dismal Frankie Avalon records to London housewives? Or is he yet another alter ego of the multi-talented novelist and writer Julian Barnes?

18 August 1989

Bob's your unctuous

Prescriptions of a Pox Doctor's Clerk ROBERT ROBINSON
(Weidenfeld and Nicolson)

WHEN Robert Robinson was gathering material for his book of pieces called *The Dog Chairman*, it is said that he went to the producer of *Stop the Week with Robert Robinson*, Michael Ember, and asked him for tapes of the programme so he could transcribe choice bits of his chat for the book. Ember revealed that he had wiped all the tapes. Robinson nearly died.

Luckily, Ember remembered that there was a faithful listener somewhere in the provinces who recorded every single programme, and it was finally only by the kind cooperation of this listener that the book appeared at all. Robinson has obviously now got a system worked out to save his conversation, because his new book contains a great deal of stuff that could only have been thrown out on the air in those moments when Milton Shulman and Michael O'Donnell were gnashing their teeth, waiting to get in.

Stop the Week is not a completely impromptu show. Nor, as many people think, is it even live. It is recorded the day previously after Robinson, Ember and the minor stars have phoned each other to sort out the topics, and who is going to lead off when. Which means that many of these little pieces are pre-rehearsed, pre-written pieces of conversation in which Robinson can show off that finely wrought, elegantly phrased conversational tone for which he is famous.

The only drawback is that the conversational elegance is used to disguise the fact that Robinson has nothing to say. He is so mesmerized by the sound of his own voice that he feels it is sufficient, and if he has a subject at all, it is the sound of his own voice. Here is the opening of a piece called Debbie.

'I was in a posh hotel on the Welsh border entirely staffed by Debbies. The first one said, "anything at all you require please don't hesitate to let me know!" I thought rather grumpily I don't imagine hesitating, the prices being what they are. A bit churlish, and I felt a little ashamed, but over my solitary dinner the thought wouldn't go away and I started to tease out the source of the faint irritation her words had promoted.'

This dreary self-absorption is mostly matched by a lack of interest in others, whose presence is normally used by Robinson only to spark off another damp chain of firework speculation about words, or phrases, or style, or those little strands of meaning which he pulls across to disguise the baldness of his thought.

It is a common conceit among humorists to start a piece with a flight of misdirected fancy, along the lines of 'Before arriving at Biggleswade, I had imagined it somehow filled entirely with 1940s RAF officers, filling the place with the sound of pranging moustaches ...', but these preludes, however long, are only preludes. With Robinson, they very often are the whole thing. He notes that Sir Michael Tippett is judging a marmalade competition, and says (after the little joke 'I was uncertain for a moment whether it wasn't Sir Michael Tiptree') 'There is a lively energetic vibration about the phrase "marmalade competition" as if the stuff was going to be thrown like a javelin. Or perhaps it was to be a new sort of 100 yards dash in special marmalade spikes, through fathoms of the stuff ...' that's all. Just a few jokes about misunderstanding the phrase 'marmalade competition' which, by the by, does *not* have a lively energetic vibration about it, unless you're desperate for a few quick jokes.

Whether you are so entranced by his juggling skills that you fail to notice he can only keep one ball in the air, or depressed by the plethora of pieces starting 'It came as a surprise to me to learn that wire coathangers were invented. I'd always thought ...' or 'I dearly love a non-sequitur if it's operatic enough', you will get a shock when you come to page 163, and a long piece called 'B. Traven: A Mystery Solved'.

It is very good indeed. It is a sober account of his TV-inspired hunt for the identity of the novelist B. Traven, and makes a rattling good detective yarn.

There are one or two other pieces like this ('No Sign of Tiptoes' on page 265, for instance), and they are all examples of pieces written for the page, not dragged out of mid-air waffle, as well as of Robinson for once getting outside the fascination with his own thought processes and seeing the outside world as more than just a peg on which to hang his own precious ramblings.

Have decades of take-the-money-and-run compering on TV and radio really addled the man's mind?

12 October 1990

Rupert Bare

Family Business ANNA MURDOCH (Collins)

MRS Rupert Murdoch's second novel is published by a firm in which her husband has a controlling stake. It has had a long and gushing review in the *Sunday Times*, which her husband owns. Small world, eh? The rest of the Murdoch press has been disloyally silent so far, but it's early days yet. Maybe the *Sun* will buy the serial rights. Certainly she shares the paper's panting obsession with sex, power and money – especially sex. Cop a load of this:

'Then he turned over and she was able to take him in her mouth and she imagined that her teeth were like the little pads of a centipede moving along a thick, smooth branch. And the centipede came to a smooth, round knob with a slit and the centipede became a tongue that explored the slit and the length of the branch and its root. And all the time the tree grew and trembled until at last it could no longer take the centipede-tongue and erupted so fiercely that its sap exploded from the branch and the branch withered away and died.'

Phew! The branch, incidentally, is married to someone other than the centipede at the time of this David Attenborough-type encounter. One mentions this only because Anna Murdoch revealed in a recent interview that she is a devout Roman Catholic.

In the same interview she said that sex in novels should be handled 'lyrically or romantically'. Quite so. One breathless seduction scene in *Family Business*, also involving the centipede, climaxes with a man whispering in her ear: 'I want to make babies.' Another woman thrilled at getting engaged to the branch-character, 'put her hand down between her legs and felt that she was as moist as a beaver in a pond'. *Very* lyrical.

Most readers will plough through the 653 pages of this drivel with one purpose in mind: to spot the Rupert character. They won't be disappointed, in spite of Anna Murdoch's insistence that it isn't a *roman à clef*. The heroine, though female and American, is transparently based on the Digger.

Just to confuse things, so is the hero.

She-Rupert is Yarrow MacLean, a centipede-tongued tycoon who starts by inheriting a newspaper in Colorado and goes on to build a huge multinational media conglomerate. Her empire is threatened only by the tiresome interference of the Federal Communications Commission (forcing her to sell a newspaper when she owns a TV station in the same city – just like Rupe) and, of course, the unions. 'She could see no way out of the imbecilic relationship between management and unions on Fleet Street except through the total destruction of one side by the other.' Fancy!

He-Rupert is a lean, ruthless, workaholic wheeler-dealer called Elliot Weyden, the guy with the exploding sap. 'His personality and enthusiasm shot off sparks like a catherine wheel spinning like a dervish.' (Like a catherine wheel *and* a dervish?) 'The doors would open and there he would be, larger than life, his eyes sparkling, his mind twirling, asking questions, probing, throwing off ideas so fast that the more timid members of the firm quaked ... If they couldn't come up with the answers, the black eyebrows would rise and one scalding phrase would sear them' – and so on. We get the picture.

Both He-Rupert and She-Rupert grow richer and richer throughout the book. They also love each other more and more. But He-Rupert is already married and his wife won't give him a divorce. So there are tears before bedtime.

And that is the entire plot, more or less. But one ought to mention a fascinating episode in the late 1960s when She-Rupert comes to London to take over a salacious Sunday paper owned by an etiolated family of old buffers. In real life, of course, the Digger did precisely this with the *News of the World*. His rival in the bitter struggle was Robert Maxwell, then a Labour MP. In the novel, She-Rupert is up against one Piers Molinski, a 'dreadful man' who came to England after the war and is now a millionaire Labour MP, though his business is 'just a house of cards' built on dodgy accounting. She-Rupert thinks him a 'pompous ass'. One trusts the lawyers of any similar figure will be firing off their customary writ.

2 September 1988

Not Carried away

Surrender the Pink CARRIE FISHER (Hutchinson)

O F course nobody minds film stars writing novels. Lots of them have and there isn't very much anyone seems to be able to do about it.

Dirk Bogarde has written some quite passable ones; Sylvester Stallone wrote one once, to the bewilderment of his publicists; even Kirk Douglas sat down at his word processor one morning, frowning at the desperate novelty of it all, and began to send some of those worrying accumulations of words – waddya know, *sentences?* – hopping around the mute, blameless screen.

No, nobody minds film stars writing novels. It's when film stars start writing novels and people go around pretending that they're art that the tired defenders of standards begin to get a little restive, a little anxious lest the joke become so prolonged that it ceases to be a joke at all.

Surrender the Pink, the second work by the star of, among others, *Star Wars* and *The Blues Brothers*, is a case in point. *It has to be a send up*, you feel as you negotiate all the crummy jokes and glum one-liners. And yet here amid the solemn ventilation of 'normal relationships', the complaints of women anxious to be 'fluent in sex', lurks a monstrous suspicion of something that appears to take itself very seriously indeed.

The seriousness has to be trailed after because, let's face it, nothing very much happens in *Surrender the Pink*. The story of a TV soap writer named Dinah Kaufman, it consists of not much more than a few self-conscious musings about – uh – sex, loosely strung together to form a plot in which Dinah meets up with her ex-husband Rudy, follows him on vacation to investigate his relationship with her replacement, has an inconclusive set-to with someone called Roy ('Captain Dream Thug') and ends up snapping the bed springs with a husky juvenile named Josh who in the TV series plays the actor 'made in Rudy's image'.

This being Hollywood, or at any rate one of its lower ledges, all the men have *problems*, notably legions of girlfriends who are upset about their ex-wives, while each of the women operates as an emotional sponge, or perhaps a better marine analogy would be a cuttlefish, spraying out endless jets of inky selfishness.

The vehicle for all this emotional megalomania, the absolute refusal of anyone to doubt the invincibility of their ego, is a kind of terminal irony. The people here don't have conversations, they simply chip away at one another, a constant metaphorical ear-tweaking which persists through dinners in restaurants, joky beddings and occasional moments of crisis.

As a style it extends to several levels: the apocalyptic ('Here is her personality: it is a pack of wild dogs on a leash, dragging her around'); the elegiac ('Her pale blue eyes had a faraway quality, like someone in the process of remembering something curious or sad from long ago'); the worryingly stretched ('She slipped herself between her envelope-like sheets and mailed herself off to sleep'). What undermines each of them is the reader's complete inability to work out what sort of a position to take up with regard to the cast.

'Don't make any jokes,' Dinah thinks when hunky Roy makes his first appearance. 'Don't make any bad jokes.' Unflustered by this sapient advice Roy and Dinah immediately make some very bad jokes indeed on the unlikely subject of muffins ('I'm afraid I don't have a strong muffin ethic', etc., etc.). There are three ways of looking at this exchange. One is that Fisher wants us to think that her characters are complete dorks. Two is that the whole thing is supposed to be sort of tender and funny. Three is that she doesn't possess the resources to make this distinction possible. On the evidence strewn elsewhere in the book the correct answer is three. Time after time the reader chances on some dumb formulation which may not, in the author's scheme of things, be a dumb formulation after all.

'If you meet an A-minus guy who doesn't like you and a B-plus guy who does, who do you like?' Dinah inquires of Roy (Rudy having sensibly skedaddled). Depending on how you look at it this is either sincere (and achingly banal) or designed to elevate Dinah to an epic level of stupidity. Perhaps in the end it's simply that Fisher doesn't want to make the choice.

Satire depends on distancing yourself from the people you're writing about – really hating them – acknowledging that the whole Hollywood/Bel Air pool party is a glorified leper pit. You leave *Surrender the Pink* thinking that at bottom it's all dreadfully serious and that Rudy, Roy and the rest of the walking penises are just regular guys after all.

1 March 1991

Better dead than read . . .

I BLAME Stephen Fry. Though there had been celebrity novels before –
does anyone remember Max Bygraves' trail-blazing mafia caper *The
Milkman's on His Way?* – it took the success of *The Liar* (60,000 in hardback,
200,000 and rising in paperback) to open the floodgates.

Since then there have been thespians (Simon Williams, Kate O'Mara);
politicians (Theresa Gorman, Edwina Currie pending), pop musicians
(Bruce Dickinson of Iron Maiden); and assorted rich people of no obvious
distinction (Ivana Trump). Newman and Baddiel are said to be writing one
(each). Lady Thatcher is almost certainly writing one.

These books have one distinguishing feature, which is that unlike *The Liar*,
whose author can hold a pen, they were generally indescribably bad. Set
down next to, say, Ivana Trump, Jack Higgins suddenly looks like a master
of the pithy phrase, and Will Self is – what? – a genius whose lustre will glow
as long as the lamp of literature continues to shine, etc., etc.

Or perhaps *two* distinguishing features. For not only are practically all
these books inept to the point of ridicule; they are also in the vast majority
of cases not written by the people whose names appear on their title pages.
Publishers get very coy about this, and there is a lot of euphemistic chatter
about 'advice' and 'collaboration', but it can confidently be stated that when
X the celebrity decides to write a novel, X's contribution will usually be
limited to a plot outline or at the very best a rough draft.

In some ways this is slightly less disgraceful than it sounds, as many a
bestselling 'proper' novelist has his or her books rewritten by a harassed
editor these days. The phenomenon, too, is age-old. Thackeray satirized it
a century and a half ago in *Pendennis*, in the person of the Hon. Percy Popjoy,
whose first novel is put together for him by a hack who in turn cribs from
an old magazine story (Percy's friends amuse themselves by congratulating
him on the merits of non-existent passages).

At least the publishers of the 1840s had the grace to pretend that what they
offered was the genuine article. One current development is for publishers
to dispense even with the illusion of authenticity. The press release
announcing the imminent arrival of a novel by (gasp) Naomi Campbell,
helpfully announced that Ms Campbell would be assisted in her lucubrations
by one 'Carly MacIntyre', the pen-name of Christopher Sinclair-
Stevenson's in-house editor Caroline Upcher. This is honest of a sort, but
a more truthful formulation might have been 'Sorry, Naomi love, we know

you couldn't write your way out of a paper bag, but here's a million quid for your name.'

Happily, though, the old ways endure. Splashed across the front cover of a recent edition of *The Bookseller* was a Hodder-Headline advert to the effect that Britt Ekland has written a novel, due out in the spring, I mean, *Britt Ekland!*

Writing is hard, darlings, as the hundreds of thousands of aspirant and unpublished scribblers scattered around the country know to their cost, and to publish 'books' by 'writers' whose only distinction is the frequency of their appearances in *Hello!* is pretty rich, especially as it comes courtesy of a group of people whose complaint about the likelihood of VAT on books was that it would amount to 'a tax on literature'.

Meanwhile, it should be put on record that the chances of Ms Ekland having had very much to with *The Sweet Life* are negligible in the extreme (something Hodder-Headline is most welcome to dispute), and that it is time some public-spirited book-buyer considered suing her publishers under the trades descriptions act.

31 December 1993

INDEX